STUDY GUIDE

GW00586775

to accompany

EIGHTH EDITION

MACROECONOMICS
PARKIN

MARK RUSH

University of Florida

PEARSON

Addison
Wesley

Boston San Francisco New York
London Toronto Sydney Tokyo Singapore Madrid
Mexico City Munich Paris Cape Town Hong Kong Montreal

ISBN-13   978-0-321-49059-9
ISBN-10   0-321-49059-2

1 2 3 4 5 6 BB 10 09 08 07

Preface

HOW TO EARN AN A!

■ Introduction

My experience has taught me that what students want most from a study guide is help in mastering course material in order to do well on examinations. I have developed this *Study Guide* to respond specifically to that demand. Using this *Study Guide* alone, however, is not enough to guarantee that you will do well in your course. In order to help you overcome the problems and difficulties that most students encounter, I have some general advice on how to study, as well as some specific advice on how best to use this *Study Guide*.

Economics requires a different style of thinking than what you may encounter in other courses. Economists make extensive use of assumptions to break down complex problems into simple, analytically manageable parts. This analytical style, while ultimately not more demanding than the styles of thinking in other disciplines, feels unfamiliar to most students and requires practice. As a result, it is not as easy to do well in economics on the basis of your raw intelligence and high-school knowledge as it is in many other courses. Many students who come to my office are frustrated and puzzled by the fact that they are getting A's and B's in their other courses but only a C or worse in economics. They have not recognized that economics is different and requires practice. In order to avoid a frustrating visit to your instructor after your first test, I suggest you do the following.

♦ *Don't rely solely on your high-school economics.* If you took high-school economics, you have seen the material on supply and demand which your instructor will lecture on in the first few weeks. Don't be lulled into feeling that the course will be easy. Your high-school knowledge of economic concepts will be very useful, but it will not be enough to guarantee high scores on exams. Your college or university instructors will demand much more detailed knowledge of concepts and ask you to apply them in new circumstances.

♦ *Keep up with the course material on a weekly basis.* Skim the appropriate chapter in the textbook *before* your instructor lectures on it. In this initial reading, don't worry about details or arguments you can't quite follow — just try to get a general understanding of the basic concepts and issues. You may be amazed at how your instructor's ability to teach improves when you come to class prepared. As soon as your instructor has finished covering a chapter, complete the corresponding *Study Guide* chapter. Avoid cramming the day before or even the week before an exam. Because economics requires practice, cramming is an almost certain recipe for failure. Indeed, based on data I have, students who crammed by intensively studying within three days of a test had higher SAT scores than the average student but did relatively poorer on the class tests than the average student who studied more consistently throughout the term. So, *don't* fall into this trap: Consistently study!

♦ *Keep a good set of lecture notes.* Good lecture notes are vital for focusing your studying. Your instructor will lecture on a subset of topics from the textbook. The topics your instructor covers in a lecture should usually be given priority when studying. Also give priority to studying the figures and graphs covered in the lecture.

Instructors differ in their emphasis on lecture notes and the textbook, so ask early on in the course which is *more* important in reviewing for exams — lecture notes or the textbook. If your instructor answers that both are important, then ask the following, typical economic question: which will be more beneficial — spending an extra hour re-reading your lecture notes or an extra hour re-reading the textbook? This question assumes that you have read each textbook chapter twice (once before lecture for a general understanding, and then later for a thorough understanding); that you have prepared a good set of lecture notes; and that you have worked through all of the problems in the appropriate *Study Guide* chapters. By applying this style of analysis to the problem of efficiently allocating your study time, you are already beginning to think like an economist!

♦ *Use your instructor and/or teaching assistants for help.* When you have questions or problems with course material, come to the office to ask questions. Remember, you are paying for your education and instructors are there to help you learn. I am often amazed at how few students come to see me during office hours. Don't be shy. The personal contact that comes from one-on-one tutoring is professionally gratifying for instructors as well as (hopefully) beneficial for you.

♦ *Form a study group.* A very useful way to motivate your studying and to learn economics is to discuss the course material and problems with other students. Explaining the answer to a question *out loud* is a very effective way of discovering how well you understand the question. When you answer a question only in your head, you often skip steps in the chain of reasoning without realizing it. When you are forced to explain your reasoning aloud, gaps and mistakes quickly appear, and you (with your fellow group members) can quickly correct your reasoning. The "You're the Teacher" questions in the *Study Guide* and the Review questions at the end of each textbook chapter are extremely good study group material. You might also get together *after* having worked the *Study Guide* problems, but *before* looking at the answers, and help each other solve unsolved problems.

♦ *Work old exams.* One of the most effective ways of studying is to work through exams your instructor has given in previous years. Old exams give you a feel for the style of question your instructor may ask, and give you the opportunity to get used to time pressure if you force yourself to do the exam in the allotted time. Studying from old exams is not cheating, as long as you have obtained a copy of the exam legally. Some institutions keep old exams in the library, others in the department. Students who have previously taken the course are usually a good source as well. Remember, though, that old exams are a useful study aid only if you use them to *understand* the reasoning behind each question. If you simply memorize answers in the hopes that your instructor will repeat the identical question, you are likely to fail. From year to year, instructors routinely change the questions or change the numerical values for similar questions.

♦ *Use the MyEconLab web site.* One of the most exciting features of the textbook is the opportunity it offers to use the MyEconLab web site. Michael Parkin, the author of the textbook, has been a leader in developing for the web site new, *useful* features that help students learn. You definitely should check out the web site because of all the help it offers. The textbook has complete details about the web site.

■ Using Your *Study Guide*

You should only attempt to complete a chapter in the *Study Guide* after you have read the corresponding textbook chapter and listened to your instructor lecture on the material. Each *Study Guide* chapter contains the following sections.

Key Concepts. This first section is a short summary, in point form, of all key definitions, concepts and material from the textbook chapter. Key terms from the textbook appear in bold. Each term in bold is in the glossary of the textbook. This first section is designed to focus you quickly and precisely on the core material that you *must* master. It is an excellent study aid for the night before an exam. Think of it as crib notes that will serve as a final check of the key concepts you have studied.

Helpful Hints. When you encounter difficulty in mastering concepts or techniques, you will not be alone. Many students find certain concepts difficult and often make the same kinds of mistakes. I have taught over 30,000 students the principles of economics and I have seen these common mistakes often enough to have learned how to help students avoid them. The hints point out these mistakes and offer tips to avoid them. The hints focus on the most important concepts, equations, and techniques for problem solving. They also review crucial graphs that appear on every instructor's exams. I hope that this section will be very useful, because instructors always ask exam questions designed to test these possible mistakes in your understanding.

Self-Test. This will be one of the most useful sections of the *Study Guide*. The questions are designed to give you practice and to test skills and techniques you must master to do well on exams.

There are plenty of multiple-choice type of questions and other types of questions in the Self-Test, each with a specific pedagogical purpose. Indeed, this book contains nearly 1,000 multiple choice questions in total!

Before I describe the four parts of the Self-Test section, here are some general tips that apply to all parts.

Use a pencil to write your answers in the *Study Guide* so you have neat, complete pages from which to study. Draw graphs wherever they are applicable. Some questions will ask explicitly for graphs; many others will not but will require a chain of reasoning that involves shifts of curves on a graph. *Always draw the graph.* Don't try to work through the reasoning in your head — you are much more likely to make mistakes that way. Whenever you draw a graph, even in the margins of the *Study Guide,* label the axes. You may think that you can keep the labels in your head, but you will be confronting many different graphs with many different variables on the axes. Avoid confusion and label. As an added incentive, remember that on exams where graphs are required, instructors will deduct points for unlabelled axes.

Do the Self-Test questions as if they were real exam questions, which means do them *without looking at the answers.* This is the single most important tip I can give you about effectively using the *Study Guide* to improve your exam performance. Struggling for the answers to questions that you find difficult is one of the most effective ways to learn. The adage "no pain, no gain" applies well to studying. You will learn the most from right answers you had to struggle for and from your wrong answers and mistakes. Only after you have attempted all the questions should you look at the answers. When you finally do check the answers, be sure to understand where you went wrong and why the right answer is correct.

There are many questions in each chapter, and it will take you somewhere between two and six hours to answer all of them. If you get tired (or bored), don't burn yourself out by trying to work through all of the questions in one sitting. Consider breaking up your Self-Test over two (or more) study sessions.

The four parts of the Self-Test section are:

True/False and Explain. These questions test basic knowledge of concepts and your ability to apply the concepts. Some of the questions challenge your understanding, to see if you can identify mistakes in statements using basic concepts. These questions will identify gaps in your knowledge and are useful to answer out loud in a study group.

When answering, identify each statement as *true,* or *false.* Explain your answer in *your words* in one sentence in the space underneath each question.

Multiple-Choice. These more difficult questions test your analytical abilities by asking you to apply concepts to new situations, manipulate information and solve numerical and graphical problems.

This is a most frequently used type of exam question, and the Self-Test contains many of them.

Read each question and all four choices carefully before you answer. Many of the choices will be plausible and will differ only slightly. You must choose the one *best* answer. A useful strategy in working these questions is first to eliminate any obviously wrong choices and then to focus on the remaining alternatives. Don't get frustrated or think that you are dim if you can't immediately see the correct answer. These questions are designed to make you work to find the correct choice.

Short Answer. Each chapter contains several Short Answer questions. Some are straightforward questions about basic concepts. They can generally be answered in a few sentences or, at most, in one paragraph. Others are problems. The best way to learn to do economics is to do problems. Problems are also the second-most popular type of exam question — practice them as much as possible!

You're the Teacher. Each chapter contains from one to three questions that either cover very broad issues or errors that are all too common among students. These questions may be the most valuable you will encounter for use in your study group. Take turns by pretending that you are the teacher and answer the questions for the rest of your group. Who knows, you may like this process so much that you actually do become a professor at a university teaching economics!

Answers. The Self-Test is followed by answers to all questions. Unlike other study guides on the market, I have included complete answers because I believe that reading complete answers will help you master the material ... and that's what this *Study Guide* is all about! But do *not* look at an answer until you have attempted a question. When you do finally look, use the answers to understand where you went wrong and why the right answer is correct.

As you work through the material, you'll find that the true/false and multiple choice questions, as well as their answers, are identified by a heading from the textbook. If you find that you are missing a lot of questions from one particular section, it is time to head back to the textbook and bone up on this material! In other words, *use* the textbook and this study guide to pull the A you want to earn!

Chapter Quiz. The last page in each chapter contains another 10 multiple questions covering the material in the chapter. These are questions that I and other instructors have included on our exams. Because these questions have been written by several instructors, they differ in style from the others in the chapter and so are a very good tool to be sure that you grasp the material. You can use the questions immediately after you finish each chapter, or else you can hoard them to help you prepare when exam time rolls around. In either case, the answers are given at the back of the book.

Part Overview Problem. Every few chapters, at the end of each of the parts of the textbook, you will find a special problem (and answer). In this section is a self-test that contains four multiple choice questions drawn from each chapter in the section. The questions are in order, with the first four from the first chapter in the section, the second four from the second chapter, and so forth. If you miss several questions from one chapter, you'll know to spend more time on that chapter when preparing for your exam. These multiple choice questions are written in a different style than those in the chapter because instructors have different ways of writing questions. By encountering different styles, you will be better prepared for *your* test.

Final Exams. At the end of the *Study Guide* are two multiple choice final exams and answers. These are final exams that I have used in my class at the University of Florida. You should use them to help you study for the final exam in your class.

If you effectively combine the use of the textbook, the *Study Guide,* the web site *MyEconLab,* and all other course resources, you will be well prepared for exams. You will also have developed analytical skills and powers of reasoning that will benefit you throughout your life and in whatever career you choose.

■ Your Future and Economics

After your class is concluded, you may well wonder about economics as a major. The last essay in this *Study Guide,* written by Robert Whaples, helps examine your future by discussing whether economics is the major for you. I invite you to read this chapter and consider the information in it. Economics is a major with a bright future so I think you'll be interested in this important chapter.

■ Final Comments

I have tried to make the *Study Guide* as helpful and useful as possible. Undoubtedly I have made some mistakes; mistakes that you may see. If you find any, I, and succeeding generations of students, would be grateful if you could point them out to me. At the end of my class at the University of Florida, when I ask my students for their advice, I point out to them that this advice won't help them at all because they have just completed the class. But, comments they make will influence how future students are taught. Thus, just as they owe a debt of gratitude for the comments and suggestions that I received from students before them, so too will students after them owe them an (unpaid and unpayable) debt. You are in the same situation. If you have questions, suggestions, or simply comments, let me know. My address is on the next page, or you can E-mail me at MARK.RUSH@CBA.UFL.EDU. Your input probably won't benefit you directly, but it will benefit following generations. And, if you give me permission, I will note your name and school in following editions so that any younger siblings (or, years down the road, maybe even your children!) will see your name and offer up thanks.

To date, students who have uncovered errors and to whom we all owe a debt of gratitude include:

- Jeanie Callen at the University of Minnesota-Twin Cities.
- Brian Mulligan at the University of Florida
- Patrick Lusby at the University of Florida
- Jonathan Baskind at the University of Florida
- Breina Polk at Cook College at Rutgers University
- Ethan Schulman at the University of Iowa
- Adrian Garza at the University of Iowa
- Curtis Hazel at the University of North Florida
- Zhang Zili at American University
- Valerie Stewart at the University of Georgia
- Rob Bleeker at The Ohio State University
- Katherine Hamilton at the University of Florida
- Dennis Spinks at The Ohio State University
- Debbie McGuffie at the University of Florida
- Daniel Glassman at the University of Florida
- Thomas Cowan at the University of Florida
- Christopher Bland at the University of Florida
- Richard Caitung at the University of Florida
- Kristin L. Thistle at the University of Florida

- Michael Benkoczy at the University of Florida
- J.B. Johns at the Johns Hopkins University
- Joshua R. Levenson at the University of Miami
- Ryan Ellis at the University of Wisconsin, Madison
- Daniel Law at Butte Community College
- Katherine Kowsh at the University of Florida
- Will Broadway at the University of Florida
- Yalcyn Bican of Turkey
- Hillary Huffmire at Brigham Young University
- Michael Lagoe, at the University of Florida

I owe Avi J. Cohen, of York University, and Harvey B. King, of University of Regina. Their superb study guide for the Canadian edition of Michael Parkin's book was a basis for this study guide. Much of what is good about this book is a direct reflection of their work.

Robert Whaples of Wake Forest University wrote the section of the *Study Guide* dealing with majoring in economics. He also checked an earlier edition of the manuscript for errors and provided questions that I use in this edition. Robert is a superb economist and this book is by far the better for this fact! Another brilliant teacher, Carol Dole of the State University of West Georgia, also supplied questions that I use with this edition. I think it fair to say that the clever questions are the work of Carol and Robert.

I also thank Michael Parkin and Robin Bade. Michael has written such a superior book that it was easy to be enthusiastic about writing the *Study Guide* to accompany it. Moreover, both Michael and Robin have played a hands on role in creating this *Study Guide* and have made suggestions that vastly improved the *Study Guide*.

I want to thank my family: Susan, Tommy, Bobby, and Katie, who, respectively: allowed me to work all hours on this book; helped me master the intricacies of FTPing computer files; let me postpone riding bicycles with him until after the book was concluded; and would run into my typing room to tell how she had advanced in her latest Zelda game. Thanks a lot!

Finally, I want to thank Lucky, Pearl, and Butterscotch who sat at my feet and next to the computer in a box (and occasionally meowed) while I typed.

Mark Rush
Economics Department
University of Florida
Gainesville, Florida 32611
January, 2007.

Table of Contents

Chapter 1

WHAT IS ECONOMICS?

■ Definition of Economics

The fundamental economic problem is **scarcity**, which is the inability to satisfy all our wants. Because the available resources are never enough to satisfy everyone's wants, choices are necessary. **Incentives**, a reward that encourages or a penalty that discourages an action, influence choices.

Economics is the social science that studies the choices that individuals, businesses, governments, and societies make as they cope with scarcity and the incentives that influence and reconcile those choices.

- **Microeconomics** is the study of choices that individuals and businesses make, the way these choices interact in markets, and the influence of governments.

- **Macroeconomics** is the study of the performance of the national economy and the global economy.

■ Two Big Economic Questions

Economics explores two big questions:

- How do choices end up determining *what*, *how*, and *for whom* goods and services get produced?

- When do choices made in the pursuit of self interest also promote the social interest?

Goods and services are the objects that people value and produce to satisfy wants. Goods and services are produced using productive resources called **factors of production.** There are four categories:

- **Land:** the "gifts of nature" such as land, minerals, and water.

- **Labor:** the work time and work effort people devote to producing goods and services. The quality

of labor depends on **human capital**, which is the knowledge and skill that people obtain from education, on-the-job training, and work experience.

- **Capital:** the tools, instruments, machines, buildings, and other constructions that businesses now use to produce goods and services.

- **Entrepreneurship:** the human resource that organizes land, labor, and capital.

For whom the goods and services are produced depends on people's incomes. To earn an income, people sell the services of the factors of production they own. Land earns **rent;** labor earns **wages;** capital earns **interest;** and entrepreneurship earns **profit.**

People make choices that are in their **self interest,** choices that they think are the best for them. Choices that are the best for society as a whole are in the **social interest.** Economists work to understand when choices made in self interest advance the social interest. For instance, does private ownership of businesses and does globalization best serve the social interest? Did the high-tech "New Economy" result from choices made in the social interest? Are the changes in production made as a result of the terror attacks on 9-11 in the social interest? And are the private choices made about the price of new drugs, about using the tropical rainforests, about fighting water shortages, about the number of people without work, and about the size of the government deficit made in the social interest?

■ The Economic Way of Thinking

A choice involves a **tradeoff.** A tradeoff is an exchange—giving up one thing to get something else. Tradeoffs include the "what" tradeoffs, the "how" tradeoffs, and the "for whom" tradeoffs.

- The **big tradeoff** is the tradeoff between equality and efficiency that occurs as a result of government programs redistributing income.

Choices being change and affect the quality of our economic lives. For instance, choices to give up current consumption in order to save mean higher consumption per person in the future, though at the cost of a lower consumption per person in the present.

The **opportunity cost** of a choice is the highest-valued alternative given up. Opportunity cost is not all the alternatives foregone, only the highest-valued alternative foregone. All tradeoffs involve an opportunity cost.

Choices are made in small steps are choices made at the **margin**.

♦ The benefit that arises from an increase in an activity is called **marginal benefit.**

♦ The cost of an increase in an activity is called **marginal cost.**

When making choices, people compare the marginal cost of an action to the marginal benefit of the action. Changes in marginal cost and/or marginal benefit affect the decisions made, so choices respond to incentives. Institutions affect whether a self-interested choice promotes the social interest.

■ Economics: A Social Science

Economists distinguish between:

♦ *Positive statements* — statements about what is. These can be shown to be true or false through observation and measurement.

♦ *Normative statements* — statements about what ought to be. These are matters of opinion.

Economic science is a collection of positive statements that are consistent with the real world. Economic science uses three steps to progress:

♦ Observation and measurement — economists observe and record economic data.

♦ Model building — an **economic model** is a description of some aspect of the economic world that includes only those features of the world that are needed for the purpose at hand.

♦ Testing — a model is tested to determine how well its predictions correspond with the real world. An **economic theory** is a generalization that summarizes what we think we understand about economic choices that people make and the performance of industries and entire economies.

When developing models and theories, economists use the idea of *ceteris paribus*, which is Latin for "other

things being equal", to focus on the effect of one particular factor.

In the development of theories and models, two fallacies are possible:

♦ Fallacy of composition — the (false) assertion that what is true of the parts must be true for the whole, or what is true for the whole must be true for the parts.

♦ *Post hoc* fallacy — the assertion that one event caused another because the first occurred before the second.

Helpful Hints

1. **CHOICES AND INCENTIVES :** The basic assumption made by economists about human behavior is that people make themselves as well off as possible. As a result, people respond to changed incentives by changing their decisions. The key idea is that an individual compares the additional (or "marginal") benefit from taking an action to the additional (or "marginal") cost of the action. If the marginal benefit from the action exceeds the marginal cost, taking the action makes the person better off, so the person takes the action. Conversely, if the marginal benefit falls short of the marginal cost, the action is not taken. Only the *additional* benefit and *additional* cost are relevant because they are the benefits and costs that the person will enjoy and incur if the action is undertaken. Keeping straight the distinction between additional benefits and costs versus total benefits and costs is a vital part of economics, particularly of microeconomics.

2. **MODELS AND SIMPLIFICATION :** In attempting to understand how and why something works (for example, an airplane or an economy), we can use description or we can use theory. A description is a list of facts about something. But it does not tell us which facts are essential for understanding how an airplane works (the shape of the wings) and which facts are less important (the color of the paint). Scientists use theory to abstract from the complex descriptive facts of the real world and focus only on those elements essential for understanding. These essential elements are fashioned into models — highly simplified representations of the real world.

In a real sense, models are like maps, which are useful precisely because they abstract from real world detail. A map that reproduced all the details of the real world (street lights, traffic signs, electric wires) would be useless. A useful map offers a simplified view, which is carefully selected according to the purpose of the map. A useful theory is similar: It gives guidance and insight into how the immensely complicated real world functions and reacts to changes.

Questions

■ True/False and Explain

Definition of Economics

1. Scarcity is a problem only for the poor.

2. Macroeconomics studies the factors that change national employment and income.

Two Big Economic Questions

3. Answering "What goods and services are produced?" automatically answers "How are goods and services produced?"

4. An example of the "how" part of the first big question is: "How does the nation decide who gets the goods and services that are produced?"

5. Capital earns profit.

6. When making choices, most people consider the social interest of their decisions.

7. Choices made in self interest sometimes advance the social interest.

The Economic Way of Thinking

8. Tradeoffs mean that you give up one thing to get something else.

9. There is no such thing as a "how" tradeoff because a business uses only one way to produce its goods and services.

10. The big tradeoff refers to the tradeoff between what goods are produced and how they are produced.

11. If Sam buys a pizza for $3 rather than a burrito for $3, the burrito is the opportunity cost of buying the slice of pizza.

12. By comparing the cost and benefit of a small change you are making your choice at the margin.

Economics: A Social Science

13. A positive statement is about what is; a normative statement is about what will be.

14. The idea of *ceteris paribus* is used whenever a *post hoc* fallacy is being examined.

■ Multiple Choice

Definition of Economics

1. The fact that wants cannot be fully satisfied with available resources reflects the definition of
   a. incentives.
   b. scarcity.
   c. the output-inflation tradeoff.
   d. for whom to produce.

2. Studying the effects choices have on the national economy is part of
   a. scarcity.
   b. microeconomics.
   c. macroeconomics.
   d. global science.

Two Big Economic Questions

3. Which of the following is <u>NOT</u> part of the first big economic question?
   a. What goods and services are produced?
   b. How are goods and services produced?
   c. For whom are goods and services produced?
   d. Why are goods and services produced?

4. The question, "Should personal computers or mainframe computers be produced?" is an example of which part of the first big economic question?
   a. "what" part
   b. "how" part
   c. "where" part
   d. "for whom" part

5. People have different amounts of income. This observation is most directly related to which part of the first big economic question?
   a. The "what" part.
   b. The "how" part.
   c. The "why" part.
   d. The "for whom" part.

6. The factor of production that earns the most income is ____.
   a. land
   b. labor
   c. capital
   d. entrepreneurship

7. If a drug executive sets the price of a new drug at $1,000 a dose because that is the price that is best for the executive, the executive is definitely making a
   a. self-interested choice.
   b. choice in the social interest.
   c. globalization choice.
   d. factors of production choice.

8. Choices made in the pursuit of self interest ____ the social interest.
   a. always further
   b. sometimes further
   c. never further
   d. are no comparable to choices made in the

The Economic Way of Thinking

9. The fact that Intel decides to produce CPU chips rather than memory chips best reflects a ____ trade-off.
   a. what
   b. how
   c. for whom
   d. standard of living

10. The choice about how much to save
    a. has no opportunity cost because saving means more future consumption.
    b. has the opportunity cost of higher future consumption.
    c. trades off current consumption for future consumption.
    d. None of the above answers is correct.

11. From 9 to 10 A.M., Fred can sleep in, go to his economics lecture, or play tennis. Suppose that Fred decides to go to the lecture but thinks that, if he hadn't, he would otherwise have slept in. The opportunity cost of attending the lecture is
    a. sleeping in *and* playing tennis.
    b. playing tennis.
    c. sleeping in.
    d. one hour of time.

12. When the government chooses to use resources to build a dam, these resources are no longer available to build a highway. This choice illustrates the concept of
    a. a market.
    b. macroeconomics.
    c. opportunity cost.
    d. marginal benefit.

13. To make a choice on the margin, an individual
    a. ignores any opportunity cost if the marginal benefit from the action is high enough.
    b. will choose to use his or her scarce resources only if there is a very large total benefit from so doing.
    c. compares the marginal cost of the choice to the marginal benefit.
    d. makes the choice with the smallest opportunity cost.

Economics: A Social Science

14. A positive statement is
    a. about what ought to be.
    b. about what is.
    c. always true.
    d. one that does not use the *ceteris paribus* clause.

15. Which of the following is a positive statement?
    a. The government must lower the price of a pizza so that more students can afford to buy it.
    b. The best level of taxation is zero percent because then people get to keep everything they earn.
    c. My economics class should last for two terms because it is my favorite class.
    d. An increase in college tuition will lead fewer students to apply to college.

16. An economic model includes
    a. only normative statements.
    b. no use of *ceteris paribus*.
    c. all known facts about a situation.
    d. only details considered essential.

17. The Latin term *ceteris paribus* means
    a. "false unless proven true."
    b. "other things the same."
    c. "after this, then because of this."
    d. "not correct, even though it is logical."

18. One student from a class of 30 can walk easily through a door. Assuming that all 30 students simultaneously therefore can walk easily through the same door is an example of the
    a. opportunity cost fallacy.
    b. fallacy of composition
    c. fallacy of substitution.
    d. *post hoc* fallacy.

19. The *post hoc* fallacy is the
    a. assertion that what is true for a part of the whole must be true for the whole.
    b. claim that one event caused another because the one event came first.
    c. use of *ceteris paribus* in order to study the impact of one factor.
    d. claim that the timing of two events has nothing to do with which event caused the other.

■ **Short Answer Problems**

1. "In the future, as our technology advances even further, eventually we will whip scarcity. In the high-tech future, scarcity will be gone." Do you agree or disagree with this claim? Explain your answer and what scarcity is. Why does the existence of scarcity require choices?

2. What are the factors of production? Focusing on the factors of production, describe the relationship between the question "How are goods and services produced?" and the question "For whom are goods and services produced?".

3. What is making a choice based on self interest? Making a choice based on social interest? Why is it important to determine if choices based on self interest are the same as choices based on social interest?

4. Why does your decision to buy a taco from Taco Bell reflect a tradeoff? Be sure to discuss the role played by opportunity cost in your answer.

5. "Education is a basic right. Just as kindergarten through 12th grade education is free, so, too, should a college education be free and guaranteed to every American." This statement can be analyzed by using the economic concepts discussed in this chapter to answer the following questions.
   a. What would be the opportunity cost of providing a free college education for everyone?
   b. Is providing this education free from the perspective of society as a whole?

6. Indicate whether each of the following statements is positive or normative. If it is normative, rewrite it so that it becomes positive. If it is positive, rewrite it so that it becomes normative.
   a. Policymakers ought to lower the inflation rate even if it lowers output.
   b. An imposition of a tax on tobacco products will decrease their consumption.
   c. Health care costs should be lower so that poorer people can afford quality health care.

7. In sciences such as chemistry, controlled experiments play a key role. How does that relate to economists' use of *ceteris paribus*?

■ **You're the Teacher**

1. Your friend asks, "Does everything have an opportunity cost?" Your friend has hit upon a very good question; provide an equally good answer!

2. "Economic theories are useless because the models on which they are based are totally unrealistic. They leave out so many descriptive details about the real world, they can't possibly be useful for understanding how the economy works." So says your skeptical friend. You'd like to keep your friend in your economics class so that you two can study together. Defend the fact that economic theories are much simpler than reality and help your friend realize that time spent studying economic theories is time well spent!

Answers

■ True/False Answers

Definition of Economics

1. **F** Scarcity exists because people's wants exceed their ability to meet those wants, and this fact of life is true for *any* person, rich or poor.

2. **T** Macroeconomics studies the entire economy; microeconomics studies separate parts of the economy.

Two Big Economic Questions

3. **F** Almost always, goods and services can be produced many different ways, so the "how" question must be answered separately from the "what" question.

4. **F** The "how" part of the first big question asks, "How are goods and services produced?"

5. **F** Capital earns interest; entrepreneurship earns profit.

6. **F** People consider the self interest of their choices, that is, they make the choices they are best f or them.

7. **T** A role of economics is to discover when choices made in the self interest advance the social interest and when they conflict with the social interest.

The Economic Way of Thinking

8. **T** The question gives the definition of a tradeoff.

9. **F** Businesses almost always can produce their products many different ways, so they face a "how" tradeoff when they choose which method they will use.

10. **F** The big tradeoff refers to the tradeoff between equality and efficiency.

11. **T** The opportunity cost is the burrito that was foregone in order to buy the pizza.

12. **T** The definition of making a choice at the margin means that choice revolves around a small change.

Economics: A Social Science

13. **F** Although a positive statement is, indeed, about what is, a normative statement tells what policies should be followed.

14. **F** *Ceteris paribus*, Latin for "other things being equal," is used in order to focus on the effect from a change in one factor alone.

■ Multiple Choice Answers

Definition of Economics

1. **b** Scarcity refers to the observation that wants are unlimited but that the resources available to satisfy these wants are limited.

2. **c** Macroeconomics studies the national economy as well as the global economy.

Two Big Economic Questions

3. **d** "Why" is not part of the first big economic question.

4. **a** The "what" part asks "What goods and services are produced?"

5. **d** People with high incomes will get more goods and services than those with low incomes.

6. **b** Labor earns wages, which together with fringe benefits are about 70 percent of total income.

7. **a** Because the choice is best for the executive, it is a self-interested choice.

8. **b** Part of the job of economists is to determine when choices made in self interest further social interest and when they come into conflict.

The Economic Way of Thinking

9. **a** The "what" tradeoff reflects Intel's decisions about "what" to produce.

10. **c** Because saving decreases current consumption, the opportunity cost of saving is the forgone current consumption.

11. **c** The opportunity cost of an action is the (single) highest-valued alternative foregone by taking the action.

12. **c** Because the resources are used to build a dam, the opportunity of using them to build a highway is given up.

13. **c** Comparing marginal cost and marginal benefit is an important technique, especially in microeconomics.

Economics: A Social Science

14. **b** Positive statements describe how the world operates.

15. **d** This statement is the only one that tries to describe how the world actually works; all the others are normative statements that describe a policy that should be pursued.

16. **d** By including only essential details, economic models are vastly simpler than reality.

17. **b** *Ceteris paribus* is the economic equivalent of a controlled experiment: Its use allows us to determine the effect from each factor alone even though many factors might play a role in affecting a variable.

18. **b** In this case, the fallacy of composition is arguing that what is true for a part must necessarily be true for the whole.

19. **b** The usual *post hoc* fallacy is to claim that one event caused another because the first event occurred before the second.

■ Answers to Short Answer Problems

1. This claim is incorrect. Scarcity will always exist. Scarcity occurs because people's wants are basically unlimited, but the resources available to satisfy these wants are finite. As a result, not all of everyone's wants can be satisfied. For instance, think about the number of people who want to spend all winter skiing on uncrowded slopes. Regardless of the level of technology, there simply are not enough ski slopes available to allow everyone who wants to spend all winter skiing in near isolation to do so. Uncrowded ski slopes are scarce and will remain so.

   Because not all the goods and services wanted can be produced, choices must be made about which wants will be satisfied and which wants will be disappointed.

2. The four factors of production are land, labor, capital, and entrepreneurship. These are the resources used to produce goods and services, so the question asking how goods and services are produced asks which factors will be used. People earn their incomes by offering factors of production for use. Land earns rent, labor earns wages, capital earns interest, and entrepreneurship earns profit. The answer to the question asking for whom the goods and services are produced depends on people's incomes. So, for example, if more land is used to produce goods and services, then landowners' incomes will be higher so they will be able to acquire more of the goods and services that have been produced.

3. A choice based on self interest is a choice that is best for the person making the choice. A choice based on social interest is a choice that is best for society. It is important to determine if choices based on self interest are the same as choices based on social interest because most choices are based on self interest. If the choices are the same, then people pursuing their own self interest advance the social interest.

4. The decision to buy a taco reflects a tradeoff because you have given up your funds in exchange for the taco. The opportunity cost of buying the taco is the highest-valued alternative given up. For instance, suppose that if you had not decided to buy the taco, you would then have used the funds to buy a burger from Burger King. In this case, the opportunity cost of buying the taco is the forgone burger because that is the highest-valued alternative given up.

5. a. Even though a college education may be offered without charge ("free"), opportunity costs still exist. The opportunity cost of providing such education is the highest valued alternative use of the resources used to construct the necessary universities and the highest valued alternative use of the resources (including human resources) used in the operation of the schools.

    b. Providing a "free" college education is hardly free from the perspective of society. The resources used in this endeavor would no longer be available for other activities. For instance, the resources used to construct a new college cannot be used to construct a hospital to provide better health care. Additionally, the time and effort spent by the faculty, staff, and students operating and attending colleges has a substantial opportunity cost, namely, that these individuals cannot participate fully in other sectors of the economy. Providing a "free" college education to everyone is not free to society!

6. a. This statement is normative. A positive statement is: "If policymakers lowered the inflation rate by 1 percentage point, then output would fall by 1 percent."

    b. This statement is positive. A normative statement is: "We should impose a tax on tobacco products in order to decrease their consumption."

c. This statement is normative. A positive statement is: "If health care costs were lower, more poor people would receive health care."

7. Chemists can check the predictions of a model by conducting controlled experiments and observing the outcomes. For instance, when determining the effect of temperature on a particular reaction, chemists can ensure that, between different experiments, *only* the temperature changes. Everything else is held constant. Economists usually cannot perform such controlled experiments and instead must change one variable at a time in a model and compare the results. This approach involves the use of *ceteris paribus*, wherein only one factor is allowed to change. So, economists face more difficult and less precise model building and testing than is possible for the controlled experiments of chemists and other scientists.

■ You're the Teacher

1. "Virtually everything has an opportunity cost. People sometimes say that viewing a beautiful sunset or using sand from the middle of the Sahara Desert have no opportunity costs. But that isn't strictly true. Viewing the sunset has an opportunity cost in terms of the time spent watching it. The time could have been utilized in some other activity and, whatever the next highest-valued opportunity might have been, that is the opportunity cost of watching the sunset. Similarly, making use of sand from the Sahara also must have some opportunity cost, be it the time spent in gathering the sand or the resources spent in gathering it. So from the widest of perspectives, the answer is: Yes, everything does have an opportunity cost."

2. "Economic theories are like maps, which are useful precisely because they abstract from real world detail. A useful map offers a simplified view, which is carefully selected according to the purpose of the map. No map maker would claim that the world is as simple (or as flat) as the map, and economists do not claim that the real economy is as simple as their theories. What economists do claim is that their theories isolate the effects of real forces operating in the economy, yield predictions that can be tested against real-world data, and result in predictions that often are correct.

"I've got a book here that my parents gave to me by Milton Friedman, a Nobel Prize winner in Economics. Here's what he says on this topic: 'A theory or its 'assumptions' cannot possibly be thoroughly 'realistic' in the immediate descriptive sense.... A completely 'realistic' theory of the wheat market would have to include not only the conditions directly underlying the supply and demand for wheat but also the kind of coins or credit instruments used to make exchanges; the personal characteristics of wheat-traders such as the color of each trader's hair and eyes, ... the number of members of his family, their characteristics, ... the kind of soil on which the wheat was grown, ... the weather prevailing during the growing season; ... and so on indefinitely. Any attempt to move very far in achieving this kind of 'realism' is certain to render a theory utterly useless.'

"I think Friedman makes a lot of sense in what he says. It seems to me that theories have to be simple in order to be powerful and so I don't see anything wrong with the fact that economic theories leave out a bunch of trivial details."

From Milton Friedman, "The Methodology of Positive Economics," in *Essays in Positive Economics*. (Chicago: University of Chicago Press, 1953), 32.

Chapter Quiz

1. The most fundamental economic problem is
   a. reducing unemployment.
   b. health and health care.
   c. scarcity.
   d. decreasing the inflation rate.

2. Studying how an individual firm decides to set its price is primarily a concern of
   a. normative economics.
   b. macroeconomics.
   c. microeconomics.
   d. all economists.

3. Which of the following is a macroeconomic topic?
   a. Why has the price of a personal computer fallen over time?
   b. How does a rise in the price of cheese affect the pizza market?
   c. What factors determine the nation's inflation rate?
   d. How does a consumer decide how many tacos to consume?

4. When the economy produces fireworks for sale at the Fourth of July, it most directly is answering the _____ question.
   a. what goods and services are produced
   b. opportunity cost
   c. for whom are goods and services produced
   d. how are goods and services produced

5. When doctors have an average income that exceeds $250,000, the economy most directly is answering the _____ part of the first big question.
   a. what goods and services are produced
   b. opportunity cost
   c. how are goods and services produced
   d. for whom are goods and services produced

6. Which of the following is microeconomic issue?
   a. How does a pharmaceutical company determine the price of a drug?
   b. What effect does a government deficit have on the unemployment rate?
   c. Is inflation harmful?
   d. Why is the unemployment rate falling?

7. The big tradeoff between equality and efficiency reflects the point that
   a. what is produced can affect people's incomes.
   b. if more of one good is produced, less of another can be produced.
   c. taxing productive activities means producing fewer goods and services.
   d. None of the above answers is correct.

8. Opportunity cost is
   a. zero for services, because services do not last for very long, and positive for goods, because goods are long lasting.
   b. paid by society not by an individual.
   c. the highest-valued alternative given up by making a choice.
   d. all the alternatives given up by making a choice.

9. In economics, positive statements
   a. are only about facts that economists are certain (are "positive") are true.
   b. tell what policy the government ought to follow.
   c. depend on value judgments.
   d. in principle, can be tested to determine if they are true or false.

10. The fallacy of composition makes the error that
    a. theory is necessary to better understand the real world.
    b. models can be normative in nature without any positive conclusions.
    c. people's free will makes predicting their behavior futile.
    d. what is true for the whole must necessarily be true for the parts.

The answers for this Chapter Quiz are on page 265

Appendix

GRAPHS IN ECONOMICS

■ Graphing Data

Graphs represent quantity as a distance on a line. On a graph, the horizontal scale line is the *x-axis*, the vertical scale line is the *y-axis*, and the intersection of the two scale lines is the *origin*.

The three main types of economic graphs are:

♦ **Time-series graphs** demonstrate the relationship between time, measured on the *x*-axis, and other variable(s), measured on the *y*-axis. Time-series graphs show the variable's level, direction of change, speed of change, and **trend**, which is its general tendency to rise or fall.

♦ **Cross-section graphs** show the values of a variable for different groups in a population at a point in time.

♦ **Scatter diagrams** plot the value of one variable against the value of another to show the relationship between two variables. Such a relationship indicates how the variables are *correlated*, not whether one variable *causes* the other.

■ Graphs Used in Economic Models

The four important relationships between variables are:

♦ **Positive relationship** or **direct relationship** — the variables move together in the same direction, as illustrated in Figure A1.1. The relationship is upward-sloping.

♦ **Negative relationship** or **inverse relationship** — the variables move in opposite directions, as shown in Figure A1.2. The relationship is downward-sloping.

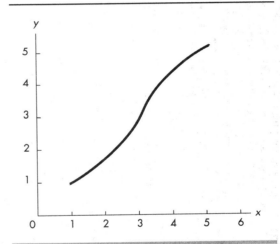

FIGURE **A1.1**
A Positive Relationship

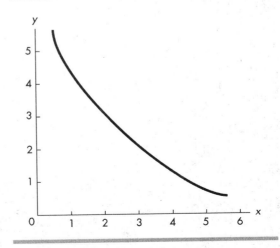

FIGURE **A1.2**
A Negative Relationship

♦ Maximum or minimum — the relationship reaches a maximum or a minimum point, then changes direction. Figure A1.3 shows a minimum.

♦ Unrelated — the variables are not related so that, when one variable changes, the other is unaffected. The graph is either a vertical or horizontal straight line, as illustrated in Figure A1.4.

A relationship illustrated by a straight line is called a **linear relationship.**

■ The Slope of a Relationship

The **slope** of a relationship is the change in the value of the variable on the *y*-axis divided by the change in the value of the variable on the *x*-axis. The formula for slope is $\Delta y/\Delta x$, with Δ meaning "change in."

A straight line (or linear relationship) has a constant slope. A curved line has a varying slope, which can be calculated two ways:

♦ *Slope at a point* — by drawing the straight line tangent to the curve at that point and then calculating the slope of the line.

♦ *Slope across an arc* — by drawing a straight line across the two points on the curve and then calculating the slope of the line.

■ Graphing Relationships Among More Than Two Variables

Relationships between more than two variables can be graphed by holding constant the values of all the variables except two (the *ceteris paribus* assumption, that is, "other things remaining the same") and then graphing the relationship between the two with, *ceteris paribus*, only the variables being studied changing. When one of the variables not illustrated in the figure changes, the entire relationship between the two that have been graphed shifts.

Helpful Hints

1. **IMPORTANCE OF GRAPHS AND GRAPHICAL ANALYSIS :** Economists almost always use graphs to present relationships between variables. This fact should not "scare" you nor give you pause.

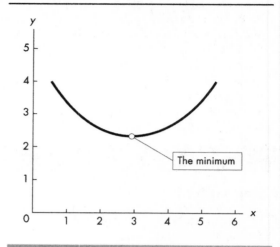

FIGURE **A1.3**
A Minimum

The minimum

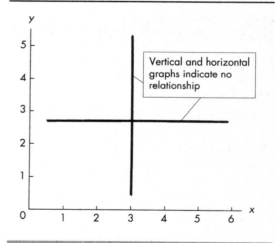

FIGURE **A1.4**
No Relationship

Vertical and horizontal graphs indicate no relationship

Economists do so because graphs *simplify* the analysis. All the key concepts you need to master are presented in this appendix. If your experience with graphical analysis is limited, this appendix is crucial to your ability to readily understand economic analysis. However, if you are experienced in constructing and using graphs, this appendix may be "old hat." Even so, you should skim the appendix and work through the questions in this *Study Guide.*

2. **CALCULATING THE SLOPE :** Often the slopes of various relationships are important. Usually what is key is the sign of the slope — whether the slope is positive or negative — rather than the actual value of the slope. An easy way to remember the formula for slope is to think of it as the "rise over the run," a saying used by carpenters and others. As illustrated in Figure A1.5, the *rise* is the change in the variable measured on the vertical axis, or in terms of symbols, Δy. The *run* is the change in the variable measured on the horizontal axis, or Δx. This "rise over the run" formula also makes it easy to remember whether the slope is positive or negative. If the rise is actually a drop, as shown in Figure A1.5, then the slope is negative because when the variable measured on the horizontal axis increases, the variable measured on the vertical axis decreases. However, if the rise actually is an increase, then the slope is positive. In this case, an increase in the variable measured on the *x*-axis is associated with an increase in the variable measured on the *y*-axis.

FIGURE **A1.5**
Rise Over The Run

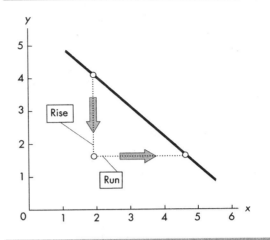

Questions

■ True/False and Explain

Graphing Data

1. The origin is the point where a graph starts.

2. A graph showing a positive relationship between stock prices and the nation's production means that an increase in stock prices causes an increase in production.

3. In Figure A1.6 the value of *y* decreased between 1998 and 1999.

4. In Figure A1.6 the value of *y* increased most rapidly between 2001 and 2002.

5. Figure A1.6 shows a trend with *y* increasing, generally speaking.

6. A cross-section graph compares the values of different groups of a variable at a single point in time.

Graphs Used in Economic Models

7. If the graph of the relationship between two variables slopes upward to the right, the relationship between the variables is positive.

FIGURE **A1.6**
True/False Questions 3, 4, 5

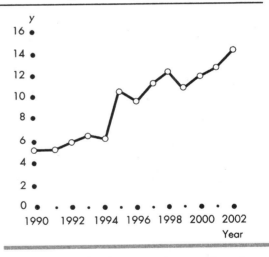

8. If the relationship between *y* (measured on the vertical axis) and *x* (measured on the horizontal axis) is one in which *y* reaches a maximum, the slope of the relationship must be negative before and positive after the maximum.

9. To the left of a minimum point, the slope is negative; to the right, the slope is positive.

10. Graphing things that are unrelated on one diagram is <u>NOT</u> possible.

The Slope of a Relationship

11. It is possible for the graph of a positive relationship to have a slope that becomes smaller when moving rightward along the graph.

12. The slope of a straight line is calculated by dividing the change in the value of the variable measured on the horizontal axis by the change in the value of the variable measured on the vertical axis.

13. For a straight line, if a large change in y is associated with a small change in x, the line is steep.

14. The slope of a curved line is <u>NOT</u> constant.

15. The slope of a curved line at a point equals the slope of a line tangent to the curved line at the point.

Graphing Relationships Among More Than Two Variables

16. *Ceteris paribus* means "everything else changes."

17. The amount of corn a farmer grows depends on its price and the amount of rainfall. The curve showing the relationship between the price of a bushel of corn and the quantity grown is the same curve regardless of the amount of rainfall.

■ Multiple Choice

Graphing Data

1. Demonstrating how an economic variable changes from one year to the next is best illustrated by a
   a. one-variable graph.
   b. time-series graph.
   c. linear graph.
   d. cross-section graph.

2. You notice that, when the inflation rate increases, the interest rate also tends to increase. This fact indicates that
   a. there might be false causality between inflation and the interest rate.
   b. higher inflation rates must cause higher interest rates.
   c. a scatter diagram of the inflation rate and the interest rate will show a positive relationship.
   d. a cross-section graph of the inflation rate and the interest rate will show a positive relationship.

3. You believe that the total amount of goods produced in the United States has generally increased. In a time-series graph illustrating the total amount produced, you expect to find
   a. an upward trend.
   b. no relationship between time and the amount of goods produced.
   c. an inverse relationship between time and the amount of goods produced.
   d. a linear relationship.

4. You hypothesize that more natural gas is sold in the Northeast when winters are colder. Which of the following possibilities would best reveal if your belief is correct?
   a. A time-series diagram showing the amount of natural gas sold in the Northeast during the last 30 years.
   b. A time-series diagram showing the average temperature in the Northeast during the last 30 years.
   c. A scatter-diagram plotting the average temperature in the Northeast against the amount of natural gas sold.
   d. A trend diagram that plots the trend in natural gas sales over the last 30 years against the average temperature in the Northeast 30 years ago and this year.

5. Which type of graph can mislead?
   a. A time-series graph.
   b. A cross-section graph.
   c. A scatter diagram.
   d. *Any* type of graph might mislead.

Graphs Used in Economic Models

6. If variables x and y move up and down together, they are
   a. positively related.
   b. negative related.
   c. unrelated.
   d. trend related.

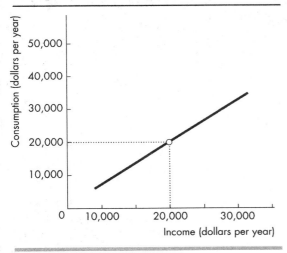

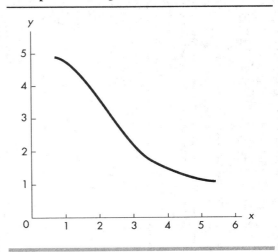

7. In Figure A1.7 when income equals $20,000, what does consumption equal?
   a. $0
   b. $10,000
   c. $20,000
   d. Impossible to tell

8. The relationship between income and consumption illustrated in Figure A1.7 is
   a. positive and linear.
   b. positive and nonlinear.
   c. negative and linear.
   d. negative and nonlinear

9. The term "direct relationship" means the same as
   a. correlation.
   b. trend.
   c. positive relationship.
   d. negative relationship.

10. Figure A1.8 shows
    a. a positive relationship.
    b. a time-series relationship.
    c. a negative relationship.
    d. no relationship between the variables.

11. The relationship between two variables, x and y, is a vertical line. Thus x and y are
    a. positively correlated.
    b. negatively correlated.
    c. not related.
    d. falsely related.

The Slope of a Relationship

12. The slope of a negative relationship is
    a. negative.
    b. undefined.
    c. positive to the right of the maximum point and negative to the left.
    d. constant as long as the relationship is nonlinear.

13. A linear relationship
    a. always has a maximum.
    b. always has a constant slope.
    c. always slopes up to the right.
    d. never has a constant slope.

FIGURE **A1.9**
Multiple Choice Questions 14 and 15

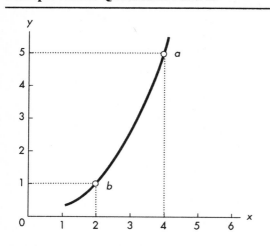

FIGURE **A1.10**
Multiple Choice Questions 16 and 17

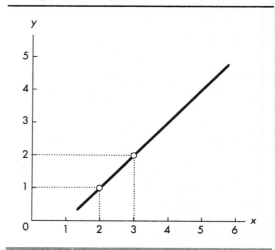

14. The relationship between x and y in Figure A1.9 is
    a. positive with an increasing slope.
    b. positive with a decreasing slope.
    c. negative with an increasing slope.
    d. negative with a decreasing slope.

15. In Figure A1.9 the slope across the arc between points a and b equals
    a. 5.
    b. 4.
    c. 2.
    d. 1.

16. In Figure A1.10, between $x = 2$ and $x = 3$, what is the slope of the line?
    a. 1
    b. −1
    c. 2
    d. 3

17. In Figure A1.10 how does the slope of the line between $x = 4$ and $x = 5$ compare with the slope between $x = 2$ and $x = 3$?
    a. The slope is greater between $x = 4$ and $x = 5$.
    b. The slope is greater between $x = 2$ and $x = 3$.
    c. The slope is the same.
    d. The slope is not comparable.

Graphing Relationships Among More Than Two Variables

FIGURE **A1.11**
Multiple Choice Questions 18, 19, 20

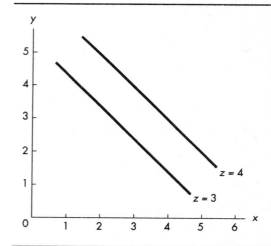

18. In Figure A1.11 x is
    a. positively related to y and negatively related to z.
    b. positively related to both y and z.
    c. negatively related to y and positively related to z.
    d. negatively related to both y and z.

19. In Figure A1.11, *ceteris paribus*, an increase in x is associated with

    a. an increase in y.
    b. a decrease in y.
    c. a decrease in z.
    d. None of the above answers is correct.

20. In Figure A1.11 an increase in z causes a

    a. movement up along one of the lines showing the relationship between x and y.
    b. movement down along one of the lines showing the relationship between x and y.
    c. shift rightward in the line showing the relationship between x and y.
    d. shift leftward in the line showing the relationship between x and y.

■ Short Answer Problems

1. a. The data in Table A1.1 show the U.S. unemployment rate between 1981 and 2003. Draw a time-series graph of these data.
    b. When was the unemployment rate the highest?

TABLE **A1.2**

Short Answer Problem 2

x	y
1	2
2	4
3	6
4	8
5	7
6	6

2. a. Use the data in Table A1.2 to graph the relationship between x and y.
    b. Over what range of values for x is this relationship positive? Over what range is it negative?
    c. Calculate the slope between $x = 1$ and $x = 2$.
    d. Calculate the slope between $x = 5$ and $x = 6$.
    e. What relationships do your answers to parts c and d have to your answer for part b?

3. a. In Figure A1.12, use the tangent line in the figure to calculate the slope at point b.
    b. Compute the slope across the arc between points b and a.
    c. Calculate the slope across the arc between points c and b.

TABLE **A1.1**

Short Answer Problem 1

Year	Unemployment rate
1981	7.6
1982	9.7
1983	9.6
1984	7.5
1985	7.2
1986	7.0
1987	6.2
1988	5.5
1989	5.3
1990	5.5
1991	6.7
1992	7.4
1993	6.8
1994	6.1
1995	5.6
1996	5.4
1997	5.6
1998	5.0
1999	4.2
2000	4.0
2001	4.7
2002	5.8
2003	6.0
2004	5.5
2005	5.1

FIGURE **A1.12**

Short Answer Problem 3

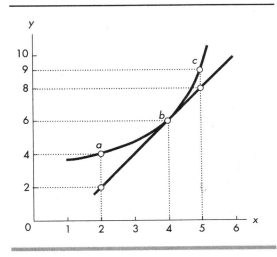

4. Can a curve have a positive but decreasing slope? If so, draw an example.

5. a. Bobby says that he buys fewer compact discs when the price of a compact disc is higher. Bobby also says that he will buy more compact discs after he graduates and his income is higher. Is the relationship between the number of compact discs Bobby buys and the price positive or negative? Is the relationship between Bobby's income and the number of compact discs positive or negative?

   b. Table A1.3 shows the number of compact discs Bobby buys in a month at different prices when his income is low and when his income is high. On a diagram with price on the vertical axis and the quantity purchased on the horizontal axis, plot the relationship between the number of discs purchased and the price when Bobby's income is low.

   c. On the same diagram, draw the relationship between the number of discs purchased and the price when Bobby's income is high.

   d. Does an increase in Bobby's income cause the relationship between the price of a compact disc and the number purchased to shift rightward or leftward?

TABLE **A1.3**

Short Answer Problem 5

Price (dollars per compact disc)	Quantity of compact discs purchased, low income	Quantity of compact discs purchased, high income
$11	5	6
12	4	5
13	3	4
14	1	3
15	0	2

■ **You're the Teacher**

1. "Hey, I thought this was an *economics* class, not a *math* class. Where's the economics? All I've seen so far is math!" Reassure your friend by explaining why the concentration in this chapter is on mathematics rather than economics.

2. "I don't understand why we need to learn all about graphs. Instead of this, why can't we just use numbers? If there is any sort of relationship we need to see, we can see it easier using numbers instead of all these complicated graphs!" Explain why graphs are useful when studying economics.

3. "There must be a relationship between the direction a curve is sloping, what its slope is, and whether the curve shows a positive or negative relationship between two variables. But I can't see the tie. Is there one? And what is it?" Help this student by answering the questions posed.

■ True/False Answers

Graphing Data

1. **F** The origin is where the horizontal and vertical axes start, *not* where the graph starts.

2. **F** The graph shows a correlation between stock prices and production, but that does not necessarily mean that an increase in stock prices causes the increase in production.

3. **T** According to the figure, *y* decreased from about 12 to about 10.

4. **F** Between 1994 and 1995, *y* rose the most.

5. **T** As the figure makes clear, there has been an upward trend in *y*. A time-series graph makes it more straightforward to identify a trend in a variable.

6. **T** This is the definition of a cross-section graph.

Graphs Used in Economic Models

7. **T** If the graph slopes upward to the right, then an increase in the variable measured along the horizontal axis is associated with an increase in the variable measured on the vertical axis.

FIGURE **A1.13**
True/False Question 8

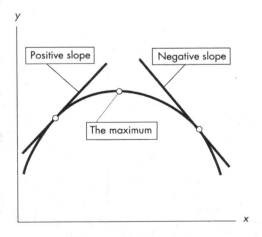

8. **F** As Figure A1.13 illustrates, before the maximum is reached, the relationship must be positive; af-

ter the maximum is attained, the relationship must be negative.

9. **T** To verify this answer, flip Figure A1.13 upside down. To the left of the minimum the line is falling, so its slope is negative; to the right the line is rising, so its slope is positive.

10. **F** If two unrelated variables are graphed on the same diagram, the "relationship" between the two is either a vertical or a horizontal straight line.

The Slope of a Relationship

FIGURE **A1.14**
True/False Question 11

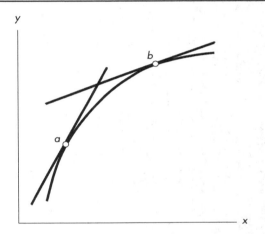

11. **T** Figure A1.14 shows a positive relationship whose slope decreases when moving rightward along it from point *a* to point *b*.

12. **F** Just the reverse is true: Divide the change in the variable on the *vertical* axis by the change in the variable on the *horizontal* axis.

13. **T** The definition of slope is $\Delta y/\Delta x$. So if a large change in *y* (the numerator) is associated with a small change in *x* (the denominator), the magnitude of the slope is relatively large. The large magnitude for the slope indicates that the line is relatively steep.

14. **T** Only the slope of a straight line is constant.

15. **T** This question tells precisely how to calculate the slope at a point on a curved line.

Graphing Relationships Among More Than Two Variables

16. **F** *Ceteris paribus* means that only the variables being studied change; all other variables do not change.

17. **F** For different amounts of rainfall, there are different curves showing the relationship between the price of a bushel of corn and the quantity that is grown.

■ Multiple Choice Answers

Graphing Data

1. **b** A time-series graph illustrates how the variable changes over time.

2. **c** A positive correlation between inflation rates and interest rates is reflected in a scatter diagram as a positive relationship; that is, the dots would tend to cluster along a line that slopes upward to the right.

3. **a** The upward trend indicates a general increase in production over time.

4. **c** A scatter diagram will show the correlation between temperature and natural gas sales.

5. **d** Any type of graph can be misleading.

Graphs Used in Economic Models

6. **a** In this case, an increase (or decrease) in x is associated with an increase (or decrease) in y, so the variables are positively related.

7. **c** Figure A1.7 shows that when income is $20,000 a year, then consumption is also $20,000 a year.

8. **a** The relationship is positive (higher income is related to higher consumption) and is linear.

9. **c** The term "positive relationship" means the same as "direct relationship."

10. **c** As x increases, y decreases; thus the relationship between x and y is negative.

11. **c** Figure A1.15 demonstrates that the change in y from 2 to 3 has no effect on x — it remains equal to 3.

The Slope of a Relationship

12. **a** A negative relationship has a negative slope; a positive relationship has a positive slope.

13. **b** A straight line — that is, a linear relationship — has a constant slope whereas nonlinear relation-

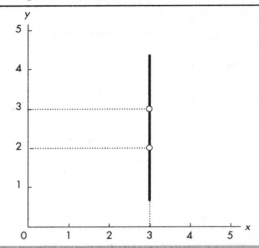

FIGURE **A1.15**
Multiple Choice Question 11

ships have slopes that vary. Thus the slope of a straight line is the same anywhere on the line.

14. **a** The slope is positive and, because the line is becoming steeper, the slope is increasing.

15. **c** The slope between the two points equals the change in the vertical distance (the "rise") divided by the change in the horizontal distance (the "run"), that is, $(5 - 1)/(4 - 2) = 2$.

16. **a** The slope equals the change in the variable measured along the vertical axis divided by the change in the variable measured along the horizontal axis, or $(2 - 1)/(3 - 2) = 1$.

17. **c** The figure shows a straight line. The slope of a straight line is constant, so the slope between $x = 4$ and $x = 5$ is the same as the slope between $x = 2$ and $x = 3$.

Graphing Relationships Among More Than Two Variables

18. **c** The curves showing the relationship between x and y demonstrate that x and y are negatively related. For any value of y, an increase in z is associated with a higher value for x, so x and z are positively related.

19. **b** Moving along one of the lines showing the relationship between x and y (say, the line with $z = 3$) shows that as x increases, y decreases.

20. **c** The higher value of z shifts the entire relationship between x and y rightward.

■ Answers to Short Answer Problems

FIGURE **A1.16**

Short Answer Problem 1

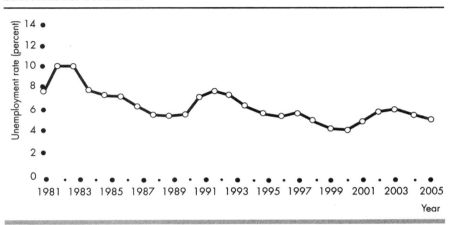

1. a. Figure A1.16 shows the time series of unemployment rates in the United States.

   b. The unemployment rate was the highest in 1982, when it equaled 9.7 percent.

FIGURE **A1.17**

Short Answer Problem 2

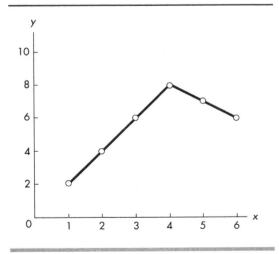

2. a. The relationship between x and y is illustrated in Figure A1.17.

   b. The relationship between x and y changes when x is 4. The relationship is positive between $x = 1$ and $x = 4$. Between $x = 4$ and $x = 6$, the relationship is negative.

   c. The slope equals $\Delta y/\Delta x$ or, in this case between $x = 1$ and $x = 2$, the slope is $(2 - 4)/(1 - 2) = 2$.

   d. Between $x = 5$ and $x = 6$, the slope is equal to $(7 - 6)/(5 - 6) = -1$.

   e. Over the range of values where the relationship between x and y is positive — from $x = 1$ to $x = 4$ — the slope is positive. Over the range where the relationship between x and y is negative — from $x = 4$ to $x = 6$ — the slope is negative. Thus positive relationships have positive slopes, and negative relationships have negative slopes.

3. a. The slope is $(8 - 2)/(5 - 2) = 2$.

   b. The slope is $(6 - 4)/(4 - 2) = 1$.

   c. The slope is $(9 - 6)/(5 - 4) = 3$.

4. Yes, a curve can have a positive, decreasing slope. Figure A1.18 (on the next page) illustrates such a relationship. In it, at relatively low values of x the slope is quite steep, indicating a high value for the slope. But as x increases, the curve becomes flatter, which means that the slope decreases. (To verify these statements, draw the tangent lines at points a and b and then compare their slopes.) This figure points out that there is a major difference between the value of a curve at some point, that is, what y equals, and what the curve's slope is at that point!

FIGURE **A1.18**
Short Answer Problem 4

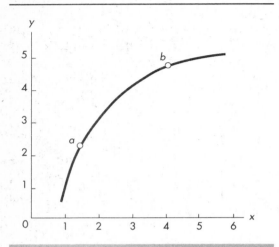

FIGURE **A1.19**
Short Answer Problem 5

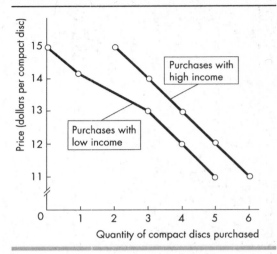

5. a. Because Bobby buys more compact discs when their price is lower, the relationship between the number of compact discs Bobby buys and the price is negative. Similarly, the relationship between Bobby's income and the number of compact discs he buys is positive.

   b. Figure A1.19 illustrates the relationship between the price of a compact disc and the number Bobby buys when his income is low.

   c. Also illustrated in Figure A1.19 is the relationship between the number of compact discs Bobby buys and their price when Bobby's income is high.

   d. An increase in Bobby's income shifts the relationship between the price of a compact disc and the number Bobby buys rightward.

■ **You're the Teacher**

1. "This *is* an economics class. But understanding some simple graphing ideas makes economics a lot easier to learn. Learning about graphing for its own sake is not important in this class; what is important is learning about graphing to help with the economics that we'll take up in the next chapter. So look at this chapter as a resource. Whether you already knew everything in it before you looked at it or even if everything in it was brand new, anytime you get confused by something dealing with a tech-

nical point on a graph, you can look back at this chapter for help. So, chill out; we'll get to the economics in the next chapter!"

2. "Graphs make understanding economics and the relationships between economic variables easier in three ways. First, graphs are extremely useful in showing the relationship between two economic variables. Imagine trying to determine the relationship between the interest rate and inflation rate if all we had was a bunch of numbers showing the interest rate and inflation rate each year for the past 30 years. We'd have 60 numbers; good luck in trying to eyeball a relationship from them! Second, graphs can help us more easily understand what an economic theory is trying to explain because they allow us to see quickly how two variables are related. By showing us the general relationship, we can be assured that any conclusions we reach don't depend on the numbers that we decided to use. Finally, graphs sometimes show us a result we might not have otherwise noticed. If all we had were numbers, we could easily become lost trying to keep track of them. Graphs make our work easier, and for this reason we need to know how to use them!"

3. "The connection between the direction a line slopes, its slope, and whether the relationship is positive or negative is easy — once you see it! Take a look at Figure A1.20. In this figure, the line slopes upward to the right. The slope of this line is posi-

FIGURE **A1.20**
You're the Teacher Question 3

FIGURE **A1.20**
You're the Teacher Question 3

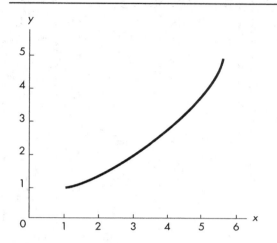

FIGURE **A1.21**
You're the Teacher Question 3

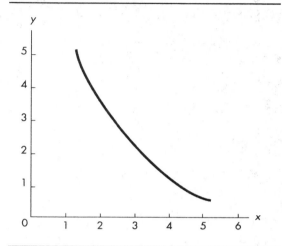

tive: an increase in x is associated with an increase in y. Because increases in x are related to increases in y, the graph shows a positive relationship between x and y.

Now look at Figure A1.21. Here the line slopes downward to the right. The slope of this line is negative: An increase in x is related to a decrease in y. Because x and y are inversely related, the relationship shown in Figure A1.21 is negative.

So, look: Positive relationships have positive slopes and negative relationships have negative slopes!

We can summarize these results for you so that you'll always be able to remember them by putting them all together:

Direction of line		Sign of slope		Type of relationship
Upward to the right	⇔	Positive	⇔	Positive
Downward to the right	⇔	Negative	⇔	Negative

This summary should help you keep everything straight. Things should be easier now."

Appendix Quiz

1. The vertical scale line of a graph is called the
   a. origin.
   b. scalar.
   c. *y*-axis.
   d. *x*-axis.

2. On a time-series graph, time is usually shown
   a. as a triangular area.
   b. as a rectangle.
   c. along the horizontal axis.
   d. at the origin.

3. A time-series diagram of the price of a purse between 1987 and 2006 has a downward trend. Hence the price of a purse
   a. is higher in 1987 than in 2006.
   b. is higher in 2006 than in 1987.
   c. definitely has fallen each year.
   d. None of the above.

4. A scatter diagram between two variables has a negative slope. Hence an increase in the variable measured on the vertical axis is associated with _____ the variable measured on the horizontal axis.
   a. an increase in
   b. no change in
   c. a decrease in
   d. no *consistent* change in

5. A graph shows the number of males and females majoring in economics in 2007. The kind of graph used to show this data would be
   a. a scatter diagram.
   b. a time-series graph.
   c. a cross-section graph.
   d. a Venn diagram.

6. Which of the following is true regarding a trend?
   a. Only a cross section graph shows trends.
   b. Both cross section and time-series graphs show trends.
   c. Only a time-series graph shows trends.
   d. Both time-series graphs and scatter plots show trends.

7. As a point on a graph moves upward and leftward, the value of its *x*-coordinate _____ and the value of its *y*-coordinate _____.
   a. rises; rises
   b. rises; falls
   c. falls; rises
   d. falls; falls

8. The slope of a line equals the
   a. change in *y* plus the change in *x*.
   b. change in *y* minus the change in *x*.
   c. change in *y* times the change in *x*.
   d. change in *y* divided by the change in *x*.

9. As a curve approaches a minimum, its slope will
   a. be positive before the minimum and negative after the minimum.
   b. be negative before the minimum and positive after the minimum.
   c. remain constant on either side of the minimum.
   d. change, but in no consistent way from one curve to the next.

10. If the change in *y* equals 10 and the change in *x* equals −5,
    a. the slope of the curve is positive.
    b. the slope of the curve is negative.
    c. the curve must be a straight line.
    d. the slope cannot be calculated without more information.

The answers for this Appendix Quiz are on page 265

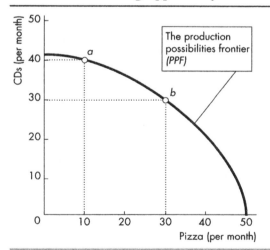

2 THE ECONOMIC PROBLEM

Key Concepts

■ Production Possibilities and Opportunity Cost

The quantities of goods and services that can be produced are limited by the available amount of resources and by technology. The **production possibilities frontier** (*PPF*) is the boundary between those combinations of goods and services that can be produced and those that cannot.

FIGURE 2.1
A *PPF* with Increasing Opportunity Costs

A *PPF* is illustrated in Figure 2.1. All production possibilities frontiers have two characteristics in common:

◆ Production points inside and on the *PPF* are attainable. Points beyond the *PPF* are not attainable.

◆ Production points on the *PPF* achieve **production efficiency** because more of one good can be obtained only by producing less of the other good.

Production points inside the *PPF* are *inefficient*, with misallocated or unused resources.

Moving between points *on* the *PPF* involves a *tradeoff* because something must be given up to get more of something else. The opportunity cost of an action is the highest-valued alternative foregone. In Figure 2.1, the opportunity cost of obtaining 20 more pizzas by moving from point *a* to point *b* is the 10 CDs that are foregone. Opportunity cost is a ratio. It equals the decrease in the production of one good divided by the increase in the production of the other. For the movement from *a* to *b* the opportunity cost is 10 CDs divided by 20 pizzas or 1/2 of a CD per pizza.

When resources are not equally productive in producing different goods and services, the *PPF* has increasing opportunity costs and bows outward, as illustrated in Figure 2.1. As more pizza is produced, the opportunity cost of a pizza increases.

■ Using Resources Efficiently

◆ The **marginal cost** of a good is the opportunity cost of producing *one* more unit of it. Because of increasing opportunity cost, when moving along the production possibilities frontier the marginal cost of an additional unit of a good increases as more is produced. So, the marginal cost curve, illustrated in Figure 2.2 on the next page, slopes upward.

◆ **Preferences** are a description of a person's likes and dislikes. Preferences can be described using the concept of marginal benefit. The **marginal benefit** from a good is the benefit a person obtains from consuming one more unit of it. The marginal benefit of a good is measured as the maximum amount someone is willing to pay for another unit of it. The marginal benefit from additional units of a good decreases as more is consumed. So the **marginal benefit curve**, which shows the relationship between the

FIGURE 2.2
Efficient Use of Resources: *MB* and *MC*

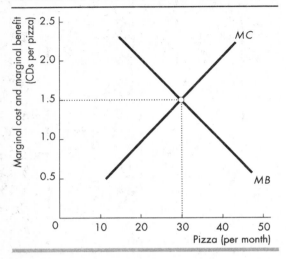

marginal benefit of a good and the quantity consumed, slopes downward as illustrated in Figure 2.2.

Allocative efficiency is reached when it is impossible to produce more of one good without giving up some other good that is valued more highly. Allocative efficiency occurs when the marginal benefit from another unit of a good equals its marginal cost. In Figure 2.2, producing 30 pizzas is the efficient allocation of resources between pizzas and CDs.

■ Economic Growth

Economic growth occurs when production expands. **Technological change,** the development of new goods and better ways of producing goods and services, and **capital accumulation,** the growth in capital resources, are two key factors that affect economic growth.

♦ Economic growth shifts the *PPF* outward. The faster it shifts, the more rapid is economic growth.

♦ The opportunity cost of economic growth is today's consumption.

♦ Nations that devote more resources to capital accumulation grow more rapidly.

■ Gains from Trade

♦ A person has a **comparative advantage** in an activity if he or she can perform the activity at a lower opportunity cost than anyone else.

♦ Comparative advantage differs from absolute advantage. **Absolute advantage** occurs when a person is more productive (can produce more goods in a given amount of time) than another person.

Specialization according to comparative advantage and trading for other goods creates gains from trade because such specialization and exchange allows consumption (not production) at points outside the *PPF*.

♦ **Learning-by-doing** occurs when people become more productive in producing a good by repeatedly producing the good.

♦ **Dynamic comparative advantage** occurs when comparative advantage is the result of specializing in a good and becoming the lowest opportunity cost provider because of learning-by-doing.

■ Economic Coordination

Firms and markets have evolved to help achieve economic coordination between the billions of individuals.

♦ A **firm** is an economic unit that hires factors of production and organizes those factors to produce and sell goods and services.

♦ A **market** is any arrangement that allows buyers and sellers to do business with each other. Markets pool information into a price, which signals buyers and sellers about the actions they should take.

Markets work only when property rights exist

♦ **Property rights** are social arrangements that set the terms of the ownership, use, and disposal of resources, goods, and services.

Goods markets are where goods and services are bought and sold; factor markets are where factors of production are bought and sold. Markets coordinate decisions in the circular flow through price adjustments.

Helpful Hints

1. **ASSUMPTIONS OF THE *PPF*:** The *PPF* provides an example of the role played by simplifying assumptions in economic analysis. No society in the world produces only two items but by assuming that there are such "two-good" nations, we gain invaluable insights into the real world. For instance, we see that once a nation is producing on its production possibilities frontier, no matter how many goods it produces, to increase the production of

one good necessarily has an opportunity cost—some other good or goods that must be foregone. In addition, we also see that countries that devote a larger proportion of their resources to capital accumulation will have more rapid growth.

2. **INEFFICIENT PRODUCTION POINTS :** Points within the *PPF* are attainable but are inefficient. Production occurs here whenever some inefficiency or misallocation emerges within the economy, such as excessive unemployment of any resource or an inefficient use of resources. Points beyond the *PPF* are unattainable. They are *not* classified as either efficient or inefficient because they are not production combinations the society can reach.

FIGURE **2.3**
A *PPF* Between Corn and Cloth

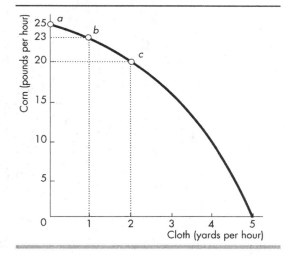

3. **CALCULATING OPPORTUNITY COST :** A helpful formula for opportunity cost results from the fact that opportunity cost is a ratio. Opportunity cost equals the quantity of goods you must give up divided by the quantity of goods you will get.

Consider the *PPF* is in Figure 2.3. If we move along the *PPF* from *a* to *b,* what is the opportunity cost of an additional yard of cloth? The nation must give up 2 pounds of corn (25 – 23) to get 1 yard of cloth (1 – 0). So the opportunity cost of the first yard of cloth is 2 pounds of corn divided by 1 yard of cloth or 2 pounds of corn per yard of cloth. Next, if we move from *b* to *c,* the opportunity cost of the second yard of cloth is calculated the same way and is 3 pounds of corn per yard of cloth.

Questions

■ True/False and Explain

Production Possibilities and Opportunity Cost

FIGURE **2.4**
True/False Questions 1 and 2

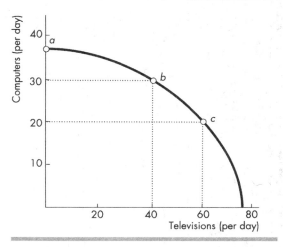

1. In Figure 2.4 point *a* is <u>NOT</u> attainable.

2. In Figure 2.4 the opportunity cost of moving from point *b* to point *c* is 10 computers.

3. From a point on the *PPF*, rearranging production and producing more of *all* goods is possible.

4. From a point within the *PPF*, rearranging production and producing more of *all* goods is possible.

5. Production efficiency requires producing at a point on the *PPF*.

6. Along a bowed-out *PPF*, as more of a good is produced, the opportunity cost of producing the good diminishes.

Using Resources Efficiently

7. The marginal cost of the 20th ton of cement equals the cost of producing all 20 tons of cement.

8. As people have more of a product, the product's marginal benefit decreases.

9. Allocative efficiency is achieved by producing the amount of a good such that the marginal benefit of

the last unit produced exceeds its marginal cost by as much as possible.

Economic Growth

10. Economic growth is illustrated by outward shifts in the *PPF*.

11. Increasing a nation's economic growth rate has an opportunity cost.

Gains from Trade

12. Daphne definitely has a comparative advantage in producing sweaters if she can produce more than can Lisa.

13. If two individuals have different opportunity costs of producing goods, both can gain from specialization and trade.

14. If the United States has an absolute advantage in growing corn and making computers, it must have a comparative advantage in growing corn.

15. Learning-by-doing can lead to dynamic comparative advantage.

Economic Coordination

16. Buyers and sellers must meet face-to-face in a market.

17. Price adjustments coordinate decisions in goods markets, but not in factor markets.

■ Multiple Choice

Production Possibilities and Opportunity Cost

1. Production points on the *PPF* itself are
   a. efficient but not attainable.
   b. efficient and attainable
   c. inefficient but not attainable.
   d. inefficient and attainable.

2. If the United States can increase its production of automobiles without decreasing its production of any other good, the United States must have been producing at a point
   a. within its *PPF*.
   b. on its *PPF*.
   c. beyond its *PPF*.
   d. None of the above are correct because increasing the production of one good without decreasing the production of another good is impossible.

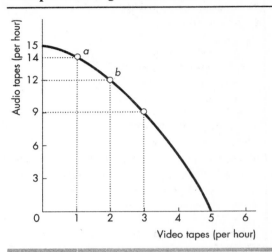

FIGURE **2.5**
Multiple Choice Questions 3 and 4

3. In Figure 2.5, at point *a* what is the opportunity cost of producing one more video tape?
   a. 14 audio tapes
   b. 3 audio tapes
   c. 2 audio tapes
   d. There is no opportunity cost.

4. In Figure 2.5, at point *b* what is the opportunity cost of producing one more video tape?
   a. 12 audio tapes
   b. 3 audio tapes
   c. 2 audio tapes
   d. There is no opportunity cost.

5. Production efficiency means that
   a. scarcity is no longer a problem.
   b. producing more of one good without producing less of some other good is not possible.
   c. as few resources as possible are being used in production.
   d. producing another unit of the good has no opportunity cost.

6. The existence of the tradeoff along the *PPF* means that the *PPF* is
   a. bowed outward.
   b. linear.
   c. negatively sloped.
   d. positively sloped.

7. The bowed-outward shape of a *PPF*
   a. is due to capital accumulation.
   b. reflects the unequal application of technology in production.
   c. illustrates the fact that no opportunity cost is incurred for increasing the production of the good measured on the horizontal axis but it is incurred to increase production of the good measured along the vertical axis.
   d. is due to the existence of increasing opportunity cost.

A nation produces only two goods — yak butter and rutabagas. Three alternative combinations of production that are on its *PPF* are given in Table 2.1. Use this information to answer the next three questions.

TABLE **2.1**

Production Possibilities

Possibility	Pounds of yak butter	Number of rutabagas
a	600	0
b	400	100
c	0	200

8. In moving from combination *a* to *b*, the opportunity cost of producing more rutabagas is
   a. 6 pounds of yak butter per rutabaga.
   b. 4 pounds of yak butter per rutabaga.
   c. 2 pounds of yak butter per rutabaga.
   d. 0 pounds of yak butter per rutabaga.

9. In moving from combination *b* to *a*, the opportunity cost of producing more pounds of yak butter is
   a. 0.10 rutabaga per pound of yak butter.
   b. 0.50 rutabaga per pound of yak butter.
   c. 1.00 rutabaga per pound of yak butter.
   d. 2.00 rutabagas per pound of yak butter.

10. Producing 400 pounds of yak butter and 50 rutabagas is
    a. not possible for this nation.
    b. possible and is an efficient production point.
    c. possible, but is an inefficient production point.
    d. an abhorrent thought.

Using Resources Efficiently

11. Moving along a bowed-out *PPF* between milk and cotton, as more milk is produced the marginal cost of an additional gallon of milk
    a. rises.
    b. does not change.
    c. falls.
    d. probably changes, but in an ambiguous direction.

12. The most anyone is willing to pay for another purse is $30. Currently the price of a purse is $40, and the cost of producing another purse is $50. The marginal benefit of a purse is
    a. $50.
    b. $40.
    c. $30.
    d. An amount not given in the answers above.

13. If the marginal benefit from another computer exceeds the marginal cost of the computer, then to use resources efficiently,
    a. more resources should be used to produce computers.
    b. fewer resources should be used to produce computers.
    c. if the marginal benefit exceeds the marginal cost by as much as possible, the efficient amount of resources are being used to produce computers.
    d. none of the above is correct because marginal benefit and marginal cost have nothing to do with using resources efficiently.

Economic Growth

14. Economic growth
    a. creates unemployment.
    b. has no opportunity cost.
    c. shifts the *PPF* outward.
    d. makes it more difficult for a nation to produce on its *PPF*.

15. The *PPF* shifts if
    a. the unemployment rate falls.
    b. people decide they want more of one good and less of another.
    c. the prices of the goods and services produced rise.
    d. the resources available to the nation change.

16. An increase in the nation's capital stock will
    a. shift the *PPF* outward.
    b. cause a movement along the *PPF* upward and leftward.
    c. cause a movement along the *PPF* downward and rightward.
    d. move the nation from producing within the *PPF* to producing at a point closer to the *PPF*.

17. One of the opportunity costs of economic growth is
    a. capital accumulation.
    b. technological change.
    c. reduced current consumption.
    d. the gain in future consumption.

18. In general, the more resources that are devoted to technological research, the
    a. greater is current consumption.
    b. higher is the unemployment rate.
    c. faster the *PPF* shifts outward.
    d. more the *PPF* will bow outward.

Gains from Trade

19. In order to achieve the maximum gains from trade, people should specialize according to
    a. property rights.
    b. *PPF*.
    c. absolute advantage.
    d. comparative advantage.

In one day Brandon can either plow 40 acres of land or plant 20 acres. In one day Christopher can either plow 28 acres of land or plant 7 acres. Use this information to answer the next four questions.

20. Which of the following statements about absolute advantage is correct?
    a. Brandon has an absolute advantage in both plowing and planting.
    b. Brandon has an absolute advantage only in plowing.
    c. Brandon has an absolute advantage only in planting.
    d. Christopher has an absolute advantage both in plowing and planting.

21. Brandon has
    a. a comparative advantage both in plowing and planting.
    b. a comparative advantage only in plowing.
    c. a comparative advantage only in planting.
    d. a comparative advantage in neither in plowing and planting.

22. Christopher has
    a. an absolute advantage only in planting.
    b. an absolute advantage only in plowing.
    c. a comparative advantage only in planting.
    d. a comparative advantage only in plowing.

23. Brandon and Christopher can
    a. both gain from exchange if Brandon specializes in planting and Christopher in plowing.
    b. both gain from exchange if Brandon specializes in plowing and Christopher in planting.
    c. exchange, but only Brandon will gain from the exchange.
    d. exchange, but only Christopher will gain from the exchange.

24. A nation can *produce* at a point outside its *PPF*
    a. when it trades with other nations.
    b. when it is producing products as efficiently as possible.
    c. when there is no unemployment.
    d. at no time ever.

25. A nation can *consume* at a point outside its *PPF*
    a. when it trades with other nations.
    b. when it is producing products as efficiently as possible.
    c. when there is no unemployment.
    d. at no time ever.

Economic Coordination

26. Which of the following does <u>NOT</u> help achieve economic coordination?
    a. Firms
    b. Markets
    c. The production possibilities frontier
    d. None of the above because all these answers given help organize trade.

27. In markets, people's decisions are coordinated by
    a. specialization according to absolute advantage.
    b. changes in property rights.
    c. learning-by-doing.
    d. adjustments in prices.

■ Short Answer Problems

1. What does the negative slope of the *PPF* mean? Why is a *PPF* bowed out?

2. In Figure 2.6 indicate which points are production efficient and which are inefficient. Also show which points are attainable and which are not attainable.

FIGURE **2.6**
Short Answer Problem 2

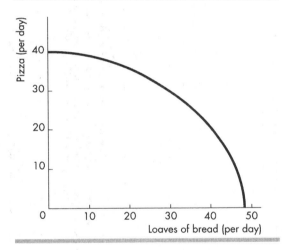

3. Sydna is stranded on a desert island and can either fish or harvest dates. Six points on her production possibilities frontier are given in Table 2.2.

   a. In Figure 2.7 plot these possibilities, label the points, and draw the *PPF*.

   b. If Sydna moves from possibility *c* to possibility *d*, what is the opportunity cost per fish?

   c. If Sydna moves from possibility *d* to possibility *e*, what is the opportunity cost per fish?

   d. In general, what happens to the opportunity cost of a fish as more fish are caught?

   e. In general, what happens to the opportunity cost of dates as more dates are harvested?

   f. Based on the original *PPF* you plotted, is a combination of 40 dates and 1 fish attainable? Is this combination an efficient one? Explain.

TABLE **2.2**
Sydna's Production Possibilities

Possibility	Dates gathered (per day)	Fish caught (per day)
a	54	0
b	50	1
c	42	2
d	32	3
e	20	4
f	0	5

FIGURE **2.7**
Short Answer Problem 3

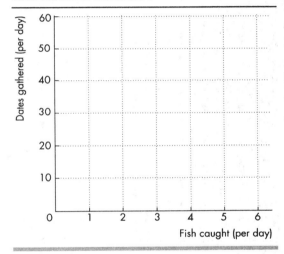

4. If the following events occurred (each is a separate event, unaccompanied by any other event), what would happen to the *PPF* in Problem 3?

   a. A new fishing pond is discovered.

   b. The output of dates is increased.

   c. Sydna finds a ladder that enables her to gather slightly more dates.

   d. A second person, with the same set of fishing and date-gathering skills as Sydna, is stranded on the island.

TABLE **2.3**
Marginal Benefit and Marginal Cost of Pizza

Slice of pizza	Marginal benefit of slice	Marginal cost of slice	Marginal benefit minus marginal cost
1	6.0	1.5	____
2	5.0	2.0	____
3	4.0	2.5	____
4	3.0	3.0	____
5	2.0	3.5	____
6	1.0	4.0	____

TABLE **2.4**
Production in France and the United States

	Computers produced in an hour	Bottles of wine produced in an hour
United States	10,000	20,000
France	12,000	8,000

TABLE **2.5**
Short Answer Problem 7 (c)

	Opportunity cost of one computer	Opportunity cost of one bottle of wine
United States	____	____
France	____	____

5. A nation produces only pizza and tacos. Table 2.3 shows the marginal benefit and marginal cost schedules for slices of pizza in terms of tacos per slice of pizza.

  a. Complete Table 2.3.

  b. For the first slice of pizza, after paying the marginal cost, how much marginal benefit — if any — is left?

  c. For the second slice, after paying the marginal cost, how much marginal benefit — if any — is left? How does your answer to this question compare to your answer to part (b)?

  d. Should the first slice of pizza be produced? Should the second one be produced? Explain you answers, especially your answer about the second slice.

  e. In a diagram, draw the marginal cost curve and the marginal benefit curve. Indicate the quantity of pizza slices that uses resources efficiently.

6. Bearing in mind the point that resources are limited, explain why is it important for a nation to use its resources efficiently.

7. Suppose that both the United States and France produce computers and wine. Table 2.4 shows what each country can produce in an hour.

  a. On graph paper, draw the *PPF* for the United States for one hour.

  b. On graph paper, draw the *PPF* for France for one hour.

  c. Complete Table 2.5.

  d. In what good(s) does the United States have a comparative advantage? France?

  e. Initially the United States uses half its resources to produce wine and half to produce computers.

How much wine and how many computers are produced in an hour in the United States? France also devotes half her resources to computers and half to wine. How many computers and bottles of wine does France produce in an hour? What is the total amount of wine produced by France and the United States in an hour? The total number of computers?

  f. Suppose that the United States specializes in wine and France in computers. What is the total amount of wine produced by France and the United States now? The total number of computers?

  g. What do your answers to parts (e) and (f) show?

8. How do property rights affect people's incentives to create new music?

■ You're the Teacher

1. "The idea of the production possibilities frontier is stupid. I mean, after all, who ever heard of a nation that produces only two goods. Come on, every nation produces millions, probably billions of goods. Why do I have to bother to learn about the production possibilities frontier when it is so unrealistic?" One reason for this student to learn about the production possibilities frontier is that it will probably be on the exams. But there are other reasons, too. Explain some of them to help motivate this student.

Answers

■ True/False Answers

Production Possibilities and Opportunity Cost

1. **F** *Any* point on the production possibilities frontier is attainable, even points where the *PPF* intersects the axes.

2. **T** The opportunity cost equals the number of computers foregone, in this case the fall from 30 computers at point *b* to 20 at point *c*.

3. **F** Points on the frontier are production efficient, so increasing the production of one good necessarily requires producing fewer of some other good.

FIGURE **2.8**
True/False Question 4

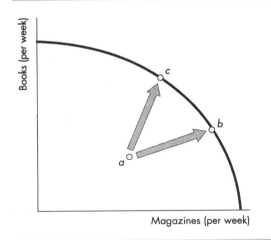

4. **T** Points within the frontier are inefficient, which means its possible to rearrange production and boost the production of all goods and services. This condition is illustrated in Figure 2.8, where from (the inefficient) point *a*, it is possible to move to points such as *b* or *c* where more of both books and magazines are produced.

5. **T** Production efficiency implies that the production of one good can be increased *only if* the production of another good is decreased, which is true only on the *PPF* itself.

6. **F** As more of a good is produced, the opportunity cost of additional units increases.

Using Resources Efficiently

7. **F** The marginal cost is the cost of the 20th ton itself, not the cost of producing all 20 tons.

8. **T** As people have more of a product, they are willing to pay less for additional units, which means that the marginal benefit of the product will decrease.

9. **F** For resources to be allocated efficiently, it is necessary for the marginal benefit of the last unit produced to equal the marginal cost of the unit.

Economic Growth

10. **T** As the *PPF* shifts outward, the nation is able to produce more of all goods.

11. **T** The opportunity cost is the loss of current consumption.

Gains from Trade

12. **F** Based on the information in the problem, Daphne definitely has an absolute advantage, but without more information we cannot tell whether she has a comparative advantage.

13. **T** A key observation is that *both* individuals gain.

14. **F** Comparative advantage requires *comparing* the opportunity cost of producing corn in the United States with the opportunity cost of producing it elsewhere.

15. **T** Learning-by-doing means that the cost of producing a good falls as more is produced, so the nation (or person) ultimately acquires a comparative advantage in making the good.

Economic Coordination

16. **F** Buyers and sellers communicate with each other in markets, but in most markets they do not meet face-to-face.

17. **F** Price adjustments coordinate decisions in markets.

■ Multiple Choice Answers

Production Possibilities and Opportunity Cost

1. **b** *Only* points on the frontier are both attainable and efficient.

2. **a** Only from points within the frontier can the production of a good increase without decreasing the production of another good.

3. **c** By producing 1 more video tape, audio tape production falls by 2 (from 14 to 12), so the opportunity cost of the video tape is the ratio of 2 audio tapes to the 1 video tape, that is, 2 audio tapes per video tape.

4. **b** As more video tapes are produced, the opportunity cost of an additional video tape gets larger.

5. **b** This answer is the definition of production efficiency.

6. **c** When production is on the *PPF*, the tradeoff is that if more of one good is produced, then some other good must be foregone. This result means that the *PPF* has a negative slope.

7. **d** Increasing opportunity cost means that, as more of a good is produced, its opportunity cost increases. As a result, the *PPF* bows outward.

8. **c** Moving from *a* to *b* gains 100 rutabagas and loses 200 pounds of yak butter, so the opportunity cost is (200 pounds of yak butter)/(100 rutabagas), or 2 pounds of yak butter per rutabaga.

9. **b** 100 rutabagas are foregone, so the opportunity cost is (100 rutabagas)/(200 pounds of yak butter), or 0.50 rutabagas per pound of yak butter. Note how the opportunity cost of a rutabaga is the inverse of the opportunity cost of a pound of yak butter, as calculated in the answer to the previous question.

10. **c** When 400 pounds of yak butter are produced, a maximum of 100 rutabagas can be produced; if only 50 rutabagas are produced, the combination is inefficient.

Using Resources Efficiently

11. **a** Along a bowed-out *PPF*, as more of a good is produced, its marginal cost — the opportunity cost of producing another unit — rises.

12. **c** The marginal benefit from a good is the maximum that a person is willing to pay for the good.

13. **a** The benefit from the computer exceeds the cost of producing the computer, so society will gain if resources are allocated so that the computer is produced.

Economic Growth

14. **c** Economic growth makes attainable previously unattainable production levels.

15. **d** An increase in resources shifts the *PPF* outward; a decrease shifts it leftward. (A decrease in the unemployment rate moves the nation from a point in the interior of the *PPF* to a point closer to the frontier.)

16. **a** Increases in a nation's resources create economic growth and shift the nation's *PPF* outward.

17. **c** If a nation devotes more resources to capital accumulation or technological development, which are the main sources of growth, fewer resources can be used to produce goods for current consumption.

18. **c** The more resources used for technological research, the more rapid is economic growth.

Gains from Trade

19. **d** Specializing according to comparative advantage reduces the opportunity cost of producing goods and services.

20. **a** Brandon can produce more of both goods than Christopher, so Brandon has an absolute advantage in both goods.

21. **c** Brandon's opportunity cost of planting an acre of land is plowing 2 acres, whereas Christopher's opportunity cost of planting an acre is plowing 4 acres.

22. **d** Christopher's opportunity cost of plowing an acre is planting 1/4 an acre, while Brandon's opportunity cost is planting 1/2 an acre.

23. **a** By specializing according to their comparative advantages, both can gain from exchange.

24. **d** The *PPF* shows the maximum amounts that can be produced.

25. **a** When a nation specializes according to its comparative advantage and trades with another specialist nation, both can consume at levels beyond their *PPF*s.

Economic Coordination

26. **c** The production possibilities frontier shows the limits to production and does not help achieve economic coordination.

27. **d** Changes in prices create incentives for people to change their actions.

■ Answers to Short Answer Problems

1. The negative slope of the *PPF* indicates that increasing the production of one good means that the production of some other good decreases.

   A *PPF* is bowed out because the existence of nonidentical resources creates an increasing opportunity cost as the production of a good is increased. Because resources are not identical, some are better suited for producing one good than another. So when resources are switched from producing items for which they are well suited to producing goods for which they are ill suited, the opportunity cost of increasing the output of these goods rises.

FIGURE **2.9**
Short Answer Problem 2

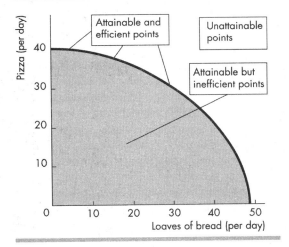

2. Figure 2.9 shows the efficient/inefficient points and attainable/not attainable points. The attainable but inefficient points are shaded; the attainable and efficient points lie on the *PPF* itself; and the unattainable points are located beyond the *PPF*.

3. a. Figure 2.10 shows the *PPF*.

   b. Moving from *c* to *d* increases the number of fish caught by 1 and decreases the number of dates gathered from 42 to 32. Catching 1 fish costs 10 dates, so the opportunity cost of the fish is 10 dates. The opportunity cost of this fish is:

   $$\frac{42 \text{ dates} - 32 \text{ dates}}{3 \text{ fish} - 2 \text{ fish}} = 10 \text{ dates per fish.}$$

   c. Moving from *d* to *e* indicates that the opportunity cost of the fish is 12 dates: The number of

FIGURE **2.10**
Short Answer Problem 3

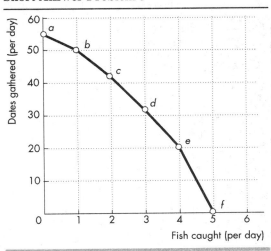

dates gathered falls from 32 to 20 while the number of fish caught increases by 1.

   d. As more fish are caught, the opportunity cost of an additional fish rises. In particular, the first fish has an opportunity cost of only 4 dates; the second, 8 dates; the third, 10 dates; the fourth, 12 dates; and the fifth, 20 dates.

   e. As more dates are gathered, the opportunity cost of a date rises. Moving from *f* to *e* shows that the first 20 dates cost only 1 fish so that the opportunity cost of a date here is 1/20 of a fish. Going from *e* to *d*, however, makes the opportunity cost of a date 1/12 of a fish. This pattern continues so that as more dates are gathered, their opportunity cost increases. Finally, moving from *b* to *a* has the largest opportunity cost for a date, 1/4 of a fish.

   As parts (d) and (e) demonstrate, there is increasing opportunity cost moving along the *PPF*. That is, as more fish are caught, their opportunity cost — in terms of foregone dates — increases and as more dates are gathered, their opportunity cost — in terms of foregone fish — also increases. It is these increasing opportunity costs that account for the bowed-outward shape of the *PPF*.

   f. This combination is within the *PPF* and is attainable. It is inefficient because Sydna could produce more of either or both goods. Sydna is not organizing her activities efficiently.

FIGURE **2.11**

FIGURE **2.11**
Short Answer Problem 4 (a)

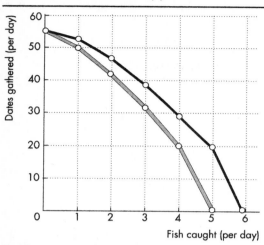

that she can catch. As a result, the maximum number of dates increases, but the maximum number of fish does not change. The *PPF* shifts in the same general pattern as shown in Figure 2.12.

FIGURE **2.13**
Short Answer Problem 4 (d)

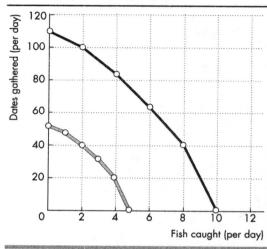

4. a. A new fishing pond increases the number of fish Sydna can catch, but it does not affect the maximum number of dates she can gather. Her *PPF* shifts generally as shown in Figure 2.11.

    b. Increasing her output of dates does not affect the *PPF*. Sydna might increase her gathering of dates either by moving from a point within the *PPF* to a point on (or closer to) the frontier or by moving along the frontier. Neither of these actions shifts the *PPF*.

FIGURE **2.12**
Short Answer Problem 4 (c)

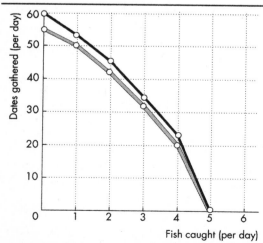

d. Having a second worker on the island boosts both the number of dates that can be gathered *and* the number of fish that can be caught. If the second person has the same set of skills as Sydna, the *PPF* shifts out in a "parallel" manner, as illustrated in Figure 2.13. Be sure to note that the scales on the axes in Figure 2.13 are different from those on the axes in Figures 2.10–2.12.

TABLE **2.6**
Marginal Benefit and Marginal Cost of Pizza

Slice of pizza	Marginal benefit of slice	Marginal cost of slice	Marginal benefit minus marginal cost
1	6.0	1.5	4.5
2	5.0	2.0	3.0
3	4.0	2.5	1.5
4	3.0	3.0	0.0
5	2.0	3.5	−1.5
6	1.0	4.0	−3.0

c. The ladder increases the number of dates that Sydna can gather, but has no effect on the fish

5. a. Table 2.6 shows the answers.

    b. For the first slice of pizza, after paying the marginal cost, there is 4.5 of marginal benefit left.

c. For the second slice of pizza, after paying the marginal cost, there is 3.0 of marginal benefit left over. There is less left over for the second slice than the first slice because the marginal benefit of the second slice is less than that of the first slice and the marginal cost the second slice is more than that of the first one.

d. The first slice should be produced because the marginal benefit from the first slice exceeds its marginal cost. The second slice also should be produced for the same reason. As long as the marginal benefit from a slice of pizza exceeds its marginal cost, society benefits if the slice is produced. The "net benefit" from the first slice is more than that of the second slice, but as long as there is a positive net benefit, society benefits.

FIGURE **2.14**
Short Answer Problem 5 (e)

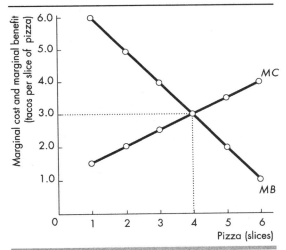

e. Figure 2.14 shows the marginal cost and marginal benefit curves. Four slices of pizza are the allocatively efficient quantity, that is the quantity that uses resources efficiently, because the marginal benefit from the fourth slice equals its marginal cost. The marginal benefit for any greater quantity of pizza slices is less than the marginal cost of the slice, so producing these units would result in a net loss for society.

6. A nation should use its resources efficiently because it has only a limited quantity of them. If resources are used inefficiently, there is waste and fewer of people's wants can be satisfied. By using its resources efficiency and thereby producing at the point of allocative efficiency, society ensures that as many of the most important wants, measured by the marginal benefit from the goods that satisfy those wants, are satisfied.

FIGURE **2.15**
Short Answer Problem 7 (a)

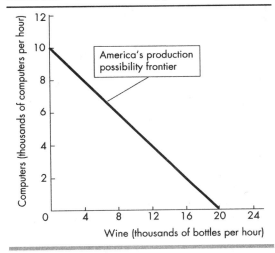

7. a. Figure 2.15 shows the *PPF* for the United States. The maximum amount of wine that can be produced is 20,000 bottles and the maximum number of computers that can be produced is 10,000.

FIGURE **2.16**
Short Answer Problem 7 (b)

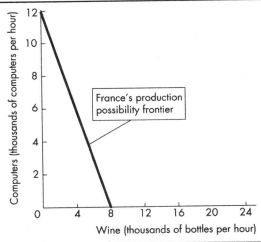

b. Figure 2.16 shows the French *PPF*.

TABLE **2.7**

Short Answer Problem 7 (c)

	Opportunity cost of one computer	Opportunity cost of one bottle of wine
United States	2 bottles of wine	½ computer
France	2/3 bottles of wine	1½ computer

c. Table 2.7 shows the opportunity costs for the goods. To illustrate how this table was obtained, we can use the opportunity cost of a computer in the United States as an example. To produce one computer in the United States requires that resources work for 1/10,000 of an hour at manufacturing computers. So to produce an additional computer, resources must be switched from the wine industry to the computer industry for 1/10,000 of an hour. During this time, if left in the wine industry, the resources could otherwise have produced (1/10,000) × (20,000 bottles of wine) or 2 bottles of wine. Hence to produce one additional computer in the United States, 2 bottles of wine are foregone. Two bottles of wine, then, are the opportunity cost of the computer. The rest of the opportunity costs are calculated similarly.

d. The United States has a comparative advantage in wine because the opportunity cost of a bottle of wine in the United States — 1/2 computer — is less than the opportunity cost of a bottle of wine in France —1½ computer. France has a comparative advantage in the production of computers, because its opportunity cost —2/3 of a bottle of wine — is less than that in the United States — 2 bottles of wine.

e. In the United States, 5,000 computers and 10,000 bottles of wine are produced in an hour. In France, 6,000 computers and 4,000 bottles of wine are produced in an hour. Overall, 11,000 computers and 14,000 bottles of wine are produced in an hour.

f. With the United States specializing in wine, 20,000 bottles of wine are produced in an hour. Because France specializes in computers, 12,000 computers are produced in an hour.

g. With specialization, world computer production rises by 1,000 computers per hour and world production of wine rises by 6,000 bottles per hour. The fact that world production of wine and computers *both* increase demonstrates that specialization, according to comparative advantage, can boost world output of all goods.

8. Property rights play a key role in shaping the incentive to create new music or, more generally, to create *any* new computer program, book, pharmaceutical drug, and so forth. Creation is costly because resources, time, and effort must be devoted to this process. By securing the property right to new music, the musician stands to benefit greatly from the resources expended. But if the person cannot obtain a property right, anyone can copy the new music. In that case the musician's return will be dissipated when a lot of people copy the music and, indeed, someone else might reap the rewards. Property rights, by promising that the musician will personally benefit from the effort involved in creating the music, motivate significantly more new music than would occur in the absence of property rights.

■ You're the Teacher

1. "*All* economic models vastly simplify the complex reality. But that is no reason to throw them away. The lessons that can be learned from the simple two-good *PPF* carry over to the real world. For instance, the two-good *PPF* shows that there are limits to production. These limits are represented by the *PPF* curve, which divides attainable from unattainable production points. Now, just as you say, in the real world billions of goods are produced. But there are still limits. But no matter how many goods a nation produces, every nation faces a limit of how much it can produce, just as in the simple two-good *PPF* case.

"Plus, the simple *PPF* model demonstrates that production can be efficient or inefficient. This result is also true in the real world. "And, the two-good *PPF* shows that once production is efficient — a point on the *PPF* — increasing the output of one good has an opportunity cost because the production of the other good must be reduced. The same is true in our real world. If we are producing efficiently, if we want to produce more of one good, we have to give up other goods. So, based on the assumption that there are only two goods, the *PPF* teaches us stuff that we can apply everywhere, not just on the next test."

Chapter Quiz

1. Consider a constant slope *PPF* with a vertical intercept of 80 guns and a horizontal intercept of 120 tons of butter. The opportunity cost of increasing butter output from 30 to 31 tons is
   a. 1/2 of a gun.
   b. 2/3 of a gun.
   c. 1 gun.
   d. 1 1/2 guns.

2. A nation can produce at a point outside its *PPF*
   a. when it trades with other nations.
   b. when it produces inefficiently.
   c. when it produces efficiently.
   d. never.

3. Which of the following statements is true?
   a. All resources are made by people.
   b. Human resources are called labor.
   c. Capital is made only by labor.
   d. Human capital is a contradiction in terms.

4. A situation in which some resources are used inefficiently is represented in a *PPF* diagram by
   a. any point on either the vertical or horizontal axis.
   b. the midpoint of the *PPF*.
   c. a point outside the *PPF*.
   d. a point inside the *PPF*.

5. Robert has decided to write the essay that is due in his economics class rather than watch a movie. The movie he will miss is Robert's _____ of writing the essay.
   a. opportunity cost
   b. explicit cost
   c. implicit cost
   d. discretionary cost

6. The cost of textbooks _____ and the earnings foregone because of attending college _____ part of the opportunity cost of attending college.
   a. is; are
   b. is; are not
   c. is not; are
   d. is not; are not

7. The best alternative foregone from an action is called the action's
   a. "loss."
   b. "money cost."
   c. "direct cost."
   d. "opportunity cost."

8. The marginal benefit of a product is the
   a. benefit that the product gives to someone other than the buyer.
   b. maximum someone is willing to pay for that unit of the product.
   c. benefit of the product that exceeds the marginal cost of the product.
   d. benefit of the product divided by the total number of units purchased.

9. A marginal benefit curve has a _____ slope; a marginal cost curve has a _____ slope.
   a. positive; positive
   b. positive; negative
   c. negative; positive
   d. negative; negative

10. The production possibilities frontier will shift inward as a result of
    a. an increase in the production of consumption goods.
    b. an increase in R&D expenditure.
    c. an increase in population.
    d. destruction of part of the nation's capital stock.

The answers for this Chapter Quiz are on page 265

1 INTRODUCTION

Mid-Term Examination

■ **Chapter 1**

1. Willy makes $25 an hour as a carpenter. He must take two hours off from work (unpaid) to go to the dentist to have a tooth pulled. The dentist charges $60. In terms of dollars, the opportunity cost of Willy's visit to the dentist is
   a. $25.
   b. $50.
   c. $60
   d. $110.

2. A company produces 100 units of a good at a cost of $400 or produces 101 units of the same good at a cost of $415 dollars. The $15 difference is
   a. the marginal benefit of producing 101 units.
   b. the marginal cost of producing the 101st unit.
   c. the marginal cost of producing the first unit.
   d. less than the average cost.

3. Positive statements are statements about
   a. prices.
   b. quantities.
   c. what is.
   d. what ought to be.

4. The branch of economics that studies individual markets within the economy is called
   a. macroeconomics.
   b. microeconomics.
   c. individual economics.
   d. market economy.

■ **Chapter 2**

5. Output combinations beyond the production possibility frontier
   a. result in more rapid growth.
   b. are associated with unused resources.
   c. are attainable only with the full utilization of all resources.
   d. are unattainable.

6. The *PPF* shifts inward as a result of
   a. a decrease in the production of consumption goods.
   b. an increase in R&D expenditure.
   c. an increase in population.
   d. the destruction of a portion of the capital stock.

7. Whenever a person can produce less of all goods than anyone else, that person
   a. should specialize in nothing.
   b. still has a comparative advantage in something.
   c. should be self-sufficient.
   d. has a comparative advantage in nothing.

8. To obtain all the gains available from comparative advantage, individuals or countries must do more than trade, they must also
   a. specialize.
   b. save.
   c. invest.
   d. engage in research and development.

Answers

■ Mid-Term Exam Answers

1. d;   2. b;   3. c;   4. b;   5. d;   6. d;   7. b;   8. a.

Chapter 3

DEMAND AND SUPPLY

Markets and Prices

A **competitive market** is one that has so many buyers and sellers so that no single buyer or seller can influence the price. The ratio of the money price of one good to the money price of another good is the **relative price**. The relative price of a good is the good's opportunity cost. The demand for and supply of a product depend, in part, on its relative price.

Demand

The **quantity demanded** of a good is the amount that consumers plan to buy during a time period at a particular price. The **law of demand** states that "other things remaining the same, the higher the price of a good, the smaller is the quantity demanded." Higher prices decrease the quantity demanded for two reasons:

♦ *Substitution effect* — a higher relative price raises the opportunity cost of buying a good and so people buy less of it.

♦ *Income effect* — a higher relative price reduces the amount of goods people can buy. Usually this effect decreases the amount people buy of the good that rose in price.

Demand is the entire relationship between the price of a good and the quantity demanded. A **demand curve** shows the inverse relationship between the quantity demanded and price, everything else remaining the same. For each quantity, a demand curve shows the highest price someone is willing to pay for that unit. This highest price is the *marginal benefit* a consumer receives for that unit of output.

FIGURE 3.1
Demand Curves

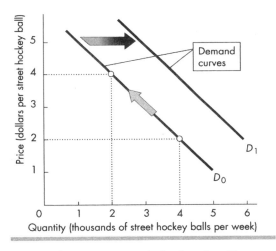

♦ Demand curves are negatively sloped, as illustrated in Figure 3.1.

♦ A change in the price of the good or service leads to a **change in the quantity demanded** and *a movement along the demand curve*. The higher the price of a good or service, the lower is the quantity demanded. This relationship is shown in Figure 3.1 with the movement along D_0 from 4,000 to 2,000 street hockey balls demanded per week in response to a rise in price from $2 to $4 for a street hockey ball.

A **change in demand** and *a shift in the demand curve*, occur when any factor that affects buying plans, other than the price of the product changes. An increase in demand means that the demand curve shifts rightward, such as the shift from D_0 to D_1 in Figure 3.1; a decrease in demand refers to the demand curve shifting leftward.

The demand curve shifts with changes in:

♦ *prices of related goods* — a rise in the price of a **substitute** increases demand and shifts the demand curve rightward; a rise in the price of a **complement** decreases demand and shifts the demand curve leftward.

♦ *expected future prices* — if the price of a good is expected to rise in the future, the current demand for it increases and the demand curve shifts rightward.

♦ *income* — for a **normal good**, an increase in income increases demand and shifts the demand curve rightward; for an **inferior good** an increase in income decreases demand and shifts the demand curve leftward.

♦ *expected future income* — when expected future income increases, the current demand might increase.

♦ *population* — an increase in population increases demand and shifts the demand curve rightward.

♦ *preferences* — if people like a good more, its demand increases so the demand curve shifts rightward.

■ Supply

The **quantity supplied** of a good or service is the amount that producers plan to sell during a given time period at a particular price.

The **law of supply** states that "other things remaining the same, the higher the price of a good, the greater is the quantity supplied." **Supply** is the entire relationship between the quantity supplied and the price of a good. A **supply curve** shows the positive relationship between the price and the quantity supplied. For each quantity, the supply curve shows the minimum price a supplier must receive in order to produce that unit of output.

♦ Supply curves are positively sloped, as shown in Figure 3.2.

♦ A change in the price of the product leads to a **change in the quantity supplied** and a *movement along the supply curve*. In Figure 3.2, the movement along S_0 from 2,000 street hockey balls supplied per week to 4,000 balls when the price rises from $2 for a ball to $4 is a change in the quantity supplied.

When any factor that influences selling plans other than the price of the good changes, there is a **change in supply,** which is illustrated *as a shift in the supply curve.* An increase in supply shifts the supply curve rightward, shown in Figure 3.2 as the shift from S_0 to S_1; a decrease in supply shifts the supply curve leftward.

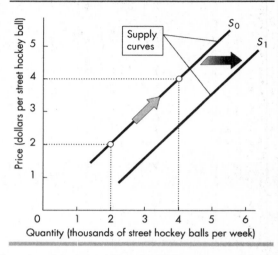

FIGURE **3.2**
Supply Curves

There is a change supply and a shift in the supply curve in response to changes in the following:

♦ *prices of the productive resources used to produce the good* — a rise in the price of an input decreases supply and the supply curve shifts leftward.

♦ *prices of related goods produced* — a rise in the price of a *substitute in production* decreases supply and the supply curve shifts leftward; a rise in the price of a *complement in production* increases supply and the supply curve shifts rightward.

♦ *expected future prices* — if the price is expected to rise in the future, the current supply decreases and the supply curve shifts leftward.

♦ *number of suppliers* — an increase in the number of suppliers increases supply and the supply curve shifts rightward.

♦ *technology* — an advance in technology increases supply and the supply curve shifts rightward.

■ Market Equilibrium

The **equilibrium price** is the price at which the quantity demanded equals the quantity supplied. It is determined by the intersection of the demand and supply curves. The **equilibrium quantity** is the quantity bought and sold at the equilibrium price. Figure 3.3 shows the equilibrium price, $3, and the equilibrium quantity, 3,000 street hockey balls per week. At prices below the equilibrium price, a shortage exists and the

FIGURE **3.3**

The Equilibrium Price and Quantity

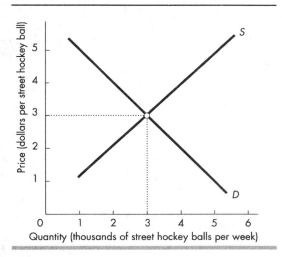

price rises. At prices above the equilibrium price, a surplus exists and the price falls. Only at the equilibrium price does the price not change.

■ Predicting Changes in Price and Quantity

When either the demand *or* supply changes so that *one* of the demand or supply curves shifts, the effect on both the price (P) and quantity (Q) can be determined:

♦ An increase in demand (a rightward shift in the demand curve) raises P and increases Q.

♦ A decrease in demand (a leftward shift in the demand curve) lowers P and decreases Q.

♦ An increase in supply (a rightward shift in the supply curve) lowers P and increases Q.

♦ A decrease in supply (a leftward shift in the supply curve) raises P and decreases Q.

When both the demand and supply change so that both the demand and supply curves shift, the effect on the price *or* the quantity can be determined, but without information about the relative sizes of the shifts, the effect on the other variable is ambiguous.

♦ If both demand and supply increases (both curves shift rightward), the quantity increases but the price might rise, fall, or remain the same.

♦ If demand decreases (the demand curve shifts leftward) and supply increases (the supply curve shifts rightward), the price falls but the quantity might increase, decrease, or not change.

Helpful Hints

1. **DEVELOPING INTUITION ABOUT DEMAND :** When you are first learning about demand and supply, think in terms of concrete examples. Have some favorite examples in the back of your mind. For instance, when you hear "complementary goods" (goods used together), think about hot dogs and hot dog buns because few people eat hot dogs without using a hot dog bun. For "substitute goods" (things that take each other's place) think about hot dogs and hamburgers because they are obvious substitutes.

2. **DEVELOPING INTUITION ABOUT SUPPLY :** An easy and concrete way to identify with suppliers is to think of "profit": Anything that increases the profit from producing a product (except for the price of the good itself) increases the supply and shifts the supply curve rightward, whereas anything that decreases profit decreases the supply and shifts the supply curve leftward.

3. **SHIFT IN A CURVE VERSUS A MOVEMENT ALONG A CURVE :** Failing to distinguish correctly between a shift in a curve and a movement along a curve can lead to error and lost points on examinations. The difference applies equally to both demand and supply curves.

   The important point to remember is *that a change in the price of a good does not shift its demand curve; it leads to a movement along the demand curve. If one of the other factors affecting demand changes, the demand curve itself shifts.*

   Similarly, the supply curve shifts if some relevant factor that affects the supply, *other than the price of the good,* changes. A change in the price of the good leads to a movement along the supply curve.

4. **RULES FOR USING A SUPPLY/DEMAND DIAGRAM :** The safest way to solve any demand and supply problem is always to draw a graph. A few mechanical rules can make using demand and supply graphs easy. First, when you draw the graph, be sure to label the axes. As the course progresses, you will encounter many graphs with different variables on the axes. You can become confused if you do not develop the habit of labeling the axes. Second, draw the demand and supply curves as straight lines. Third, be sure to indicate and label the initial equilibrium price and quantity.

Now come two more difficult parts that you must practice. Suppose that you are dealing with a situation in which one influence changes. First, determine whether the influence shifts the demand or the supply curve. Aside from the effect of the expected future price, most factors generally shift only one curve and you must decide which one. Second, determine whether the curve that is affected shifts rightward (increases) or shifts leftward (decreases). From here on, it's more straightforward: Take the figure you have already drawn, shift the appropriate curve, and read off the answer!

FIGURE **3.4**
The Effect of an Increase in Demand

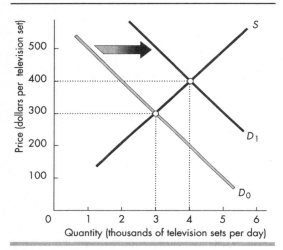

5. **CHANGES IN DEMAND DO NOT CAUSE CHANGES IN SUPPLY ; CHANGES IN SUPPLY DO NOT CAUSE CHANGES IN DEMAND :** Do not make the common error of believing that an increase in demand, that is, a rightward shift in the demand curve, causes an increase in supply, a rightward shift in the supply curve. Use Figure 3.4, which illustrates the market for television sets, as an example. An increase in demand shifts the demand curve rightward, as shown. This shift means the equilibrium price of a television rises (from $300 for a set to $400) and the equilibrium quantity increases (from 3,000 sets per day to 4,000). But the shift in the demand curve does not cause the supply curve to *shift*. Instead, there is a *movement along* the unchanging supply curve.

Questions

■ True/False and Explain

Markets and Prices

1. A good with a high relative price must have a low opportunity cost.

2. A product's relative price can fall even though its money price rises.

Demand

3. The law of demand states that, if nothing else changes, as the price of a good rises, the quantity demanded decreases.

4. A decrease in income decreases the demand for all products.

5. "An increase in demand" means a movement down and rightward along a demand curve.

6. New technology for manufacturing computer chips shifts the demand curve for computer chips.

Supply

7. A supply curve shows the maximum price required in order to have the last unit of output produced.

8. A rise in the price of chicken feed decreases the supply of chickens.

9. A rise in the price of orange juice shifts the supply curve of orange juice rightward.

Market Equilibrium

10. Once a market is at its equilibrium price, unless something changes, the price will not change.

11. If there is a surplus of a good, its price falls.

Predicting Changes in Price and Quantity

12. If the expected future price of a good rises, its current price rises.

13. A rise in the price of a product decreases the quantity demanded, so there can never be a situation with both the product's equilibrium price rising and equilibrium quantity increasing.

14. If both the demand and supply curves shift rightward, the equilibrium quantity definitely increases.

15. If both the demand and supply curves shift rightward, the equilibrium price definitely rises.

■ Multiple Choice

Markets and Prices

1. The opportunity cost of a good is the same as its
   a. money price.
   b. relative price.
   c. price index.
   d. None of the above.

2. The money price of a pizza is $12 per pizza and the money price of a taco is $2 per taco. The relative price of a pizza is
   a. $12 per pizza.
   b. $24 per pizza.
   c. 6 tacos per pizza.
   d. 1/6 pizza.

Demand

3. The law of demand concludes that a rise in the price of a golf ball _____ the quantity demanded and
   _____.
   a. increases; shifts the demand curve for golf balls rightward.
   b. decreases; shifts the demand curve for golf balls leftward.
   c. decreases; creates a movement up along the demand curve for golf balls.
   d. increases; creates a movement down along the demand curve for golf balls.

4. If a rise in the price of gasoline decreases the demand for large cars,
   a. gasoline and large cars are substitutes in consumption.
   b. gasoline and large cars are complements in consumption.
   c. gasoline is an inferior good.
   d. large cars are an inferior good.

5. A normal good is one
   a. with a downward sloping demand curve.
   b. for which demand increases when the price of a substitute rises.
   c. for which demand increases when income increases.
   d. None of the above.

6. Some sales managers are talking shop. Which of the following quotations refers to a movement along the demand curve?
   a. "Since our competitors raised their prices our sales have doubled."
   b. "It has been an unusually mild winter; our sales of wool scarves are down from last year."
   c. "We decided to cut our prices, and the increase in our sales has been remarkable."
   d. None of the above.

FIGURE **3.5**
Multiple Choice Question 7

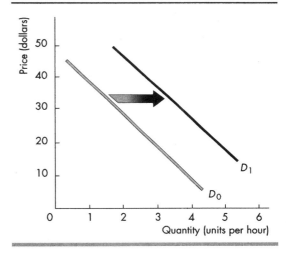

7. Which of the following could lead to the shift in the demand curve illustrated in Figure 3.5?
   a. An increase in the quantity demanded
   b. A rise in the price of a substitute good
   c. A rise in the price of a complement
   d. A fall in the price of the product

Supply

8. A fall in the price of a good leads to producers decreasing the quantity of the good supplied. This statement reflects
   a. the law of supply.
   b. the law of demand.
   c. a change in supply.
   d. the nature of an inferior good.

9. Which of the following influences does <u>NOT</u> shift the supply curve?
    a. A rise in the wages paid workers
    b. Development of new technology
    c. People deciding that they want to buy more of the product
    d. A decrease in the number of suppliers

10. The price of jet fuel rises, so the
    a. demand for airplane trips increases.
    b. demand for airplane trips decreases.
    c. supply of airplane trips increases.
    d. supply of airplane trips decreases.

11. In addition to showing the quantity that will be supplied at different prices, a supply curve can be viewed as the
    a. willingness-and-ability-to-pay curve.
    b. marginal benefit curve.
    c. minimum-supply price curve.
    d. maximum-supply price curve.

12. An increase in the number of producers of gruel _____ the supply of gruel and shifts the supply curve of gruel _____.
    a. increases; rightward
    b. increases; leftward
    c. decreases; rightward
    d. decreases; leftward

13. An increase in the price of the cheese used to produce pizza shifts the supply curve of pizza _____ and shifts the demand curve for pizza _____.
    a. rightward; leftward
    b. leftward; leftward
    c. leftward; not at all
    d. not at all; leftward

14. To say that "supply increases" for any reason, means there is a
    a. movement rightward along a supply curve.
    b. movement leftward along a supply curve.
    c. shift rightward in the supply curve.
    d. shift leftward in the supply curve.

Market Equilibrium

15. If the market for Twinkies is in equilibrium, then
    a. Twinkies must be a normal good.
    b. producers would like to sell more at the current price.
    c. consumers would like to buy more at the current price.
    d. the quantity supplied equals the quantity demanded.

16. If there is a shortage of a good, the quantity demanded is _____ than the quantity supplied and the price will _____.
    a. less; rise
    b. less; fall
    c. greater; rise
    d. greater; fall

FIGURE **3.6**
Multiple Choice Question 17

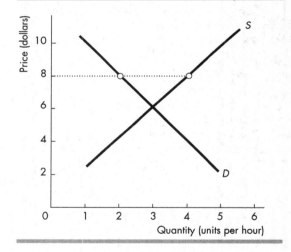

17. In Figure 3.6 at the price of $8 there is a
    a. shortage and the price will rise.
    b. shortage and the price will fall.
    c. surplus and the price will rise.
    d. surplus and the price will fall.

18. In a market, at the equilibrium price,
    a. neither buyers nor sellers can do business at a better price.
    b. buyers are willing to pay a higher price, but sellers do not ask for a higher price.
    c. buyers are paying the minimum price they are willing to pay for any amount of output and sellers are charging the maximum price they are willing to charge for any amount of production.
    d. None of the above is true.

Predicting Changes in Price and Quantity

19. For consumers, pizza and hamburgers are substitutes. A rise in the price of pizza _____ the price of a hamburger and _____ in the quantity of hamburgers.
    a. raises; increases
    b. raises; decreases
    c. lowers; increases
    d. lowers; decreases

20. How does an unusually cold winter affect the equilibrium price and quantity of anti-freeze?
    a. It raises the price and increases the quantity.
    b. It raises the price and decreases the quantity.
    c. It lowers the price and increases the quantity.
    d. It lowers the price and decreases the quantity.

21. You notice that the price of wheat rises and the quantity of wheat increases. This set of observations can be the result of the
    a. demand for wheat curve shifting rightward.
    b. demand for wheat curve shifting leftward.
    c. supply of wheat curve shifting rightward.
    d. supply of wheat curve shifting leftward.

22. A technological improvement lowers the cost of producing coffee. As a result, the price of a pound of coffee _____ and the quantity of coffee _____.
    a. rises; increases
    b. rises; decreases
    c. falls; increases
    d. falls; decreases

23. The number of firms producing computer memory chips decreases. As a result, the price of a memory chip _____ and the quantity of memory chips _____.
    a. rises; increases
    b. rises; decreases
    c. falls; increases
    d. falls; decreases

For the next five questions, suppose that the price of paper used in books rises and simultaneously (and independently) more people decide they want to read books.

24. The rise in the price of paper shifts the
    a. demand curve rightward.
    b. demand curve leftward.
    c. supply curve rightward.
    d. supply curve leftward.

25. The fact that more people want to read books shifts the
    a. demand curve rightward.
    b. demand curve leftward.
    c. supply curve rightward.
    d. supply curve leftward.

26. The equilibrium quantity of books
    a. definitely increases.
    b. definitely does not change.
    c. definitely decreases.
    d. might increase, not change, or decrease.

27. The equilibrium price of a book
    a. definitely rises.
    b. definitely does not change.
    c. definitely falls.
    d. might rise, not change, or fall.

28. Suppose that the effect from people deciding they want to read more books is larger than the effect from the increase in the price of paper. In this case, the equilibrium quantity of books
    a. definitely increases.
    b. definitely does not change.
    c. definitely decreases.
    d. might increase, not change, or decrease.

29. Which of the following definitely raises the equilibrium price?
    a. An increase in both demand and supply.
    b. A decrease in both demand and supply.
    c. An increase in demand combined with a decrease in supply.
    d. A decrease in demand combined with an increase in supply.

30. Is it possible for the price of a good to stay the same while the quantity increases?
    a. Yes, if both the demand and supply of the good increase by the same amount.
    b. Yes, if the demand increases by the same amount the supply decreases.
    c. Yes, if the supply increases and the demand does not change.
    d. No, it is not possible.

■ Short Answer Problems

1. a. This year the price of a hamburger is $2 and the price of a compact disc is $12. In terms of hamburgers, what is the relative price of a compact disc? In terms of hamburgers, what is the opportunity cost of buying a compact disc? How are the two answers related?
   b. Next year the (money) price of a compact disc doubles to $24 and the (money) price of a hamburger remains at $2. Now what is the relative price of a compact disc?
   c. The following year the (money) price of a compact disc stays at $24 and the (money) price of a hamburger doubles to $4. What is the relative price of a compact disc?
   d. In the next year, the (money) price of a compact disc doubles to $48 and the money price of a hamburger triples to $12. What is the relative price of a compact disc?
   e. Can a product's relative price fall even though its money price has risen? Why or why not?

2. a. When drawing a demand curve, what six influences are assumed not to change?
   b. If any of these influences change, what happens to the demand curve?
   c. When drawing a supply curve, what five influences are assumed not to change?
   d. If any of these influences change, what happens to the supply curve?

3. a. Table 3.1 presents the demand and supply schedules for comic books. Graph these demand and supply schedules in Figure 3.7. What is the equilibrium price? The equilibrium quantity?
   b. What is the marginal benefit received by the consumer of the 12,000,000th comic book? What is the minimum price for which a producer is willing to produce the 12,000,000th comic book?

TABLE **3.1**
Demand and Supply Schedules

Price (per comic book)	Quantity demanded (per month)	Quantity supplied (per month)
$2.50	14,000,000	8,000,000
3.00	13,000,000	10,000,000
3.50	12,000,000	12,000,000
4.00	11,000,000	13,000,000
4.50	10,000,000	14,000,000

FIGURE **3.7**
Short Answer Problem 3

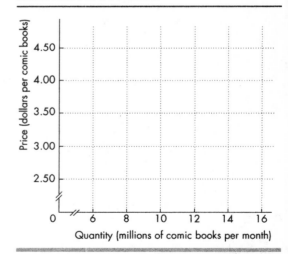

c. Suppose that the price of a movie, a substitute for comic books, rises so that at every price of a comic book consumers now want to buy 2,000,000 more comic books than before. That is, at the price of $2.50, consumers now will buy 16,000,000 comics; and so on. Plot this new demand curve in Figure 3.7. What is the new equilibrium price? The new equilibrium quantity?

4. New cars are a normal good. Suppose that the economy enters a period of strong economic expansion so that people's incomes increase substantially. Use a demand and supply diagram to determine what happens to the equilibrium price and quantity of new cars.

5. DVDs and video tapes are substitutes. Use a supply and demand diagram to determine what happens to the equilibrium price and quantity of video tapes when the price of a DVD falls because of an increase in the supply of DVDs.

6. Suppose we observe that the consumption of peanut butter increases at the same time its price rises. What must have happened in the market for peanut butter? Is the observation that the price rose and the quantity increased consistent with the law of demand? Why or why not?

7. Suppose that the wages paid oil workers fall. Use a demand and supply diagram to determine the effect this action has on the equilibrium price and quantity of gasoline.

8. Chemical companies discover a new, more efficient technology for producing benzene. Use a demand and supply model to determine the impact that this new method has on the equilibrium price and quantity of benzene.

9. The price of a personal computer has continued to fall in the face of increasing demand. Explain.

10. a. The market for chickens initially is in equilibrium. Suppose that eating buffalo wings (which, contrary to the name, are made from chicken wings) becomes so stylish that people eat them for breakfast, lunch, and dinner. Use a demand

and supply diagram to determine how the equilibrium price and quantity of chicken change.

b. Return to the initial equilibrium, before eating buffalo wings became stylish. Now suppose that a heat wave occurred and caused tens of thousands of chickens to die or commit suicide. Keeping in mind that dead chickens cannot be marketed, use a demand and supply diagram to determine what happens to the equilibrium price and quantity of chicken.

c. Now assume that both the heat wave and fad strike at the same time. Use a demand and supply diagram to show what happens to the equilibrium price and quantity of chicken. (Hint: Can you tell for sure what happens to the price? The quantity?)

■ You're the Teacher

1. When you and a friend are studying Chapter 3, the friend says to you, "I really don't understand the difference between a 'shift in a curve' and a 'movement along' a curve. Can you help me? It's probably important to understand this, so what's the difference?" Explain the difference to your friend.

2. "This demand and supply model is nonsense. It says that if demand for some product decreases, the price of that good falls. But, come on — except for computers, how many times have you actually seen a price fall? Prices *always* rise, so don't try telling me that that they fall." The demand and supply model is sound; it is this statement that is nonsense. Show the speaker the error in that analysis.

Answers

■ True/False Answers

Markets and Prices

1. **F** A product's relative price is its opportunity cost.

2. **T** A good's relative price will fall if its money price rises less than the money prices of other goods.

Demand

3. **T** The law of demand points out the negative relationship between a product's price and the quantity demanded.

4. **F** Demand decreases for normal goods but increases for inferior goods.

5. **F** The term "increase in demand" refers to a rightward shift in the demand curve.

6. **F** Changes in technology are not a factor that shifts the demand curve. (Changes in technology will shift the supply curve.)

Supply

7. **F** The supply curve shows the *minimum* price that suppliers must receive in order to produce the last unit supplied.

8. **T** Chicken feed is a resource used to produce chickens, so a rise in its price shifts the supply curve of chickens leftward.

9. **F** The rise in the price of orange juice creates a movement along the supply curve to a larger quantity supplied (that is, upward and rightward), but it does not shift the supply curve.

Market Equilibrium

10. **T** Once at the equilibrium price, because the opposing forces of demand and supply are in balance, the situation can persist indefinitely until something changes.

11. **T** A surplus of a product results in its price falling until it reaches the equilibrium price.

Predicting Changes in Price and Quantity

12. **T** The rise in the future price shifts the demand curve rightward and the supply curve leftward, unambiguously raising the current price.

13. **F** The inverse relationship between the price and quantity demanded holds along a fixed demand curve. But if the demand curve shifts rightward, the equilibrium price rises and the equilibrium quantity increases.

14. **T** The equilibrium quantity definitely increases when both the demand and supply increase.

15. **F** The price rises if the shift in the demand curve is larger than that in the supply curve; but if the shifts are the same size, the price does not change and if the supply shift is larger, the price falls.

■ Multiple Choice Answers

Markets and Prices

1. **b** A product's relative price tells how much of another good must be foregone to have another unit of the product, which is the opportunity cost of the product.

2. **c** The relative price of the pizza is its money price relative to the money price of a taco, which equals ($12 per pizza)/($2 per taco) or 6 tacos per pizza.

Demand

3. **c** The law of demand points out that a higher price decreases the quantity demanded and creates a movement up along the demand curve for golf balls.

4. **b** The definition of complementary goods is that a rise in the price of one decreases the demand for the other.

5. **c** This is the definition of a "normal good."

6. **c** A reduction in the price of the product leads to a movement along its demand curve.

7. **b** A rise in the price of a substitute shifts the demand curve rightward.

Supply

8. **a** The law of supply points out the positive relationship between the price of a product and the quantity supplied.

9. **c** A change in preferences shifts the demand curve, not the supply curve.

10. **d** Jet fuel is a resource used to produce airplane trips, so a rise in the price of this resource decreases the supply of airplane trips.

11. **c** For any unit of output, the supply curve shows the minimum price for which a producer is willing to produce and sell that unit of output.

12. **a** An increase in supply is reflected by a rightward shift of the supply curve.

13. **c** A change in the price of a resource used to produce a good shifts the supply curve but does not shift the demand curve.

14. **c** An "increase in supply" means that the supply curve shifts rightward; a "decrease in supply" means the supply curve shifts leftward.

Market Equilibrium

15. **d** At equilibrium, consumers and suppliers are simultaneously satisfied insofar as the quantity consumers are willing to buy matches the quantity producers are willing to sell.

16. **c** A shortage occurs when the price is below the equilibrium price. The quantity demanded exceeds the quantity supplied and the resulting shortage means the price rises until it reaches its equilibrium.

FIGURE **3.8**
Multiple Choice Question 17

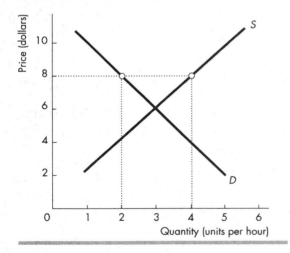

17. **d** There is surplus because, as illustrated in Figure 3.8, the quantity supplied at the price of $8 is 4. This quantity exceeds 2, the quantity demanded.

18. **a** Buyers cannot find anyone willing to sell to at a lower price and sellers cannot find anyone willing to buy at a higher price.

Predicting Changes in Price and Quantity

19. **a** The rise in the price of a pizza increases the demand for hamburgers, which results in a rise in the price of a hamburger and an increase in the quantity of hamburgers.

20. **a** The cold winter shifts the demand curve rightward, as consumers increase their demand for antifreeze; the supply curve does not shift. As a result, the equilibrium price rises and the quantity increases.

FIGURE **3.9**
Multiple Choice Question 21

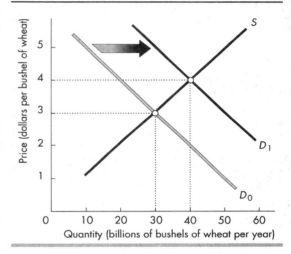

21. **a** Figure 3.9 shows that an increase in the demand for wheat, so that the demand curve shifts from D_0 to D_1, raises the price of wheat from $3 a bushel to $4 and increases its quantity from 30 billion bushels of wheat a year to 40 billion.

22. **c** The technological improvement increases the supply, that is, the supply curve shifts rightward. As a result, the quantity increases and the price falls.

23. **b** The decrease in the number of firms producing memory chips decreases the supply of memory chips, which raises the price and decreases the quantity of chips.

24. **d** Paper is a resource used in the manufacture of books, so a rise in the price of paper shifts the supply curve of books leftward.

25. **a** When people's preferences change so that they want to read more books, the demand curve for books shifts rightward.

26. **d** The equilibrium quantity increases if the increase in demand is larger than the decrease in

supply, decreases if the change in supply is larger, and does not change if the changes are the same size.

27. **a** Both the increase in demand and decrease in supply lead to a rise in the price, so the equilibrium price unambiguously rises.

FIGURE 3.10
Multiple Choice Question 28

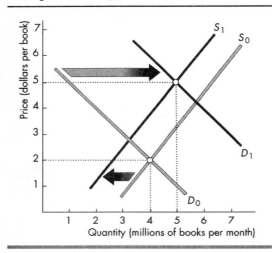

28. **a** If the shift in the demand curve exceeds the shift in the supply curve, the equilibrium quantity increases. This result is illustrated in Figure 3.10, where the quantity increases from 4 to 5 million.

29. **c** Separately, the increase in demand and decrease in supply both raise the price, so the two of them occurring together definitely raise the price.

30. **a** If both the demand and supply increase by the same amount, the price will not change and the quantity will increase.

■ Answers to Short Answer Problems

1. a. The money price of a compact disc is $12 per compact disc; the money price of a hamburger is $2 per hamburger. The relative price of a compact disc is the ratio of the money prices, $12 per compact disc/$2 per hamburger, or 6 hamburgers per compact disc. For the opportunity cost, buying 1 compact disc means using the funds that otherwise could purchase 6 hamburgers. Hence the opportunity cost of buying 1 compact disc is 6 hamburgers. The relative price and the opportunity cost are identical.

b. The relative price of a compact disc is $24 per compact disc/$2 per hamburger or 12 hamburgers per compact disc.

c. The relative price of a compact disc is $24 per compact disc/$4 per hamburger, or 6 hamburgers per compact disc.

d. The relative price of a compact disc is $48 per compact disc/$12 per hamburger, or 4 hamburgers per compact disc.

e. Yes, a product's relative price can fall even though its money price rises. Part (d) gives an example of how that can occur: If a good's money price rises by a smaller percentage than the money price of other goods, then the product's relative price falls. Keep this result in mind when you use the demand and supply model because when the model predicts that the equilibrium price will fall, it means that the *relative* price, and not necessarily the money price, falls.

2. a. The six influences that do not change along a demand curve are prices of related goods, expected future prices, income, expected future income, population, and preferences.

b. If any of these factors change, the demand curve shifts.

c. The five influences that are held constant when you draw a supply curve are prices of resources used to produce the good, prices of related goods produced, expected future prices, the number of suppliers, and technology.

d. If any of these influences change, the supply curve shifts. It is very important to remember what influences shift a supply curve and what shift a demand curve.

3. a. Figure 3.11 (on the next page) shows the graph of the demand and supply schedules as S and D_0. The equilibrium price is $3.50 a comic book, and the equilibrium quantity is 12,000,000 comic books.

b. The person who buys the 12,000,000th comic book pays $3.50 for the comic book, and so $3.50 is the benefit this person receives from this comic book. The firm that produces the 12,000,000th comic book receives $3.50 for the book, and the supply curve shows that $3.50 is the minimum price for which this firm is willing to produce and sell the comic book.

FIGURE **3.11**
Short Answer Problem 3

FIGURE **3.11**
Short Answer Problem 3

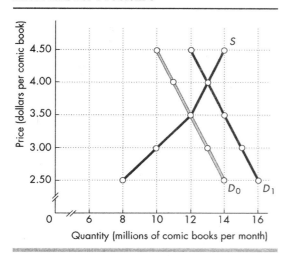

c. The new demand curve is plotted in Figure 3.11 as D_1. The new equilibrium price is $4, and the new equilibrium quantity is 13 million.

FIGURE **3.12**
Short Answer Problem 4

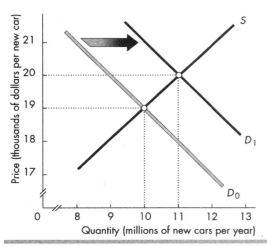

4. Because new cars are a normal good, an increase in income increases the demand for them. Hence the demand curve shifts rightward, as shown in Figure 3.12. As a result, the equilibrium price rises (from $19,000 to $20,000 in the figure) and the equilibrium quantity also increases (from 10 million a year to 11 million in the figure).

FIGURE **3.13**
Short Answer Problem 5

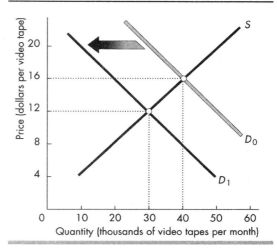

5. The fall in the price of a DVD, a substitute for video tapes, decreases the demand for video tapes. This change means the demand curve for video tapes shifts leftward, as shown in Figure 3.13. As a result, the price of a video tape falls, (from $16 a tape to $12 in the figure) and the quantity decreases (from 40,000 per month to 30,000 in the figure). Note that it is the shift in the demand curve that changed the price and that the shift in the demand curve did *not* shift the supply curve.

6. In order for both the equilibrium price and quantity of peanut butter to increase, the demand for peanut butter must have increased. The increase in demand leads to a rise in the price and an increase in the quantity of peanut butter.

The observation that both the price rose and the quantity increased is not at all inconsistent with the law of demand. The law of demand states that "other things remaining the same, the higher the price of a good, the smaller is the quantity demanded." A key part of this law is the "other things remaining the same" clause. When the demand curve for peanut butter shifts rightward, something else that increased the demand for peanut butter changed. Hence "other things" have not remained the same and by changing have resulted in a higher price and increased quantity of peanut butter.

FIGURE **3.14**

Short Answer Problem 7

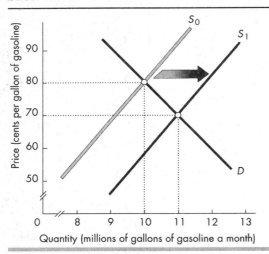

Quantity (millions of gallons of gasoline a month)

7. Lower wages reduce the price of a resource (labor) used to produce gasoline. As a result, the supply of gasoline increases. This change is illustrated in Figure 3.14, where the supply curve shifts rightward from S_0 to S_1. The increase in supply lowers the price of gasoline (from 80 cents a gallon to 70 cents in the figure) and increases the quantity (from 10 million gallons a month to 11 million).

FIGURE **3.15**

Short Answer Problem 8

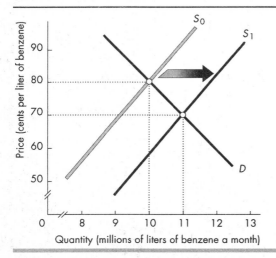

Quantity (millions of liters of benzene a month)

8. New technology increases the supply, so the supply curve shifts rightward. Then, as Figure 3.15 shows, the price falls (from 80 cents a liter to 70 cents in the figure) and the equilibrium quantity increases

from (10 million liters of benzene a month to 11 million).

This answer and the figure are virtually the same as those in problem 7. Even though a fall in wages and the development of new technology appear dissimilar, the demand and supply model reveals that both have the same effect on the price and quantity of the product. This model can easily accommodate these quite different changes. For this reason the demand and supply model is a very important economic tool.

FIGURE **3.16**

Short Answer Problem 9

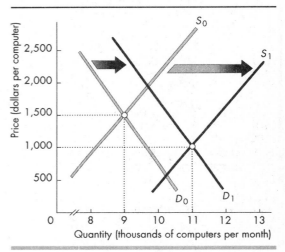

Quantity (thousands of computers per month)

9. Personal computers have fallen in price although the demand for them has increased because the supply has increased even more rapidly. Figure 3.16 illustrates this situation. From one year to the next the demand curve shifted from D_0 to D_1. But over the year the supply curve shifted f from S_0 to S_1. Because the supply has increased more than the demand, the price of a personal computer fell (in the figure, from $1,500 for a personal computer to $1,000). The quantity increased (from 9,000 personal computers a month to 11,000 in the figure).

10. a. With the change in people's preferences — so that they want more chicken wings and hence more chickens — the demand for chickens increases. The increase in the demand for chickens means that the demand curve for chickens shifts rightward. Figure 3.17 (on the next page) shows this change. As it demonstrates, the equilibrium

FIGURE **3.17**
Short Answer Problem 10 (a)

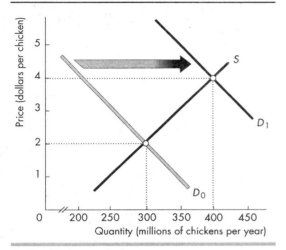

price rises (from $2 to $4 per chicken) and the equilibrium quantity of chickens increase (from 300 million to 400 million). Note that the change in people's preferences does not affect the supply of chicken, so the supply curve does *not* shift.

FIGURE **3.18**
Short Answer Problem 10 (b)

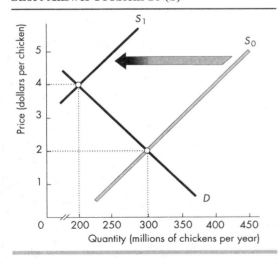

b. The heat wave decreases the number of chickens that can be supplied. This change shifts the supply curve for chickens leftward, as Figure 3.18 shows. As a result, the heat wave raises the price

FIGURE **3.19**
Short Answer Problem 10 (c)

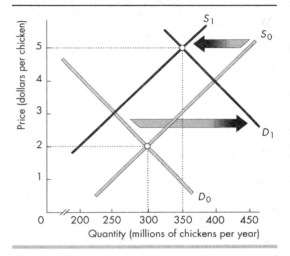

FIGURE **3.20**
Short Answer Problem 10 (c)

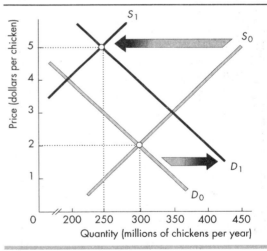

of a chicken (from $2 to $4) and decreases the quantity (from 300 million to 200 million).

c. If the demand increases *and* the supply decreases, the equilibrium price of a chicken rises. But the effect on the quantity is ambiguous. Figures 3.19 and 3.20 reveal the nature of this ambiguity. In Figure 3.19, the demand shift is larger than the supply shift, and the equilibrium quantity increases to 350 million chickens. But in Figure 3.20, the magnitude of the shifts is reversed, and the supply shift exceeds the demand shift. Because the supply shift is larger, the equilibrium quantity decreases to 250 million chickens. So unless you know which shift is larger, you cannot determine whether the quantity increases (when the demand shift is larger); decreases (when the supply shift is larger); or stays the same (when both shifts are the same size). However, regardless of the relative sizes, Figures 3.19 and 3.20 show that the price will unambiguously rise, coincidentally to $5 in both figures.

■ You're the Teacher

1. "The distinction between a 'shift in a curve' and a 'movement along a curve' is really crucial. Let's think about the demand curve; once you understand the difference for the demand curve, understanding it for the supply curve is easier. Take movies, OK? A lot of things affect how many movies we see in a month: the ticket price, our income, and so on. Start with the price. Obviously, if the price of a movie ticket rises, we'll buy fewer. The slope of a demand curve shows this effect. For the demand curve in Figure 3.21, when the price rises from $5 to $6 for a movie, the movement is from point a on the demand curve to point b. Our quantity demanded decreases from 5 movies a month to 4. So the rise in the price of the product has lead to a movement along the demand curve. The negative slope of the demand curve shows the negative effect that higher prices have on the quantity demanded.

"Now, let's suppose that our incomes fall and that as a result we're going to go to fewer movies. The demand curve's slope can't show us this effect because the slope indicates the relationship between the price and the quantity demanded. Instead, the whole demand curve is going to shift. That is, at any price we'll buy fewer tickets. Look at Figure 3.22 for instance. If the price stays at $6 a movie, the quantity we demand decreases from 4 movies a month to 2.

"But the same is true if the price is $5: If the price stays at $5 the quantity we demand decreases from 5 movies a month to only 3. Now, I don't mean to say that the price has to stay at $6 or at $5. All I'm saying is that at any possible price, the number of movies we'll see has decreased and I'm just using $6 and $5 as examples. So we're going to decrease the quantity demanded at $6 and at $5, *and* at every

FIGURE **3.21**
You're the Teacher Question 1

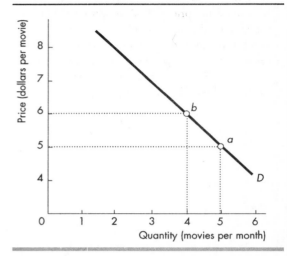

FIGURE **3.22**
You're the Teacher Question 1

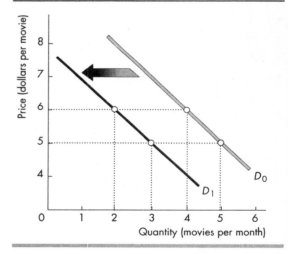

other possible price. That means that we can draw a new demand curve (D_1) to show how much we demand at every price after our incomes fall. So, the drop in income has shifted the demand curve from D_0 to D_1. And, that's all there is to the difference between a 'movement along the demand curve' and a 'shift in the demand curve.' "

2. "You're missing a key point about the demand and supply model. This model predicts what happens to *relative* prices, not *money* prices. You're certainly right when you say that we don't often see a money

price fall. We live in inflationary times and most money prices usually rise. But when the demand and supply model says that the price falls, it means that the *relative* price falls. A good's relative price can fall even though its money price rises. For instance, if the money price of some product rises by 2 percent when the money prices of all other goods are rising by 4 percent, the first product's relative price has fallen. That is, its money price relative to every other money price is lower. If you think about it, relative prices change all the time, and at least half the time relative prices fall. Drops in relative prices aren't rare; they're common. So, don't be too hasty to throw away the demand and supply model. Not only are we going to see it on tests in this class, but it also works well to help us understand what happens to a product's (relative) price and quantity whenever there's a change in a relevant factor."

Chapter Quiz

1. When demand increases, the
   a. price falls and the quantity decreases.
   b. price falls and the quantity increases.
   c. price rises and the quantity decreases.
   d. price rises and the quantity increases.

2. Wants differ from demands insofar as
   a. wants are limited by income but demands are unlimited.
   b. wants require a plan to acquire a good, while demands require no such plan.
   c. wants imply a decision about which demands to satisfy, while demands require no such specific plans.
   d. wants are unlimited and involve no specific plan to acquire the good, while demands reflect a decision about which wants to satisfy and a plan to buy the good.

3. A complement is a good
   a. that can be used in place of another good.
   b. that is used with another good.
   c. of lower quality than another.
   d. of higher quality than another.

4. Suppose that people buy less of good 1 when the price of good 2 falls. These goods are
   a. complements.
   b. substitutes.
   c. normal.
   d. inferior.

5. A change in the price of a good _____ its supply curve and _____ a movement along its supply curve.
   a. shifts; results in
   b. shifts; does not result in
   c. does not shift; results in
   d. does not shift; does not result in

6. Which of the following shifts the supply curve of plywood leftward?
   a. A situation in which the quantity demanded of plywood exceeds the quantity supplied.
   b. An increase in the price of machinery used to produce plywood.
   c. A technological improvement in the production of plywood.
   d. A decrease in the wages of workers employed to produce plywood.

7. A surplus results in the
   a. demand curve shifting rightward.
   b. supply curve shifting rightward.
   c. price falling.
   d. price rising.

8. If a product is a normal good and people's incomes rise, then the new equilibrium quantity is _____ the initial equilibrium quantity.
   a. greater than
   b. equal to
   c. less than
   d. perhaps greater than, less than, or equal to depending on how suppliers react to the change in demand.

9. In the market for oil, the development of a new deep sea drilling technology _____ the demand curve for oil and _____ the supply curve of oil.
   a. shifts rightward; shifts rightward
   b. does not shift; shifts rightward
   c. shifts leftward; shifts leftward
   d. does not shift; shifts leftward

10. Taken by itself, an increase in supply results in
    a. the price rising.
    b. the price falling.
    c. the demand curve shifting rightward.
    d. the demand curve shifting leftward.

The answers for this Chapter Quiz are on page 265

2 HOW MARKETS WORK

Mid-Term Examination

■ Chapter 3

1. The law of demand states that, other things remaining the same, the higher the price of a good, the
   a. smaller will be the demand for the good.
   b. larger will be the demand for the good.
   c. smaller will be the quantity of the good demanded.
   d. larger will be the quantity of the good demanded.

2. Which of the following shifts the supply curve?
   a. An increase in income but only if the good is a normal good.
   b. An increase in income regardless of whether the good is normal or inferior.
   c. A rise in the price of the good.
   d. An increase in the cost of producing the product.

3. A shortage of wheat
   a. shifts the demand curve for wheat leftward.
   b. shifts the supply curve of wheat rightward.
   c. leads to the price of wheat falling.
   d. leads to the price of wheat rising.

4. When supply of blouses increases, the equilibrium quantity of blouses _____ and the equilibrium price of a blouse _____.
   a. increases; rises
   b. decreases; falls
   c. increases; falls
   d. decreases; rises

Answers

■ Mid-Term Exam Answers

1. c;   2. d;   3. d;   4. c

Chapter 4 A FIRST LOOK AT MACROECONOMICS*

Key Concepts

■ Origins and Issues of Macroeconomics

Modern macroeconomics began during the **Great Depression**, 1929–1939. The **Great Depression** was a decade of high unemployment and stagnant production throughout the world. Macroeconomics initially focused on short-term problems, such as high unemployment. Recently long-term problems, such as economic growth, have come to be considered vital.

■ Economic Growth and Fluctuations

Economic growth is the expansion of the economy's production possibilities. It is measured by the increase in **real gross domestic product**, also called **real GDP**. Real GDP is the value of the total production of all the nation's farms, factories, shops, and offices measured in the prices of a single year.

Potential GDP is the quantity of real GDP that is produced when all the economy's labor, capital, land, and entrepreneurial ability are fully employed.

◆ The **productivity growth slowdown** was the slowing of the growth rate of output per person that occurred during the 1970s.

The periodic but irregular up-and-down movement in production is the **business cycle**. It occurs as real GDP fluctuates irregularly around potential GDP. A business cycle has four parts:

◆ *Trough* — the lower turning point, when a recession ends and an expansion begins.

◆ **Expansion** — a period of time during which real GDP increases.

◆ *Peak* — the upper turning point, when an expansion ends and a recession begins.

◆ **Recession** — a period during which real GDP decreases for at least two successive quarters.

The most recent recession began in the first quarter of 2001 and ended in the fourth quarter of 2001. This recession was milder than previous recessions. A depression is a severe recession.

◆ Between 1976 and 2006, the growth rate of real GDP in the United States was about equal to that of the rest of the world but was more variable.

◆ Between 1996 and 2006, of the advanced economies Japan grew the slowest and the newly industrialized nations of Asia grew the fastest.

The **Lucas wedge** is the accumulated loss of output that results from a slowdown in the growth rate of real GDP per person. The productivity growth slowdown of the 1970s has created a Lucas wedge of $72 trillion. The **Okun gap** (the *output gap*) is the gap between real GDP and potential GDP. The recessions since 1973 have created an accumulated Okun gap of $3.3 trillion.

Economic growth expands future consumption possibilities. However, economic growth allows less current consumption as resources must be devoted to capital accumulation and might lead to more rapid depletion of resources and more pollution.

■ Jobs and Unemployment

In 2006, 143 million people had jobs. More new jobs are created during expansions and jobs are lost during recessions.

A person is unemployed if he or she does not have a job but is looking for work. The **unemployment rate** is the number of unemployed workers as a percentage of all the people who have jobs or are looking for one.

◆ Unemployment increases during a recession and decreases during an expansion.

◆ The average unemployment rate in the United States is higher than in Japan, but lower than in Canada and Western Europe.

---

* This chapter is Chapter 20 in *Economics*.

Unemployment is a serious problem because unemployed workers lose income and can find their future job prospects limited.

■ Inflation and the Dollar

The **price level** is the average of the prices people pay for all the goods and services they buy. **Inflation** occurs when prices rise. The **inflation rate** is the annual percentage change in the price level. **Deflation** occurs when the inflation rate is negative so that the price level falls. In recent years, deflation has been rare in the United States.

Inflation was high in the 1970s and early 1980s, but has been lower since then, though it has been on an uptick since 2002. The U.S. experience with inflation has been similar to that of other industrialized nations. Inflation in developing countries is generally higher than that in developed countries.

Inflation reduces the value of money, so unpredictable inflation makes transactions spread over time more difficult to carry out. In times of high inflation, people use resources to predict inflation rather than to produce goods and services. A **hyperinflation** is a period when the inflation rate exceeds 50 percent per month. At such rates, inflation causes economic chaos.

The **exchange rate** is the value of the U.S. dollar in terms of other currencies. The exchange rate fluctuates, sometimes rising in value—*appreciating*—and sometimes falling in value—*depreciating*.

■ Surpluses, Deficits, and Debts

A **government budget surplus** occurs when the government collects more in taxes than it spends; a **government budget deficit** occurs when the government spends more than it collects in taxes. The U.S. federal government had a surplus between 1998 to 2000 and a deficit after 2001.

The **current account** balance equals exports minus imports plus interest income received from the rest of the world minus interest expense paid to the rest of the world. Payments (for, say, imports) greater than receipts (from, say, exports) create a current account deficit. The United States has had a current account deficit since 1980.

The government debt is the **national debt**. The national debt is the total amount the government owes. A government budget deficit increases the national debt.

The U.S. international debt is the amount U.S. residents owe to foreigners. Current account deficits increase the U.S. international debt.

■ Macroeconomic Policy Challenges and Tools

Five widely agreed upon challenges for macroeconomic policy are:

♦ Boost economic growth
♦ Keep inflation low
♦ Stabilize the business cycle
♦ Reduce unemployment
♦ Reduce the government and international deficits

Achieving these challenges will help the economy.

The two general macroeconomic policy tools the government has at hand to help attain the policy goals are:

♦ **Fiscal policy** — setting and changing tax rates and the amount of government spending. The federal government can use fiscal policy in efforts to accomplish some of the policy challenges.

♦ **Monetary policy** — changes in the interest rate and the amount of money in the economy. Monetary policy is under the control of the Federal Reserve, or Fed. The Federal Reserve can use monetary policy to try to meet some of the policy challenges.

Helpful Hints

1. **THE MACROECONOMIC CHALLENGES :** The chapter discusses five widely agreed upon macroeconomic challenges. As you study the forthcoming chapters, keep these challenges in mind because ultimately we return to see what policies, if any, the government might adopt to help meet these goals. While these challenges are widely agreed upon, there is dispute among economists about ranking their importance as well as dispute about the proper polices necessary to attain some of them. The first disagreement matters because at times the goals collide, so that achieving one causes setbacks in others. The second area of contention arises even with agreement on the ranking of the goals because there is disagreement amongst macroeconomists about how to meet the macroeconomic challenges and that this can lead to different policy advice.

Questions

■ True/False and Explain

Origins and Issues of Macroeconomics

1. Modern macroeconomics was developed during the decade of the Great Depression.

2. All macroeconomic goals are long-term goals.

Economic Growth and Fluctuations

3. Real GDP is the amount of goods and services that are produced in a year when resources are fully employed.

4. Real GDP per person grew slowly in the 1960s and quite rapidly in the 1970s.

5. The trough is the lower turning point of the business cycle.

6. Since 1996, the growth rate of real GDP has been lower in Japan than in the United States.

Jobs and Unemployment

7. Unemployment rates in recent years have been lower than those during the Great Depression.

8. In the recession phase of a business cycle, the unemployment rate rises.

Inflation and the Dollar

9. The inflation rate can never be negative.

10. Inflation in the United States has been similar to that in other industrialized nations.

Surpluses, Deficits, and Debts

11. Ignoring interest income and expense, if U.S. exports exceed U.S. imports, the United States has a current account deficit.

12. A current account deficit definitely harms the nation.

Macroeconomic Policy Challenges and Tools

13. The government can use fiscal policy and monetary policy to pursue its macroeconomic goals.

14. Fiscal policy includes government engineered changes in the interest rate.

■ Multiple Choice Questions

Origins and Issues of Macroeconomics

1. During the Great Depression,
   a. the major focus of macroeconomics switched to preventing inflation.
   b. the productivity growth slowdown occurred.
   c. economists switched their focus so that macroeconomics began to emphasize business cycles.
   d. long-term economic growth was the major problem facing capitalist nations.

Economic Growth and Fluctuations

2. Real GDP
   a. measures only the output of real goods, such as machines and food, not "unreal" things such as services.
   b. includes all the goods and services produced in the economy, including those produced in the home.
   c. is measured in the prices of a single year in order to eliminate the effects of inflation.
   d. is the amount of goods and services that the nation is able to produce when its resources are fully employed.

3. Which is the proper order for the business cycle?
   a. Peak, recession, trough, expansion
   b. Peak, trough, expansion, recession
   c. Peak, expansion, trough, recession
   d. Peak, recession, expansion, trough

4. Real GDP rose in all four quarters of 2003; thus 2003 was definitely a year
   a. of expansion.
   b. with a business cycle peak.
   c. of recession.
   d. with a business cycle trough.

5. Which of the following statements about the productivity growth slowdown is correct?
   a. The productivity growth slowdown was confined to the United States.
   b. The productivity growth slowdown occurred in the 1960s.
   c. The growth of potential GDP slowed during the productivity growth slowdown.
   d. Extremely low oil prices were a major cause of the productivity growth slowdown.

6. Since 1976, compared to the rest of the world, real GDP growth in the United States was _____ variable than in the rest of the world and was _____ the world growth rate.
   a. more; greater than
   b. less; equal to
   c. more; slightly less than
   d. less; equal to

7. The accumulated loss of output that results from a slowdown in the growth rate of real GDP per person is called the _____
   a. Lucas wedge.
   b. Okun gap.
   c. output gap.
   d. growth gap.

8. Which of the following is <u>NOT</u> a cost of more rapid economic growth?
   a. Current consumption must be foregone in order to develop new technology or new capital.
   b. Environmental damage may increase because of economic growth.
   c. Consumption possibilities expand in the future because of economic growth.
   d. The Lucas wedge increases in size.

Jobs and Unemployment

9. In 2006, _____ people had jobs in the United States.
   a. 1,000,000
   b. 143,000,000
   c. 85,000,000
   d. 180,000,000

10. The unemployment rate generally rises during _____ in the business cycle.
    a. a peak
    b. a recession
    c. a trough
    d. an expansion

11. Comparing the United States, Western Europe, and Japan, in recent years the unemployment rate has been highest in
    a. the United States.
    b. Western Europe.
    c. Japan.
    d. the United States and Japan.

Inflation and the Dollar

12. In the United States, the average inflation rate was highest over the decade of the
    a. 1960s.
    b. 1970s.
    c. 1990s.
    d. 2000s.

13. Which of the following is a cost of unpredictable inflation?
    a. People use resources to predict inflation rather than to produce output.
    b. It becomes too easy to obtain loans.
    c. Deflation becomes an increasing problem.
    d. All of the above are costs of unpredictable inflation.

Surpluses, Deficits, and Debts

14. Which of the following statements about the government budget is correct?
    a. Whenever tax revenues exceed government spending, the government has a budget deficit,
    b. As a fraction of GDP, the budget deficit has increased steadily since 1980.
    c. The government has had a budget deficit every year since 1970.
    d. None of the above are correct.

15. Since 1980, the U.S. current account has had
    a. a deficit that has been large at times and small at other times.
    b. a surplus that has been consistently large.
    c. a deficit that has gotten consistently larger.
    d. alternating small surpluses and deficits.

Macroeconomic Policy Challenges and Tools

16. Which of the following is <u>NOT</u> a policy challenge?
    a. Boosting long-term growth.
    b. Lowering unemployment.
    c. Stabilizing the business cycle.
    d. Raising the government budget deficit.

17. Which of the following is an example of monetary policy?
    a. Changing the interest rate.
    b. Changing government spending.
    c. Changing tax rates.
    d. Changing the government's deficit.

■ Short Answer Problems

1. What was the productivity growth slowdown? Why is it important?

2. Suppose that real GDP per person in the United States in 2007 is $30,000.

   a. If the U.S. real GDP per person grows at 2 percent per year, what is real GDP per person in 2008? In 2009? In 2012? In 2017?

   b. If the U.S. real GDP per person grows at 3 percent per year, what is real GDP per person in 2008? In 2009? In 2012? In 2017?

   c. In 2017 what is the difference in real GDP per person if the growth rate is 3 percent per year versus 2 percent? What does this result illustrate?

3. Between 1996 and 2006, how has the growth rate of real GDP in the United States compared to that in Japan? To that of the European Union? To that of the newly industrialized nations of Asia?

4. What happens to real GDP and the unemployment rate during each of the four phases of the business cycle?

5. What are the costs of unemployment?

6. How has inflation in the United States compared to inflation in other countries?

■ You're the Teacher

1. After class, your friend asks you: "You know, I wonder what's more important: stabilizing the business cycle or boosting long-term economic growth. Both seem important, and it would be cool if we could achieve both of these goals, but do you think one is more important than the other? You know, what I mean is that if we can actually achieve only one of these goals, which one do you think it ought to be?" Your friend has posed a very thoughtful question; what is your equally thoughtful response?

Answers

True/False Answers

Origins and Issues of Macroeconomics

1. **T** The initial focus of modern macroeconomics was on overcoming the very high unemployment that existed in the Great Depression.

2. **F** Short-term goals, such as avoiding a depression, as well as long term goals, such as the rate of economic growth, are both important parts of macroeconomics.

Economic Growth and Fluctuations

3. **F** Potential real GDP is the amount of goods and services produced when all resources are fully employed.

4. **F** Real GDP per person started growing more slowly in the 1970s. Indeed, that was the "productivity growth slowdown."

5. **T** After the trough, the economy enters the expansion phase of the business cycle.

6. **T** Between 1996 and 2006, the United States has grown more rapidly than Japan.

Jobs and Unemployment

7. **T** In the Great Depression, unemployment rates approximated 25 percent; during the past 50 years, at its monthly peak, the unemployment rate was approximately 12 percent.

8. **T** As real GDP falls during a recession, the unemployment rate rises.

Inflation and the Dollar

9. **F** The inflation rate can be negative (called deflation), though in recent years inflation has rarely been negative.

10. **T** In industrial nations worldwide, the inflation rate was very high in the 1970s and lower in recent years.

Surpluses, Deficits, and Debts

11. **F** If exports exceed imports, the United States has a current account *surplus*.

12. **F** If the current account deficit occurs because the nation is buying capital equipment and other investments from abroad, the deficit can help the nation; if the nation is buying consumption goods and services, it can prove harmful to the nation.

Macroeconomic Policy Challenges and Tools

13. **T** In chapters to come, we explore fiscal and monetary policy in detail.

14. **F** Interest rate changes are part of monetary policy.

Multiple Choice Answers

Origins and Issues of Macroeconomics

1. **c** During the Great Depression, the extraordinarily high unemployment rates caused economists to stress short-term goals, such as reducing the severity of recessions or depressions.

Economic Growth and Fluctuations

2. **c** By measuring prices in a single year, real GDP eliminates the effects of inflation.

3. **a** Keep in mind that the business cycle is not a "smooth" cycle; some expansions last longer than others, some troughs are deeper than others, and so on.

4. **a** By definition, an expansion is a period of time during which real GDP increases.

5. **c** The slowdown in productivity growth is reflected in the slower growth rate of potential GDP.

6. **c** On average the United States has grown only slightly less rapidly than the rest of the world, so the U.S. share of world GDP has fallen only slightly from 21 percent to 20 percent.

7. **d** The question gives the definition of the Lucas wedge.

8. **c** The expansion of future consumption possibilities is a benefit of economic growth.

Jobs and Unemployment

9. **b** In recessions, jobs are destroyed and in expansions more jobs are created.

10. **b** As real GDP falls in a recession, the unemployment rate rises.

11. **b** Relatively high unemployment rates in Western Europe have emerged as a major economic problem in those countries.

Inflation and the Dollar

12. **b** The inflation rate was markedly highest during the 1970s.

13. **a** By becoming "amateur inflation predictors," people take time and effort away from their occupations and so the nation produces fewer goods and services.

Surpluses, Deficits, and Debts

14. **d** Until 1998 to 2000, when it had a budget surplus, the government had had a budget deficit every year since 1970.

15. **a** The United States has had a deficit that initially became large, diminished in size, and then became even larger than before.

Macroeconomic Policy Challenges and Tools

16. **d** *Lowering* any government budget deficit is the macroeconomic policy challenge.

17. **a** Monetary policy includes changing the interest rate and/or the nation's money supply. The other answers are examples of fiscal policy.

■ Answers to Short Answer Problems

1. The productivity growth slowdown refers to period that started in the 1970s when growth in real GDP fell. During the 1970s, growth in real GDP slowed and has remained lower since than. Growth in real GDP is important because economic growth increases people's consumption possibilities; the larger real GDP, then the more goods and services people can consume. Basically, because of the productivity growth slowdown, today we all have smaller incomes than we would have had if productivity growth had not slowed.

2. a. In 2008 real GDP per person equals $30,600; in 2009 it equals $31,212; in 2012 it equals $33,122.42; and in 2017 it equals $36,569.83.

    b. In 2008 real GDP per person equals $30,900; in 2009 it equals $31,827; in 2012 it equals 34,778.22; and in 2017 it equals $40,317.49.

    c. The difference is $3,747.66, or almost $4,000 per person. This result illustrates the point of the Lucas wedge, that a relatively small difference in the growth rate of real GDP per person can eventually make a large difference in the total amount of real GDP per person.

3. Between 1996 and 2006, real GDP has grown most rapidly in the new industrialized nations of Asia and has grown most slowly in Japan. The growth rate of real GDP in the European Union tops that in Japan, but the growth rate of real GDP in the United States exceeds that in the European Union.

4. During the recession phase of the business cycle, real GDP falls. During this phase of the cycle, the unemployment rate rises, although the rise in unemployment starts somewhat after the time that real GDP starts falling. At the trough, real GDP reaches its lowest point below potential GDP, and soon thereafter the unemployment rate is at its highest point over the business cycle. The trough is the turning point between the recession phase and the expansion phase. During the expansion, real GDP grows and the unemployment rate generally falls. At the end of an expansion, the economy reaches the peak of the business cycle. The peak is characterized by real GDP at its highest point above potential GDP and the rate of unemployment is either then or soon thereafter at its lowest point over the business cycle.

5. There are two important costs of unemployment: one "paid" immediately and the other incurred over a longer time horizon. First, and immediately, unemployed workers suffer a loss of income and the nation loses production. Second, and perhaps equally significant, when workers are unemployed for long periods of time, their skills and abilities deteriorate, which hurts their future job prospects.

6. Inflation in the United States has been similar to that in other industrialized countries. In particular, inflation rates rose in the 1970s and early 1980s and have fallen substantially since then.

■ You're the Teacher

1. ""You are talking about the Lucas wedge and the Okun gap and it's an excellent question. I asked our teacher about it, and our teacher said that economists don't agree about which of these macroeconomic challenges is more important.

"Some economists think that boosting long-term growth is most important. They point to the Lucas wedge—it's $72 trillion!! That's an immense amount. They also point out that if we are able to increase the growth rate of potential real GDP by 1 percentage point, after one generation, or two decades, real GDP per person would be over 22 percent higher than otherwise. That means that our consumption possibilities would expand by 22 percent so that, on the average, we could buy 22 percent more goods and services than otherwise. These economists also point out that this 22 percent increase in consumption possibilities dwarfs the fall of real GDP per person in a recession. So they argue that increasing the growth rate of potential GDP is more important than eliminating business cycles.

"Other economists disagree. Although they agree that boosting the growth rate of potential real GDP is important, they point out that sustaining even a 1 percent increase in real GDP over 20 years is extremely difficult. And they say that eliminating the Lucas wedge simply isn't possible. Instead, they ar-

gue that taming the business cycle should be considered the major goal of macroeconomic policy. They contend that this task is easier than increasing the growth rate of potential real GDP. Indeed, some of these economists suggest that we have tamed the business cycle a bit because there hasn't been a recession nearly as severe as the Great Depression since 1940.

"But our teacher says that *neither* of these objectives is easy to meet because if either were easy, we'd already be doing it. But, both challenges really are important. You know, I learned that our instructor became an economist exactly because these are crucial challenges and that by becoming a professional economist, our instructor hoped to help resolve these issues."

Chapter Quiz

1. The unemployment rate was approximately 25 percent
   a. during the Great Depression.
   b. during the most recent recession.
   c. during the 1974-1975 recession.
   d. in most years during the 1990s.

2. If the price level is rising, then the inflation rate
   a. is positive.
   b. is zero.
   c. is negative.
   d. could be positive, negative, or zero depending on the speed with which prices are rising.

3. Economic growth can be viewed as outward shifts the nation's *PPF*. Economic growth is the expansion in the economy's real GDP.
   a. Both sentences are true.
   b. The first sentence is true and the second is false.
   c. The first sentence is false and the second is true.
   d. Both sentences are false.

4. Which of the following statements is correct?
   a. Real GDP is the same as potential GDP.
   b. Real GDP can be larger or smaller than potential GDP.
   c. In the United States, real GDP generally grows at rate of 10 percent per year.
   d. Since 1960, real GDP has decreased about as many years as it has increased.

5. The productivity growth slowdown refers to the
   a. increase in output growth during the 1970s.
   b. decrease in output per person growth during the 1970s.
   c. increase in employment growth in the 1990s.
   d. recession that occurred in 2001.

6. You notice that over the last year the unemployment rate has gone from 7.2 percent to 5.8 percent and growth in real GDP has increased. So over this year the economy is likely
   a. in a recession.
   b. at the trough of a business cycle.
   c. in an expansion.
   d. at the peak of a business cycle.

7. Unemployment is a problem because
   a. it leads to higher inflation.
   b. it leads to deflation.
   c. there is lost income and production.
   d. real GDP does not measure the unemployment rate.

8. One of the costs of increasing growth in GDP is
   a. it does not increase the wealth available for all.
   b. it makes too many goods available for consumption in the future.
   c. people must give up current consumption.
   d. inflation must rise.

9. In recent decades, unemployment in the United States has been
   a. higher than in Western Europe.
   b. lower than in Japan.
   c. lower than in Canada.
   d. None of the above answers are correct.

10. The government collects $2,500 billion in taxes and spends $2,550 billion. The government has
    a. a budget surplus of $2,500 billion.
    b. a budget surplus of $50 billion.
    c. a budget deficit of $2,550 billion.
    d. a budget deficit of $50 billion.

The answers for this Chapter Quiz are on page 265

Chapter 5 MEASURING GDP AND ECONOMIC GROWTH*

Key Concepts

■ Gross Domestic Product

Gross domestic product, GDP, is the market value of all the final goods and services produced within in a country in a given time period.

♦ A **final good or service** is an item that is bought by its final user during a specified time period. In contrast, an **intermediate good** is an item produced by one firm, bought by another and used as a component of a final good or service. Intermediate goods are not directly included in real GDP.

The circular flow of income and expenditure shows real and monetary flows in the economy. The circular flow involves:

♦ Four economic sectors — households, firms, governments, and the rest of the world.

♦ Three major markets — factor markets, goods markets, and financial markets.

In these markets people make their economic decisions by choosing the amounts of key economic variables:

♦ **Consumption expenditures** (C) — total household spending on consumption goods and services.

♦ **Investment** (I) — firms' purchase of new plants, equipment, buildings, and additions to inventories.

♦ **Government expenditure** (G) — government expenditure on goods and services. **Net taxes** (T) are taxes paid to the government minus transfer payments received from governments and minus interest payments on the government's debt.

♦ **Net exports** (NX) — **exports** (X, sales of U.S. goods and services abroad) minus **imports** (M, purchases of foreign good and services).

Aggregate expenditure, $C + I + G + NX$, equals aggregate production, GDP, and also equals aggregate income, Y. This equality is the basis for measuring GDP.

♦ **National saving** equals saving by households and businesses plus government saving: $S + (T - G)$.

♦ Borrowing from the rest of the world equals $M - X$.

Investment is financed by national saving plus borrowing from the rest of world, $I = S + (T - G) + M - X$.

A *flow* is a quantity over a unit of time. A *stock* is a quantity that exists at a moment in time. Wealth and capital are stocks; saving and investment are flows.

♦ **Wealth**, the value of things that people own, is a stock; *income*, what people earn, is a flow.

♦ Saving is the amount of income remaining after spending on consumption. Saving is a flow that adds to wealth.

♦ *Capital*, the amount of plant, equipment, and inventories used to produce other goods, is a stock.

♦ **Depreciation** (also called *capital consumption*) is the decrease in the capital stock because of wear and tear and obsolescence. **Gross investment** is the total amount of investment. **Net investment** is the amount by which the capital stock changes. Net investment equals gross investment minus depreciation.

Gross domestic product includes depreciation and so on the income side includes firms' gross profit (before subtracting depreciation) and on the expenditure side includes gross investment. Net domestic product excludes (subtracts) depreciation so it includes firms' net profits and net investment.

---

* This chapter is Chapter 21 in *Economics*.

■ Measuring U.S. GDP

In 2006, U.S. GDP equaled $13,008 billion.

♦ The *expenditure approach* measures GDP by adding final expenditures, $C + I + G + NX$. Of these expenditures, personal consumption expenditure is the largest, at about 70 percent. Gross private investment is about 17 percent, government expenditures on goods and services is about 19 percent, and net exports is about negative 6 percent.

♦ The *income approach* adds the compensation of employees, net interest, rental income, corporate profits and proprietors' income to give *net domestic income at factor cost*. Indirect taxes and depreciation are added and subsidies subtracted to obtain GDP.

■ Real GDP and the Price Level

Real GDP is the value of final goods and services produced in a given year when valued at constant prices. **Nominal GDP** is the value of the final goods and services produced in a given year valued at the prices that prevailed in that same year.

The base year prices method, which is the traditional method of calculating real GDP, values the quantities produced in each year using the prices of the base year. The **chain-weighted output index** method, which is the new method of calculating real GDP, uses the prices of two adjacent years to calculate the real GDP growth rate. The chain-weighted output index:

♦ First calculates the value of GDP for this year and last year, using prices from last year to value both year's outputs and then calculates the growth rate of GDP between the two years.

♦ Next calculates the value of GDP for this year and last year, this time using prices from this year to value both year's outputs and again calculates the growth rate of GDP between the two years.

♦ Finally the two growth rates are averaged. This average growth rate is used to scale up last year's real GDP by multiplying last year's real GDP by the average growth rate.

The **price level** is the average level of prices. One measure is of the price level is the **GDP deflator,** which is an average of current-year prices as a percentage of base-year prices. The GDP deflator equals (Nominal GDP ÷ Real GDP) × 100.

■ The Uses and Limitations of Real GDP

Real GDP is used for economic welfare comparisons, for making international comparisons of output, and for business cycle forecasting.

Economic welfare is a comprehensive measure of general economic well being. Real GDP is an imperfect measure of economic welfare because real GDP:

♦ Over adjusts for inflation — many quality improvements that lead to higher prices are counted as only price hikes.

♦ Omits household production — all household production is omitted.

♦ Omits the underground economy — the underground economy (transactions hidden from the government) is not included.

♦ Omits health and life expectancy — neither people's health nor life expectancy are indicated by real GDP.

♦ Omits leisure time — the value of leisure time is not included.

♦ Omits environmental quality — the consequences of adverse and beneficial environmental changes are omitted.

♦ Ignores political freedom and social justice — the extent of political freedom or social justice within a nation is not measured.

Making international comparisons of real GDP can be tricky because the real GDP of one country must be converted into the other nation's currency. Using exchange rates for such conversions might understate the real GDP in less developed nations. However, use of purchasing power parity prices might give a more accurate comparison. Using purchasing power parity prices puts U.S. GDP 5 times higher than China's GDP whereas using the market exchange rate to change Chinese prices into their equivalent U.S. prices puts U.S. GDP 28 times higher than China's GDP.

Though real GDP probably overstates the size of fluctuations in total production and economic welfare, it is a reasonably good indicator of the phase of the business cycle, e.g., expansion, peak, and so on.

Helpful Hints

1. **GDP, AGGREGATE EXPENDITURE, AND AGGREGATE INCOME :** Some of the most important

results in this chapter show the equality between GDP, aggregate expenditure, and aggregate income. A key point about these equalities is that GDP, aggregate expenditure, and aggregate income are linked. For instance, the production of output (GDP) creates income (aggregate income) as firms pay their workers and also creates expenditure (aggregate expenditure) as households use their incomes to buy goods and services.

2. **THE DIFFERENCE BETWEEN GOVERNMENT EXPENDITURES AND GOVERNMENT TRANSFER PAYMENTS :** Government expenditures on goods and services (G) and government transfer payments are fundamentally different. Both involve outlays by the government, but transfer payments are not payments for goods and services. Instead, they are simply a flow of money. Transfer payments are like gifts; they do not buy a good or service for the government in exchange. Transfer payments are not payment for a good or service, so they are not part of the G component of aggregate expenditure, $C + I + G + NX$, because aggregate expenditure measures *purchases of goods and services*.

Questions

■ True/False and Explain

Gross Domestic Product

1. The market value of *all* the goods and services produced within a country in a given time period are included in GDP.

2. Wages paid to households for their labor is part of aggregate income.

3. Transfer payments are included in the government expenditures component of aggregate expenditure.

4. Aggregate income equals aggregate expenditure.

5. Capital is a stock; investment is a flow.

6. Gross domestic product is larger than net domestic product.

Measuring U.S. GDP

7. GDP can be measured only one way.

8. The expenditure approach to measuring GDP adds firms' expenditures on wages, rent, interest, and profit.

Real GDP and the Price Level

9. The chain-weighted output index method is how real GDP is calculated.

10. The GDP deflator is calculated as real GDP divided by nominal GDP, multiplied by 100.

11. If prices rise, nominal GDP is smaller than real GDP.

The Uses and Limitations of Real GDP

12. If two nations have the same GDP, economic welfare must be the same in each.

13. Real GDP is a good measure of economic welfare in less developed nations, but is a bad measure in developed nations.

14. Real GDP is a good measure of the phase of the business cycle.

■ Multiple Choice

Gross Domestic Product

1. Which of the following is <u>NOT</u> a final good?
   a. a new computer sold to an NYU student
   b. a new car sold to Avis for use in their fleet of rental cars
   c. a purse sold to a foreign visitor
   d. a hot dog sold to a spectator at a Chicago Bears football game

2. GDP equals
   a. aggregate expenditure.
   b. aggregate income.
   c. the value of the aggregate production in a country during a given time period.
   d. all of the above.

3. A nation's investment must be financed by
   a. national saving only.
   b. the government's budget deficit.
   c. borrowing from the rest of the world only.
   d. national saving plus borrowing from the rest of the world.

4. Which of the following is a flow?
   a. GDP
   b. Wealth
   c. The amount of money in a savings account
   d. Capital

5. Which of the following is a stock?
   a. Income
   b. Depreciation
   c. Investment
   d. Capital

Measuring U.S. GDP

6. Gross private domestic investment is a component of which approach to measuring GDP?
   a. Incomes approach
   b. Expenditure approach
   c. Linking approach
   d. Output approach

7. Which of the following is <u>NOT</u> a component of the incomes approach to GDP?
   a. Net exports
   b. Wages and salaries
   c. Corporate profits
   d. Proprietors' income

Use Table 5.1 for the next eight questions. Assume there are no indirect taxes, subsidies, or depreciation.

TABLE **5.1**
Multiple Choice Questions 8–15

Consumption expenditure	$200 billion
Government expenditures	60 billion
Net taxes	50 billion
Investment	50 billion
Corporate profits	30 billion
Imports	20 billion
Exports	10 billion

8. How much is aggregate expenditure?
   a. $440 billion
   b. $330 billion
   c. $300 billion
   d. $270 billion

9. How much is GDP?
   a. $440 billion
   b. $330 billion
   c. $300 billion
   d. $270 billion

10. How much is aggregate income?
    a. $440 billion
    b. $330 billion
    c. $300 billion
    d. $270 billion

11. How much is net exports?
    a. $20 billion
    b. $10 billion
    c. $0
    d. −$10 billion

12. How much is household saving?
    a. $300 billion
    b. $200 billion
    c. $100 billion
    d. $50 billion

13. How much is government saving?
    a. $60 billion
    b. $50 billion
    c. $0
    d. −$10 billion

14. How much is national saving?
    a. $200 billion
    b. $50 billion
    c. $40 billion
    d. −$10 billion

15. How much is the borrowing from the rest of the world?
    a. $20 billion
    b. $10 billion
    c. $0
    d. −$10 billion

Real GDP and the Price Level

16. Currently, real GDP is calculated using
    a. the quantities only method.
    b. base year prices method.
    c. current year prices method.
    d. chain-weighted output index method.

17. Real GDP in 2006 is $100. Between 2006 and 2007, using 2006 prices GDP grew 8 percent and using 2007 prices real GDP grew 4 percent. What does real GDP in 2007 equal?
    a. $104
    b. $106
    c. $108
    d. None of the above answers is correct.

Use Table 5.2 for the next two questions.

TABLE **5.2**

Multiple Choice Questions 18 and 19

Year	Nominal GDP (billions of dollars)	Real GDP (billions of 2000 dollars)	GDP deflator
2006	$4,500	_____	150
2007	_____	$3,100	156

18. What is real GDP in 2006?
    a. $675,000 billion
    b. $4,500 billion
    c. $3,100 billion
    d. $3,000 billion

19. What is nominal GDP in 2007?
    a. $4,836 billion
    b. $3,100 billion
    c. $3,000 billion
    d. $1,987 billion

The Uses and Limitations of Real GDP

20. Pollution is a by-product of some production processes, so real GDP as measured
    a. is adjusted downward to take into account the pollution.
    b. is adjusted upward to take into account the expenditures that will be made in the future to clean up the pollution.
    c. tends to overstate economic welfare.
    d. tends to understate economic welfare.

21. Which of the following is <u>NOT</u> a reason that real GDP is a poor measure of a nation's economic welfare?
    a. Real GDP omits measures of political freedom.
    b. Real GDP does not take into account the value of people's leisure time.
    c. Real GDP does not include the underground economy.
    d. Real GDP overvalues household production.

22. Which of the following statements about the comparison between GDP in China and in the U.S. is correct?
    a. Using the exchange rate to value China's GDP in dollars shows that China's GDP per person exceeds the GDP per person in the United States.
    b. Using purchasing power parity prices to value China's GDP in dollars shows that China's GDP per person exceeds the GDP per person in the United States.
    c. China's GDP per person is higher using purchasing power parity prices rather than the exchange rate when valuing China's GDP in dollars.
    d. None of the above answers are correct because they are all false statements.

■ Short Answer Problems

1. Robert buys 100 shares of stock in Microsoft and pays a total of $10,000. Is his expenditure of $10,000 part of GDP? Explain your answer.

2. How can we measure gross domestic product, GDP, with either the expenditure or the incomes approach, when neither of these approaches actually measures production?

3. Betty receives a Social Security check for $1,500 from the government. Is her check part of the government purchases component of GDP? Explain your answer.

4. How is a nation's investment financed? Define national saving and borrowing from the rest of world in your answer.

TABLE **5.3**

Data From Mallville

Consumption expenditure	$400 billion
Government expenditures	120 billion
Net taxes	100 billion
Investment	80 billion
Corporate profits	50 billion
Imports	50 billion
Exports	60 billion

5. Table 5.3 shows data for the nation of Mallville. Depreciation in Mallville is zero. Using these data, what is the value of Mallville's

a. GDP?

b. aggregate expenditure?

c. net exports?

d. aggregate income?

e. household saving?

f. government saving?

g. national saving?

h. borrowing from the rest of world?

6. Use the data and your answers from problem 6 to show how Mallville's investment of $80 billion is financed.

7. Igor has been hired to use the chain-weighted output index method for calculating real GDP for Transylvania's real GDP in 2007. Igor likes chains, so he thought he would be good at his new job, but he needs help. Real GDP in 2006 was $500. Igor calculates that GDP using 2006 prices is $1,000 in 2006 and $1,100 in 2007. He also calculates that GDP using 2007 prices is $1,200 in 2006 and $1,440 in 2007. Help Igor avoid chains himself by calculating real GDP in 2007.

■ You're the Teacher

1. "Even though I studied this chapter a lot, just like our teacher told us to, I don't understand why I had to study it so much. What's the big deal? Do you know why?" Your friend probably didn't study this chapter quite enough. Because you did, you can help your friend by explaining why this chapter is worthy of study.

Answers

■ True/False Answers

Gross Domestic Product

1. **F** The market value of only *final* goods and services is included in GDP; the market value of intermediate goods is not included.

2. **T** Compensation of employees (wages) is the single largest component of aggregate income.

3. **F** The government expenditures part of aggregate expenditure is the goods and services the government buys. Transfer payments buy no good or service and so they are not part of the government expenditures part of aggregate expenditure.

4. **T** Aggregate income equals aggregate expenditure and both equal GDP.

5. **T** Investment is the flow that adds to the stock of capital.

6. **T** Gross domestic product includes depreciation.

Measuring U.S. GDP

7. **F** Because of the equality between aggregate expenditure, aggregate income, and GDP, GDP can be measured using the expenditure approach or using the income approach.

8. **F** The expenditure approach to measuring GDP adds consumption expenditure, investment, government expenditure, and net exports.

Real GDP and the Price Level

9. **T** The chain-weighted output index method is the new method used to calculate real GDP. The base year prices method is the older method that is no longer in use.

10. **F** The GDP price deflator is equal to (Nominal GDP ÷ Real GDP) × 100.

11. **F** When prices rise, nominal GDP is larger than real GDP and must be deflated to equal real GDP.

The Uses and Limitations of Real GDP

12. **F** Economic welfare depends on more than just real GDP, so even if the nations' real GDPs are equal, their economic welfare can be different.

13. **F** In developed nations real GDP is not a perfect measure of economic welfare and is an even poorer measure in less developed nations.

14. **T** Real GDP generally is a reliable indicator of business cycle phases.

■ Multiple Choice Answers

Gross Domestic Product

1. **b** The new car sold to Avis is an intermediate good.

2. **d** The equality of these three measures of GDP is a key result developed in this chapter.

3. **d** A nation's investment can be financed through borrowing from foreigners and/or saving by domestic citizens.

4. **a** GDP is the flow of production during a year.

5. **d** Capital is the total amount of plant, equipment, and inventories that exists at a moment in time.

Measuring U.S. GDP

6. **a** The expenditures approach adds the expenditures made on all final goods and services.

7. **a** Net exports is a component of the expenditure approach to measuring GDP.

8. **c** Aggregate expenditure equals the sum of consumption expenditure ($200 billion) plus gross investment ($50 billion) plus government expenditure ($60 billion) plus net exports (–$10 billion, exports minus imports).

9. **c** GDP equals aggregate expenditure.

10. **c** Aggregate income equals GDP.

11. **d** Net exports equals exports ($10 billion) minus imports ($20 billion).

12. **d** Household saving equals aggregate income ($300 billion) minus consumption expenditure ($200 billion) and net taxes ($50 billion), so household saving is $50 billion.

13. **d** Government saving equals net taxes ($50 billion) minus government expenditures ($60 billion) so government saving is –$10 billion.

14. **c** National saving equals the sum of household saving plus government saving. From question 12, household saving is $50 billion. From question 13, government saving is –$10 billion. So, national saving is $40 billion.

15. **b** Borrowing from the rest of the world equals the negative of net exports.

Real GDP and the Price Level

16. **d** The base year prices method is the old method for calculating real GDP; currently the chain-weighted output index is the method used to calculate real GDP.

17. **b** The average growth rate between these years is 6 percent, so real GDP grew 6 percent to $106.

18. **d** Real GDP equals nominal GDP deflated by (divided by) the GDP deflator, then multiplied by 100.

19. **a** Nominal GDP equals real GDP multiplied by the GDP deflator, then divided by 100.

The Uses and Limitations of Real GDP

20. **c** Because pollution is not subtracted from real GDP, real GDP overstates economic welfare.

21. **d** Real GDP omits household production.

22. **c** When the exchange rate is used to value China's GDP, GDP per person in the United States is 34 times larger than China's GDP per person. If purchasing power parity prices are used to value China's GDP, U.S. GDP per person is 6 times larger than China's GDP per person.

■ Answers to Short Answer Problems

1. No, Robert's purchase of Microsoft stock is not part of GDP. GDP includes the purchase of final goods and services. Included in GDP would be, say, Microsoft's purchase of a new telephone system because this is the purchase of a piece of capital. When Robert purchased Microsoft stock, no good or service changed hands. So it is excluded from GDP because the expenditures in GDP represent the purchase of goods or services.

2. The analysis of the circular flow showed that firms produce goods and services (what we want to measure, GDP); sell them (what the expenditure approach measures); and then use the proceeds to pay incomes, such as rents, profits, and the like (what the incomes approach measures). Therefore aggregate expenditure = aggregate income = production = GDP.

3. No, Betty's $1,500 Social Security check is not part of the government expenditure (G) component of GDP. That measures the government's expenditures on goods and services. The government is not buying a good or service when it gives Betty her Social Security check. Instead, the check is a transfer payment, that is, a transfer of income from the people who paid Social Security taxes to Betty. Transfer payments are not part of the government expenditure component of GDP.

4. Investment can be financed by national saving and/or borrowing from the rest of the world. National saving equals the sum of household saving, S, plus government saving, $T - G$. Hence national saving equals $S + (T - G)$. Borrowing from the rest of world is $M - X$. So investment must equal what is saved in the nation plus what is borrowed from abroad, which in terms of a formula is equal to $S + (T - G) + M - X$.

5. a. GDP in Mallville equals the sum of consumption expenditure (C, $400 billion) plus investment (I, $80 billion) plus government expenditure (G, $120 billion) plus net exports (NX), which equals exports (X, $60 billion) minus imports (M, $50 billion). So GDP in Mallville is $610 billion.

   b. Aggregate expenditure equals GDP, so aggregate expenditure is $610 billion.

   c. Net exports, NX, is equal to exports ($60 billion) minus imports ($50 billion), or $10 billion.

   d. Aggregate income, Y, equals GDP, or $610 billion.

   e. Household saving equals aggregate income ($610 billion) minus net taxes ($100 billion) minus consumption expenditure ($400 billion), or $110 billion.

   f. Government saving is net taxes minus government expenditures, or $T - G$. So government saving equals $100 billion − $120 billion, or −$20 billion.

   g. National saving equals household saving plus government saving. From parts (e) and (f), national saving in Mallville is $90 billion.

   h. Borrowing from the rest of the world equals imports minus exports, $M - X$. Therefore Mallville's borrowing from the rest of the world is $50 billion − $60 billion = −$10 billion, that is, Mallville's residents *loan* $10 billion to the rest of the world.

6. Investment is financed by national saving and borrowing from the rest of the world. In Mallville's case, gross investment is $80 billion. That equals the sum of national saving, $90 billion plus borrowing from the rest of world, −$10 billion. Basically, Mallville has national saving of $90 billion, but only $80 billion of investment. Hence the difference, $10 billion, is loaned to the rest of the world.

7. Using 2006 prices, Transylvania's GDP grew from $1,000 in 2006 to $1,100 in 2007, so the percentage increase is 10 percent, $\frac{\$1,100 - \$1,000}{\$1,000} \times 100$.

    Using 2007 prices, GDP increased from $1,200 in 2006 to $1,440 in 2007, for a 20 percent increase. The average percent increase is 15 percent. As a result, real GDP is calculated as growing 15 percent between 2006 and 2007, so real GDP in 2007 is (15 percent) × ($500) = $575.

■ You're the Teacher

1. "Yes, I have an idea why this chapter is important. Basically, it is a lot of the foundation for the next 10 or so chapters!

    "That statement sure got your attention! Now, listen: We're trying to learn what factors affect the aggregate economy in order to discover what makes our economy grow more or less rapidly and what causes business cycles and other stuff. Look, these are important issues! I don't know about you, but I sure hope the economy's not in a recession when we graduate and have to look for jobs. At least I sure hope there's no recession going on when *I* have to look for a job! And once we get jobs, I sure hope that the economy grows rapidly so that our incomes grow rapidly along with it.

    "Anyway, we have to know what GDP is in order to understand growth and business cycles. After all, how would we measure these things if we didn't know what the GDP is? So, we're going to be studying what makes GDP grow faster and what makes it fluctuate. And, when we do, a lot of the stuff we learned in this chapter will be important, like the idea that aggregate expenditure equals aggregate income and both equal GDP. So, I'm glad you studied this stuff, because if you'd blown it off, I'd be alone, without any friends, in the last half of the class."

Chapter Quiz

1. Which of the following is an example of a flow variable?
   a. Capital.
   b. GDP.
   c. Inventories.
   d. The money in your wallet.

2. Two factors that both directly change the amount of capital are
   a. consumption and government expenditure.
   b. exports and net exports.
   c. depreciation and investment.
   d. investment and government expenditure.

3. In the national income accounts, government expenditures on goods and services exclude
   a. transfer payments.
   b. state and local government spending.
   c. spending on national defense.
   d. local government spending, though it does include state government spending.

4. A government budget surplus equals
   a. net taxes minus government expenditure on goods and services.
   b. government expenditure on goods and services minus investment.
   c. consumption expenditure minus net taxes.
   d. None of the above.

5. Real GDP
   a. measures only real things, such as goods but not services.
   b. is the value of final goods and services using current prices.
   c. measures the change in production.
   d. is always larger than nominal GDP.

6. Which component of GDP has been negative in recent years?
   a. Consumption expenditure.
   b. Investment.
   c. Government expenditure on goods and services.
   d. Net exports.

7. Gross investment equals
   a. depreciation minus net investment.
   b. net investment plus depreciation.
   c. net investment minus depreciation.
   d. saving.

8. As a measure of economic welfare, real GDP takes account of
   a. household production.
   b. the value of leisure time.
   c. the underground economy.
   d. None of the above answers is correct because real GDP does not take account of any of them.

9. Which of the following is correct?
   a. Aggregate production, GDP, equals aggregate expenditure.
   b. Aggregate production, GDP, equals aggregate income.
   c. Investment can be financed by national saving or borrowing from the rest of the world.
   d. All of the above answers are correct.

10. GDP equals
   a $C + I - S - T.$
   b. $C + S - NX.$
   c. $C + I + G + NX.$
   d. $C + S + G.$

The answers for this Chapter Quiz are on page 265

Chapter 6 MONITORING JOBS AND THE PRICE LEVEL*

Key Concepts

■ Jobs and Wages

The U.S. Census Bureau divides the **working-age population** (those people aged 16 years and over who are not in jail, hospital, or other institution) into categories:

♦ Employed — people working at a full-time or part-time job.

♦ Unemployed — people who are (1) without a job but have made efforts to find a job within the past four weeks; or, (2) waiting to be called back to work from a layoff; or, (3) waiting to start a new job within 30 days.

♦ Not in the labor force — people who are not employed and not looking for work, that is, are not unemployed.

The **labor force** equals the sum of employed plus unemployed workers. **Discouraged workers** are people who are available and willing to work but have not made specific efforts to find a job within the previous four weeks. Discouraged workers are not in the labor force.

♦ **Unemployment rate** — percentage of people in the labor force who are unemployed. The unemployment rate equals

$$\frac{\text{Number of people unemployed}}{\text{Labor force}} \times 100$$

The unemployment rate in 2006 was 4.8 percent. From 1960 to 2006, the average unemployment rate has been about 5.9 percent. It rises during recessions.

♦ **Labor force participation rate** — percentage of the working-age population who are members of

the labor force. This rate is

$$\frac{\text{Labor force}}{\text{Working-age population}} \times 100$$

Since 1960, the labor force participation rate has generally increased and in 2006 was 66.7 percent. It falls during recessions because of **discouraged workers**, who temporarily leave the labor force during the recession and then rejoin it during expansions.

♦ **Employment-to-population ratio** — the percentage of working age people who have jobs. This ratio has generally increased since 1960 and in 2006 is 63.5 percent. The employment-to-population ratio falls during recessions.

Both the labor force participation rate and the employment-to-population ratio have increased because more women are working at market jobs.

A measure of labor input is **aggregate hours**, the total number of hours worked by all the people employed, both full time and part time, during a year. Aggregate hours have maintained an upward trend, but have increased less rapidly than the number of people employed because the average hours per worker has become shorter. Aggregate hours fall during recessions.

The **real wage rate** is the quantity of goods and services an hour's work can buy. It equals the money wage rate divided by the price level. Real wage rate growth was rapid in the 1990s, slowed with the recession in 2001, and has since resumed growing.

■ Unemployment and Full Employment

Unemployed workers include:

♦ **Job losers,** workers who are laid off or fired;

♦ **Job leavers,** workers who voluntarily quit;

---

* This is Chapter 22 in *Economics*.

◆ Labor force **entrants** and **reentrants,** people who are entering the labor force for the first time or are returning to it after leaving.

Job losers are the largest source of unemployment; job leavers are the smallest. Unemployment ends when a person is hired, recalled, or leaves the labor force. The duration of unemployment increases during recessions.

Unemployment rates are highest for young workers and black workers.

Unemployment is classified into three types:

◆ **Frictional unemployment** — the result of normal labor market turnover, such as people entering the labor force and leaving the labor force and businesses expanding or contracting. Frictionally unemployed workers are searching for good job matches. The length of their searches can be influenced by the amount of unemployment compensation payments.

◆ **Structural unemployment** — the result of changes in technology or international competition that change the skills needed to perform jobs or change the location of jobs.

◆ **Cyclical unemployment** — the fluctuating unemployment over the business cycle. Cyclical unemployment increases during recessions and decreases during expansions.

Full employment occurs when there is no cyclical unemployment. The **natural unemployment rate** is the unemployment rate when there is full employment. It equals the sum of the frictional and structural unemployment rates. The quantity of GDP at full employment is called **potential GDP.**

◆ Over the business cycle, unemployment fluctuates around the natural rate and real GDP fluctuates around potential GDP. When the unemployment rate is higher than the natural rate, real GDP is less than potential GDP and when the unemployment rate is lower than the natural rate, real GDP exceeds potential GDP.

■ The Consumer Price Index

The **Consumer Price Index (CPI)** is a measure of the average of the prices paid by urban consumers for a fixed "basket" of consumer goods and services. The CPI is defined to equal 100 for a period called the **reference base period.**

◆ The CPI basket contains the goods and services purchased by urban consumers. Each month the cost of the CPI basket is determined by a monthly price survey.

The CPI equals the current cost of basket divided by the cost in the base period multiplied by 100.

The **inflation rate** is the percentage change in the price level from one year to the next and equals:

$$\frac{(\text{CPI this year}) - (\text{CPI last year})}{(\text{CPI last year})} \times 100.$$

The CPI overstates the actual inflation rate for four reasons:

◆ New goods bias — when new, higher priced goods replace older goods.

◆ Quality change bias — failing to take account of quality improvements that raise prices.

◆ Commodity substitution bias — when consumers shift their purchases away from goods whose relative prices rise toward lower priced goods.

◆ Outlet substitution bias — with higher prices, people switch to low-cost discount stores.

The CPI is estimated to overstate inflation by 1.1 percentage points per year.

Helpful Hints

1. **FULL EMPLOYMENT :** Remember that full employment does not mean that everyone has a job. Rather, it means that the only unemployment is frictional and structural in nature so that there is no cyclical unemployment. When there is no cyclical unemployment, the unemployment rate is the natural unemployment rate.

   The actual rate of unemployment can be less than the natural unemployment rate, so that the employment can exceed full employment. In these situations, people are spending too little time searching for jobs, and therefore less productive job matches are being made. Conversely, the actual rate of unemployment can exceed the natural unemployment rate, so that employment is less than full employment. In this case, too many workers are searching for jobs and so the economy is able to produce fewer goods and services.

Questions

True/False and Explain

Jobs and Wages

1. Full-time students not looking for work are counted as unemployed.

2. The unemployment rate equals the total number of unemployed workers divided by the total working-age population.

3. Lesline lost her job and looked for a new job for eight months. She stopped looking for work because she believes she cannot find a job. Lesline is counted as unemployed.

4. The labor force participation rate has generally risen over the past several decades because more women are working in the marketplace.

5. The aggregate hours worked in the United States have not grown as quickly as the number of people employed.

6. The real wage rate is the wage rate including all fringes, that is, the wage rate that workers "really" receive.

7. The growth rate of real wages accelerated during the 1970s and 1980s.

Unemployment and Full Employment

8. More unemployed workers have quit their previous jobs than were fired or laid off.

9. In a recession, the duration of unemployment generally increases.

10. Bill has just graduated from high school and is looking for his first job. Bill is frictionally unemployed.

11. The natural unemployment rate equals the sum of frictional and structural unemployment.

12. At full employment, there is no unemployment.

13. Real GDP can never be greater than potential GDP.

The Consumer Price Index

14. The CPI basket used in calculating the CPI changes each year.

15. Consumers shift their purchases away from goods whose relative prices increase and thereby cause the CPI to overstate the actual inflation rate.

■ Multiple Choice

Jobs and Wages

1. In a country with a working-age population of 200 million, 130 million workers are employed and 10 million are unemployed. The labor force equals
   a. 200 million.
   b. 140 million.
   c. 130 million.
   d. 10 million.

2. In a country with a working-age population of 200 million, 130 million workers are employed and 10 million are unemployed. The unemployment rate is
   a. 5.0 percent.
   b. 7.1 percent.
   c. 7.7 percent.
   d. 65.0 percent.

3. In a country with a working-age population of 200 million, 130 million workers are employed and 10 million are unemployed. The labor force participation rate is
   a. 100 percent.
   b. 70 percent.
   c. 65 percent.
   d. 5 percent.

4. Over the past 30 years, the labor force participation rate for men has _____ and for women has _____.
   a. increased; increased
   b. increased; decreased
   c. decreased; increased
   d. decreased; decreased

5. Suppose that the money wage rate is $5 per hour, and that the price level is 100. If the money wage rate rises to $10 per hour and the price level does not change, what happens to the real wage rate?
   a. The real wage rate doubles.
   b. The real wage rate rises, but does not double.
   c. The real wage rate does not change.
   d. The real wage rate falls.

6. Suppose that the money wage rate is $5 per hour and that the price level is 100. If the money wage rate rises to $10 per hour and simultaneously the price level rises to 200, what happens to the real wage rate?
   a. The real wage rate doubles.
   b. The real wage rate rises but does not double.
   c. The real wage rate does not change.
   d. The real wage rate falls.

7. During the last 40 years,
   a. the average hours of work per week has declined.
   b. the unemployment rate generally has increased.
   c. aggregate hours of work have declined.
   d. the real wage rate increased most rapidly in the 1970s and early 1980s.

Unemployment and Full Employment

8. Which of the following accounts for largest amount of unemployment?
   a. Job leavers
   b. Job losers
   c. New entrants to the labor force
   d. Reentrants to the labor force

9. For which of the following groups is the unemployment rate the lowest?
   a. Black teenagers
   b. White teenagers
   c. Blacks, 20 years old and older
   d. Whites, 20 years old and older

10. Unemployment resulting from a recession is called
    a. cyclical unemployment.
    b. frictional unemployment.
    c. structural unemployment.
    d. cycle unemployment.

11. Who of the following is a discouraged worker?
    a. Cara, who lost her job because of foreign competition and is unemployed until retrained.
    b. Omar, a fishery worker who is searching for a better job closer to home.
    c. Eugene, a steelworker who was laid off but has stopped looking for a new job because the economy is in a recession and he thinks he won't be able to find a job.
    d. Amanda, an office worker who lost her job because of a slowdown in economic activity.

12. Who of the following is frictionally unemployed?
    a. Cara, who lost her job because of foreign competition and is unemployed until retrained.
    b. Omar, a fishery worker who is searching for a better job closer to home.
    c. Eugene, a steelworker who was laid off but has stopped looking for a new job because the economy is in a recession and he thinks he won't be able to find a job.
    d. Amanda, an office worker who lost her job because of a slowdown in economic activity.

13. Who of the following is structurally unemployed?
    a. Cara, who lost her job because of foreign competition and is unemployed until retrained.
    b. Omar, a fishery worker who is searching for a better job closer to home.
    c. Eugene, a steelworker who was laid off but has stopped looking for a new job because the economy is in a recession and he thinks he won't be able to find a job.
    d. Amanda, an office worker who lost her job because of a slowdown in economic activity.

14. Who of the following is cyclically unemployed?
    a. Cara, who lost her job because of foreign competition and is unemployed until retrained.
    b. Omar, a fishery worker who is searching for a better job closer to home.
    c. Eugene, a steelworker who was laid off but has stopped looking for a new job because the economy is in a recession and he thinks he won't be able to find a job.
    d. Amanda, an office worker who lost her job because of a slowdown in economic activity.

15. At the natural unemployment rate, there is no
    a. frictional unemployment.
    b. structural unemployment.
    c. cyclical unemployment.
    d. unemployment.

16. If the economy is at full employment,
    a. the entire population is employed.
    b. the entire labor force is employed.
    c. the only unemployment is frictional unemployment plus discouraged workers.
    d. real GDP equals potential GDP.

The Consumer Price Index

17. At the end of last year, the CPI equaled 120. At the end of this year, the CPI equals 132. What is the inflation rate over this year?
    a. 6 percent.
    b. 10 percent.
    c. 12 percent.
    d. None of the above answers are correct because more information is needed to calculate the inflation rate.

18. The commodity substitution bias is that
    a. consumers substitute high-quality goods for low-quality goods.
    b. government spending is a good substitute for investment expenditures.
    c. national saving and foreign borrowing are interchangeable.
    d. consumers decrease the quantity they buy of goods whose relative prices rise and increase the quantity of goods whose relative price falls.

■ Short Answer Problems

TABLE **6.1**

Short Answer Question 1

Employed workers	Unemployed workers	Labor force	Unemployment rate
100	10	____	____
80	____	100	____
____	____	200	5.0%
130	8	____	____

1. Complete Table 6.1.
2. Can the unemployment rate increase while the total amount of employment also increases? Be sure to take account of the behavior of discouraged workers in your answer.
3. Describe the trends in the labor force participation rate and employment-to-population ratio since 1960. Is there any difference in these trends for men and women?
4. Describe the trends in aggregate hours and total employment since 1960. How do they behave during recessions?

5. For the following time periods, describe Igor's labor market status. When Igor is unemployed, tell whether it is frictional, structural, or cyclical unemployment.
    a. From January 1 through June 30, 2007, Igor was a full-time student pursuing his bachelor's degree.
    b. On July 1, Igor graduated with his degree in body building. He spent three months looking for work before Dr. Frankenstein hired him on October 1.
    c. From October 1 to January 1, 2008, Igor worked full-time on the night shift.
    d. On January 1, because of generally worsening economic conditions, Igor was put on part-time on the night-shift even though he wanted to work full time.
    e. On February 28, as economic conditions worsened, Dr. Frankenstein fired Igor. Igor looked for work until May 1.
    f. On May 1, Igor became convinced that he couldn't find a job, so until October 31 Igor tended house and dug in his garden but did not look for work.
    g. On October 31, Count Dracula dropped by for a bite and offered Igor a job, which Igor accepted.

TABLE **6.2**

Consumption in Snowville

	2007		2008	
	Price	Quantity	Price	Quantity
Rutabaga	$0.50	200	$0.70	110
Parka	$50.00	2	$75.00	1
Book	$40.00	5	$30.00	10

6. In 2007, consumers in Snowville consumed only rutabagas, parkas, and books. The prices and quantities for 2007 and 2008 are listed in Table 6.2. The reference base period for Snowville's CPI is 2007.
    a. What is the CPI for Snowville in 2007?
    b. What is the CPI for Snowville in 2008?
    c. What is the inflation rate between 2007 and 2008?

■ **You're the Teacher**

1. "I really don't understand why we bother with the ideas of 'frictional,' 'structural,' and 'cyclical' unemployment. I mean, unemployment is unemployment, so who really cares about these types?" Your friend is being unnecessarily negative; explain why understanding these different types of unemployment is useful.

2. "Okay, now I see that the book is right — we should divide unemployment into frictional, structural, and cyclical. But, I still can't see why we should have any unemployment. I think that the government should reduce the unemployment rate to zero because that has to be best for the nation!" Your friend sees some of the lessons from the book, but your friend's vision is far from 20/20. Help this student by explaining why a goal of zero unemployment is neither realistic nor desirable.

Answers

■ True/False Answers

Jobs and Wages

1. **F** These students are not in the labor force.

2. **F** The unemployment rate equals the total number of unemployed workers divided by the labor force, not the total working-age population.

3. **F** Lesline is a discouraged worker because she stopped looking for a job and discouraged workers are not counted as unemployed.

4. **T** The labor force participation rate for men has generally fallen, but it has generally risen for women. The increase in the female labor force participation rate has been enough so that the overall participation rate has risen.

5. **T** The average hours per worker has gotten shorter, so the growth in total employment has been greater than the growth in aggregate hours of work.

6. **F** The real wage is the purchasing power of the wage, so the real wage rate shows the quantity of goods and services that can be purchased with an hour's work.

7. **F** The growth rate of real wages fell in the 1970s and 1980s.

Unemployment and Full Employment

8. **F** The greatest number of unemployed workers were fired or laid off.

9. **T** The duration of unemployment refers to length of time workers are unemployed, and the duration increases during a recession.

10. **T** Bill is part of the normal turnover in the labor market and thus is frictionally unemployed.

11. **T** The natural unemployment rate is *defined* to equal the sum of frictional and structural unemployment.

12. **F** At full employment, the unemployment rate equals the natural rate, comprising frictional and structural unemployment.

13. **F** When the unemployment rate is less than the natural unemployment rate, real GDP is greater than potential GDP.

The Consumer Price Index

14. **F** The CPI basket stays the same, that is, the quantities used in the basket do not change. However, the prices used change.

15. **T** The CPI is based on a fixed market basket, which assumes that people continue to buy the same quantities of goods and services whose relative prices have increased.

■ Multiple Choice Answers

Jobs and Wages

1. **b** The labor force equals the sum of employed workers (130 million) and unemployed workers (10 million), or 140 million.

2. **b** The unemployment rate equals the number of unemployed workers divided by the labor force, multiplied by 100.

3. **b** The labor force participation rate equals the percentage of the working-age population in the labor force, that is, the total labor force (140 million) divided by the total working-age population (200 million), multiplied by 100.

4. **c** The increase for women has been larger than the decrease for men, so the overall labor force participation rate has increased.

5. **a** The real wage rate equals the money wage rate divided by the price level, so when the money wage rate doubles and the price level does not change, the real wage rate doubles.

6. **c** The real wage rate equals the money wage rate divided by the price level. Thus when both the money wage rate and price level double, the real wage rate does not change.

7. **a** The average work week has declined in length primarily because the number of part-time jobs has increased.

Unemployment and Full Employment

8. **b** Job losers include workers who have been fired or laid off, and these workers account for the majority of unemployment.

9. **d** The unemployment rate for whites, 20 years old or older is the lowest and for teenage blacks is the highest.

10. **a** Cyclical unemployment is positive when the economy is in a recession and negative when it is an expansion.

11. **c** Eugene has stopped looking for work, so he is no longer considered an unemployed worker.

12. **b** Omar is part of the normal turnover in the labor force, so he is frictionally unemployed.

13. **a** Cara lost her job because of structural change (more foreign competition) in the economy, so she is structurally unemployed.

14. **d** Amanda's job was lost because of a recession, so Amanda is cyclically unemployed.

15. **c** The natural rate consists of only frictional and structural unemployment.

16. **d** At full employment, the amount of real GDP that is produced is potential GDP.

The Consumer Price Index

17. **b** The inflation rate is the percentage change in the price index, $\frac{132 - 120}{120} \times 100$, or 10 percent.

18. **d** In part because of the commodity substitution bias, the CPI overstates the true increase in the cost of living.

■ Answers to Short Answer Problems

TABLE **6.3**
Short Answer Question 1

Employed workers	Unemployed workers	Labor force	Unemployment rate
100	10	110	9.1%
80	20	100	20.0%
190	10	200	5.0%
130	8	138	5.8%

1. The answers are in Table 6.3. To calculate them, recall that the labor force equals the sum of employed and unemployed workers. Hence in the first line the total labor force equals 100 + 10 or 110. In the second line, the number of unemployed workers equals the labor force, 100, minus the total number of employed workers, 80. So unemployed workers number 20. The unemployment rate equals the total number of unemployed workers divided by the labor force,

multiplied by 100. So in the first row the unemployment rate equals (10 ÷ 110) × 100 = 9.1 percent. In the third row, rearranging the definition of the unemployment rate shows that the total number of unemployed workers equals the unemployment rate multiplied by the labor force. Hence in the third row the total number of unemployed workers is (5.0 percent) × (200) so that unemployment is 10. The number of employed workers in that row therefore is 190.

2. Although uncommon, both the number of employed workers and the unemployment rate can increase at the same time. This situation occurs most often just after the trough of the business cycle when the economy moves into an expansion. In these months, the economy is growing, and real GDP is expanding, so the total amount of employment rises. In addition, previously discouraged workers begin to perceive that they may now be able to find a job. A large number of discouraged workers may rejoin the labor force, start searching for jobs, and add significantly to the number of unemployed workers. (Recall that as discouraged workers, they were not counted as unemployed; rather they were not in the labor force.) Hence the unemployment rate may increase even though the total number of employed workers increases.

3. Both the labor force participation rate and the employment-to-population ratio have increased since 1960. The primary reason is more women in the labor force. The female labor force participation rate and the female employment-to-population ratio each have increased substantially since 1960. In contrast, the male labor force participation rate and the male employment-to-population ratio both have decreased slightly.

4. Both aggregate hours and total employment have increased since 1960. However, the changes have not been steady; during recessions, they have increased at a slower rate or have even decreased, but in total both have increased significantly over the past three decades. The growth in employment has exceeded the growth in total hours because the average work week has shortened.

5. a. As a full-time student, Igor was not in the labor force.
   b. While Igor searched for his first job, he was frictionally unemployed.

c. When working full-time for Dr. Frankenstein, Igor was an employed worker.

d. Even though Igor wanted full-time work, he nonetheless was still counted as (fully) employed when he was on the part-time night shift.

e. From February 28 to May 1, Igor was cyclically unemployed because his unemployment was the result of a downturn in the economy.

f. From May 1 to October 31, Igor was not in the labor force because he was not looking for work. Igor was a discouraged worker.

g. Igor is employed after October 31.

TABLE **6.4**

Consumption in Snowville

	2007		2008	
	Price	Quantity	Price	Quantity
Rutabaga	$0.50	200	$0.70	110
Parka	$50.00	2	$75.00	1
Book	$40.00	5	$30.00	10

6. a. The CPI in 2007 is 100. This answer can be calculated in two ways. First, the CPI in *any* reference base period equals 100. Alternatively, the CPI can be calculated directly. From Table 6.4, in 2007, the CPI basket cost ($0.50 per rutabaga) × (200 rutabagas) + ($50.00 per parka) × (2 parkas) + ($40.00 per book) × (5 books) or $400. The CPI is defined as 100 times the ratio of the cost of the basket in the current year divided by the cost of the basket in the reference base period. So, the CPI equals

$$\frac{(\$400)}{(\$400)} \times 100, \text{ or } 100.$$

b. As the first step in calculating the CPI for 2008, calculate the cost using 2008 prices of the 2007 CPI basket: ($0.70 per rutabaga) × (200 rutabagas) + ($75.00 per parka) × (2 parkas) + ($30 per book) × (5 books) or $440. The CPI equals 100 times the ratio of the cost of the basket in the current year divided by the cost of the basket in the reference base period, or $\frac{(\$440)}{(\$400)} \times 100 = 110$.

c. The inflation rate between 2007 and 2008 equals $(110 - 100) \div (100)$, or 10 percent.

■ **You're the Teacher**

1. "You're right, it probably doesn't make any difference to the unemployed worker whether he or she is frictionally, structurally, or cyclically unemployed. And determining which classification a particular unemployed worker falls into is difficult — perhaps impossible. But, this division can be *very* useful for us, as students, because it makes clear some of the causes of unemployment. And, once we know the causes, we can get insight into what we can do.

"Take the idea of structural unemployment, for instance. Helping workers who are structurally unemployed has to take a different tack than helping those who are cyclically unemployed. A worker who is cyclically unemployed doesn't necessarily need a lot of retraining. But one who is structurally unemployed may well benefit from this type of training. So, by recognizing that structural reasons are one cause of unemployment, we can see that offering retraining may be a good idea if we want to reduce the unemployment rate.

"Now, if we hadn't divided unemployment into different types, we may very well have thought that all unemployment was cyclical in nature. And in this case, we would probably have completely overlooked retraining. So dividing unemployment into three categories is helpful because it helps us think more deeply about unemployment."

2. "Look, here's another case where the division of unemployment into frictional, structural, and cyclical unemployment can help you avoid these outlandish statements. Think about frictional unemployment: What would it take to reduce this type of unemployment to zero? I mean, the laws and regulations would be awful! For instance, you'd need a law that says you couldn't graduate from college until you already had a job lined up because if you had to look for a job after graduation, you'd be frictionally unemployed. And once you had a job, you couldn't leave it until you had another job lined up. I don't know about you, but even though I like college, I don't want to

spend the rest of my life as a student and, if I get stuck in a job I hate, I want to be able to quit to look for a better one.

"You can see that reducing frictional unemployment to zero would be way too costly. The laws it would take are too strict and would really hurt our economy! It would probably be equally impossible to reduce structural unemployment to zero. But cyclical unemployment is a different issue. The more we can tame the business cycle, the more we can reduce cyclical unemployment. So, possibly what we want to aim for is to reduce cyclical unemployment to zero. In other words, forget the idea of eliminating *all* unemployment; let's concentrate instead on eliminating cyclical unemployment."

Chapter Quiz

1. The unemployment rate
   a. rises during an expansion and falls during a recession.
   b. measures the percentage of the working-age population who can't find a job.
   c. includes workers who have quit looking for work because they think they cannot find a job, that is, the unemployment rate includes discouraged workers.
   d. equals the percentage of the labor force that is without a job.

2. Over the last four decades, the labor force participation rate _____ and the employment-to-population ratio _____.
   a. increased; increased
   b. increased; decreased
   c. decreased; increased
   d. decreased; decreased

3. In a country with a working-age population of 200 million, 90 million workers are employed and 10 million are unemployed. What is the unemployment rate?
   a. 45.0 percent
   b. 11.1 percent
   c. 10.0 percent
   d. 5.0 percent

4. If money wages rise by a greater percentage than the price level, real wages
   a. increase.
   b. do not change.
   c. decrease.
   d. probably change, but without knowledge of the labor demand and labor supply, it is impossible to tell the direction.

5. Most unemployed people are
   a. job leavers.
   b. job losers.
   c. discouraged workers.
   d. new entrants into the labor force.

6. Unemployment that is associated with changing jobs in a normally changing economy is best characterized as
   a. cyclical unemployment.
   b. structural unemployment.
   c. frictional unemployment.
   d. long-term unemployment.

7. When thirty workers are laid off because the economy has entered a recession, _____ unemployment has increased.
   a. cyclical
   b. structural
   c. frictional
   d. discouraged worker

8. When thirty workers enter the labor force after graduation from school, _____ unemployment has increased.
   a. cyclical
   b. structural
   c. frictional
   d. discouraged worker

9. When thirty workers are laid off and cannot find new jobs because they lack the necessary skills, _____ unemployment has increased.
   a. cyclical
   b. structural
   c. frictional
   d. discouraged worker

10. Which of the following is correct?
    a. Aggregate hours have increased more rapidly than employment so the average work week has lengthened.
    b. Aggregate hours have increased more rapidly than employment so the average work week has shortened.
    c. Aggregate hours have increased less rapidly than employment so the average work week has lengthened.
    d. Aggregate hours have increased less rapidly than employment so the average work week has shortened.

The answers for this Chapter Quiz are on page 265

■ **Chapter 4**

1. Potential GDP is the
   a. the value of production with fully employed resources.
   b. current value of production in the economy.
   c. value of production when the economy is in a recession.
   d. value of production when the economy is at a peak.

2. The unemployment rate generally _____ during recessions and _____ during expansions.
   a. rises; falls
   b. rises; rises
   c. falls; rises
   d. falls; falls.

3. A cost of inflation to the economy is that
   a. predictable inflation is difficult to avoid.
   b. inflation requires foregone consumption.
   c. inflation leads to discouraged workers and increased unemployment.
   d. unpredictable inflation leads to uncertainty

4. A policy created change in _____ is an example of monetary policy.
   a. tax rates
   b. federal government spending
   c. the interest rate
   d. the budget deficit

■ **Chapter 5**

5. All of the following are included in GDP <u>EXCEPT</u>
   a. purchases of the services of attorneys.
   b. purchases of short-lived goods such as cotton candy.
   c. steel production.
   d. production in the underground economy.

6. Gross investment
   a. is the purchase of new capital.
   b. includes only replacement investment.
   c. does not include additions to inventories.
   d. Both answers A and B are correct.

7. Let *C* equal consumption expenditure, *S* saving, *I* investment, *G* government expenditures, and *NX* net exports. Then GDP equals
    a. $C + S + G + NX$
    b. $C + S + G - S$
    c. $C + I + G + NX$
    d. $C + I + G - NX$.

8. Which of the following is a component of the incomes approach to GDP?
    a. Consumption expenditure.
    b. Wages and salaries.
    c. Investment.
    d. Government expenditures on goods and services.

■ **Chapter 6**

9. What is the proper order for a business cycle?
    a. recession, peak, expansion, trough
    b. recession, expansion, peak, trough
    c. recession, expansion, trough, peak
    d. recession, trough, expansion, peak

10. The working age population is 150 million, there are 120 million employed workers and 10 million unemployed workers. The unemployment rate equals
    a. 80.0 percent.
    b. 25.0 percent.
    c. 8.3 percent.
    d. 7.7 percent.

11. The natural unemployment rate includes
    a. only frictional unemployment.
    b. only structural unemployment.
    c. only frictional and structural unemployment.
    d. frictional, structural, and cyclical unemployment.

12. If the CPI in 2006 is 100 and the CPI in 2007 is 105, then the inflation rate is
    a. 1.5 percent.
    b. 5 percent.
    c. 100 percent.
    d. 105 percent.

Answers

■ Mid-Term Exam Answers

1. a; 2. a; 3. d; 4. c; 5. d; 6. a; 7. c; 8. b; 9. d; 10. d; 11. c; 12. b.

Chapter 7 AT FULL EMPLOYMENT: THE CLASSICAL MODEL*

■ The Classical Model: A Preview

Real variables, such as real GDP, employment, unemployment, the real wage rate, saving, investment, and consumption tell us what is really happening to economic wellbeing. Nominal variables, such as the price level, the inflation rate, and nominal GDP, tell us how dollar values and the cost of living are changing.

The **classical dichotomy** is the discovery that at full employment, the forces that determine real variables are independent of those that determine nominal variables.

The **classical model** is a model of an economy that determines the real variables at full employment. Most economists agree that the economy fluctuates around full employment, but classical economists think that the economy is always at full employment.

■ Real GDP and Employment

A production possibilities frontier between real GDP and leisure shows that GDP can be increased if time spent at leisure is decreased, that is, if employment is increased.

The **production function** is the relationship between real GDP and the quantity of labor employed when all other influences on production remain the same. A production function is illustrated in Figure 7.1.

◆ When employment increases, there is a movement along the production function, as illustrated by the movement from point *a* to point *b* along *PF*.

■ The Labor Market and Potential GDP

The demand for labor and the supply of labor depend

FIGURE **7.1**
Production Function

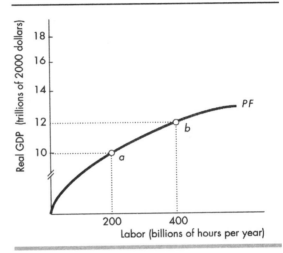

on the **real wage rate**, the quantity of goods and services an hour of labor earns. The **money wage rate** is the number of dollars an hour of labor earns.

◆ The real wage rate equals the money wage rate divided by the price level multiplied by 100.

The **demand for labor** is the relationship between the real wage rate and the quantity of labor firms demand, where the *quantity of labor demanded* is the number of labor hours hired by all the firms in the economy. As the real wage rate increases, the quantity of labor demanded decreases.

◆ The **marginal product of labor** is the additional real GDP produced by an additional hour of labor. The **law of diminishing returns** states that as the quantity of labor increases, other things remaining the same, the marginal product of labor diminishes.

---

* This chapter is Chapter 23 in *Economics*.

♦ Because the marginal product of labor diminishes as employment increases, firms hire additional workers only if the real wage rate falls. So the demand for labor curve, *LD* illustrated in Figure 7.2, slopes downward.

♦ The demand for labor increases and the demand for labor curve shifts rightward when the marginal product of labor increases.

The *quantity of labor supplied* is the number of labor hours that all the households plan to work. The **supply of labor** is the relationship between the quantity of labor supplied and the real wage rate when all other influences on work plans remain the same.

♦ The supply of labor curve, *LS*, slopes upward, as illustrated in Figure 7.2. A higher real wage rate increase the amount of goods and services that can be purchased for an hour's work and increases the quantity of labor supplied for two reasons: For most households, an increase in the real wage rate increases the hours of labor per person. In addition, an increase in the real wage rate raises the labor force participation rate.

In Figure 7.2 the equilibrium real wage rate is $35 per hour and equilibrium employment is 200 billion hours.

♦ The equilibrium quantity of employment, determined in the labor market, together with the production function determine potential GDP.

■ Unemployment at Full Employment

Two factors explain why unemployment is always present even at full employment (when the unemployment rate equals the natural unemployment rate):

♦ **Job search** — the activity of looking for an acceptable vacant job. The length of time spent searching increases when more young people enter the labor market; when unemployment compensation payments be come more generous; and when structural change in the economy increases.

♦ **Job rationing** — paying workers a real wage rate above the equilibrium level and then rationing jobs by some method. Jobs can be rationed because of **efficiency wages** (a real wage rate that is set above the full-employment equilibrium wage rate that balances the costs and benefits of this higher wage to maximize the firm's profit) or because of a **minimum wage** law (which sets the lowest wage rate at which a firm may legally hire labor).

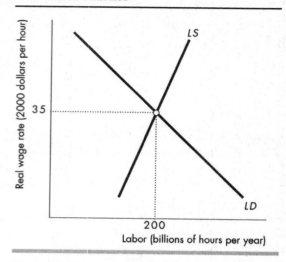

FIGURE 7.2
The Labor Market

■ Loanable Funds and the Real Interest Rate

The **capital stock** is the total quantity of plant, equipment, buildings, and inventories. Investment increases the capital stock. The funds that finance investment are obtained in the loanable funds market. The **market for loanable funds** is the market in which households, firms, governments, banks, and other financial institutions borrow and lend. Loanable funds are used for investment, a government budget deficit, and international investment or lending. Loanable funds come from private saving, a government budget surplus, and international borrowing.

The quantity of loanable funds demanded depends on the real interest rate, the expected profit rate, and government and international factors.

♦ The **real interest rate** is the quantity of goods and services that a unit of capital earns. The **nominal interest rate** is the number of dollars that a unit of capital earns.

♦ The real interest rate (approximately) equals the nominal interest rate minus the inflation rate.

♦ The **demand for loanable funds** is the relationship between the quantity of loanable funds demanded and the real interest rate when all other influences on borrowing plans remain the same. As illustrated in Figure 7.3 (on the next page) the demand for loanable funds curve, *DLF*, is downward sloping.

Investment demand is the main item that makes up the demand for loanable funds. Any government budget

FIGURE **7.3**
The Loanable Funds Market

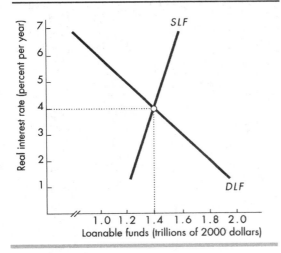

deficit and international lending add to investment to give the total demand for loanable fund. Investment depends on two factors:

♦ *Real interest rate* — the opportunity cost of the funds used to make an investment.

♦ *Expected profit rate* — the profit rate from an investment. The expected profit rate depends on technology. An increase in the expected profit rate increases investment demand.

A change in the interest rate leads to a movement along the demand for loanable funds curve. A change in the expected profit rate changes investment and shifts the demand for loanable funds curve.

Loanable funds supplied depends on the real interest rate, disposable income, wealth, future expected income, and government and international factors.

♦ The **supply of loanable funds** is the relationship between the quantity of loanable funds supplied and the real interest rate when all other influences on borrowing plans remain the same. As illustrated in Figure 7.3 the supply of loanable funds curve, *SLF*, is upward sloping.

Saving is the main item that makes up the supply of loanable funds. Any government budget surplus and international borrowing add to saving. Saving depends on:

♦ *Real interest rate* — the lower the real interest rate, the smaller is the quantity of saving.

♦ *Disposable income* — the higher a household's disposable income, the more it saves.

♦ *Wealth* — wealth equals assets minus debts. The higher a household's wealth, the lower is its saving.

♦ *Expected future income* — the lower a household's expected future income, the greater is its (current) saving.

A change in the interest rate leads to a movement along the supply of loanable funds curve. A change in disposable income, wealth, or expected future income changes saving and shifts the supply of loanable funds curve.

The demand for loanable funds and the supply of loanable funds determine the real interest rate. In Figure 7.3, the equilibrium real interest rate is 4 percent and the equilibrium quantity of loanable funds is $1.4 trillion.

■ Using the Classical Model

The classical model applies when the economy is at full employment, so it shows the average state of the economy over a business cycle.

In the United States, since 1986 both the demand for labor and supply of labor have increased. The demand for labor increased more than the supply, so the real wage rate increased. the quantity of employment has increased, from 198 billion hours per year to 254 billion hours per year. Advances in technology and capital accumulation shifted the U.S. production function upward, as illustrated in Figure 7.4 by the shift from PF_{86} to PF_{05}. As a result of these changes, potential U.S. GDP increased from $6.0 trillion in 1986 to $11.8 trillion in 2005.

FIGURE **7.4**
Shift of the U.S. Production Function

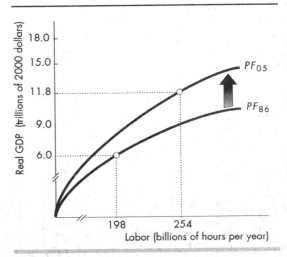

Helpful Hints

1. **THE SUPPLY AND DEMAND MODEL ONCE AGAIN:**
    The labor market and capital market function like
    the "typical" supply and demand markets you stud-
    ied in Chapter 3. Everything you learned there
    about how to use the supply and demand model
    applies to these two markets. For instance, the
    equilibrium point is where the two curves cross. In
    addition, the key difference between shifts in a
    curve versus movements along a curve continues to
    apply. In the labor market, changes in the real wage
    rate create movements along the labor demand and
    labor supply curves while other relevant factors
    shift the curves. And in the capital market, changes
    in the real interest rate create movements along the
    investment demand and saving supply curves while
    other relevant factors shift the curves.

2. **PRODUCTION FUNCTION :** The production func-
    tion links the labor market and the aggregate out-
    put market. The equilibrium level of employment
    is determined in the labor market and then the
    production function shows how much output re-
    sults from that level of employment.

Questions

■ True/False and Explain

The Classical Model: A Preview

1. Investment and unemployment are real variables.

2. The classical dichotomy states that the inflation
    rate is determined by the same factors that deter-
    mine employment.

Real GDP and Employment

3. If the production possibilities frontier does not
    shift, real GDP can be increased only if leisure is
    increased.

4. An increase in employment results in a movement
    along the production function.

The Labor Market and Potential GDP

5. The demand for labor curve is downward sloping.

6. As more workers are employed, the marginal prod-
    uct of labor increases.

7. A rise in the real wage rate increases the quantity of
    labor supplied.

8. When employment equals the equilibrium quan-
    tity, the economy is producing potential GDP.

9. An increase in the demand for labor raises the real
    wage rate.

Unemployment at Full Employment

10. When the unemployment rate equals the natural
    rate, there is no job search.

11. An increase in unemployment compensation de-
    creases job search.

12. Efficiency wages can lead to unemployment.

Loanable Funds and the Real Interest Rate

13. The real interest rate equals the nominal interest
    rate plus the inflation rate.

14. The real interest rate is the opportunity cost of
    investment.

15. An increase in the real interest rate increases the
    quantity of people's saving.

16. An increase in the expected profit rate shifts the
    supply of loanable funds curve rightward.

17. The equilibrium real interest rate sets the quantity
    of loanable funds demanded equal to the quantity
    of loanable funds supplied.

Using the Classical Model

18. An increase in the demand for labor increases po-
    tential GDP.

19. An increase in the nation's physical capital stock
    decreases the demand for labor.

20. An increase in labor productivity shifts the produc-
    tion function downward and decreases the quantity
    of employment.

■ Multiple Choice

The Classical Model: A Preview

1. Of the following, which is a real variable?
    a. employment
    b. the price level
    c. the inflation rate
    d. nominal wage rate

Real GDP and Employment

2. The production possibilities frontier between real GDP and leisure
   a. shifts inward when the capital stock increases because unemployment rises.
   b. shows that increasing leisure will decrease real GDP.
   c. shifts if employment increases.
   d. All of the above answers are correct.

3. An increase in employment
   a. shifts the nation's production function upward.
   b. shifts the nation's production function downward.
   c. leads to a movement along the nation's production function to a higher level of real GDP.
   d. leads to a movement along the nation's production function to a higher price level.

The Labor Market and Potential GDP

4. The money wage rate is $10 per hour and the price level is 100. If the price level rises to 200 and the money wage rate does not change, what happens to the real wage rate?
   a. The real wage rate doubles.
   b. The real wage rate rises, but does not double.
   c. The real wage rate does not change.
   d. The real wage rate falls.

5. Five workers produce total output of $200; six workers produce total output of $222. The marginal product of the sixth worker equals
   a. $40.
   b. $37.
   c. $22.
   d. None of the above answers is correct.

6. The demand for labor curve is downward sloping because the
   a. marginal product of labor diminishes as more workers are employed.
   b. supply curve of labor is upward sloping.
   c. demand curve shifts when capital increases.
   d. None of the above answers are correct because the demand for labor curve is upward sloping.

7. As the real wage rate increases, the quantity of labor supplied increases
   a. only because people already working increase the quantity of labor they supply.
   b. only because the higher wage rate increases labor force participation.
   c. because people already working increase the quantity of labor they supply *and* because the higher wage rate increases labor force participation.
   d. None of the above answers is correct because an increase in the real wage rate decreases the quantity of labor supplied.

8. A rise in the real wage rate
   a. shifts the labor demand curve rightward.
   b. shifts the labor demand curve leftward.
   c. shifts the labor supply curve leftward.
   d. does not shift the labor demand or labor supply curve.

9. At potential GDP,
   a. the labor market is in equilibrium so that the quantity of labor demanded equals the quantity supplied.
   b. the labor market might or might not be in equilibrium.
   c. the real wage has adjusted so that it equals the money wage.
   d. the real wage rate must be rising because otherwise people will not work.

10. An increase in population shifts the
    a. labor demand curve rightward.
    b. labor demand curve leftward.
    c. labor supply curve rightward.
    d. labor supply curve leftward.

Unemployment at Full Employment

11. An increase in unemployment compensation payments will
    a. decrease the extent of search unemployment.
    b. lead to more job rationing.
    c. decrease the extent of demographic change.
    d. increase the length of time a worker searches for a job.

12. Which of the following is a reason that jobs might be rationed?
    a. Efficiency wages
    b. Equilibrium real wage rate
    c. Efficiently rationed jobs
    d. An increase in the demand for labor

13. An efficiency wage refers to
    a. workers being paid wages below the equilibrium wage rate in order to increase the economy's efficiency.
    b. wages being set to generate the efficient level of unemployment.
    c. workers being paid wages above the equilibrium wage rate in order to increase their productivity.
    d. None of the above.

14. Suppose that the real wage rate is above the equilibrium real wage rate. Then the quantity demanded of labor ____ the quantity supplied of labor and there _____ unemployment.
    a. is more than; is
    b. is more than; is not
    c. is less than; is not
    d. is less than; is

Loanable Funds and the Real Interest Rate

15. If the nominal interest rate is 8 percent and the inflation rate is 2 percent, the real interest rate is
    a. 16 percent.
    b. 10 percent.
    c. 6 percent.
    d. 4 percent.

16. The expected profit rate rises
    a. when the real interest rate falls.
    b. during business cycle recessions.
    c. when sales fall so that the company has time to make investments.
    d. when technology advances make firms optimistic about future profits.

17. An increase in the real interest rate ____ the demand for loanable funds curve.
    a. results in a movement along
    b. results in a rightward shift of
    c. results in a leftward shift of
    d. has no effect on

18. An increase in disposable income shifts the ____.
    a. demand for loanable funds curve rightward.
    b. demand for loanable funds curve leftward.
    c. supply of loanable funds curve leftward.
    d. supply of loanable funds curve rightward.

19. If the real interest rate in the loanable funds market is less than the equilibrium real interest rate, the quantity of loanable funds supplied is ____ than the quantity of loanable funds demanded and the real interest rate ____.
    a. greater; rises
    b. greater; falls
    c. less; rises
    d. less; falls

Using the Classical Model

20. An increase in population shifts the
    a. labor demand curve rightward.
    b. labor demand curve leftward.
    c. labor supply curve rightward.
    d. labor supply curve leftward.

21. An advance in technology that increases the marginal product of labor shifts the production function ____ and shifts the demand for labor curve ____.
    a. upward; rightward
    b. upward; leftward
    c. downward; rightward
    d. downward; leftward

22. An increase in the demand for labor ____ the real wage and ____ the quantity of employment.
    a. raises; increases
    b. raises; decreases
    c. lowers; increases
    d. lowers; decreases

23. In the United States, from 1986 to 2005, the demand for labor has
    a. increased more than the supply of labor has increased.
    b. increased less than the supply of labor increased.
    c. increased while the supply of labor has decreased.
    d. decreased while the supply of labor has increased

■ Short Answer Problems

1. What is the importance of the classical dichotomy?

2. What is the connection between the production possibilities frontier showing the relationship between leisure and real GDP and the production function showing the relationship between employment and real GDP?

3. a. What does diminishing returns mean?

   b. Moving along a production function, why does the marginal product of labor diminish as employment increases?

4. Why is the marginal product of labor curve the same as the demand for labor curve? What does this equality imply for the slope of the demand for labor curve?

5. a. What is the real wage rate? How does it differ from the money rate? How is the real wage rate constructed?

   b. Why does the supply of labor depend on the real wage rate rather than the money wage rate?

FIGURE **7.5**

Short Answer Problem 6

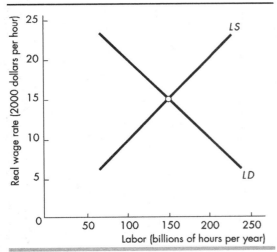

6. In Figure 7.5 what is the equilibrium real wage rate? Illustrate a real wage rate at which jobs are rationed. Indicate the amount of unemployment.

7. What can account for job rationing?

8. The nominal interest rate in 1974 was 12 percent; thirty two years afterwards, in 2006, the nominal interest rate was 6 percent. Based on this information

tion alone, can you determine in which year the real interest rate was the highest? Why?

FIGURE **7.6**

Short Answer Problem 9

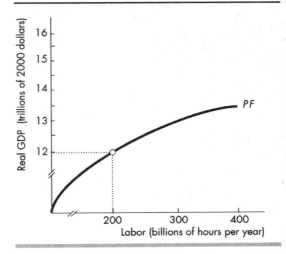

FIGURE **7.7**

Short Answer Problem 9

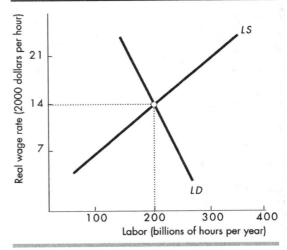

9. Suppose that new technology shifts the production function upward and increases the marginal product of labor. Using Figures 7.6 and 7.7, show what happens in both. Does the equilibrium quantity of employment rise or fall? Does real GDP increase or decrease?

■ You're the Teacher

1. "I really don't understand one thing about this chapter: Why does investment decrease when the real interest rate rises? I just don't get this! After all, if I could get more interest, I'd sure invest more in my savings account at my bank!" Your friend is making a fundamental error. Correct it and perhaps you can earn your friend's undying gratitude ... or your friend's help in another course you're both taking!

Answers

■ True/False Answers

The Classical Model: A Preview

1. **T** Real variables tell what is *really* happening to the real economy and people's wellbeing.

2. **F** According to the classical dichotomy, real variables, such as employment, are determined by forces that are independent of nominal variables, such as the inflation rate.

Real GDP and Employment

3. **F** Increasing leisure decreases employment and hence *decreases* real GDP.

4. **T** An increase in employment causes a movement along the production function to a higher level of real GDP.

The Labor Market and Potential GDP

5. **T** The demand for labor curve is downward sloping because the marginal product of labor diminishes as more workers are employed.

6. **F** As more workers are employed, the marginal product diminishes.

7. **T** If the real wage rate rises, more workers enter the labor force and workers already in the labor force supply more hours of work.

8. **T** Equilibrium employment is full employment, which means the economy is at potential GDP.

9. **T** An increase in the demand for labor raises both the real wage rate and employment.

Unemployment at Full Employment

10. **F** Job search *always* exists.

11. **F** An increase in unemployment compensation creates more job search and hence increases unemployment.

12. **T** When wages are set above the equilibrium level, unemployment results.

Loanable Funds and the Real Interest Rate

13. **F** The real interest rate equals the nominal interest rate *minus* the inflation rate.

14. **T** Because the real interest rate is the opportunity cost of investment, an increase in the real interest rate decreases the quantity of investment.

15. **T** As the real interest rate rises, the "reward" from saving increases, so people increase the amount they save.

16. **F** An increase in the expected profit rate increases investment and shifts the demand for loanable funds curve rightward; it does not shift the supply of loanable funds curve.

17. **T** At the equilibrium real interest rate, there is neither a shortage nor a surplus of loanable funds.

Using the Classical Model

18. **T** Because an increase in the demand for labor increases employment, it also increases potential GDP.

19. **F** An increase in capital raises the marginal product of labor, which increases the demand for labor.

20. **F** An increase in productivity shifts the production function upward and increases the quantity of employment.

■ Multiple Choice Answers

The Classical Model: A Preview

1. **a** Employment is the real variable; the others are dollar values and so are nominal variables.

Real GDP and Employment

2. **b** If leisure increases, people are spending less time at work. As a result, real GDP decreases.

3. **c** An increase in employment creates a movement along the production function and, with more people employed, real GDP increases.

The Labor Market and Potential GDP

4. **d** The real wage rate equals the money wage rate divided by the price level so when the price level rises and the money wage rate does not change, the real wage rate falls

5. **c** The marginal product of labor equals the change in output divided by the change in employment, or, in this case, ($222 − $200) ÷ (6 − 5) = $22.

6. **a** The demand for labor curve is the same as the marginal product of labor curve.

7. **c** For both reasons given in the answer, the supply of labor curve is upward sloping, indicating that an increase in the real wage rate increases the quantity of labor supplied.

8. **d** A change in the real wage rate creates a movement along the labor demand and labor supply curves but does not shift either curve.

9. **a** When the labor market is in equilibrium — the quantity of labor supplied equals the quantity of labor demanded — the economy is producing its potential GDP.

10. **c** With more people, the supply of labor increases.

Unemployment at Full Employment

11. **d** Unemployment compensation payments reduce the cost of being unemployed, so an increase in these payments makes unemployed workers willing to search for longer periods of time to find better jobs.

12. **a** Efficiency wages and the minimum wage both can lead to job rationing.

13. **c** Answer (c) is the definition of an efficiency wage.

14. **d** With the real wage rate above the equilibrium wage rate, there are workers who cannot find jobs and these workers are unemployed.

Loanable Funds and the Real Interest Rate

15. **c** The real interest rate equals the nominal interest rate, 8 percent, minus the inflation rate, 2 percent.

16. **d** As the expected profit rate rises, investment increases.

17. **a** An increase in the real interest rate decreases investment and creates a movement along the demand for loanable funds curve.

18. **d** An increase in disposable income increases saving, so the supply of loanable funds curve shifts rightward.

19. **c** The quantity of loanable funds supplied is less than the quantity of loanable funds demanded, which forces the real interest rate to rise toward its equilibrium.

Using the Classical Model

20. **c** With more people, the supply of labor increases.

21. **a** The increase in the marginal product of labor shifts the demand for labor curve rightward.

22. **a** As Figure 7.8 illustrates, the increase in the demand for labor is reflected in the rightward shift in the demand curve from LD_0 to LD_1. The wage rate rises from $10 an hour to $15 and

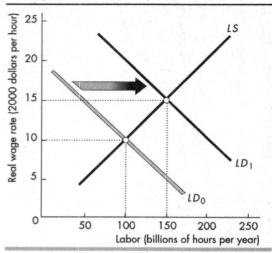

FIGURE 7.8
Multiple Choice Question 22

employment increases from 100 billion hours to 150 billion. In combination with the last question, which showed how an increase in the marginal product of labor increases the demand for labor, this question shows how the increase in the marginal product results in a higher real wage rate.

23. **a** Because the demand for labor has increased more than the supply of labor, the real wage rate has risen.

■ Answers to Short Answer Problems

1. The classical dichotomy states that at full employment, the forces that determine real variables are independent of those that determine nominal variables. This statement means that if we want to study why real GDP differs among nations or why real GDP has grown over the years, we need study only factors that influence real variables and do not need to study the factors that influence nominal variables.

2. The production possibilities frontier and the production function are basically opposite sides of the same coin.

   The production possibilities frontier shows that if leisure is decreased — so that employment is increased — then real GDP increases. Because of increasing opportunity cost, the production possibilities frontier also shows that as more additional time is spent in employment, the additional GDP that results diminishes.

The production function shows similar results. The production function demonstrates that if employment increases, real GDP increases. Because of diminishing returns, the production function also shows that as employment increases, the additional GDP that results diminishes.

3. a. Diminishing returns means that as the quantity of labor increases, the additional GDP that results diminishes. In other words, the 1,000,001st hour of labor by itself creates less additional GDP than does the 1,000,000th hour of labor.

   b. Moving along a production function, the marginal product of labor diminishes because along the production function the amount of the capital stock and technology are constant. Thus additional labor must work with the same number of factories, assembly lines, and so forth. In this situation, an added worker will not create as much additional output because the assembly lines, machine tools, and so forth are already efficiently stocked with enough workers.

4. The marginal product of labor curve is the same as the demand for labor curve because firms want to earn the maximum possible profit. When a firm is considering hiring another worker, the firm looks at two factors: How much it costs to hire the worker and how much the worker adds to the firm's output. If the worker adds more to the firm's output than it costs to hire the worker, the firm will employ the worker.

   The cost of hiring another worker is the real wage rate. And, the amount of output that the worker produces is the marginal product of labor. If the marginal product exceeds the real wage rate, the firm hires the worker because it is profitable. As the firm hires more and more workers, the marginal product of labor diminishes. But as long as the marginal product exceeds the real wage rate, the firm hires the workers because by so doing the firm raises its profit. Eventually the firm hires enough workers so that the marginal product of an additional worker just equals the real wage. The firm will hire this worker but will hire no more workers because for all additional workers the marginal product of labor would be less than the real wage rate. So the quantity of workers that the firm hires is determined by the marginal product of labor curve. The quantity of workers the firm hires is the same as the quantity it demands. Therefore the marginal product of labor curve is the same as the demand for labor curve.

5. a. The real wage rate shows the quantity of goods and services that can be purchased with an hour's labor. The money wage rate is the quantity of money received for an hour's labor. The real wage rate is defined as the money wage rate divided by the price level.

   b. The supply of labor depends on the real wage rate because workers are interested in what they can buy in exchange for their work. The money wage rate just shows the number of dollar bills that the worker will receive for an hour's labor. But the worker is concerned with what can be purchased with these dollar bills, which is what the real wage rate indicates.

FIGURE **7.9**

Short Answer Problem 6

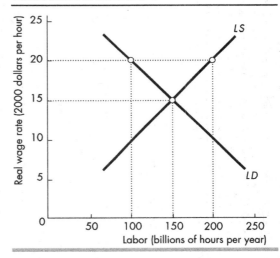

6. In Figure 7.9 the equilibrium wage rate is $15 an hour. Any wage rate higher than the equilibrium wage rate creates some job rationing. For instance, at the wage rate of $20 an hour, the demand for labor is only 100 billion hours of labor, yet at this wage rate 200 billion hours of labor are supplied. At this wage rate unemployment is 100 billion hours of labor. More generally, at any wage rate, the extent of unemployment equals the difference between the quantity of labor supplied and the quantity demanded.

7. Two factors can account for job rationing: efficiency wages and the minimum wage.

Efficiency wages occur when firms pay above-equilibrium wage rates to increase their workers' productivity. Firms might pay a wage rate that exceeds the equilibrium wage rate knowing that, although the higher wage rate increases their costs, this effect is more than offset by the higher productivity of the workers receiving the higher wage rate.

The minimum wage can be at a level that is above the equilibrium wage rate. In this case the quantity of labor demanded is less than that supplied, and jobs are rationed because not everyone who wants to work at the going (minimum) wage rate can find employment.

8. From what is given, determining when the real interest rate is the highest is impossible. The real interest rate equals the nominal interest rate minus the inflation rate. If the inflation rates in the two years were the same, the real interest rate in 1974 was higher. But if the inflation rate was enough higher in 1974 than in 2006, the real interest rate in 1974 was lower than in 2006. For instance, suppose that the inflation rate in 1974 was 11 percent and in 2006 was 3 percent. Then the real interest rate in 1974 is 1 percent and in 2006 is 3 percent. Indeed, in the United States, nominal interest rates in 1974 generally were higher than in 2006, but the inflation rate in 1974 was much higher than in 2006, so the real interest rate in 1974 was lower than in 2006.

9. Start with the production function, illustrated in Figure 7.10. The upward shift is illustrated.

A key feature of this change is that the marginal product of labor increased, so the change increases the demand for labor. So in Figure 7.11, the demand for labor curve has shifted rightward, from LD_0 to LD_1. As a result, the equilibrium quantity of employment increases, to 300 billion hours, and the equilibrium real wage rate rises, to $21 per hour in the figure. In Figure 7.10, GDP changes for two reasons: First, the production function has shifted upward, so even if employment did not change, GDP would increase. But, employment *does* increase. Thus as Figure 7.10 demonstrates, GDP increases from $12 trillion to $14.5 trillion as the economy moves from point a on production function PF_0 to point b on production function PF_1.

FIGURE 7.10
Short Answer Problem 9

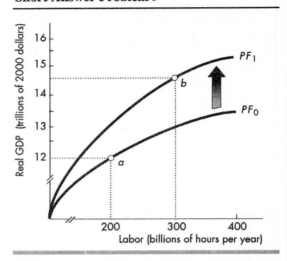

FIGURE 7.11
Short Answer Problem 9

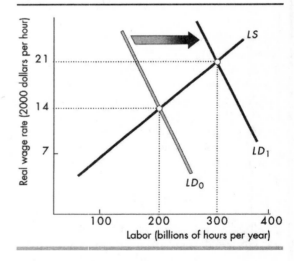

■ You're the Teacher

1. 1. "No, you're making a fundamental error. Once you get the point here, I bet the chapter will be a *lot* easier! Anyway, the deal is that you're confusing investment and saving. 'Investment' means the purchase of new capital goods; that is, investment refers to buying the actual capital good. When you think about your funds in a savings account, you're thinking about 'saving.' And, yeah, I agree with you that if the real interest rate you get on your savings in-

creases, you'll save more. In fact, that's exactly what our book says! But when you think about investment, you have to realize that the real interest rate is a cost of investment. It's the same way with you and me: If the real interest rate goes up, I know that I am less likely to borrow to buy a car or anything else. Companies behave the same way: If the real interest rate goes up, companies will borrow less, cutting back on their investments. So, you can see, that when the real interest rate rises, the quantity of investment demanded decreases."

Chapter Quiz

1. If the nominal interest rate is 8 percent and the inflation rate is 2 percent, the real interest rate is approximately
   a. 16 percent.
   b. 10 percent.
   c. 6 percent.
   d. 4 percent.

2. Diminishing marginal product of labor means that
   a. the supply of labor curve is upward sloping so that a higher real wage increases the quantity of labor supplied.
   b. as more labor is employed, GDP decreases.
   c. the demand for labor curve is upward sloping.
   d. as more labor is employed, the additional amount of GDP produced diminishes.

3. If the money wage rate rises and the price level does not change, the real wage rate
   a. increases.
   b. does not change.
   c. decreases.
   d. probably changes, but without knowledge of the labor demand and labor supply, it is impossible to tell the direction.

4. The supply of loanable funds curve has a negative slope. The demand for loanable funds curve has a positive slope.
   a. Both sentences are true.
   b. The first sentence is true and the second is false.
   c. The first sentence is false and the second is true.
   d. Both sentences are false.

5. If the demand for labor increases, the equilibrium quantity of employment ___ and potential GDP ____.
   a. increases; increases
   b. increases; decreases
   c. decreases; increases
   d. decreases; decreases

6. If firms become more optimistic about the future, the expected profit rate ____ and the demand for loanable funds curve shifts ____.
   a. rises; rightward
   b. rises; leftward
   c. falls; rightward
   d. falls; leftward

7. The demand for labor curve is ____ sloped; the supply of labor curve is ____ sloped.
   a. positively; positively
   b. positively; negatively
   c. negatively; positively
   d. negatively; negatively

8. If the supply of labor increases more than the demand for labor, then the real wage rate ____ and the level of employment ____.
   a. rises; increases
   b. rises; decreases
   c. falls; increases
   d. falls; decreases

9. Job search occurs
   a. only when the supply of labor increases.
   b. only when the quantity of labor demanded exceeds the quantity of labor supplied.
   c. only when the quantity of labor supplied exceeds the quantity of labor demanded.
   d. at all times.

10. Job search increases if
    a. the minimum wage falls.
    b. efficiency wage rates are lowered.
    c. unemployment compensation payments increase.
    d. the demand for labor increases.

The answers for this Chapter Quiz are on page 265

Chapter 8

ECONOMIC GROWTH*

Key Concepts

The Basics of Economic Growth

The **economic growth rate** is the annual percentage change real GDP.

♦ The growth rate of real GDP equals

$$\frac{\text{Real GDP in current year} - \text{Re al GDP in past year}}{\text{Re al GDP in past year}} \times 100$$

The standard of living depends on **real GDP per person** (also called *per capita* real GDP), which is real GDP divided by the population.

♦ The growth rate of real GDP per person can be calculated using the same formula as above. It also approximately equals the growth rate of real GDP minus the population growth rate.

♦ The **Rule of 70** is a mathematical relationship which states that the number of years it takes for the level of any variable to double is approximately 70 divided by the annual percentage growth rate of the variable.

Economic Growth Trends

♦ Over the past 100 years, growth in real GDP per person in the United States has averaged 2 percent per year. The growth rate varies from one period to the next. It slowed between 1973 and 1983 and has since increased.

♦ Among the seven richest nations in the world, the United States has the highest level of real GDP per person. The gaps between U.S. GDP per person

and those in Canada and Europe's Big 4 have been almost constant so these nations are not catching up to the U.S. level of real GDP per person.

♦ Many poor nations in Central and South America and in Africa are not catching up to the U.S. level of real GDP per person.

♦ Hong Kong, Korea, Singapore, and Taiwan are generally growing more rapidly than the United States and so they are catching up. China also is catching up but from a long way behind

The Sources of Economic Growth

Real GDP grows when the quantities of the factors of production grow or when persistent advances in technology make the factors increasingly productive. Focusing on labor, real GDP increases with increases in aggregate hours and labor productivity.

♦ *Aggregate hours* — The total number of hours worked. Aggregate hours increase when the working-age population grows, when the employment-to-population ratio increases, or when average hours per worker rises. Only growth in the working-age population can create sustained growth in aggregate hours.

Labor productivity is the quantity of real GDP produced by an hour of labor; it equals real GDP divided by aggregate labor hours. Growth in labor productivity depends on growth in physical capital, growth in human capital, and technological advances.

♦ Saving and investment in new capital — the accumulation of capital adds to the nation's productivity and level of output.

♦ Investment in human capital — human capital, the skills and talents people possess, is a key ingredient

---

* This chapter is Chapter 24 in *Economics*.

for economic growth. Some human capital is acquired through education; some is obtained through doing the same task over and over.

♦ Discovery of new technologies — technological advancement is crucial to economic growth.

Three institutions are the basic precondition for economic growth:

♦ Markets — enable buyers and sellers to conduct transactions. They also convey information (in the form of prices) that create incentives for people to change their quantities demanded and supplied.

♦ Property rights — social arrangements that govern the ownership, use, and disposal of productive resources and goods and services.

♦ Monetary exchange — facilitates buying and selling of goods and services.

Markets, property rights, and monetary exchange create the conditions necessary for economic growth but do not guarantee that economic growth will occur.

■ Growth Accounting

Growth accounting is a tool used to calculate the quantitative contribution to real GDP growth of each of its components, growth in labor and capital and technological change.

The **law of diminishing returns** states that as the quantity of one input increases with the quantities of the other inputs remaining the same, output increases but by increasingly smaller amounts. The **one third rule** states that on the average a 1 percent increase in capital per hour of labor yields a *one third of 1 percent* increase in real GDP per hour of labor. The one-third rule divides growth in productivity into growth resulting from increases in capital per hour of labor and growth resulting from advances in technology.

Growth in real GDP per person slowed from 3.7 percent per year between 1960 and 1973 to only 1.7 percent per year between 1973 and 1983. The one-third rule shows that the slowdown in productivity growth between 1973 and 1983 occurred because technological change was offsetting energy price shocks and increasing environmental protection. Productivity growth has since speeded up a bit and was 2.4 percent per year between 1993 and 2005.

Policies for increasing the economic growth rate are:

♦ Stimulate saving — tax incentives could be directed at increasing saving.

♦ Stimulate research and development — inventions can be copied, so government subsidies can lead to more inventions that spread throughout the economy.

♦ Target high-technology industries — by encouraging such industries, a country temporarily can earn above-average profits.

♦ Encourage international trade — free international trade encourages economic growth because free trade extracts all the possible gains from specialization and exchange.

♦ Improve the quality of education — education creates benefits beyond the ones enjoyed by the students who receive education, so without government action, too little education is provided.

■ Growth Theories

FIGURE 8.1

An Increase in Labor Productivity

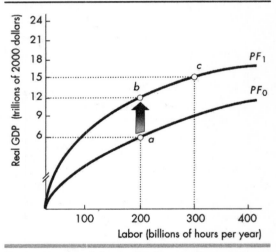

Economic growth is sustained, year-after-year increases in potential GDP. Increases in labor productivity are a key aspect of economic growth. The classical model from Chapter 7 shows that an increase in labor productivity resulting from an increase in physical or human capital or an advance in technology increases the demand for labor and shifts the aggregate production function upward, as illustrated in Figure 8.1.

♦ The upward shift in the production function moves the economy from point *a* to point *b*, thereby increasing potential GDP.

♦ The increase in productivity raises the demand for labor and increases the full employment quantity of labor. This effect moves the economy from point *b* to point *c* along the new production function, which also increases potential GDP.

♦ The real wage rises and real GDP per person grows.

Population growth increases potential GDP but, by itself, decreases real GDP per hour of work.

♦ An increase in population increases the supply of labor. The real wage rate falls and the full employment quantity of labor increases. The increase in full employment moves the economy along its aggregate production function so that potential GDP increases.

♦ The aggregate production function does not shift, so diminishing returns while moving along it means that real GDP per person falls.

Three theories of economic growth are *classical, neoclassical*, and *new growth*.

The **classical growth theory** is the view that real GDP growth is temporary and that when real GDP per person rises above subsistence level, a population explosion eventually brings real GDP per person back to the subsistence level.

♦ As productivity increases, income per person rises, which raises the population growth rate.

♦ The increase in population increases labor supply, which drives the real wage rate back to the **subsistence real wage rate,** the minimum real wage rate necessary to maintain life.

♦ Economic growth ceases until new technological change occurs.

♦ Even if capital growth occurs, *anything* (including capital growth) that raises real GDP per hour of labor above the subsistence level leads to a population explosion that eventually forces real GDP per hour of labor back to the subsistence level.

Contrary to the classical theory assumption, the population growth rate is approximately independent of the economic growth rate.

The **neoclassical growth theory** stresses that real GDP per person grows because technological changes increase saving and investment so that the capital stock grows. Technological change is determined by factors outside the model, such as luck.

♦ Technological change increases investment so that the real interest rate rises above people's target rate of return. With the interest rate above the target rate of return, saving increases.

♦ More saving increases the capital stock and, as capital accumulates, diminishing returns lowers the return from additional capital and lowers the real interest rate. Eventually saving decreases so that no new capital is accumulated.

♦ Real GDP per person remains higher after the technological change than before, but unless technology keeps advancing economic growth ceases.

One difficulty with the neoclassical model is that it predicts all nations will converge to the same level of per capita income.

The **new growth theory** is based on the idea that technological change results from the choices that people make in the pursuit of profit and growth can persist. Four facts about market economies are important:

♦ Discoveries result from people's choices, such as whether to look for something new and, if so, how intensively to look.

♦ A new discovery brings the discovered high profits but eventually competitors emerge and the above-average profit is competed away.

♦ Discoveries can be used by everyone without reducing their availability to others, so the benefits from a new discovery spread everywhere.

♦ Knowledge is not subject to the law of diminishing returns so the incentive to innovate new and better products and production methods never decreases.

The new growth theory concludes that economic growth can persist indefinitely because of the capacity for people to continually innovate.

Helpful Hints

1. **THE ONE-THIRD RULE :** The one-third rule is used to divide economic growth into growth resulting from increases in capital per hour of labor and growth resulting from advances in technology. The basic idea is that is impossible to directly measure growth resulting from technological innovations. So, the growth attributed to technology is the growth that cannot be attributed to increases in capital. The one-third rule says that the economic growth resulting from growth in capital per hour of labor equals one third of the growth in capital per hour of labor. Subtract this calculated growth from the actual economic growth rate to obtain the growth resulting from technological advances.

2. **CLASSICAL VERSUS NEW GROWTH THEORY:**
   Economics is sometimes called the "dismal science." This nickname came about because of the classical growth theory. The main conclusion from the classical approach is that, in the long run, workers are bound to earn only a subsistence wage, a truly dismal result!

   The fact that the classical model of growth was developed right at the beginning of the industrial revolution is ironic. The classical model focuses on population growth and does not allow for continuing technological change and capital growth, two features of the industrial revolution that were to become an increasingly important aspect of our world. It is these omissions that account for the dismal, subsistence-wage conclusion of the classical model.

   New growth theory examines the factors that lead to technological change. In this theory, economic growth can persist indefinitely because the incentive to accumulate more capital persists indefinitely. Perhaps the nickname for economics should be changed to the "happy science"!

Questions

■ True/False and Explain

The Basics of Economic Growth

1. Increases in real GDP always increase real GDP per person.

2. If real GDP grows at an annual rate of 2 percent, then real GDP will double in 50 years.

Economic Growth Trends

3. Over the past 100 years, real GDP per person in the United States has grown at an average rate of 5 percent per year.

4. Because real GDP per person is highest in the United States, over the past 30 years economic growth has been most rapid in the United States.

The Sources of Economic Growth

5. Population growth is the only source of persistent growth in aggregate hours.

6. Discovery of new technologies helps generate economic growth.

7. Once a nation has in place markets, property rights, and monetary exchange, economic growth is inevitable.

Growth Accounting

8. The law of diminishing returns states that as more capital is used, total output produced diminishes.

9. Productivity growth slowed between 1973 and 1983 because capital per hour of labor did not grow during this period.

10. Energy price hikes are one of the causes of the productivity growth slowdown.

Growth Theories

11. An increase in labor productivity increases the full employment quantity of labor.

12. An assumption of the classical growth theory is that an increase in real wages and incomes increase the population growth rate.

13. In the neoclassical theory of growth, a technological advance can create perpetual economic growth.

14. The neoclassical growth theory stresses the role played by people's incentives for discovering new technology.

15. In the new theory of economic growth, economic growth can continue indefinitely.

■ Multiple Choice

The Basics of Economic Growth

1. If the annual average growth rate of real GDP is 3 percent, then the level of real GDP will double in approximately _____ years.
   a. 100
   b. 33
   c. 23
   d. 10

Economic Growth Trends

2. For the last 100 years in the United States, growth in real GDP per person
   a. has averaged 2 percent per year.
   b. has accelerated in the last half century because of the technological revolution.
   c. was never negative for any year.
   d. has averaged about 8 percent per year.

3. Which of the following best describes the facts?

   a. Almost all rich and poor nations are catching up to the level of U.S. GDP per person.
   b. Almost all rich nations are growing fast enough to catch up to the level of U.S. GDP per person, but virtually no poor nation is growing fast enough to catch up.
   c. Some poor nations are catching up to the level of U.S. GDP per person, but many poor nations are not catching up.
   d. No nation is growing fast enough to catch up to the level of U.S. GDP per person.

The Sources of Economic Growth

4. An increase in aggregate hours _____ real GDP and an increase in labor productivity _____ real GDP.

   a. increases; increases
   b. increases; does not increase
   c. does not increase; increases
   d. does not increase; does not increase

5. Which of the following does <u>NOT</u> increase labor productivity?

   a. saving and investment in new capital
   b. an increase in aggregate hours
   c. investment in human capital
   d. discovery of new technologies

Growth Accounting

6. Growth accounting divides changes in productivity into changes resulting from

   a. markets and property rights.
   b. saving and investment.
   c. capital per hour of labor and technology.
   d. human capital and other capital.

7. The law of diminishing returns

   a. holds that additional workers produce less additional output.
   b. applies only to labor and not to capital.
   c. explains why the productivity curve shifts upward when technology increases.
   d. does not apply to labor.

8. The one-third rule states that

   a. one third of all technology helps replace capital per hour of labor.
   b. an increase in productivity can be traced to one third of the firms in the nation.
   c. a 1 percent increase in capital per hour of labor creates a 3 percent increase in productivity.
   d. a 1 percent increase in capital per hour of labor creates a 1/3 percent increase in productivity.

9. Suppose that capital per hour of labor increases by 30 percent and that real GDP per hour of labor increases by 18 percent. The increase in capital per hour of labor increased real GDP per hour of labor by _____.

   a. 30 percent
   b. 18 percent
   c. 10 percent
   d. 8 percent

10. Suppose that capital per hour of labor increases by 30 percent while real GDP per hour of labor increases by 18 percent. The change in technology increased real GDP per hour of labor by _____.

    a. 30 percent
    b. 18 percent
    c. 10 percent
    d. 8 percent

11. When did productivity grow most rapidly?

    a. 1963 to 1973
    b. 1973 to 1983
    c. 1983 to 1997
    d. 1963 to 1983

12. Helping create the 1973-1983 slowdown in productivity growth was

    a. a large increase in capital per hour of labor.
    b. large increases in the price of oil.
    c. passing fewer environmental protection laws.
    d. All of the above helped create the slowdown in productivity growth.

13. Economic growth can be increased by
   a. taxing savings.
   b. limiting international trade.
   c. using government funds to help finance basic research.
   d. decreasing the length of time for which a patent is effective.

Growth Theories

14. Technological advances that shift the nation's production function upward by increasing labor productivity _____ the real wage rate and _____ real GDP per person.
   a. do not change; increase
   b. raise; do not change
   c. lower; decrease
   d. raise; increase

15. Increases in population _____ the real wage rate and _____ real GDP per person.
   a. do not change; increase
   b. raise; do not change
   c. lower; decrease
   d. raise; increase

16. An assumption of the classical growth theory is that
   a. the population growth rate increases when real GDP per person increases.
   b. saving is more important than investment in determining economic growth.
   c. capital plays a major role in determining how rapidly the economy grows.
   d. human capital is the ultimate cause of economic growth.

17. A factor that turned out to be a weakness of the classical theory of growth is its
   a. emphasis on saving and investment.
   b. assumption that the growth rate of the population increases when income increases.
   c. reliance on constant growth in technology.
   d. neglect of the subsistence real wage.

18. In the neoclassical theory of growth, growth in _____ is the result of luck.
   a. saving
   b. income
   c. technology
   d. the real interest rate

19. A key assumption of new growth theory is that
   a. all technological change is the result of luck.
   b. higher incomes lead to a higher birth rate.
   c. a successful innovator has the opportunity to earn a temporary, above-average profit.
   d. the target interest rate is lower than the real interest rate.

20. Which theory of economic growth concludes that in the long run people will be paid only a subsistence real wage?
   a. The classical growth theory
   b. The neoclassical growth theory
   c. The new growth theory
   d. All of the theories

21. Which theory of economic growth concludes that growth can continue indefinitely?
   a. The classical growth theory
   b. The neoclassical growth theory
   c. The new growth theory
   d. All of the theories

■ Short Answer Problems

1. a. In 2007 real GDP per person in the nation of Slow is $2,000 and is growing at the rate of 1 percent per year. After 1 year, what is real GDP per person? After 2 years? After 10 years? After 30 years?

   b. In 2007 real GDP per person in Fast is half of that in Slow, $1,000, but is growing at the rate of 3 percent per year. After 1 year, what is real GDP per person? After 2 years? After 10 years? After 30 years?

   c. Initially the ratio of GDP per person in Fast to GDP per person in Slow is 0.50. What is the ratio after 1 year? After 30 years?

2. What are the three basic preconditions for economic growth? Explain the role that each plays in promoting economic growth. Are these preconditions sufficient for economic growth to continue forever? Why or why not?

3. Would the slowdown in productivity growth in the United States have been as large if real GDP included the value of improving the environment? Explain your answer.

4. Igor was recently named economic minister. His first assigned task is to predict his nation's long-term growth prospects. Igor expects that capital per hour of labor will grow at 1 percent per year. Moreover, he expects technological change of 1 percent per year. What growth rate for real GDP per hour of labor will Igor predict?

5. After Igor announces his prediction from question 8, the nation's president suggests to Igor that Igor's current position will be short-lived unless productivity growth picks up. Igor likes his current job because it involves no night work and very little digging. What government policies to speed up growth might Igor suggest and why?

6. Why can't a high level of GDP per person persist in classical growth theory? In particular, what mechanism drives the economy back to the situation in which workers receive only a subsistence wage?

7. Figure 8.2 shows the situation in which the nation's production function constantly shifts upward. This figure best illustrates which theory of economic growth? Why?

8. What is the driving factor behind economic growth in the neoclassical model of economic growth?

■ You're the Teacher

1. "This is a really great chapter, but you know, there's one thing that puzzles me just a bit. I just don't get the relationship between saving supply, which we talked about in the last chapter, and the amount of capital per hour of labor, which we talked about in this chapter. I know these things have to be related, but I just can't see how and it's really bugging me!" Help debug your friend by explaining the relationship between the two.

FIGURE 8.2

Short Answer Problem 7

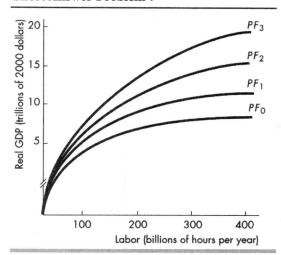

Answers

■ True/False Answers

The Basics of Economic Growth

1. **F** If the population growth exceeds growth in real GDP, real GDP per person falls.

2. **F** The Rule of 70 shows that with 2 percent annual growth, real GDP will double in approximately 35 years.

Economic Growth Trends

3. **F** Real GDP growth per person has averaged 2 percent per year, not 5 percent.

4. **F** Other nations have grown more rapidly and these nations are catching up to the level of GDP per person in the United States.

The Sources of Economic Growth

5. **T** Increases in the employment-to-population ratio or in average hours per worker increase aggregate hours, but these two factors cannot increase forever. Only population growth can continue indefinitely.

6. **T** The discovery of new technologies is a key method of creating growth in GDP per person.

7. **F** Markets, property rights, and monetary exchange are necessary for economic growth, but they do not guarantee that it will occur.

Growth Accounting

8. **F** The law of diminishing returns states that as more capital is used the *additional* output produced diminishes.

9. **F** The main cause of the productivity growth slowdown was the failure of technological change to contribute to increasing productivity.

10. **T** As a result of massive hikes in the price of energy, technological development was devoted to reducing the amount of energy used in production rather than increasing overall productivity.

Growth Theories

11. **T** An increase in labor productivity increases the demand for labor, thereby raising the real wage rate and increasing the full employment quantity of labor.

12. **T** The data, however, show that increases in real wages and incomes is associated with little change in the population growth rate.

13. **F** In the neoclassical theory, a technological advance raises real GDP but does not create persist economic growth.

14. **F** The neoclassical growth theory stresses the role played by saving and investment; the new growth theory emphasizes people's incentives.

15. **T** Economic growth can persist forever because the return from knowledge does not diminish.

■ Multiple Choice Answers

Economic Growth Trends

1. **c** The Rule of 70 shows that the level of real GDP will double in 70 ÷ 3, or approximately 23 years.

Economic Growth Trends

2. **a** Over the last 100 years, growth in real GDP per person in the United States has averaged 2 percent per year.

3. **c** If a nation *grows* more rapidly than the United States, eventually that nation's *level* of GDP per person will catch up to that in the United States.

The Sources of Economic Growth

4. **a** Increases in both aggregate hours and labor productivity increase real GDP but only increases in labor productivity increase real GDP per person.

5. **b** An increases in aggregate hours might be a result of an increase in labor productivity but it does not cause an increase in labor productivity.

Growth Accounting

6. **c** Growth accounting is used to divide changes in productivity into different factors so that the factors responsible for growth can be identified.

7. **a** Answer (a) is the law of diminishing returns applied to labor.

8. **d** Answer (d) states the one-third rule.

9. **c** The one-third rule states that the increase in real GDP per hour of labor from the increase in capital per hour of labor is (1/3) × (30 percent), or 10 percent.

10. **d** Based on the answer to question 9, the increase in capital per hour of labor raised productivity

by 10 percent, leaving technology to account for the remaining 8 percent.

11. **a** Between 1963 and 1973, rapid technological progress shifted the productivity curve upward and productivity growth was high.

12. **b** Energy prices jumped upward and so research was devoted to saving energy rather than increasing productivity.

13. **c** Private markets will allocate too few funds to basic research because an inventor's profit can be limited by copying the inventions.

Growth Theories

14. **d** The increase in labor productivity increases the demand for labor which raises the real wage rate. The upward shift of the production function raises real GDP per person.

15. **c** The increase in population increases the supply of labor which lowers the real wage rate and increases the full employment quantity of labor. The increase in full employment raises real GDP but diminishing returns means that real GDP per person falls.

16. **a** This assumption is important because it leads to the (dismal!) conclusion that people are paid only a subsistence wage.

17. **b** The previous answer pointed out the importance of the assumption that population growth increases when income increases. However, this assumption is a weakness because the data show it to be false: Population growth does not change when income increases.

18. **c** Technological growth is the driving force behind economic growth in the neoclassical theory. However, because technological growth depends on chance and luck in this approach, the neoclassical model advanced no reasons for the occurrence of technological growth.

19. **c** The opportunity to earn an above-average profit gives innovators the incentive to develop new technologies.

20. **a** This long-run conclusion of the classical theory was based on the (faulty!) assumption that the population growth rate rises when income increases.

21. **c** Only in the new theory can economic growth continue forever as the natural course of the economy.

■ Answers to Short Answer Problems

1. a. After 1 year, real GDP per person in Slow is ($2,000.00)(1.01) or $2,020.00. After 2 years, real GDP per person in is ($2,000.00)$(1.01)^2$ or $2,040.20. Similarly, after 10 years real GDP per person is $2,209.24 and after 30 years is $2,695.70.

   b. Real GDP per person in Fast after 1 year is $1,030.00; after 2 years is $1,060.90; after 10 years is $1,343.92; after 30 years is $2,427.26.

   c. After 1 year the ratio of real GDP per person in Fast to real GDP per person in Slow is equal to $1,030.00/$2,020.00 = 0.51. After 30 years the ratio is $2,427.26/$2,695.70 = 0.90. By growing more rapidly than Slow, the nation of Fast has been able to close a large part of the gap in the GDP per person. In other words, by growing more rapidly than the (advanced) nation of Slow, the (poorer) nation of Fast is able to catch up to the (higher) level of GDP in Slow. In fact, after these 30 years, the level of GDP in Fast will equal that in Slow in less than 6 more years!

2. Three necessary preconditions for economic growth are markets, property rights, and monetary exchange. Markets enable people to buy and sell at low cost and markets create and convey important information in the form of prices. Monetary exchange also facilitates buying and selling. Markets and monetary exchange help promote specialization, which can vastly increase the amount of goods and services produced. Secure property rights are a key to specialization. Without secure property rights, people would be less willing to specialize because what they produce might be taken from them without their deriving any personal benefit from it. In this case, people likely would not specialize.

   These preconditions are not sufficient for growth to continue forever. To have persistent growth, saving, investing in new capital (both physical and human), and developing new technologies must occur. Without the necessary three preconditions, saving, investing, and developing new technologies will not occur. But simply having the three preconditions in place is no guarantee that saving, investing, and developing new technologies will occur.

3. No, the slowdown in productivity growth would not have been as large. One of the reasons for the slowdown was that the value of an improved envi-

ronment is not included in real GDP. During the 1970s, investment often was aimed at reducing pollution. If the benefit of the resulting cleaner environment had been included, real GDP would have been larger and, as a result, productivity, which equals real GDP divided by aggregate hours of work, also would have been larger.

4. Use the one-third rule to predict the productivity growth rate: Capital per hour of labor is growing at 1 percent and will contribute productivity growth of 1/3 percent. Technological change contributes another 1 percent, so Igor will predict that total productivity growth will be 1 1/3 percent.

5. Igor can suggest five policies. First, he can recommend that his nation stimulate saving by using tax incentives. By increasing saving, his country can increase its growth rate of capital per hour. Second, Igor can recommend that the government subsidize research and development. Research and development will spur technological advances. Third, Igor can propose a government policy of targeting high-tech industries with, say, favorable tax treatment. This policy also should translate into more rapid technological growth. Fourth, Igor can recommend encouraging international trade. Finally, Igor can suggest that his nation undertake policies to improve the quality and increase the quantity of education.

6. High levels of real GDP per person do not persist in classical growth theory because an assumption of classical growth theory is that population growth is directly related to people's real wage or real income. In particular, an increase in productivity raises peo-

ple's real wage. Real GDP per person increases. But in response to the higher real wage, the classical theory holds that the population growth rate increases. As a result, the supply of labor increases, which depresses the real wage. As long as the real wage rate is above the subsistence real wage, population growth remains rapid and the real wage ultimately is driven back to its subsistence level. A high level of real GDP per person is only temporary.

7. The figure best describes the new growth theory because it shows the production function persistently shifting upward. Only the new growth theory concludes that technological advances will constantly occur so only the new growth theory predicts that economic growth can persist indefinitely.

8. The factor that creates economic growth in the neoclassical model is technological progress. As long as technology continues to advance, the economy continues to grow. However the neoclassical model had no explanation for the forces that lead to growth in technology.

■ You're the Teacher

1. "You know, I had to think about this subject a bit myself, and then I finally figured out what's going on. The amount of capital per hour of labor basically gives us the amount of capital in the economy. Saving basically goes to increasing the quantity of capital. So if we save more, maybe because the real interest rate exceeds the target rate of return, then we increase our capital more so that the amount of capital per hour of labor increases."

Chapter Quiz

1. Over the last 100 years, U.S. economic growth per person has averaged about _____ percent per year.
   a. 15
   b. 10
   c. 5
   d. 2

2. For the past decade, among Canada, Germany, and the United States, the nation with the highest GDP per person has been _____ and Japan grew _____ rapidly than this nation.
   a. Canada; less
   b. the United States; more
   c. Germany; less
   d. the United States; less

3. Markets, property rights, and monetary exchange
   a. guarantee that economic growth will occur.
   b. are unrelated to economic growth.
   c. lead nations to trade with each other.
   d. are needed for economic growth to occur, but do not guarantee that growth takes place.

4. Continuing economic growth requires
   a. investment in human capital.
   b. saving and investment in new capital.
   c. technological progress.
   d. All of the above.

5. The purpose of growth accounting is to
   a. estimate the production function for the United States
   b. verify the one-third rule.
   c. measure how much economic growth is the result of technological progress, increased labor, and increased capital.
   d. determine whether the United States is saving and investing enough in new capital.

6. A movement along the production function occurs when
   a. technological progress takes place.
   b. the amount of capital in the nation increases.
   c. the amount of labor employed increases.
   d. the amount of real GDP produced does not change.

7. The slope of the production function becomes less steep as the quantity of labor increases, which reflects the effects of
   a. capital accumulation.
   b. technological progress.
   c. diminishing returns.
   d. population growth.

8. Capital per hour of labor rises by 6 percent and technology has increased output per hour of labor by 9 percent. Hence the total increase in output per hour of labor equals
   a. 15 percent.
   b. 11 percent.
   c. 9 percent.
   d. None of the above.

9. The new theory of economic growth assumes that
   a. the supply of labor increases whenever the wage rate exceeds the subsistence level.
   b. technological change is the result of luck.
   c. knowledge does not have diminishing returns.
   d. people save as long as the real interest rate is less than the target interest rate.

10. Which theory of economic growth predicts that nations eventually converge to the same level of real GDP per person?
    a. The classical growth theory.
    b. The neoclassical growth theory.
    c. The new theory of economic growth.
    d. None of the theories makes this prediction.

The answers for this Chapter Quiz are on page 265

Chapter 9

MONEY, THE PRICE LEVEL, AND INFLATION*

Key Concepts

■ What is Money?

Money is anything generally acceptable as a **means of payment,** that is, a method of settling a debt. Money has three functions:

♦ Medium of exchange — money is accepted in exchange for goods and services. Without money, **barter** (exchanging one good directly for another) would be necessary.

♦ Unit of account — prices are measured in units of money.

♦ Store of value — money is exchangeable at a later date. A low inflation rate makes money as useful as possible as a store of value.

Currency is the bills and coins we use. Money consists of currency plus deposits at banks and other depository institutions. The two major measures of money in the United States are:

♦ M1 — currency outside of banks plus travelers checks plus checking deposits.

♦ M2 — M1 plus saving and time deposits, money market mutual funds, and other deposits.

Liquidity means that an asset can be instantly converted into a means of payment with little loss of value. The assets in M2 that are not directly a means of payment are very liquid.

The deposits at depository institutions are money, but the checks transferring these deposits from one person to another are not money. Credit cards are not money; they are a way to get an instant loan.

■ Depository Institutions

A **depository institution** is a firm that takes deposits from households and firms and then uses the deposits to make loans. Depository institutions include commercial banks, thrift institutions (savings and loan associations, savings banks, and credit unions) and money market mutual funds.

Banks keep only a small fraction of their funds as reserves. They divide the rest of their assets into three broad components: liquid assets, such as U.S. Treasury bills and commercial bills; investment securities, such as longer-term U.S. government bonds and other bonds; and loans. These assets pay the bank interest.

Depository institutions provide four economic services:

♦ Create liquidity — bank deposits are highly liquid, that is, easily convertible into money.

♦ Minimize cost of obtaining funds — borrowing from one bank is cheaper than borrowing from a variety of lenders.

♦ Minimize cost of monitoring borrowers — depository institutions specialize in monitoring borrowers.

♦ Pool risk — depository institutions reduce risk by making loans to many borrowers.

Developing new ways of borrowing and lending is called *financial innovation*. Financial innovation was rapid in the 1980s and 1990s. The extent of financial innovation depends on the economic environment, technology, and regulation. Checking deposits at S&Ls, savings banks, and credit unions to become an increasingly large fraction of M1 because of financial innovation.

---

* This chapter is Chapter 25 in *Economics*.

■ The Federal Reserve System

The **Federal Reserve System** (or the **Fed**) is the central bank for the United States. A **central bank** is a bank for banks and a public authority that regulates the nation's depository institutions and controls the quantity of money. The Fed is responsible for monetary policy, so it adjusts the quantity of money in circulation. To conduct its monetary policy, the Fed pays attention to interest rates, especially the **federal funds rate**, which is the interest rate banks charge each other on overnight loans of reserves. The Fed sets a target for the federal funds rate that will allow it to met its goals, such as low inflation and moderating the business cycle.

Three key players in the Fed are:

♦   The Board of Governors — seven members appointed by the President and confirmed by the Senate for 14-year terms. This group oversees operations of the Fed.

♦   The regional Federal Reserve Banks —12 regional banks, each of which has a president.

♦   The **Federal Open Market Committee** (FOMC) — the Fed's main policy-making group. Voting members are the Board of Governors, the president of the Federal Reserve Bank of New York and, on a rotating basis, presidents of four other regional Federal Reserve banks.

The Fed has three policy tools:

♦   Required reserve ratio — the Fed sets the **required reserve ratio**, the minimum percentage of deposits that depository institutions must hold as reserves.

♦   **Discount rate** — the interest rate at which the Fed will lend reserves to depository institutions.

♦   **Open market operation** — the purchase or sale of government securities—U.S. Treasury bills and bonds—by the Fed in the open market.

The major assets on the Fed's balance sheet are gold and foreign exchange, U.S. government securities, and loans to banks. The major liabilities are Federal Reserve notes in circulation (currency) and banks' deposits (reserves). The **monetary base** is the sum of Federal Reserve notes, coins, and banks' deposits at the Fed.

■ How Banks Create Money

Banks (more generally, depository institutions) create money by making loans. The process by which they create money involves:

♦   The monetary base.

♦   The **deserved reserve ratio** is the ratio of reserves to deposits that banks *want* to hold. A bank's *actual reserves* are the notes and coins in its vaults and its deposit at the Fed. The fraction of a bank's total deposits held as reserves is the **reserve ratio**. **Excess reserves** are actual reserves minus desired reserves.

♦   Desired currency holding — the amount of money people want to hold as currency. The **currency drain** is the ratio of currency to deposits.

When the monetary base increases, banks gain reserves. If actual reserves exceed desired reserves, banks loan the excess reserves, increasing borrowers' deposits. This lending creates new deposits, that is, new money. Some of the funds loaned, however, are held as currency and not deposited back in banks. The ultimate increase in the amount of money exceeds the initial increase in excess reserves.

♦   The **money multiplier** — the ratio of the change in the quantity of money to the change in the monetary base. In terms of a formula, the money multiplier equals $[(1 + a)/(a + b)]$, where b is the desired reserve ratio and a is the currency drain, the ratio of currency to deposits.

■ The Market for Money

Four factors influence the demand for money:

♦   *The price level* — An increase in the price level increases the *nominal* demand for money.

♦   *The nominal interest rate* — An increase in the nominal interest rate raises the opportunity cost of holding money and decreases the quantity of real money demanded.

♦   *Real GDP* — An increase in real GDP increases the demand for money.

♦   *Financial innovation* — Innovations that lower the cost of switching between money and other assets decrease the demand for money.

The **demand for money** is the relationship between the quantity of real money demanded and the nominal interest rate when all other influences on the amount of money that people wish to hold remain the same. Figure 9.1 (on the next page) shows the demand for money curve (*MD*). The *real* quantity of money equals the nominal quantity divided by the price level. Changes in the nominal interest rate create movements along the demand curve; changes in the other relevant factors change the demand and shift the demand curve.

FIGURE **9.1**
Money Demand

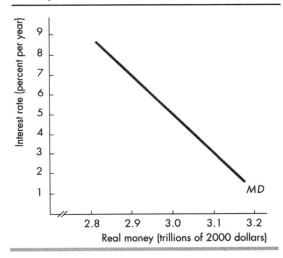

FIGURE **9.2**
The Equilibrium Interest Rate

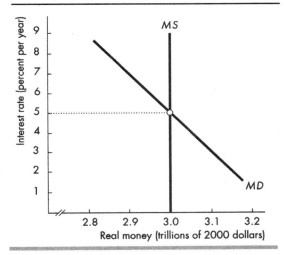

Equilibrium in the money market occurs when the quantity of money demanded equals the quantity of money supplied.

♦ In the short run, the interest rate is determined by the equilibrium in the market for money, as illustrated in Figure 9.2. The real supply of money is $3.0 trillion, so the supply curve of money is *MS*. The demand curve for money is *MD*, and the equilibrium interest rate is 5 percent.

♦ In the long run, supply and demand in the loanable funds market determines the real interest rate. The nominal interest rate then equals the real interest rate plus the expected inflation rate. The variable that adjusts to establish equilibrium in the money market is the price level because changes in the price level change the quantity of real money.

■ The Quantity Theory of Money

The **quantity theory of money** holds that, in the long run, an increase in the quantity of money brings an equal percentage increase in the price level.

The **velocity of circulation** is the average number of times a dollar of money is used in a year to buy goods and services in GDP. In terms of a formula, velocity of circulation, *V*, is given by $V = PY/M$, where *P* is the price level, *Y* is real GDP, and *M* is the quantity of money.

The *equation of exchange* shows that the quantity of money multiplied by velocity equals (nominal) GDP, or

$$MV = PY.$$

The quantity theory makes two assumptions:

♦ Velocity is not affected by the quantity of money.

♦ Potential GDP is not affected by the quantity of money.

In growth rates, the equation of exchange is that

Money growth rate + Rate of velocity change =
Inflation rate + Real GDP growth rate

If, in the long run, velocity growth is zero, then the quantity theory concludes that

Inflation rate=Money growth rate − Real GDP growth rate

Historical evidence from the United States and international evidence both show that in the long run, the money growth rate and inflation rate are positively related and that the year-to-year relationship is weaker.

Helpful Hints

1. **MONEY VERSUS INCOME :** Ordinary use of the term "money" does not make the important distinction that is made in economics. We often talk about income as the amount of money we earn, say, in a year. But this informal use of the term is not what is meant by the word in economics. In

economics, "money" means M1 or M2. Informally, when we talk about the money we earn, actually we are talking about our "income." Keep this distinction in mind, that money means M1 or M2.

2. **How Banks Create Money :** One of the most important concepts presented in this chapter is the process by which banks create money. There are two fundamental facts that allow banks to create money.

First, banks create money by creating new checking deposits. Second, banks hold fractional reserves. That is, when a bank receives a deposit, it holds only part of it as reserves and loans the rest. When that loan is spent, part of the proceeds will likely be deposited in another bank, creating a new deposit (money).

The key part of this process follows from this last point: Banks make loans when they receive new deposits; these loans are spent; and the proceeds are deposited in another bank, creating a new deposit. The process then repeats itself, adding more deposits (but in progressively smaller amounts) in each round. Practice going through examples until the process becomes clear to you.

3. **Use of the Quantity Theory :** Analysts often use the quantity theory to help shape their thinking about the future inflation rate by using the rate of growth of the quantity of money to help predict whether the inflation rate is likely to rise or fall. Even though the relationship between the growth rate of the quantity of money and the inflation rate might not be one-to-one as suggested by the quantity theory, nonetheless the correlation between higher monetary growth rates and higher inflation rates is quite substantial.

You, too, can use this relationship to help predict the inflation rate. For instance, if you note that the growth rate of the quantity of money has jumped sharply higher, you should expect higher inflation rates to occur. Because interest rates tend to increase with the inflation rate, you would want to obtain loans with fixed (nominal) interest rates as quickly as possible. Conversely, you would not want to enter into long-term savings contracts with fixed interest rates.

Questions

■ True/False and Explain

What is Money?

1. Money is anything that is generally acceptable as a means of payment.

2. Checking accounts in banks are part of M1.

3. The amount of M2 money is more than the amount of M1 money.

4. In modern economies, credit cards are money.

Depository Institutions

5. A bank's reserves consist of cash in its vault plus its deposits at Federal Reserve banks.

6. A savings and loan association is an example of a depository institution.

7. Depository institutions help minimize the cost of borrowing funds.

The Federal Reserve System

8. The presidents of each of the Federal Reserve banks are nominated by the President of the United States and confirmed by the Senate.

9. As voting members, the FOMC comprises all the presidents of the Federal Reserve regional banks, the chairman of the Federal Reserve, and, on a rotating basis, four of the members of the Board of Governors.

10. The discount rate is the interest rate banks charge the Fed on the reserves the Fed borrows from banks.

11. Federal Reserve notes in circulation are an asset to the Federal Reserve.

How Banks Create Money

11. If a depositor withdraws currency from a bank, that bank's total reserves decrease.

12. A bank helps create money by loaning excess reserves.

13. The larger the currency ratio, the small the money multiplier.

14. The larger the required reserve ratio, the larger the money multiplier.

The Market for Money

15. The price level is the opportunity cost of holding money.

16. An increase in real GDP increases the demand for money.

17. In the short run, if the supply of money increases, the nominal interest rate falls.

The Quantity Theory of Money

18. Velocity equals *MY/P*.

19. The quantity theory of money predicts that inflation is the result of rapidly growing velocity.

20. Almost surely, high inflation rates cause high monetary growth rates.

■ Multiple Choice

What is Money?

1. Which of the following is <u>NOT</u> a function of money?
   a. Medium of exchange
   b. Barter
   c. Unit of account
   d. Store of value

2. The fact that prices are quoted in terms of money reflects money's role as a
   a. cause of inflation.
   b. medium of exchange.
   c. unit of account.
   d. store of value.

3. Which is the largest component of M1 money?
   a. Currency
   b. Traveler's checks
   c. Checking deposits
   d. Savings deposits

4. U.S. currency is
   a. part of M1 only.
   b. part of M2 only.
   c. part of M1 and M2.
   d. part of neither M1 nor M2.

5. Which of the following is a component of M2 but not of M1?
   a. Currency
   b. Checking accounts at banks
   c. Traveler's checks
   d. Savings accounts at banks

6. Which of the following is money?
   a. A check written for $200.
   b. A $200 checking deposit at a bank.
   c. A credit card with a $200 line of credit.
   d. All of the above.

Depository Institutions

7. A bank's reserves equal its
   a. cash in its vaults.
   b. cash in its vaults plus its deposits at the Federal Reserve banks.
   c. cash in its vaults plus its liquid deposits.
   d. cash in its vaults plus its liquid deposits plus its deposits at the Federal Reserve banks.

8. Depository institutions do all the following <u>EXCEPT</u>
   a. minimize the cost of obtaining funds.
   b. create liquidity.
   c. pool risks.
   d. create required reserve ratios.

9. Of the following, which can create an incentive for financial innovation?
   a. Technological change
   b. Removal of government regulation
   c. Low inflation and interest rates
   d. Liquidity creation.

The Federal Reserve System

10. Which group makes decisions about the course of the nation's monetary policy?
   a. The Fed's Board of Governors
   b. The FOMC
   c. The presidents of the Fed's regional banks
   d. The President and the Senate

11. The discount rate is the interest rate
   a. the Fed charges when it loans reserves to banks.
   b. banks charge their finest loan customers.
   c. banks pay on savings accounts.
   d. the Fed pays on reserves held by banks.

12. The purchase of $1 billion of government securities by the Fed is an example of
    a. the discount rate being affected.
    b. a multiple contraction of the quantity of money.
    c. an open market operation.
    d. a change in the required reserve ratio.

13. ____ is a liability of the Federal Reserve.
    a. Government securities
    b. Loans to banks
    c. Banks' deposits at the Fed
    d. Foreign exchange

How Banks Create Money

14. The desired reserve ratio on deposits is 10 percent. A bank has $2 million of deposits and reserves of $300,000. The bank has excess reserves of
    a. $300,000.
    b. $200,000.
    c. $100,000.
    d. $0.

15. A bank has desired reserves of $10 million and actual reserves of $9 million. Its excess reserves are equal to
    a. $10 million.
    b. $1 million.
    c. −$1 million.
    d. $0.

16. When a bank helps create money, it does so by
    a. selling some of its investment securities.
    b. increasing its reserves.
    c. lending its excess reserves.
    d. printing more checks.

17. If the desired reserve ratio is 0.05 and the currency drain ratio is 0.50, then the money multiplier equals
    a. 2.73.
    b. 1.91.
    c. 2.05.
    d. 1.85.

18. If the money multiplier is 2.5, a $10 billion increase in the monetary base raises the quantity of money by
    a. $25 billion.
    b. $10 billion.
    c. $4.0 billion.
    d. $2.5 billion.

The Market for Money

19. An increase in ____ decreases the quantity of money people want to hold.
    a. the price level
    b. real GDP
    c. the interest rate
    d. the quantity of money

20. Which of the following does NOT directly shift the demand for money curve?
    a. A change in GDP.
    b. A change in the quantity of money.
    c. Financial innovation.
    d. None of the above because they all directly shift the demand for money curve.

21. Since 1970, in the United States the demand curve for M2 money has shifted
    a. rightward in all but 2 years.
    b. leftward in all but 2 years.
    c. rightward in most years until 1989, then leftward for a few years, and rightward most years afterwards.
    d. leftward in most years until 1989 and then rightward in some years and leftward in others.

22. If the interest rate exceeds the equilibrium interest rate, then the quantity of money demanded is ____ than the quantity of money supplied and the interest rate ____.
    a. less; rises
    b. less; falls
    c. greater; rises
    d. greater; falls

The Quantity Theory of Money

23. The quantity theory of money is the idea that
    a. the quantity of money is determined by banks.
    b. the quantity of money serves as a good indicator of how well money functions as a store of value.
    c. the quantity of money determines real GDP.
    d. in the long run, an increase in the quantity of money causes an equal percentage increase in the price level.

24. The equation of exchange is
    a. $MV = PY$.
    b. $MP = VY$.
    c. $MY = PV$.
    d. $M/Y = PV$.

25. Velocity equals
    a. YM/P.
    b. PM/Y.
    c. PY/M.
    d. M/PY.

26. Nominal GDP, PY, is $6 trillion. The quantity of money is $2 trillion. Velocity is
    a. 6 trillion.
    b. 12.
    c. 3.
    d. 2.

27. Historical evidence shows that higher monetary growth rates are associated with
    a. higher inflation rates.
    b. no change in the inflation rate.
    c. lower inflation rates.
    d. higher growth rates of real GDP.

■ Short Answer Problems

1. Explain why credit cards are not money. Be sure to mention the role actually played by credit cards, that is, what they allow their owner to do.

2. Briefly explain how banks create money.

3. While digging in a local cemetery, Igor uncovers a musty chest containing $1,000 in currency. He rushes to deposit all $1,000 in his checking account at his bank. The desired reserve ratio is 10 percent. How does Igor's deposit affect the bank's actual reserves and excess reserves? What is the maximum amount that the bank can loan? Will Igor's bank's actions play any role in creating more money?

4. How does an increase in the required reserve ratio affect banks' excess reserves?

5. The desired reserve ratio is 0.05 and the currency drain ratio is 0.30.
   a. What is the money multiplier?
   b. Suppose the Federal Reserve raises the required reserve ratio so that the desired reserve ratio increases to .010. The currency drain ratio remains equal to 0.30. What now is the money multiplier?
   c. With the desired reserve ratio equal to 0.10, suppose people decide they want to hold more currency, so the currency drain ratio rises to 0.45. Now what is the money multiplier?

d. How does an increase in the desired reserve ratio affect the money multiplier? An increase in the currency drain ratio?

TABLE **9.1**

The Demand For Money

Interest rate (percent per year)	Quantity of money demanded (billions of dollars)
3	$600
4	500
5	400
6	300

6. Table 11.1 gives data on the demand for money. Suppose that the equilibrium nominal interest rate is 6 percent. What is the quantity of money?
   b. Suppose that the Fed wants to lower the interest rate to 4 percent. By how much must it change the quantity of money?

FIGURE **9.3**

Short Answer Problem 7

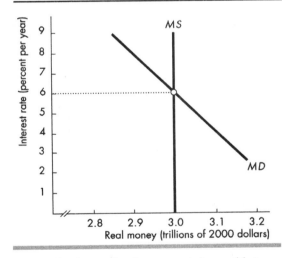

7. Initially, the market for money is in equilibrium, as illustrated in Figure 9.3. Then, the Fed increases the quantity of money by $100 billion.
   a. Draw this increase in Figure 9.3.
   b. What was the initial equilibrium interest rate? What happens to the equilibrium interest rate?
   c. Explain, in general, the adjustment process to the new equilibrium interest rate.

TABLE 9.2

Quantity Theory

Money, M (billions of dollars)	Velocity, V	Price level, P	Real GDP, Y (trillions of dollars)
_____	6	1.00	$6
$500	6	_____	3
550	6	_____	3
605	6	_____	3

8. a. Complete Table 9.2.

 b. Between the second and third rows of Table 9.2, what is the percentage increase in the quantity of money? What is the inflation rate?

 c. Between the third and fourth rows of Table 9.2, what is the percentage increase in the quantity of money? What is the inflation rate?

 d. Comment on your answers to parts (b) and (c).

■ **You're the Teacher**

1. "I couldn't believe what I read in this chapter! Do you mean to tell me that when I deposit $100 in my checking account at my bank that the bank doesn't keep all $100? That should be illegal! I mean, how can this work? How can I ever get my money back?" Your friend has just discovered "fractional reserve banking." Your friend also has some strong opinions. Making sure to stay out of arm's reach — or at least, fist's reach — explain to your friend how fractional reserve banking works and how the $100 deposited in the bank will be there, awaiting your friend's withdrawal.

Answers

■ True/False Answers

What is Money?

1. **T** This is the general definition of money.
2. **T** Checking accounts are a large component of M1.
3. **T** M2 equals M1 plus additional "savings" assets, so the amount of M2 must be larger than the amount of M1.
4. **F** Credit cards give their owners the ability to obtain a loan but are not money.

Depository Institutions

5. **T** This is the definition of bank reserves.
6. **T** Intermediaries, such as savings and loan associations, stand between — are intermediate to — savers and borrowers.
7. **T** Minimizing the cost of borrowing is a service provided by depository institutions.

The Federal Reserve System

8. **F** The members of the Board of Governors are nominated by the President and confirmed by the Senate.
9. **F** As voting members, the FOMC comprises all the members of the Board of Governors, the president of the New York Federal Reserve Bank and, on a rotating basis, the presidents of four other regional Federal Reserve banks.
10. **F** The discount rate is the interest rate the Fed charges banks for the reserves that banks borrow from the Fed.
11. **F** Federal Reserve notes in circulation are a liability to the Federal Reserve.

How Banks Create Money

12. **T** Part of the bank's reserves is its currency, so if a depositor withdraws currency, the bank loses reserves.
13. **T** The process of loaning (and then reloaning) excess reserves is the method by which banks create money.
14. **T** The larger the currency ratio, at each round in the money creation process the smaller the fraction of each loan that is deposited in banks and so the less loans banks can make in the next round of the money creation process.
14. **F** The larger the required reserve ratio, the less banks are able to loan from each deposit and so the smaller is the money multiplier.

The Market for Money

15. **F** The interest rate is the opportunity cost of holding money.
16. **T** An increase in real GDP means more transactions occur and increases the demand for money.
17. **T** When the supply of money increases, in the short run the supply of money curve shifts rightward and the interest rate falls.

The Quantity Theory of Money

18. **F** Velocity equals PY/M.
19. **F** The quantity theory predicts that inflation is caused by growth in the quantity of money.
20. **F** Almost surely, the reverse is true: High monetary growth rates cause high inflation rates.

■ Multiple Choice Answers

What is Money?

1. **b** Money eliminates the use of barter.
2. **c** A unit of account is the factor in which prices are given (e.g., 3 dollars per slice of pizza).
3. **c** Checking deposits are approximately 50 percent of M1.
4. **c** U.S. currency is part of M1 and M1 is part of M2.
5. **d** Savings accounts are not part of M1.
6. **b** Checking accounts, not the checks themselves, represent money. In addition, credit cards simply allow loans to be made quickly and are not money.

Depository Institutions

7. **b** Answer (b) is the definition of a bank's reserves.
8. **d** Required reserve ratios are set by regulators, in particular, by the Federal Reserve.
9. **a** Technological change can help foster innovation.

The Federal Reserve System

10. **b** The FOMC is an important committee because it makes decisions about the nation's monetary policy.

11. **a** The discount rate is the interest rate that banks must pay when they borrow reserves from the Fed.

12. **c** An open market operation occurs whenever the Fed buys or sells government securities.

13. **c** Banks' deposits are a Fed liability because banks own the deposits, and the Fed must return the funds to a bank that wants to make a withdrawal from its deposit.

How Banks Create Money

14. **c** Desired reserves equal 10 percent of deposits, or $(0.10) \times (\$2$ million$) = \$200,000$. The bank has reserves of \$300,000, so its excess reserves are \$300,000 − \$200,000, which is \$100,000.

15. **c** Excess reserves equal actual reserves (\$9 million) minus desired reserves (\$10 million), or −\$1 million.

16. **c** By lending its reserves, the loan becomes deposits in another bank and, because deposits are part of money, the loan has helped create money.

17. **a** The money multiplier in the problem is equal to $(1 + 0.50)/(0.50 + 0.05)$, which is 2.73.

18. **a** The change in the quantity of money equals the money multiplier multiplied by the change in the monetary base or, in this case, $(2.5) \times (\$10$ billion$) = \$25$ billion.

The Market for Money

19. **c** The interest rate is the opportunity cost of holding money, so an increase in the interest rate reduces the quantity of money demanded.

20. **b** Changes in the quantity of money create movements along the demand for money curve; they do not shift the curve.

21. **c** Until about 1989, growth in real GDP generally increased the demand for M2. Since 1989, innovation has decreased the demand for M2 while GDP growth has increased it.

22. **b** When the interest rate exceeds the equilibrium interest rate, the quantity of money demanded is less than the quantity supplied and the interest rate falls to restore the equilibrium.

The Quantity Theory of Money

23. **d** The quantity theory traces the cause of inflation to monetary growth.

24. **a** This answer is the definition of the equation of exchange.

25. **c** The equation of exchange, $MV = PY$, can be rearranged to show that velocity equals PY/M.

26. **c** The answer to this question can be calculated using the formula in the previous question. Intuitively, velocity equals the number of times an average dollar is spent on goods and services in GDP.

27. **a** Historical evidence supports the general thrust of the quantity theory.

■ Answers to Short Answer Problems

1. A credit card is not money, but a mechanism for borrowing money, which must be repaid. In other words, a credit card is merely a mechanism for rapidly arranging a loan. Repayment of the loan takes place when the credit card bill is repaid with money.

2. Banks create money by making new loans. When the loans are spent, the person receiving the funds deposits much of it in a bank, which is new money.

3. Deposits at Igor's bank have increased by \$1,000. Igor's bank wants to keep 10 percent, or \$100 as additional reserves. The entire \$1,000 increases the bank's total reserves, so the bank now has \$900 of excess reserves. The maximum amount the bank can loan is equal to its excess reserves, or \$900. The bank will help create additional money by loaning the excess reserves.

4. An increase in the required reserve ratio means that for every dollar of deposits banks must keep more reserves either in their vault or at the Federal Reserve. The increase in the required reserve ratio will increase banks' desired reserve ratio. As a result, banks' excess reserves — the reserves over and above the desired reserves — fall. Because banks will keep more reserves on hand for each dollar of deposits, they can make fewer loans. Then, with fewer loans, the quantity of money decreases.

5. a. The money multiplier equals $[(1 + a)/(a + b)]$, where b is the desired reserve ratio and a is the ratio of currency to deposits, the currency drain ratio. When b is 0.05 and a is 0.30, the money multiplier equals 1.30/0.35, or 3.71.

   b. When b is 0.10 and a is 0.30, the money multiplier equals 1.30/0.40, or 3.25.

   c. When b is 0.10 and a is 0.45, the money multiplier equals 1.45/0.55, or 2.64.

   d. An increase in the desired reserve ratio decreases the money multiplier. An increase in the currency drain ratio also decreases the money multiplier.

6. a. When the nominal interest rate is 6 percent, the quantity of money demanded is $300 billion. Hence the quantity supplied also must be $300 billion.

   b. In order to reduce the nominal interest rate to 4 percent, the Fed must increase the quantity of money supplied to $500 billion. So the quantity of money must increase by $200 billion.

FIGURE **9.4**

Short Answer Problem 7

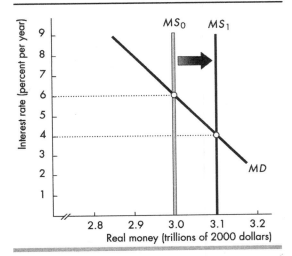

7. a. Figure 9.4 shows the $100 billion increase in the quantity of money as the rightward shift from MS_0 to MS_1.

   b. The initial nominal interest rate was 6 percent; after the increase in the quantity of money, the nominal interest rate fell, to 4 percent.

   c. An increase in the quantity of money means

that, at the initial nominal interest rate (6 percent), the quantity of money supplied is greater than the quantity of money demanded. Money holders want to reduce their money holdings and do so by buying financial assets, such as bonds. The increase in the demand for financial assets raises the price of financial assets and thereby lowers their interest rate. As the interest rate falls, the quantity of money demanded increases, which reduces the excess supply of money. This process continues until the interest rate has fallen sufficiently so that the quantity of money demanded is the same as the quantity of money supplied. The interest rate that sets the new quantity of money supplied equal to the quantity of money demanded is the (new) equilibrium interest rate.

TABLE **9.3**

Quantity Theory

Money, M (billions of dollars)	Velocity, V	Price level, P	Real GDP, Y (trillions of dollars)
$1000	6	1.00	$6
500	6	1.00	3
550	6	1.10	3
605	6	1.21	3

---

8. a. Table 9.3 completes Table 9.2. All the answers were calculated with the equation of exchange, $MV = PY$. For the first row, to calculate M, the equation of exchange was rearranged as $M = PY/V$ so that M equals $1,000 billion ($1 trillion). For the following rows, the equation of exchange was rearranged to show that $MV/Y = P$.

   b. Going from the second to the third row, the quantity of money grows by 10 percent, and (with constant velocity and real GDP) the price level grows by 10 percent, that is, the inflation rate is 10 percent.

   c. Moving from the third to the fourth row shows that another 10 percent increase in the quantity of money results in another 10 percent growth in the price level.

   d. The last three rows illustrate the quantity theory of money conclusion: A 10 percent increase in the quantity of money raises the price level by 10 percent.

■ You're the Teacher

1. "Look, don't worry. It's not illegal and you'll get your money back! Here's the deal: What you're talking about is called 'fractional reserve banking.' Banks have been doing this for a long time. Seventy or so years ago, some risk *was* involved in this procedure, but today it's safe. In fact, if it weren't for fractional banking and the banks lending out part of your deposits, they wouldn't be able to pay you interest on your account. Instead, they'd charge you for the cost of storing your money!

"Anyway, you're right that banks don't set aside the $100 you deposit with them. They do keep a fraction of the $100 in reserves but, just as you said, the majority of the deposit is loaned to people who want to borrow. But this isn't a problem for you when you want to get your cash back. On any day, banks have thousands of people who deposit cash and also thousands who want to withdraw it. And, on most days these amounts roughly balance. That is, the cash deposited will about equal the cash withdrawn. So, although you won't get back the exact same $100 you deposited with your bank, you will get back $100 that other customers have deposited.

"As I said, this process doesn't give a problem today. But I remember from my U.S. history class about the bank runs during the Great Depression. In those days, bank deposits weren't insured like they are today. Back then, if a bank failed, its depositors might lose all their deposits. So if depositors thought a bank was likely to fail, all the depositors would run to the bank to withdraw their money. When this sort of thing happened, the bank wouldn't have enough cash on hand because the amount deposited that day was a lot less than the amount that people wanted to withdraw. And because the bank didn't have the cash on hand, the bank would fail. Bank runs were a self-fulfilling prophecy: If people thought that a bank might fail, they would make a run on the bank, and the bank would fail. Today, the deposit insurance our book talks about prevents bank panics because depositors know that, even if their bank fails, they will get back their deposits. Today fractional reserve banking is safe, so you probably ought to worry more about your grade in our economics class than losing your money in the bank."

Chapter Quiz

1. The most direct way that money replaces barter is through money's use as a
   a. medium of exchange.
   b. store of value.
   c. unit of account.
   d. trade mechanism.

2. Juan takes $100 dollars from his checking account and transfers it to his saving account. As a result, M1 _____ and M2 _____.
   a. increases; increases
   b. decreases; does not change
   c. does not change; increases
   d. does not change; does not change

3. Juan takes $100 dollars from his wallet and deposits it in his checking account. As a result, M1 _____ and M2 _____.
   a. increases; increases
   b. increases; does not change
   c. does not change; increases
   d. does not change; does not change

4. Depository institutions create liquidity. Depository institutions pool risk.
   a. Both sentences are true.
   b. The first sentence is true and the second sentence is false.
   c. The first sentence is false and the second sentence is true.
   d. Both sentences are false.

5. The smaller the desired reserve ratio,
   a. the larger the money multiplier.
   b. the smaller the money multiplier.
   c. the smaller M1 is relative to M2.
   d. None of the above.

6. Reserve requirements are rules setting
   a. the minimum percentage of deposits that must be kept as reserves.
   b. the minimum amount of the owners' wealth that must be invested in the depository institution.
   c. what sort of loans the depository institution can make.
   d. the types of assets a bank can purchase.

7. A bank's reserves include the _____ and the _____.
   a. deposits it has accepted; cash it keeps in its vault
   b. liquid loans it has made; deposits it keeps at the Federal Reserve
   c. liquid securities it has purchased; liquid loans it has made
   d. deposits it keeps at the Federal Reserve; cash it keeps in its vault

8. The U.S. central bank is the
   a. Federal Central Bank.
   b. Federal Open Market Committee.
   c. Federal Reserve System.
   d. U.S. Treasury.

9. Using data from different countries, it is apparent that a high growth rate of the quantity of money is associated with a
   a. high growth rate of real GDP.
   b. high inflation rate.
   c. low growth rate of velocity.
   d. low unemployment rates.

10. Velocity grows at 2 percent, the quantity of money at 6 percent and real GDP at 3 percent. Hence the inflation rate equals
    a. 11 percent.
    b. 7 percent.
    c. 5 percent.
    d. 3 percent.

The answers for this Chapter Quiz are on page 265

Chapter 10 THE EXCHANGE RATE AND THE BALANCE OF PAYMENTS*

■ Currencies and the Exchange Rate

To buy products produced in other countries, the other country's money must be used. **Foreign currency** is defined as the money of other countries regardless of whether that money is in the form of notes, coins, or bank deposits. The **foreign exchange market** is the market in which the currency of one nation is traded for the currency of another. The price at which the currency exchanges for another is the **exchange rate.** The exchange rate rises and falls:

◆ *Depreciation of the dollar* — when the exchange rate falls so the dollar falls in value.

◆ *Appreciation of the dollar* — when the exchange rate rises so the dollar rises in value.

The **nominal exchange rate** is the value of the U.S. dollar expressed in units of foreign currency per U.S. dollar. The nominal exchange rate tells how many units of a foreign currency we get for a dollar, such as 1118 yen per dollar. The **real exchange rate** is the relative price of foreign-produced goods and services to U.S.-produced goods and services. The real exchange rate tells how many units of a foreign country's real GDP we get for a unit of U.S. real GDP. The real exchange rate is equal to:

$$RER = E \times (P/P^*)$$

Where *RER* is the real exchange rate, *E* is the nominal exchange rate, *P* is the U.S. price level, and *P** is the foreign price level. The real exchange rate does not change if the foreign price level and the exchange rate rise by the same proportion.

---

* This is Chapter 26 in *Economics*.

The **trade-weighted index** is the average exchange rate of the U.S. dollar against other currencies, with individual currencies weighted by their importance in U.S. international trade. Both the trade-weighted real and nominal exchange rates generally rose (appreciated) from 1995 to 2001, after which they generally fell (depreciated).

■ The Foreign Exchange Market

The exchange rate is determined by demand and supply in the foreign exchange market. When people demand dollars, they supply foreign currency.

FIGURE **10.1**

A Foreign Exchange Market

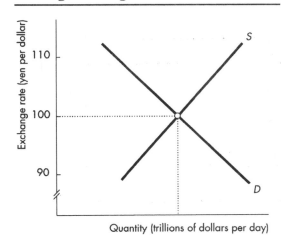

Quantity (trillions of dollars per day)

As illustrated in Figure 10.1 the demand for U.S. dollars is negatively related to the U.S. exchange rate. There are two reasons for this relationship:

◆ Exports effect — when the exchange rate falls, the quantity of U.S. exports increases and so the quantity of dollars demanded increases.

♦ Expected profit effect — for a given expected value of the U.S. exchange rate in the future, the higher the current exchange rate, the smaller the profit from holding U.S. dollars, so the quantity of dollars demanded decreases.

People supply dollars when they buy other currencies to pay for U.S. imports or to buy foreign assets. As illustrated in Figure 10.1, the supply of U.S. dollars is positively related to the exchange rate, that is, the supply curve has a positive slope. There are two reasons for the positive relationship:

♦ Imports effect — when the exchange rate rises, the quantity of U.S. imports increases, which increases the quantity of U.S. dollars supplied.

♦ Expected profits effect — for a given value of the expected exchange rate in the future, the higher the current exchange rate, the greater the profit from buying foreign currency, so the greater is the quantity of U.S. dollars supplied.

Figure 10.1 illustrates how demand and supply determine the equilibrium exchange rate, 100 yen in the figure.

■ Changes in Demand and Supply: Exchange Rate Fluctuations

Three factors change the demand for U.S. dollars and shift the demand curve for U.S. dollars:

♦ The world demand for U.S. exports— an increase in the demand for U.S. exports increases the demand for U.S. dollars and shifts the demand curve for U.S. dollars rightward.

♦ The **U.S. interest rate differential** — The U.S. interest rate differential equals the U.S. interest rate minus the foreign interest rate. A rise in the U.S. interest rate differential increases the demand for U.S. dollar assets and shifts the demand curve for U.S. dollars rightward.

♦ The expected future exchange rate — a rise in the expected future exchange rate increases the demand for U.S. dollars and shifts the demand curve for U.S. dollars rightward.

The factors change the supply of U.S. dollars changes and shift the supply curve of U.S. dollars:

♦ U.S. demand for imports— an increase in the U.S. demand for imports increases the supply of U.S.

dollars and shifts the supply curve of U.S. dollars rightward.

♦ The U.S. interest rate differential — an increase in this differential decreases the demand for foreign assets and thereby decreases the supply of U.S. dollars.

♦ The expected future exchange rate — a rise in the expected future exchange rate decreases the current supply of U.S. dollars as people hold the dollars to sell later at the higher exchange rate.

Shifts in the demand curve and/or supply curve of dollars change the exchange rate.

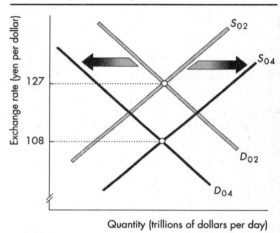

FIGURE **10.2**
The Foreign Exchange Market in 2002-2004

Quantity (trillions of dollars per day)

Figure 10.2 shows the foreign exchange market in 2002-2004.

♦ The U.S. interest rate differential and also the expected future exchange rate fell, which decreased the demand for dollars and increased the supply.

Two basic fundamentals help drive the foreign exchange market:

♦ **Interest rate parity** — "equal rates of return," that is, the exchange rate adjusts so that the return from investing in assets in different nations is the same. The exchange rate adjusts immediately so that interest rate parity always holds.

♦ **Purchasing power parity** — "equal value of money," that is, the exchange rate adjusts so that one currency can buy the same amount of goods and services as another currency. Purchasing power parity holds in the long run but not necessarily in the short run.

The real exchange and nominal exchange are linked by the formula $RER = E \times (P/P^*)$. Rearranging the formula to $E = RER \times (P^*/P)$ shows how the nominal exchange rate is determined in the long run. The quantity of money determines the price levels in each county (P and P^*) and the real exchange rate (RER) is determined by supply and demand in markets for goods and services. So in the long run, the nominal exchange rate must equal $RER \times (P^*/P)$. A change in the quantity of money changes the price level and also changes the nominal exchange rate. In the long run, the nominal exchange rate is a monetary phenomenon.

■ Financing International Trade

The **balance of payments accounts** record a country's international trading, borrowing, and lending in three accounts:

♦ **Current account** — records receipts for exports, payments for imports, net interest, and net transfers. The current account balance equals exports minus imports, net interest, and net transfers.

♦ **Capital account** — records foreign investment in the United States and U.S. investment abroad. Any statistical discrepancy is recorded in this account.

♦ **Official settlements account** — shows changes in **U.S. official reserves,** the government holdings of foreign currency.

The current account balance plus capital account balance plus official settlements account must sum to zero. In 2005 the United States had a current account deficit that was nearly equal to its capital account surplus. The United States has had a current account deficit for most years since 1980.

♦ A nation that is borrowing more from the rest of the world than it is loaning to the rest of the world is a **net borrower;** a country that is loaning more to the rest of the world than it is borrowing from the rest of the world is a **net lender.** The United States is a net borrower.

♦ A **debtor nation** is a country that during its entire history has borrowed more from the rest of the world than it has lent to it; a **creditor nation** is a country that during its entire history has invested more in the rest of the world than other countries have invested in it. The United States is a debtor nation.

National income accounting provides a framework for analyzing the current account. Combining the national income accounts result that GDP = $C + I + G + X - M$ and that GDP = $C + S + T$ gives:

$$X - M = (T - G) + (S - I),$$

where $X - M$ is **net exports,** $T - G$ is the **government surplus or deficit,** and $S - I$ is the **private sector surplus or deficit.** In 2006, the government sector deficit was $313 billion and the private sector deficit was $471 billion, so the net exports deficit was $784 billion.

In the United States, there is not a strong relationship between net exports and the other two sector balances separately. Instead, net exports respond to the sum of the other two sector balances.

In the long run, a change in the nominal exchange rate does not affect the real exchange rate so, in the long run, the nominal exchange rate has no influence on the current account balance.

■ Exchange Rate Policy

Government's and central banks must have an exchange rate policy. Three possible policies are:

♦ **Flexible exchange rate** — a policy that permits the exchange rate to be determined by demand and supply with no direct intervention in the foreign exchange market by the central bank. The United States follows a flexible exchange rate policy.

♦ **Fixed exchange rate**— a policy that pegs the exchange rate at a value decided by the government or central bank and that blocks the unregulated forces of demand and supply by direct intervention in the foreign exchange market. If the Fed wanted to pursue a fixed exchange rate, it could intervene in the foreign exchange market by selling dollars — which drives the exchange rate lower — or by buying dollars — which drives the exchange rate higher. These policies would allow the Fed to fix the exchange rate. However the Fed could not buy dollars forever because it would run out of the foreign exchange it is using to buy the dollars.

♦ **Crawling peg** — a policy that selects a target path for the exchange rate with intervention in the foreign exchange market to achieve that path. A crawling peg is like a fixed exchange whose target value for the exchange rate changes.

China had a fixed exchange rate until 2005, after which it has had a crawling peg. The People's Bank of China purchased $200 billion dollars a year to fix (and now peg) its exchange rate. By fixing its exchange rate, China anchored its inflation rate to the low U.S. inflation rate.

Helpful Hints

1. **BASICS OF THE FOREIGN EXCHANGE MARKET :** There is an important difference between trade within a single country and trade between countries — currency. Individuals trading in the same country use the same currency and trade is straightforward. But international trade is complicated by the fact that individuals in different countries use different currencies. For example, a Japanese seller of goods will want payment in Japanese yen, but a U.S. buyer likely will be holding only U.S. dollars.

2. **DEMAND FOR U.S. DOLLARS :** The demand for U.S. dollars in the foreign exchange market arises from the desire on the part of foreigners to purchase U.S. goods and services (which requires dollars) and U.S. financial or real assets (which also requires dollars). So a Japanese importer of U.S. rice demands dollars to pay to U.S. rice farmers. And a Japanese investor who wants to buy a U.S. security also demands dollars to pay the current American owner.

   Foreign exchange rates are prices determined by supply and demand. Hence any factor that changes the demand for U.S. dollars will change the exchange rate. And, the influences that change the demand for U.S. dollars are the factors that change either the quantity of American goods (such as U.S. rice) or change the quantity of U.S. assets that foreigners buy.

Questions

■ True/False and Explain

Currencies and Exchange Rates

1. If the exchange rate between the U.S. dollar and the Japanese yen changes from 100 yen per dollar to 80 yen per dollar, the U.S. dollar has appreciated.

2. The nominal exchange rate measures how much of one money exchanges for a unit of another money.

3. The formula for the real exchange rate is $RER = E \times (P \times P^*)$ where RER is the real exchange rate, E is the nominal exchange rate, P is the U.S. price level, and P^* is the foreign price level.

4. If the nominal exchange rate rises 10 percent and the foreign price level rises 10 percent, the real exchange rate also rises by 10 percent.

5. If the U.S. price level rises and the foreign price level and real exchange rate do not change, then the nominal exchange rate falls.

The Foreign Exchange Market

6. If the U.S. exchange rate rises, the demand for foreign exchange curve shifts rightward.

7. The lower the exchange rate, the cheaper foreigners find U.S.-produced goods and services.

8. .The supply curve for U.S. dollars is vertical in the market for foreign exchange.

Changes in Demand and Supply: Exchange Rate Fluctuations

9. If the U.S. interest rate differential rises, the demand for U.S. dollars increases.

10. If the U.S. exchange rate is expected to appreciate in the future, the current supply of U.S. dollars decreases.

11. An increase in the U.S. demand for imports increases the demand for U.S. dollars.

12. An increase in the U.S. interest rate differential raises the U.S. exchange rate.

13. If the demand for U.S. dollars decreases and the supply increases, the exchange rate definitely falls.

14. Purchasing power parity means that if the U.S. dollar can buy more goods in Japan than in the United States, the U.S. exchange rate will fall.

15. If the U.S price level and real exchange rate do not change while the foreign price level rises 10 percent, the nominal exchange rate rises by 10 percent.

Financing International Trade

16. The sum of the current account plus capital account plus official settlements account is positive for a nation that is a net lender.

17. A debtor nation must be a net borrower nation.

18. If investment is greater than saving, the private sector has a deficit.

19. $X - M$ equals $(T - G) + (S - I)$.

20. For the last ten years, the United States has had both a current account deficit and a capital account deficit.

21. In the United States, a larger government sector deficit immediately leads to a larger net exports deficit.

Exchange Rate Policy

22. If the Federal Reserve buys U.S. dollars, the exchange rate rises.

23. The United States uses a crawling peg exchange rate policy.

24. In order to keep its exchange rate fixed, over the last decade the People's Bank of Chin has been forced to buy billions of yuan per year.

■ Multiple Choice

Currencies and Exchange Rates

1. Foreigners demand U.S. dollars to
   a. sell the goods imported into the United States.
   b. buy the goods exported from the United States.
   c. take advantage of higher U.S. prices.
   d. for reasons that are not given in the previous answers.

2. If the exchange rate _____, then the exchange rate has _____.
   a. falls; depreciates
   b. falls; appreciates
   c. rises; depreciates
   d. None of the above answers is correct.

3. The real exchange rate
   a. changes only when the nominal exchange rate changes.
   b. must be calculated using a trade-weighted index of exchange rates.
   c. is the relative price of foreign-produced goods and services to U.S. produced goods and services.
   d. cannot depreciate.

4. Suppose the U.S. price level is 120, the European price level is 130, and the exchange rate is 1.15 euros per dollar. Then the U.S. real exchange rate is
   a. 1.25.
   b. 0.94.
   c. 1.36.
   d. 1.06.

The Foreign Exchange Market

5. When the exchange rate rises, the demand curve for foreign exchange shifts _____ and the supply curve of foreign exchange shifts _____.
   a. rightward; rightward
   b. leftward; leftward
   c. rightward; leftward
   d. None of the above answers is correct because a change in the exchange rate does not shift either curve.

6. If the U.S. exchange rate falls, the price to foreigners of U.S.-produced goods and services _____ and the quantity of U.S. dollars demanded _____.
   a. rises; increases
   b. rises; decreases
   c. falls; increases
   d. falls; decreases

7. If the U.S. exchange rate falls and expected future exchange rate does not change, the _____ the expected profit from selling U.S. dollars today and so the _____ the quantity of U.S. dollars supplied today.
   a. larger; larger
   b. larger; smaller
   c. smaller; larger
   d. smaller; smaller

Changes in Demand and Supply: Exchange Rate Fluctuations

8. An increase in the demand for U.S. exports _____ the demand for U.S. dollars and shifts the demand curve for U.S. dollars _____.
   a. increases; rightward
   b. increases; leftward
   c. decreases; rightward
   d. decreases; leftward

9. An increase in the expected future exchange rate shifts the demand curve for U.S. dollars _____ and the supply curve of U.S. dollars _____.
   a. rightward; rightward
   b. rightward; leftward
   c. leftward; rightward
   d. leftward; leftward

10. Which of the following increases the supply of U.S. dollars?
    a. A increase in foreigners' demand for goods and services made in the United States.
    b. An increase in the demand for U.S. assets by foreigners.
    c. The U.S. dollar is expected to appreciate in the future.
    d. The U.S. dollar is expected to depreciate in the future.

Use Figure 10.3 for the next two questions.

FIGURE 10.3
Multiple Choice Questions 11 and 12

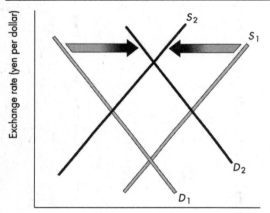

Quantity (trillions of dollars per day)

11. As illustrated in Figure 10.3, which influence might have shifted the demand curve?
    a. An increase in the U.S. exchange rate.
    b. An expectation that the U.S. dollar exchange rate will depreciate in the future.
    c. An increase in the U.S. interest rate differential.
    d. None of the above.

12. As illustrated in Figure 10.3, which influence might have shifted the supply curve?
    a. An increase in the U.S. exchange rate.
    b. An expectation that the U.S. dollar exchange rate will depreciate in the future.
    c. An increase in the U.S. interest rate differential.
    d. None of the above.

13. Of the following, when would the U.S. exchange rate fall the most?
    a. When the supply of and demand for U.S. dollars increase.
    b. When the supply of U.S. dollars increases and the demand for them decreases.
    c. When the supply of U.S. dollars decreases and the demand for them increases.
    d. When the supply of and demand for U.S. dollars decrease.

14. Which of the following would lead the exchange rate to fall against the yen?
    a. A decrease in U.S. demand for Japanese imports.
    b. An increase in American interest rates.
    c. A decrease in interest rates in Japan.
    d. The dollar is expected to depreciate against the yen in the future.

15. Interest rate parity means that
    a. interest rates in two nations must be equal.
    b. interest rates in two nations can never be equal.
    c. a nation with a high interest rate has an exchange rate that is expected to depreciate.
    d. a nation with a high interest rate has an exchange rate that is expected to appreciate.

16. Suppose the exchange rate between the U.S. dollar and the British pound is 0.5 pounds per dollar. If a radio sells for 38 pounds in Britain, what is the dollar price of the radio?
    a. $19
    b. $26
    c. $38
    d. $76

17. Purchasing power parity means
    a. that interest rates in different nations are the same.
    b. that interest rates in different nations adjusted by the expected change in the exchange rate are the same.
    c. that the purchasing power of different currencies is the same.
    d. something other than the answers given above.

18. Suppose the Federal Reserve announces it will increase interest rates next week. As a result, the U.S. exchange rate will
    a. slowly fall.
    b. rapidly fall.
    c. slowly rise.
    d. rapidly rise.

19. In the long run, the U.S. price level is 120, the European price level is 130, and the real exchange rate is 1.40. Then the U.S. nominal exchange rate is
    a. 1.25 euros per dollar.
    b. 1.11 euros per dollar.
    c. 1.52 euros per dollar.
    d. 1.06 euros per dollar.

Financing International Trade

20. Which of the following is one of the balance of payments accounts?
    a. Current account
    b. Borrowing account
    c. Official lending account
    d. Net transfer interest account

21. Foreign investment in the United States and U.S. investment abroad are recorded in
    a. the current account.
    b. the capital account.
    c. the official settlements account.
    d. a balance of payments account that is not mentioned above.

22. Suppose the United States initially has no trade surplus or deficit. Then U.S. firms increase their imports from Canada, financing that increase by borrowing from Canada. The United States now has a current account _____ and a capital account _____.
    a. surplus; surplus
    b. surplus; deficit
    c. deficit; surplus
    d. deficit; deficit

23. If the official settlements account is $0 and the United States has a current account deficit of $100 billion, then the
    a. capital account necessarily has a deficit of $100 billion.
    b. capital account necessarily has a surplus of $100 billion.
    c. government necessarily has a budget deficit of $100 billion.
    d. government necessarily has a budget surplus of $100 billion.

24. In recent years, the United States has been a _____ and a _____.
    a. net lender; creditor nation
    b. net lender; debtor nation
    c. net borrower; debtor nation
    d. net borrower; creditor nation

25. This year a nation is currently a net lender and is also a debtor nation. Which of the following statements accurately describes the nation's current situation?
    a. It has loaned more capital than it has borrowed abroad this year, but it has borrowed more than it has loaned during its history.
    b. It has borrowed more capital abroad than it has loaned this year and it also has borrowed more than it has loaned during its history.
    c. It has loaned more capital than it has borrowed abroad this year and it has loaned more than it has borrowed during its history.
    d. It has borrowed more capital abroad than it has loaned this year and it has loaned more than it has borrowed during its history.

Table 10.1 presents several national income accounts for a nation. Use the table for the next three questions.

TABLE **18.1**

Multiple Choice Questions 26, 27, 28

Component	Billions of dollars
Government purchases, G	$600
Net taxes, T	500
Investment, I	250
Saving, S	400

26. What does the government's surplus equal?
    a. $600 billion
    b. $500 billion
    c. −$100 billion
    d. $0

27. What does the private sector surplus equal?
    a. $400 billion
    b. $250 billion
    c. $150 billion
    d. $0

28. What does the net exports balance equal?
    a. A deficit of $600 billion
    b. A deficit of $250 billion
    c. A surplus of $50 billion
    d. A surplus of $1,650 billion

29. The government sector deficit is $100 billion and the private sector deficit is $25 billion. Hence net exports equals
    a. −$125 billion.
    b. −$100 billion
    c. −$75 billion.
    d. $75 billion.

30. In the United States, net exports respond
    a. only to the government sector balance.
    b. only to the private sector balance.
    c. to the sum of the government sector balance plus private sector balance.
    d. to the difference between the government sector balance minus the private sector balance..

Exchange Rate Policy

31. Which of the following is <u>NOT</u> a possible exchange rate policy?
    a. flexible exchange rate policy
    b. official intervention policy
    c. crawling peg policy
    d. fixed exchange rate policy

32. If a country's central bank does not intervene in the foreign exchange market, the country has
    a. a flexible exchange rate policy.
    b. no exchange rate policy.
    c. a crawling peg exchange rate policy.
    d. a fixed exchange rate policy.

33. If the Fed buys U.S. dollars, the exchange rate
    a. rises.
    b. does not change.
    c. falls.
    d. changes, but the direction depends on whether the Fed's action affected the demand for dollars or the supply of dollars.

34. If the Fed buys U.S. dollars in the exchange market, it pays for the dollars with
    a. foreign currency.
    b. more U.S. dollars.
    c. imports.
    d. government securities.

35. Since 1995, the People's Bank of China has purchased _____ in order to prevent the yuan-U.S. dollar exchange rate from _____.
    a. yuan; rising
    b. yuan; falling
    c. dollars; rising
    d. dollars; falling

■ Short Answer Problems

1. Igor has moved to Japan. He wants to buy 100 bats a year and can buy either American or Japanese bats. Igor thinks both are identical; hence he will buy the cheapest ones. The price of a bat in the United States is 5 dollars and in Japan is 500 yen.
    a. If the exchange rate between the U.S. and Japan is 110 yen per dollar, from where will Igor buy his bats — the United States or Japan? What is Igor's demand for U.S. dollars?

b. If the exchange rate between the U.S. and Japan falls to 90 yen per dollar, from which country will Igor purchase his bats? What is Igor's demand for U.S. dollars?

c. How does the quantity of U.S. dollars Igor demands change as the U.S. exchange rate falls from 110 yen per dollar to 90 yen per dollar?

2. Why does a rise in U.S. interest rates change the value of the exchange rate?

FIGURE **10.4**

Short Answer Problem 3

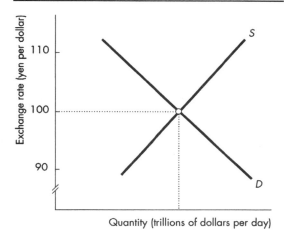

3. In Figure 10.4, show what happens to the demand for and supply of U.S. dollars if the U.S. exchange rate is expected to fall in the future. Does the current exchange rate rise or fall?

TABLE **10.2**

Supply and Demand of U.S. Dollars

U.S. exchange rate (yen per dollar)	Quantity of U.S. dollars demanded (trillions of dollars)	Quantity of U.S. dollars supplied (trillions of dollars)
130	$5.6	$6.0
120	5.7	5.9
110	5.8	5.8
100	5.9	5.7
90	6.0	5.6

4. Table 10.2 presents the supply and demand schedules for U.S. dollars.

a. Graph the supply and demand curves in Figure 10.5. What is the equilibrium exchange rate?

FIGURE **10.5**

Short Answer Problem 4

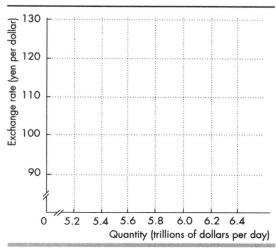

b. Suppose the Federal Reserve buys $200 billion of foreign securities. In Figure 10.5 illustrate the effect of this increase in supply of U.S. dollars on the equilibrium foreign exchange rate.

c. Suppose when the Federal Reserve purchased $200 billion of foreign securities, the U.S. interest rate fell. Further, suppose that the fall in the U.S. interest rate decreases the demand for U.S. dollars by $200 billion. Now illustrate the effect of the *combined* increase in supply and decrease in demand for U.S. dollars in Figure 10.5.

d. Is the change in the exchange rate larger when the supply alone changes, or when both the supply and demand change?

5. What is the relationship between a country's net exports deficit, its government budget deficit, and its private sector deficit?

TABLE **10.3**

Short Answer Problem 6

Component	Billions of dollars
Government expenditures, G	$1,000
Net taxes, T	800
Investment, I	900
Saving, S	800

6. Table 10.3 shows data for a nation.

a. What is the government surplus or deficit?

b. What is the private sector surplus or deficit?

c. What is the net exports balance?

d. Suppose that the government decreased its net taxes by $100 billion and people responded by increasing their private saving by $100 billion. How do these changes affect the net exports balance?

TABLE **10.4**

International Lending and Borrowing

Year	Lending to foreigners (dollars)	Borrowing from abroad (dollars)
2004	$2,000	$3,000
2005	3,000	3,000
2006	5,000	1,000
2007	5,000	6,000

7. The nation of Sega is newly formed in 2004. Table 10.4 shows Sega's international borrowing and lending from 2004 through 2007.

a. In 2004 was Sega a net borrower or lender? In 2005? In 2006? In 2007?

b. At the end of 2004 was Sega a net creditor or debtor nation? At the end of 2005? At the end of 2006? At the end of 2007?

■ **You're the Teacher**

1. "Haven't I read somewhere that a current account deficit is called an 'unfavorable balance of trade'? Do you have any idea what this means, or why a current account deficit is called 'unfavorable'?" Your friend is indeed correct that a current account deficit is often called "unfavorable." Explain to your friend why you think a current account deficit has this name.

Answers

■ True/False Answers

Currencies and Exchange Rate

1. **F** The fall in the exchange rate means that the U.S. dollar has depreciated.

2. **T** A nominal exchange rate such as 120 yen per dollar means that one dollar exchanges for 120 yen.

3. **F** The formula for the real exchange rate is $RER = E \times (P/P^*)$.

4. **F** If both the nominal exchange rate and foreign price level change by the same percentage, the real exchange does not change.

5. **T** The formula for the real exchange rate, which is $RER = E \times (P/P^*)$, shows that a rise in the U.S. price level leads to a fall in the nominal exchange rate if the foreign price level and real exchange rate do not change.

The Foreign Exchange Market

6. **F** There is a movement upward along the demand curve but the demand curve does not shift.

7. **T** The lower the exchange rate, are fewer units of foreign currency needed to buy a U.S. dollar and so the less expensive are U.S.-produced goods and services to foreigners.

8. **F** The supply curve for U.S. dollars is upward sloping, not vertical.

Changes in Demand and Supply: Exchange Rate Fluctuations

9. **T** An increase in the U.S. interest rate differential means that the interest rate paid on U.S. assets has risen relative to interest rates paid on foreign assets, which increases the demand for U.S. dollars.

10. **T** Suppliers want to hold — not sell — more U.S. dollars in order to reap the expected profit from the dollar's expected appreciation, so the current supply of dollars decreases.

11. **F** An increase in the U.S. demand for imports increases the *supply* of demand U.S. dollars.

12. **T** The demand for U.S. dollars increases and the supply decreases, both of which appreciate the U.S. exchange rate.

13. **T** The changes outlined in the question occurred in 2002-2004 when the U.S. dollar exchange rate depreciated.

14. **T** In the case outlined in the question, U.S. residents will supply more dollars to buy yen, which thereby drives down the U.S. exchange rate.

15. **T** In the long run, the nominal exchange rate is determined by $E = RER \times (P^*/P)$ so any increase in the foreign price level results in a proportionate rise in the nominal exchange rate.

Financing International Trade

16. **F** The sum of the current account, capital account, and official settlements account is *always* zero.

17. **F** A debtor nation might currently be a net loaner nation, which would thereby reduce its overall indebtedness.

18. **T** The private sector's surplus equals $S - I$, so if investment exceeds saving, the private sector has a deficit.

19. **T** The result that $X - M = (T - G) + (S - I)$ provides a framework for understanding what factors affect the net exports balance, $X - M$.

20. **F** Setting aside changes in official reserves, a current account deficit must be matched by an equal capital account surplus. In the 1990s and into the 2000s, the United States had a current account deficit and a capital account surplus.

21. **F** The net exports deficit is only weakly related to the government sector's surplus or deficit.

Exchange Rate Policy

22. **T** By buying U.S. dollars, the Fed increases the demand for dollars, thereby raising the U.S. exchange rate.

23. **F** The United States follows a flexible exchange rate policy; the United States has never used a crawling peg policy.

24. **F** The People's Bank was forced to buy billions of dollars *not* billions of yuan.

■ Multiple Choice Answers

Currencies and Exchange Rate

1. **b** The demand for U.S. dollars is derived from the demand from foreigners for U.S. goods and U.S. assets.

2. **a** When the exchange rate falls, it has depreciated; when it rises, it has appreciated.

3. **c** Answer c correctly defines the real exchange rate.

4. **d** The real exchange rate equals $E \times (P/P^*)$, which in this case is $1.15 \times (120/130)$.

The Foreign Exchange Market

5. **d** A change in the exchange rate leads to a movement along the demand and supply curves *not* a shift in the curves.

6. **c** When the U.S. exchange rate falls, the price to foreigners of U.S.-produced products falls, so their demand for U.S.-produced products increases which increases the quantity of U.S. dollars demanded.

7. **d** The fall in the exchange rate with no change in the expected future exchange rate means that the expected profit from holding dollars rises. The rise in the expected profit decreases the quantity of dollars supplied because investors see a higher expected profit from holding dollars.

Changes in Demand and Supply: Exchange Rate Fluctuations

8. **a** To buy U.S.-produced products, foreigners need U.S. dollars, so the demand for U.S. dollars increases.

9. **b** The increase in the future expected exchange rate raises the profit from owning U.S. dollars, which increases the demand and decreases the supply of dollars.

10. **d** This expectation increases the supply of dollars as people try to decrease the quantity of dollars they hold in order to limit their loss from the expected future depreciation.

11. **c** The rise in the U.S. interest rate differential influences foreigners to demand more U.S. assets and fewer foreign assets, thereby increasing the demand for U.S. dollars.

12. **c** Similar to the previous answer, the rise in the U.S. interest rate differential influences U.S. residents to demand more U.S. assets and fewer foreign assets, thereby decreasing the supply of U.S. dollars.

13. **b** Both an increase in the supply of U.S. dollars and a decrease in the demand for U.S. dollars lower the U.S. exchange rate.

14. **d** This expected depreciation decreases the demand for dollars and increases the supply.

15. **c** The expected depreciation "offsets" the higher interest rate.

16. **d** It takes 2 dollars to purchase 1 pound, so the U.S. dollar cost of the British radio is (38 pounds) × (2 dollars per pound) = 76 dollars.

17. **c** Answer (c) is essentially the definition of purchasing power parity.

18. **c** In order to profit from the anticipated rise in the exchange rate, traders increase their current demand for dollars and decrease their current supply, so the exchange rate rises immediately.

19. **c** In the long run, the nominal exchange rate equals $RER \times (P^*/P)$ where RER is the real exchange rate, P^* is the foreign price level, and P is the U.S. price level.

Financing International Trade

20. **a** The current account records net exports, net transfers, and interest income from abroad minus interest payments to foreigners.

21. **b** The capital account records all investment accounts.

22. **c** The current account deficit reflects the excess of imports over exports while the capital account surplus reflects the excess of borrowing from foreigners over loaning to foreigners.

23. **b** With the official settlements account equal to zero, a current account deficit is balanced by an equal capital account surplus.

24. **c** Answer (c) correctly describes the recent situation with the United States.

25. **a** "Net lender" means that the nation is currently loaning more abroad than it is borrowing; "debtor" means that in the past the nation has borrowed more abroad than it has loaned. So, in total, the nation owes foreigners more than they owe it.

26. **c** The government surplus equals the difference between its net taxes and its spending, which in this case is –$100 billion. The negative sign indicates that the "surplus" is actually a deficit, so the government's deficit is $100 billion.

27. **c** The private sector surplus is the difference between the private sector's saving and investment.

28. **c** The net exports balance equals the sum of the government's (or public sector's) surplus, –$100 billion, plus the private sector's surplus, $150 billion, for a net exports surplus of $50 billion.

29. **a** Net exports equals the government sector deficit (the government budget deficit) plus the private sector deficit.

30. **c** The government sector balance and private sector balance tend to offset each other, so net exports does not respond strongly to either alone.

Exchange Rate Policy

31. **b** There is no such thing as an "official intervention policy."

32. **a** By not intervening, the central bank is allowing the exchange rate to respond to supply and demand.

33. **a** When the Fed buys dollars, it increases the demand for dollars, thereby raising the exchange rate.

34. **a** By purchasing dollars, the Fed must pay for the purchases with foreign currency. The Fed has only a certain amount of foreign currency, so eventually the Fed would run out of foreign currency, at which time it would be forced to stop buying dollars.

34. **c** By purchasing dollars, the People's Bank of China supplied yuan, which kept the yuan-U.S. dollar exchange rate from rising.

■ Answers to Short Answer Problems

1. a. If Igor buys his bats from the United States, he will need 5 dollars per bat. With the exchange rate of 110 yen per dollar, a U.S. bat would cost 550 yen. A Japanese bat, however, costs only 500 yen. Hence Igor will buy from his Japanese supplier. Because Igor does not buy American bats, Igor's demand for U.S. dollars is zero.

    b. After the fall in the exchange rate, bats in the United States cost 450 yen. (5 dollars times 90 yen per dollar.) Thus bats are less expensive in the United States, so Igor buys from his American supplier. In order to pay this supplier, Igor demands 500 U.S. dollars.

    c. As the exchange rate fell, the quantity of U.S. dollars Igor demands increased. This result illustrates the downward slope of the demand curve

for dollars: As the U.S. exchange rate falls, the quantity of U.S. dollars demanded increases.

2. A rise in U.S. interest rates changes the U.S. interest rate differential. More fundamentally, a rise in the U.S. interest rate increases the desirability of U.S. financial assets relative to foreign assets. In turn, this change affects the demand for U.S. dollars, which are necessary to buy American assets. In particular, foreigners increase their demand for U.S. dollars in order to buy more U.S. assets. The increase in the U.S. interest rate differential also decreases the supply of U.S. dollars because U.S. residents will buy fewer foreign assets. The increase in demand and decrease in supply both serve to raise the U.S. exchange rate.

FIGURE 10.6
Short Answer Problem 3

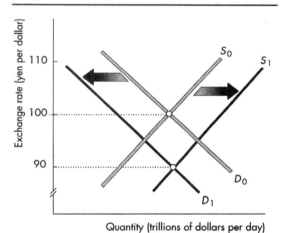

Quantity (trillions of dollars per day)

3. If people expect that the U.S. exchange rate will fall in the future, they do not want to hold dollars because they will suffer a loss when the dollar falls in value. Hence the supply increases, as those people who currently own U.S. dollars try to sell them. And the demand decreases because buyers do not want to own the dollars when they fall in value. Figure 10.6 illustrates these responses. The demand curve shifts leftward, from D_0 to D_1 while the supply shifts rightward from S_0 to S_1. (Your figure does not need to be identical to Figure 10.6, but the direction of the shifts must be the same.) As Figure 10.6 shows, as a result of these changes the current exchange rate falls.

FIGURE 10.7
Problem 4 (a)

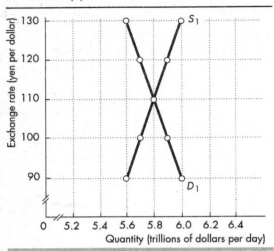

4. a. Figure 10.7 shows the demand and supply curves. The equilibrium exchange rate is 110 yen per dollar because this is the exchange rate at which the quantity of U.S. dollars demanded equals the quantity supplied.

FIGURE 10.8
Short Answer Problem 4 (b)

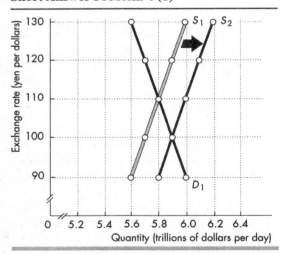

b. When the Federal Reserve buys $200 billion of foreign securities, the quantity of U.S. dollars supplied increases by $200 billion. Thus, as illustrated in Figure 10.8, the supply curve of U.S. dollars shifts rightward by $200 billion. The increase in U.S. dollars depreciates the U.S. exchange rate to 100 yen per dollar.

FIGURE 10.9
Short Answer Problem 4 (c)

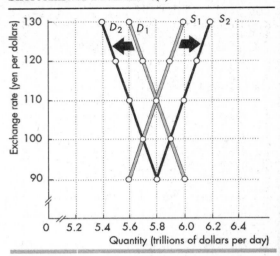

c. Figure 10.9 illustrates the situation when the supply increases and demand decreases. The decrease in demand shifts the demand curve for U.S. dollars leftward by $200 billion, from D_1 to D_2. With both the shift in the supply and demand curves the exchange rate falls to 90 yen per dollar.

d. The exchange rate falls more when both the demand and supply curves shift. This result illustrates why exchange rates can be volatile: Factors that change the supply also affect the demand. In the case at hand, the Fed's actions affect *both* the supply for and demand of dollars. This situation is unlike that in most markets, in which the factors that influence the supply are generally different from those that affect the demand.

5. The national income accounting identities show that a country's net export deficit is equal to the sum of its government budget deficit and its private sector deficit. In particular, the relationship is $X - M = (T - G) + (S - I)$ where $X - M$ is the net exports balance, $T - G$ is the government surplus or deficit and $S - I$ is the private sector surplus or deficit.

6. a. The government surplus (or deficit) equals $T - G$. Hence, in the problem the government "surplus" is $800 billion minus $1,000 billion or –$200 billion, that is, a government deficit of $200 billion.

b. The private sector surplus (or deficit) is equal to

$S - I$. Thus this formula yields a private sector "surplus" of $800 billion – $900 billion, that is, a deficit of $100 billion.

c. The net exports balance, $X - M$, can be determined from the national income accounts formula $X - M = (T - G) + (S - I)$. Using the answers from parts (a) and (b) for the government deficit and private sector deficit gives the net exports balance equal to –$300 billion. That is, there is a deficit on the net exports balance of $300 billion.

d. If taxes fall by $100 billion and private saving increases by $100 billion, using the formula $X - M = (T - G) + (S - I)$ shows that the net exports balance remains at $300 billion.

7. a. In 2004, Sega is a net borrower: its borrowing from the rest of world, $3,000, exceeds its lending to the rest of the world, $2,000. In 2005, Sega is neither a net borrower nor a net lender because its borrowing just equals its lending. In 2006 Sega is a net lender because its lending to the rest of the world, $5,000, exceeds its borrowing from the rest of the world, $1,000. In 2007 Sega is a net borrower.

b. At the end of 2004, Sega is a debtor nation. It owed the rest of the world $3,000 (its borrowing to date), but the rest of the world owed Sega only $2,000 (its loans to the rest of the world to date). At the end of 2005 Sega is still a debtor nation: It owed the rest of the world a total of $6,000 ($3,000 borrowed in 2004 plus $3,000 borrowed in 2005) and the rest of the world owed Sega only $5,000 ($2,000 loaned by Sega in 2004 plus $3,000 loaned in 2005). At the end of 2006, Sega is a creditor nation because the amount it owed the rest of the world, $7,000, is less than what the rest of the world owed Sega, $10,000. Even though in 2007 Sega is a net borrower, at the end of 2007 Sega is still a creditor nation because the amount it owed the rest of the world ($13,000) is less than the amount the rest of the world owed Sega ($15,000).

■ You're the Teacher

1. "You know, you're right, a current account deficit sometimes is called 'unfavorable.' I think there might be three reasons for this name. And actually all are rather silly!

"First, if we are running a current account deficit, it almost always means that the value of our imports exceeds the value of our exports; that is, the United States is importing more than it's exporting. Some observers claim that this situation costs us jobs in the United States. But look, we know from this chapter that this claim is wrong. I mean, we know that a current account deficit must be matched by a capital account surplus. So if our country runs a current account deficit, foreigners must be using the 'excess' funds to invest in the United States. Foreigners are buying U.S. financial assets, and that way they are keeping our interest rates lower than otherwise. And, by keeping U.S. interest rates lower, American businesses spend more on investment, which means that there are more people employed in industries that make investment goods, such as automobiles or machine tools. On net, a current account deficit doesn't seem likely to reduce jobs overall in the United States.

"Another reason that I can think of why a current account surplus is called 'unfavorable' is even sillier than the last. I bet some people think that foreigners actually keep the dollars abroad, that is, the United States runs an official settlements surplus. Now, we know from this chapter that the official settlements balance is very small, so the idea that foreigners keep our money rather than use it to invest in the United States is *really* silly. But, if they did, I think this would be great! We'd get their goods in exchange for paper! Boy, I'd sure like to be able to buy the stuff I want and only have to give the stores paper on which I've scribbled some sort of design! If I could do this, I sure wouldn't call this situation 'unfavorable'!

"The last reason that comes to mind is the fact that if we're running a current account deficit, we must be running a capital account surplus. Thus foreigners are buying our assets. Some people think that when foreigners own enough of our assets, they can then control us and we'll be reduced to being some other nation's colony. Personally, I think this concern is also really silly, maybe the silliest of the bunch! First, there's no one nation that is buying up all our assets. Even if buying our assets could make us some sort of colony, what do you think the odds are that, say, Japan, Korea, France, Germany, South Africa, Poland, and all the other nations that own our assets can get together and agree to make us a colony? If you think this is likely, I have a large asset that extends over water in the city of Brooklyn that I'd love to sell to you! Second, even if a bunch of our assets are owned by someone else, so what? I mean, I owe a lot of money on my student loans, but the bank doesn't control me. And keep in mind that when these other nations buy our assets, they're basically at our mercy. For instance, suppose that Germany buys a lot of U.S. government securities. We could always decide that we simply wouldn't pay the Germans back! I mean, what are they going to do? Foreclose on the White House? Now, I don't think that we'll ever do this and I don't think that it's right, but come on. If we ever thought that foreigners were controlling us too much, we could take steps to end this control.

"So, I guess I can see why some people think that a current account deficit is 'unfavorable.' But I believe that what this claim actually shows is that the people making the claim haven't actually thought about the issue too deeply."

Chapter Quiz

1. The currency used to buy goods imported into a nation is generally
   a. gold.
   b. the currency of the nation importing the goods.
   c. the currency of the nation exporting the goods.
   d. None of the above.

2. A nation's balance of payments accounts include all of the following EXCEPT
   a. current account.
   b. national defense account.
   c. capital account.
   d. official settlements account.

3. A debtor nation is a country that
   a. currently borrows more than it lends.
   b. currently lends more than it borrows.
   c. owes foreigners more than foreigners owe to it.
   d. owes foreigners less than foreigners owe to it.

4. If the U.S. exchange rate changes from 120 yen per dollar to 105 yen per dollar, the dollar has
   a. appreciated.
   b. depreciated.
   c. become a net borrower.
   d. become a net lender.

5. If the expected future value of the U.S. exchange rate rises, the demand for dollars _____ and the supply of dollars _____.
   a. increases; increases
   b. increases; decreases
   c. decreases; increases
   d. decreases; decreases

6. If the expected future value of the U.S. exchange rate rises, the current U.S. exchange rate _____.
   a. rises
   b. does not change
   c. falls
   d. probably changes but in an ambiguous direction

7. An increase in the U.S. interest rate differential _____ the demand for U.S. dollars and the U.S. exchange rate _____.
   a. increases; rises
   b. increases; falls
   c. decreases; rises
   d. decreases; falls

8. An increase in the current U.S. exchange rate
   a. shifts the supply curve of U.S. dollars rightward.
   b. does not shift the supply curve of U.S. dollars either rightward or leftward.
   c. shifts the supply curve of U.S. dollars leftward.
   d. probably shifts the supply curve of U.S. dollars, but without more information it is impossible to determine the direction.

9. $X - M$ equals
   a. $(T - G) + (S - I)$.
   b. $(T - G) - (S - I)$.
   c. $(G - T) + (S - I)$.
   d. $(G - T) + (I - S)$.

10. The idea of "equal value for different currencies" is captured by
    a. interest rate parity.
    b. appreciation of all currencies.
    c. purchasing power parity.
    d. None of the above.

The answers for this Chapter Quiz are on page 265

4 THE ECONOMY IN THE LONG RUN

Mid-Term Examination

■ **Chapter 7**

1. If unemployment compensation benefits are reduced in amount, then the opportunity cost of search for unemployed workers will _____ and the natural unemployment rate will _____.
   a. increase; increase
   b. increase; decrease
   c. decrease; decrease
   d. decrease; increase

2. Which of the following is an example of economic practices that leads to unemployment?
   a. Efficiency wages.
   b. Real wages.
   c. The downward sloping demand curve for labor.
   d. People not being in the labor force.

3. An increase in the supply of labor _____ employment and _____ potential GDP.
   a. does not change; increases
   b. increases; decreases
   c. increases; does not change
   d. increases; increases

4. The quantity of loans supplied exceeds the quantity of loans demanded if
   a. the real interest rate exceeds the equilibrium real interest rate.
   b. the real interest rate equals the equilibrium real interest rate.
   c. the real interest rate is less than the equilibrium real interest rate.
   d. savers' incomes exceed investors' incomes.

■ **Chapter 8**

5. An example of capital is
   a. land owned by IBM.
   b. a factory owned by IBM.
   c. 100 shares of stock in IBM.
   d. a $1000 bond issued by IBM.

6. If the amount of capital decreases, then generally
   a. labor productivity declines.
   b. long-term economic growth increases.
   c. labor productivity increases.
   d. potential GDP increases.

7. The one-third rule means that if capital per hour of labor increases by 6 percent and technological changes raise real GDP per hour of labor by 3 percent, then the total increase in real GDP per hour of labor equals
   a. 9 percent.
   b. 7 percent.
   c. 5 percent.
   d. 2 percent.

8. According to the new growth theory, firms are more likely to devote resources to research and development when
   a. the country is in recession.
   b. they expect to earn profits from successful R&D.
   c. it is easy to copy new techniques of other firms.
   d. the country has limited the amount of international trade it allows.

■ **Chapter 9**

9. If Daniel transfers $1,000 out of his checking account and places it in his savings account, instantly
   a. M1 and M2 fall.
   b. M1 falls and M2 rises.
   c. M1 and M2 rise.
   d. M1 falls and M2 does not change.

10. Suppose velocity is not growing and real GDP grows at 2 percent per year. The if the quantity of money grows 7 percent per year, the inflation rate equals
    a. 9 percent.
    b. 14 percent.
    c. 5 percent.
    d. 3.5 percent.

11. Which of the following is one of the Fed's policy tools?
    a. Open market operations.
    b. The tax rate on interest income.
    c. Transfer payments.
    d. The government's deficit or surplus.

12. If the currency drain ratio is 1.00 and the desired reserve ratio is 0.10, then the money multiplier equals
    a. banks' reserves and the money supply increase.
    b. 1.82.
    c. banks' reserves increase and the money supply decreases.
    d. banks' reserves and the money supply decrease.

■ **Chapter 10**

13. When selling exported goods, most often the seller wants
    a. gold.
    b. the currency of the seller's nation.
    c. the currency of the buyer's nation.
    d. bonds from the buyer's nation.

14. If a country has a current account surplus, that nation's quantity of foreign assets is
    a. increasing
    b. decreasing.
    c. not affected.
    d. zero.

15. The demand curve for U.S. dollars
    a. is vertical.
    b. is horizontal.
    c. is positively sloped.
    d. is negatively sloped.

16. If the interest rate on Japanese yen assets rises, then the supply of dollars _____ and the demand for dollars _____.
    a. increases; increases
    b. increases; decreases
    c. decreases; increases
    d. decreases; decreases

Answers

■ Mid-Term Exam Answers

1. b;   2. a;   3. d;   4. a;   5. b;   6. a;   7. c;   8. b;   9. d;   10. c;   11. a;   12 b;   13. b;   14. a;
15. d;   16. b;

11 AGGREGATE SUPPLY AND AGGREGATE DEMAND*

Key Concepts

■ The Macroeconomic Long Run and Short Run

The **macroeconomic long run** is a time frame that is sufficiently long for all prices (including the real wage rate and real interest rate) to have adjusted to achieve full equilibrium. The **macroeconomic short run** is a period during which some *money* prices are sticky so that real GDP might be below, above, or at potential GDP and the unemployment rate might be above, below, or at the natural unemployment rate.

The aggregate supply-aggregate demand model studies the behavior of real GDP and the price level in the short run. It also explains how the economy adjusts to its long-run equilibrium.

■ Aggregate Supply

Potential GDP is the quantity of real GDP at full employment. Over the business cycle, real GDP fluctuates around potential GDP. Aggregate supply is the relationship between the quantity of real GDP supplied and the price level. Aggregate supply depends on the time frame.

♦ The **long-run aggregate supply curve**, *LAS*, is the relationship between the price level and real GDP when real GDP equals potential GDP. The *LAS* curve is vertical, as illustrated in Figure 11.1. Along the *LAS* curve, both the prices of goods and services *and* the prices of productive resources change.

♦ The **short-run aggregate supply curve**, *SAS*, is the relationship between the quantity of real GDP supplied and the price level in the short run when the

* This chapter is Chapter 27 in *Economics*.

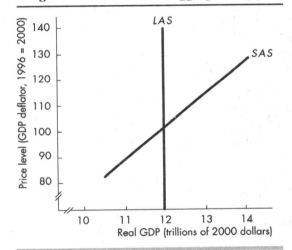

FIGURE **11.1**
Long-Run and Short-Run Aggregate Supply

money wage rate, the prices of other resources, and potential GDP remain constant. The *SAS* curve slopes upward, as illustrated in Figure 11.1. Moving along the *SAS* curve, only the price level changes; the money wage rate and other resource prices are constant.

When the *LAS* curve shifts, so does the *SAS* curve. Three factors shift the *LAS* curve:

♦ Changes in the full-employment quantity of labor.

♦ Changes in the quantity of capital, including human capital.

♦ Advances in technology.

Short-run aggregate supply changes and the *SAS* curve shifts when the money wage rate or money price of other resources changes.

♦ A rise in the money wage rate (or the money price of other factors) decreases short-run aggregate supply and shifts the *SAS* curve leftward. It does not shift the *LAS* curve.

♦ The money wage rate changes when unemployment differs from the natural rate and when expected inflation changes.

■ Aggregate Demand

The quantity of real GDP demanded equals the sum of real consumption expenditure (*C*), investment (*I*), government expenditure (*G*), and exports (*X*) minus imports (*M*).

Aggregate demand shows the relationship between the quantity of real GDP demanded and the price level. As illustrated in Figure 11.2 the aggregate demand curve, *AD*, slopes downward. It does so for two reasons:

♦ Wealth effect — A higher price level decreases the amount of *real* wealth (that is, the purchasing power of wealth), which decreases the quantity of real GDP demanded.

♦ Substitution effects — An increase in the price level raises the interest rate, which reduces the quantity of real GDP demanded. In addition, an increase in the U.S. price level raises the price of U.S. goods relative to foreign goods, which also reduces the quantity of U.S. real GDP demanded.

When aggregate demand increases, the *AD* curve shifts rightward. Three key factors shift the *AD* curve:

♦ Expectations — higher expected future incomes, higher expected inflation, or higher expected profits increase current aggregate demand.

♦ Fiscal policy and monetary policy — **Fiscal policy** is government attempts to influence the economy by changing taxes, transfer payments, and government purchases. An increase in government expenditures increases aggregate demand because government expenditures are one part of aggregate demand. Reduced taxes and increased transfer payments raise **disposable income** (aggregate income minus taxes plus transfer payments) and thereby increase consumption expenditure and hence aggregate demand. **Monetary policy** is changes in interest rates and the quantity of money. Increasing the quantity of money or lowering interest rates increases aggregate demand.

♦ World economy — a decline in the foreign exchange rate or an increase in foreign incomes increase net exports and hence aggregate demand.

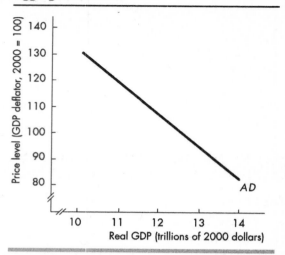

FIGURE 11.2
Aggregate Demand

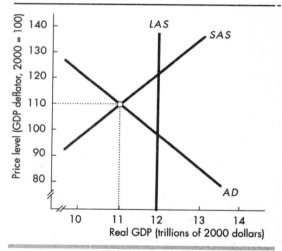

FIGURE 11.3
Macroeconomic Equilibrium

■ Macroeconomic Equilibrium

Short-run macroeconomic equilibrium occurs when the quantity of GDP demanded equals the quantity supplied, which is where the *AD* and *SAS* curves intersect. In Figure 11.3 the equilibrium real GDP is $11 trillion and the price level is 110. The price level adjusts to achieve equilibrium. Short-run equilibrium does not necessarily take place at full employment.

Long-run macroeconomic equilibrium occurs when real GDP equals potential GDP so that the economy is on the *LAS* curve.

Economic growth takes place when potential GDP increases. *Inflation* occurs when aggregate demand increases more than long-run aggregate supply. *Business cycles* result when aggregate demand and short-run aggregate supply do not grow at the same rate.

The **output gap** is the gap between real GDP and potential GDP.

♦ Figure 11.3 shows a **below full-employment equilibrium** in which potential GDP exceeds real GDP. A **recessionary gap** is the amount by which potential GDP exceeds real GDP ($1 trillion in the figure).

♦ A **full-employment equilibrium** occurs when real GDP equals potential GDP. In this case, the equilibrium occurs where the *AD* curve intersects the *SAS* curve at potential GDP.

♦ An **above full-employment equilibrium** occurs when real GDP exceeds potential GDP. The **inflationary gap** is the amount by which real GDP exceeds potential GDP.

The *AS/AD* framework illustrates how the economy responds to an increase in aggregate demand:

♦ In the short run, the *AD* curve shifts rightward and the equilibrium moves along the initial *SAS* curve. Real GDP increases and the price level rises.

♦ Eventually, the money wage rate rises to reflect the higher prices. The *SAS* curve shifts leftward, decreasing real GDP and further raising the price level.

♦ In the long run, the *SAS* curve shifts leftward enough so that real GDP returns to potential GDP. Further adjustments cease. Real GDP is at potential GDP, and the price level is permanently higher than before the increase in aggregate demand.

The *AD/AS* model also explains how the economy responds to a decrease in aggregate supply:

♦ The *SAS* curve shifts leftward, real GDP decreases and the price level rises. A period of time with combined recession and inflation is known as **stagflation**.

■ Macroeconomic Schools of Thought

Macroeconomists can be divided into three broad schools of thought, classical, Keynesian, and monetarist.

♦ **Classical** — a macroeconomist who believes that the economy is self-regulating and that it is always at full employment because the money wage is flexible and quickly adjusts to restore full employment. Real GDP always equals potential GDP. A **new classical** view is that business cycle fluctuations are the efficient responses to technological change. Classical economists think that taxes should be minimized to speed economic growth.

♦ **Keynesian** — a macroeconomist who believes that left alone, the economy would rarely operate at full employment and that to achieve full employment, active help from fiscal policy and monetary policy is needed. Aggregate demand fluctuations and sticky money wages lead to business cycle. A **new Keynesian** view holds that not only is the money wage rate sticky, but that prices of goods and services are also sticky. The Keynesian view is fiscal and monetary policy should be actively used to offset changes in aggregate demand.

♦ **Monetarist** — a macroeconomist who believes that the economy is self-regulating and that it will normally operate at full employment provided that monetary policy is not erratic and that the pace of money growth is kept steady. Changes in the quantity of money is the most significant source of aggregate demand fluctuations. Monetarists think that taxes should be kept low and quantity of money should grow at a steady pace.

Helpful Hints

1. **SHORT-RUN AND LONG-RUN AGGREGATE SUPPLY :** In the short run, the prices of resources do not change in response to change in the price level; in the long run, resource prices do change. This difference leads to the distinction between the short-run and the long-run aggregate supply curves.

   When the price level rises, in the short run resource prices do not change. Firms' profits increase because the prices of their outputs rise while the costs of their inputs do not change. They react by hiring more resources and supplying more real GDP, so the short-run aggregate supply curve slopes upward: As the price level rises, the quantity of real GDP supplied increases.

   In the long run, resource prices adjust by the same amount as the price level, which means that firms find their costs have risen by the same percentage as their revenue. These two effects offset each other, so firms do not change their supply as the price level rises. Hence the long-run aggregate supply curve is vertical.

Questions

■ True/False and Explain

Aggregate Supply

1. At full employment, there is no unemployment.

2. Along the *LAS* curve, a rise in the price level and all resource prices increase the aggregate quantity of goods and services supplied.

3. Along the *SAS* curve, a rise in the price level increases the aggregate quantity of goods and services supplied.

4. Both the long-run and short-run aggregate supply curves shift rightward when the quantity of capital increases.

5. Any factor that shifts the short-run aggregate supply curve also shifts the long-run aggregate supply curve.

Aggregate Demand

6. Aggregate demand equals consumption expenditure plus investment plus government purchases plus exports minus imports.

7. According to the wealth effect, the lower the quantity of real wealth, the larger will be the quantity of real GDP demanded.

8. The term "monetary policy" refers to the government's spending more money to purchase more goods and services.

Macroeconomic Equilibrium

9. Long-run macroeconomic equilibrium occurs when real GDP equals potential GDP.

10. In the short run, an increase in expected future profits raises the price level and increases real GDP.

11. The main forces generating persistent growth in real GDP are those that cause increases in long-run aggregate supply.

12. If the economy is in equilibrium at below full employment, there is a recessionary gap.

13. A rise in the money wage rate increases short-run aggregate supply, that is, shifts the short-run aggregate supply curve rightward.

14. If aggregate demand increases so there is an inflationary gap, then, with the passage of time, the money wage rate will rise in response to the higher price level.

15. If the aggregate demand curve shifts rightward by more than the short-run aggregate supply curve shifts rightward, the price level rises.

16. If the aggregate demand curve and the short-run aggregate supply curve both shift rightward at the same time, real GDP increases.

Macroeconomic Schools of Thought

17. All macroeconomic schools of thought agree that the economy is self-regulating and would operate at full employment if left alone.

■ Multiple Choice

Aggregate Supply

1. Long-run aggregate supply is the level of real GDP at which
   a. aggregate demand always equals short-run aggregate supply.
   b. full employment occurs.
   c. more than full employment occurs.
   d. prices are sure to rise

2. Along which curve do money wages and the price level change in the same proportion?
   a. Both the *SAS* and the *LAS* curves.
   b. Only the *SAS* curve.
   c. Only the *LAS* curve.
   d. Neither the *SAS* curve nor the *LAS* curve.

3. Long-run aggregate supply will increase for all the following reasons EXCEPT
   a. reduced money wages.
   b. increased human capital.
   c. introduction of new technology.
   d. increased capital.

4. A technological improvement shifts
   a. both the *SAS* and *LAS* curves rightward.
   b. both the *SAS* and *LAS* curves leftward.
   c. the *SAS* curve rightward, but it leaves the *LAS* unchanged.
   d. the *LAS* curve rightward, but it leaves the *SAS* curve unchanged.

5. An increase in the money wage rate shifts
   a. both the *SAS* and *LAS* curves rightward.
   b. both the *SAS* and *LAS* curves leftward.
   c. the *SAS* curve leftward, but leaves the *LAS* curve unchanged.
   d. the *LAS* curve rightward, but leaves the *SAS* curve unchanged.

Aggregate Demand

6. The aggregate demand curve (*AD*) illustrates that, as the price level falls,
   a. the quantity of real GDP demanded increases.
   b. the quantity of real GDP demanded decreases.
   c. the *AD* curve shifts rightward.
   d. the *AD* curve shifts leftward.

7. As the price level rises, the quantity of real wealth ____ and the aggregate quantity demanded ____.
   a. increases; increases
   b. increases; decreases
   c. decreases; increases
   d. decreases; decreases

8. Which of the following is classified as monetary policy?
   a. The government changing the amount of its purchases.
   b. The government changing its level of taxation.
   c. The government changing interest rates.
   d. The government financing a change in money wages.

9. Which of the following shifts the aggregate demand curve rightward?
   a. An increase in expected inflation.
   b. An increase in taxes.
   c. A fall in the price level.
   d. A rise in the price level.

Macroeconomic Equilibrium

10. Short-run macroeconomic equilibrium occurs at the level of GDP where the
    a. economy is at full employment.
    b. *AD* curve intersects the *SAS* curve.
    c. *SAS* curve intersects the *LAS* curve.
    d. *AD* curve intersects the *LAS* curve.

Use Table 11.1 for the next four questions.

TABLE 11.1

Multiple Choice Questions 11, 12, 13, 14

Price level	Aggregate demand (billions of 2000 dollars)	Short-run aggregate supply (billions of 2000 dollars)	Long-run aggregate supply (billions of 2000 dollars)
100	$800	$600	$600
110	700	700	600
120	600	800	600
130	500	900	600

11. In the short-run macroeconomic equilibrium, the price level is ____ and the level of real GDP is ____ billion.
    a. 100; $600
    b. 110; $700
    c. 120; $600
    d. 130; $600

12. In the short run, the economy is in
    a. a full-employment equilibrium and resource prices will not change.
    b. an above full-employment equilibrium and resource prices will rise.
    c. an above full-employment equilibrium and resource prices will fall.
    d. a below full-employment equilibrium and resource prices will fall.

13. In the short-run equilibrium, there is
    a. an inflationary gap of $100 billion.
    b. an inflationary gap of $50 billion.
    c. a recessionary gap of $50 billion.
    d. a recessionary gap of $100 billion.

14. Assuming no changes in aggregate demand or long-run aggregate supply, in the long-run macroeconomic equilibrium, the price level is ____ and the level of real GDP is ____ billion.
    a. 100; $600
    b. 110; $700
    c. 120; $600
    d. 130; $600

15. Persistent inflation is caused by
    a. persistent rightward shifts in the *AD* curve.
    b. persistent rightward shifts in the *SAS* curve.
    c. the tendency for long-run aggregate supply to increase faster than aggregate demand.
    d. persistent leftward shifts in the *SAS* and *AD* curves.

16. If real GDP is greater than potential real GDP, then the economy is
    a. not in macroeconomic equilibrium.
    b. in a full-employment equilibrium.
    c. in an above full-employment equilibrium.
    d. in a below full-employment equilibrium.

17. A below full-employment equilibrium can be the result of the
    a. *AD* curve shifting rightward.
    b. *SAS* curve shifting rightward.
    c. *LAS* curve shifting leftward.
    d. *AD* curve shifting leftward.

Use Figure 11.4 for the next four questions.

FIGURE 11.4
Multiple Choice Questions 18, 19, 20, 21

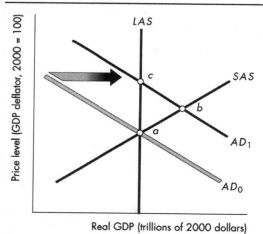

18. Which of the following factors might have shifted the aggregate demand curve rightward?
    a. Reduced taxes
    b. Less investment
    c. A decrease in government purchases
    d. Higher money wages

19. After the aggregate demand curve has shifted permanently to AD_1, the new short-run macroeconomic equilibrium is at point
    a. point *a*.
    b. point *b*.
    c. point *c*.
    d. No point identified with a letter in the figure.

20. When the economy in Figure 11.4 is moving to its long-run equilibrium, which curve shifts?
    a. The *LAS* curve shifts rightward.
    b. The *LAS* curve shifts leftward.
    c. The *SAS* curve shifts rightward.
    d. The *SAS* curve shifts leftward.

21. After the aggregate demand curve has shifted permanently to AD_1, the new long-run macroeconomic equilibrium will be at
    a. point *a*.
    b. point *b*.
    c. point *c*.
    d. No point identified with a letter in the figure.

Macroeconomic Schools of Thought

22. Which school of thought says that waves of pessimism or optimism (animal spirits) are the most important influence on aggregate demand?
    a. Keynesian school
    b. classical school
    c. monetarist school
    d. Both Keynesian and monetarist schools

23. Which school of thought believes that real GDP always equals potential GDP?
    a. Keynesian school
    b. classical school
    c. monetarist school
    d. Both classical and monetarist schools

24. Which school of thought believes that recessions are the result of inappropriate monetary policy?
    a. Keynesian school
    b. classical school
    c. monetarist school
    d. Both classical and monetarist schools

Short Answer Problems

1. Why is the *LAS* curve vertical?
2. Why does the *SAS* curve have a positive slope?
3. The international substitution effect implies that an increase in the price level will lead to a decrease in the aggregate quantity of goods and services demanded. Explain why.

FIGURE 11.5
Short Answer Problem 4

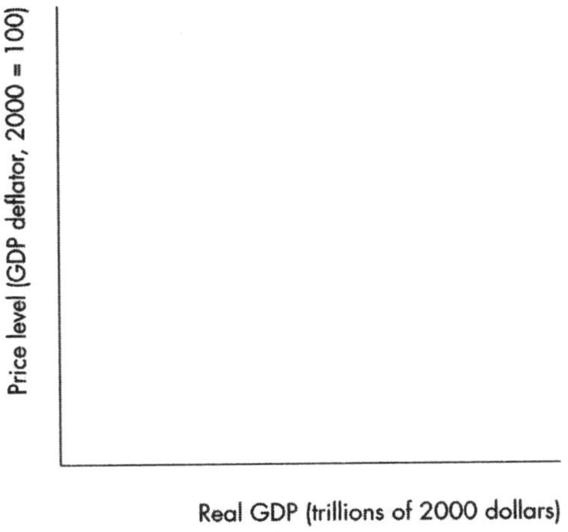

4. In Figure 11.5 illustrate an economy in long-run equilibrium, producing at the full-employment level of production. Indicate the equilibrium price level and level of real GDP. Also indicate the potential level of real GDP.

5. In Figure 11.6 illustrate an economy in short-run equilibrium producing at a below full-employment level of production. Indicate the equilibrium price level and level of real GDP and show the amount of the recessionary gap.

6. In Figure 11.7 illustrate an economy in short-run equilibrium producing at an above full-employment level of production. Indicate the equilibrium price level and level of real GDP and show the amount of the inflationary gap.

FIGURE 11.6
Short Answer Problem 5

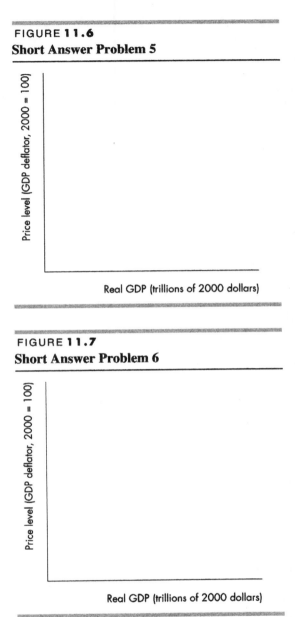

FIGURE 11.7
Short Answer Problem 6

FIGURE **11.8**
Problem 7

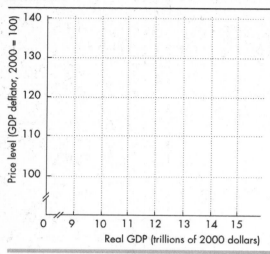

TABLE **11.2**

Short Answer Problem 7

Price level	Aggregate demand (trillions of 2000 dollars)	Short-run aggregate supply (trillions of 2000 dollars)	Long-run aggregate supply (trillions of 2000 dollars)
100	$13	$11	$12
110	12	12	12
120	11	13	12
130	10	14	12
140	9	15	12

7. Table 11.2 shows the initial aggregate demand, short-run, and long-run aggregate supply schedules for the nation of Macro.

a. Draw the *AD*, *SAS*, and *LAS* curves for Macro in Figure 11.8. Label the equilibrium point *a*. What is the equilibrium level of real GDP and price level?

b. Suppose that government purchases increase so that aggregate demand increases by $2 trillion at every price level. In Figure 11.8 draw the new aggregate demand curve. Label the new short run equilibrium point *b*. What is the equilibrium level of real GDP and price level in the short run?

c. Why is point *b* not a long-run equilibrium? In your answer, mention the level of potential real

GDP, and describe whether point *b* represents an above full-employment, a full-employment, or a below full-employment equilibrium. If either an inflationary or recessionary gap exists, calculate what it equals.

d. As time passes, what happens to move the economy back to its long-run equilibrium? Illustrate this process in Figure 11.8 by drawing any other curves you need. Label the long-run equilibrium point *c*. What is the equilibrium level of GDP and price level in the long run?

8. Suppose that the *AD* curve shifts rightward. In the long run, how does this shift affect the *SAS* curve? Why does the *SAS* change only in the long run?

FIGURE **11.9**

Short Answer Problem 9

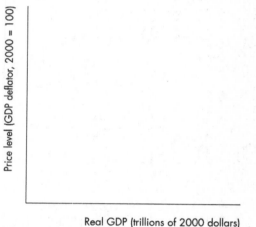

9. Suppose that new, productivity enhancing technologies are discovered. In Figure 11.9 show how these technological advances affect the equilibrium level of real GDP and the price level.

10. Keynesian economists generally believe that government fiscal and monetary policy is desirable. Classical economists generally disagree. What accounts for this difference in views?

You're the Teacher

1. "I've really tried, but I just don't see why a change in the price level doesn't shift the short-run aggregate supply curve. After all, it seems like when the price level falls, firms should decrease the amount they produce and that this should shift the *SAS*

curve. Plus, I'm a little shaky on how to use the *AS/AD* model. I sure hope the *AS/AD* model isn't too important so that I don't get hurt badly by not knowing this." In truth, your friend may be mortally wounded by not understanding the difference between a shift of a curve and a movement along a curve. Use an example in which the *AD* curve shifts leftward to help explain to your friend how to use the *AS/AD* model for the short run and also why a drop in the price level does not shift the *SAS* curve.

2. After you have helped overcome the previous problems, your friend offers an observation: "I think I'm catching on to this stuff now. And the diagram you just drew was really helpful. But, is that diagram the end of the story? Or does something else happen as more time passes?" Basically, your friend is asking you to complete the explanation you started by showing what happens in the long run. Doing so would help reinforce your friend's grasp of the *AS/AD* model. So, using another diagram, show what happens in the long run after an initial decrease in aggregate demand has occurred.

Answers

■ True/False Answers

Aggregate Supply

1. **F** Even at full employment, there is some unemployment, which is called the natural rate of unemployment.

2. **F** The *LAS* curve is vertical at the level of potential GDP. This fact indicates that the amount of potential GDP does not change when the price level *and* all resource prices rise.

3. **T** The *SAS* curve slopes upward, which means that an increase in the price level increases the quantity of real GDP supplied.

4. **T** An increase in the capital stock increases the nation's potential real GDP, thereby shifting both the *LAS* and *SAS* curves rightward.

5. **F** A change in money wages shifts the *SAS* curve, but does not shift the *LAS* curve. The *LAS* curve shifts *only* when potential GDP changes.

Aggregate Demand

6. **T** Any factor that changes consumption expenditure, investment, government purchases, exports, or imports will have an affect on aggregate demand.

7. **F** The lower the quantity of real wealth, the smaller is the quantity of real GDP demanded, which is a reason for the negative slope of the aggregate demand curve.

8. **F** Monetary policy refers to changes in the quantity of money or interest rates.

Macroeconomic Equilibrium

9. **T** At the long-run macroeconomic equilibrium, the economy is on its long-run aggregate supply curve.

10. **T** The increase in expected future profits shifts the *AD* curve rightward, thereby raising the price level and increasing real GDP.

11. **T** As the nation's potential real GDP grows, the long-run aggregate supply curve shifts rightward.

12. **T** The recessionary gap is the amount by which actual GDP falls short of potential GDP.

13. **F** An increase in money wages causes short-run aggregate supply to decrease (not increase),

which means the short-run aggregate supply curve shifts leftward (not rightward).

14. **T** If the economy is producing more than potential GDP, the amount of employment exceeds full employment. The tight labor market then puts upward pressure on money wages and money wages rise.

15. **T** As long as the shift of the *AD* curve exceeds that of the *SAS* curve, the price level rises. But if the shift of the *SAS* curve exceeds that of the *AD* curve, the price level falls.

16. **T** Both shifts increase real GDP.

U.S. Economic Growth, Inflation, and Cycles

17. **F** The Keynesian school asserts that the economy is not self-regulating and would rarely operate at full employment if left alone.

■ Multiple Choice Answers

Aggregate Supply

1. **b** Long-run aggregate supply is at potential GDP, which occurs when the economy is at full employment.

2. **c** Moving along the *LAS* curve, *both* money wages and the price level change in the same proportion. (Moving along the *SAS* curve, *only* the price level changes.)

3. **a** Along the *LAS* curve, both the price level and money wage rate change, so a change in the money wage rate does not shift the *LAS* curve.

4. **a** Any factor that shifts the *LAS* curve, such as technological advances, also shifts the *SAS* curve.

5. **c** The change in money wages shifts the *SAS* curve but not the *LAS* curve.

Aggregate Demand

6. **a** As the price level falls, a movement occurs along a stationary *AD* curve to a larger quantity of real GDP demanded.

7. **d** Real wealth equals the amount of wealth divided by the price level, so an increase in the price level decreases real wealth. In turn, this reduction decreases the quantity of real GDP demanded.

8. **c** Monetary policy includes changes in the quantity of money and interest rates.

9. **a** An increase in expected inflation causes people to increase their demand now in order to beat the higher prices expected in the future.

Macroeconomic Equilibrium

10. **b** The intersection of the *AD* and *SAS* curves always determines the equilibrium level of real GDP and price level. (In the long run, where the *AD* and *SAS* curves cross, the both also cross the *LAS* curve.)

11. **b** The equilibrium price level is 110 because that is the price level at which the quantity of real GDP demanded equals the (short-run) quantity supplied, $700 billion.

12. **b** Potential GDP is only $600 billion, so, with actual GDP greater than potential GDP, the economy is at an above full-employment equilibrium.

13. **a** The inflationary gap equals the difference between actual GDP ($700 billion) and potential real GDP ($600 billion).

14. **c** In long-run equilibrium, the price level is such that the aggregate quantity demanded equals potential real GDP. (In the long run, the *SAS* curve shifts so that it goes through the point where the *AD* and *LAS* curves cross.)

15. **a** As the *AD* curve shifts rightward, the price level rises, so persistent rightward shifts of the *AD* curve cause persistent increases in the price level; that is, cause inflation.

16. **c** Whenever real GDP exceeds potential GDP, the economy is in an above full-employment equilibrium.

17. **d** A leftward shift of the *AD* curve decreases real GDP and causes a below full-employment equilibrium.

18. **a** Lower taxes increase consumption expenditure, thereby shifting the aggregate demand curve rightward.

19. **b** The short-run equilibrium is where the *SAS* curve intersects the *AD* curve.

20. **d** At point *b*, real GDP exceeds potential GDP, so point *b* is an above full-employment equilibrium. Hence money wages rise and the *SAS* curve shifts leftward, moving the economy to its (new) long-run equilibrium.

21. **c** The long-run equilibrium occurs where the *LAS* curve crosses the *AD* curve. In the long run, the

SAS curve will have shifted so that it, too, goes through point *c*.

Macroeconomic Schools of Thought

22. **a** Keynesians believe that expectations based on herd instinct (animal spirits) are the major factor changing aggregate demand.

23. **b** Classical economists assert that the money age rate adjusts so that real GDP always equals potential GDP.

24. **c** Monetarists trace recessions to abrupt slowdowns in the growth rate of the quantity of money.

■ Answers to Short Answer Problems

1. Long-run aggregate supply is the level of real GDP supplied at full employment. Because this level of real GDP, potential GDP, is independent of the price level, the long-run aggregate supply curve is vertical. Potential real GDP is attained when prices of resources, such as the money wage rate, have had enough time to adjust so as to restore full employment in all resource markets.

2. The short-run aggregate supply curve has a positive slope because it holds prices of productive resources constant. Along this curve, when the price level rises, the prices of firms' output rises but the prices of their inputs (costs) remain unchanged. Firms increase their output because by so doing they can increase their profit. Hence, as firms increase their output, aggregate output (real GDP) increases.

3. International substitution means substituting domestically produced goods for foreign-produced ones or vice versa. If the price of domestic goods rises and foreign prices remain constant, domestic goods become relatively more expensive, and households buy fewer domestic and more foreign goods. This substitution decreases the demand for real (domestic) GDP. Thus a rise in the price level (the prices of domestic goods) leads to a decrease in the aggregate quantity of (domestic) goods and services demanded via the international price effect. Conversely, a fall in the price level leads to an increase in the aggregate quantity of domestic goods and services demanded.

FIGURE **11.10**
Short Answer Problem 4

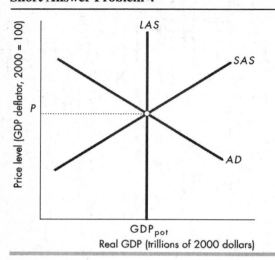

4. Figure 11.10 shows the economy in a long-run, full employment equilibrium. The equilibrium price level is P, and the equilibrium level of real GDP is GDP_{pot}. Potential real GDP also equals GDP_{pot}.

FIGURE **11.11**
Short Answer Problem 5

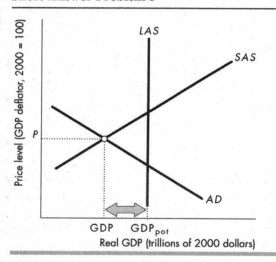

5. Figure 11.11 shows the economy when it is in a below full-employment equilibrium. The price level is P, and the level of real GDP is GDP. The recessionary gap is the difference between potential real GDP, GDP_{pot}, and the actual GDP, so it equals the length of the arrow in Figure 11.11.

FIGURE **11.12**
Short Answer Problem 6

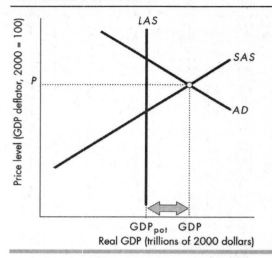

6. Figure 11.12 shows the economy in a short-run, above full-employment equilibrium. The equilibrium price level is P and the level of real GDP is GDP. The inflationary gap is the difference between actual GDP and potential real GDP, which is GDP_{pot}. The inflationary gap equals the length of the double-headed arrow in the figure.

FIGURE **11.13**
Problem 7 (a) and (b)

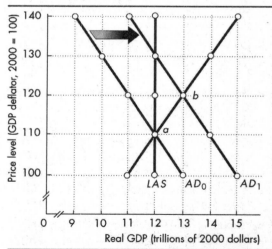

7. a. Figure 11.13 shows the initial aggregate demand curve (AD_0) the initial short-run aggregate supply curve (SAS_0), and the long-run aggregate

supply curve (*LAS*). Point *a* is the equilibrium point, where the aggregate demand curve crosses the short-run aggregate supply curve. This point also is a long-run equilibrium because it is on the *LAS* curve. The price level is 110 because this price level sets the aggregate quantity demanded equal to the aggregate quantity supplied. The level of real GDP is $12 trillion.

b. As illustrated in Figure 11.13, the increase in government purchases shifts the aggregate demand curve from AD_0 to AD_1. The new, short-run equilibrium point is labeled *b*. The price level rises to 120 and the level of real GDP increases to $13 trillion.

c. Point *b* cannot be the long-run equilibrium because the economy is producing more than the potential level of real GDP. The long-run *AS* curve shows the potential level of real GDP to be $12 trillion. Hence the situation illustrated by point *b* in Figure 11.13 is an above full-employ-ment equilibrium. The inflationary gap in Figure 11.13 equals $1 trillion, the difference between real GDP and potential real GDP.

FIGURE 11.14
Problem 7 (d)

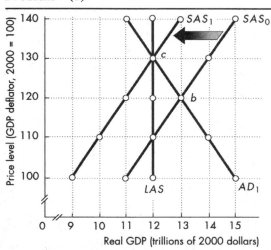

d. As the answer in part (c) just described, the short-run equilibrium at point *b* is an above full-employment equilibrium. Unemployment is below its natural rate. As a result of the tight conditions in the labor market (and other resource markets), money wages (and other resource

prices) rise. As money wages rise, the short-run aggregate supply curve shifts leftward. Figure 11.14 illustrates this process, whereby the short-run aggregate supply curve has shifted from SAS_0 to SAS_1. When the short-run aggregate supply curve is SAS_1 the economy has reached its new long-run equilibrium at point *c*. At point *c*, the price level is 130 and the level of real GDP has returned to potential real GDP, $12 trillion.

8. A rightward shift of the *AD* curve raises the price level. In the short run, the money wage rate does not change, but in the long run the money wage rate will rise to reflect the higher price level. Hence, in the long run, the increase in money wages shifts the *SAS* curve leftward. The curve does not shift in the short run because money wages do not respond immediately to higher prices. Initially, prices rise but money wages are constant. But then, over time, workers demand higher money wage rates to make up for the fact that they must pay higher prices for the goods and services they purchase. Thus in the long run, money wages rise along with prices.

FIGURE 11.15
Short Answer Problem 9

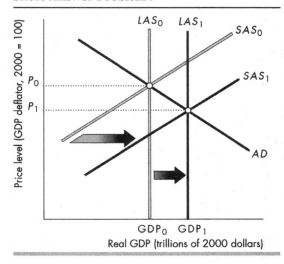

9. As Figure 11.15 shows, technological advances shift both the *LAS* and *SAS* curves rightward. However, the *AD* curve does not shift. As a result, the equilibrium price level falls from P_0 to P_1, and the level of real GDP increases, from GDP_0 to GDP_1.

10. Keynesian economists believe that the economy would rarely operate at full employment without

government fiscal and monetary policies to drive it there. Classical economists, however, believe that the economy is self-regulating and always operates at full employment. As a result, government fiscal and monetary policies are not needed to drive the economy to full employment because it is already there.

■ You're the Teacher

1. "Look, using the *AS/AD* model has to be important because a whole chapter's devoted to it and, when I flipped through the next chapters in the book, I saw *lots* of *AS/AD* figures. So, you've got to get this straight, or I won't be seeing you in class after a while.

"Here's the deal: A change in the price level does not shift the *AD* or the *AS* curves. Instead, the price level changes in response to a shift of the *AD* or *AS* curve.

"Let me give you an example to hammer this point home. I need to draw a figure — let's call it Figure 11.16. Now in Figure 11.16, the initial equilibrium is at point *a* because that's where the initial aggregate demand curve, AD_0, and short-run aggregate supply curve, SAS_0, intersect.

"Let's figure out what happens in our model when firms lose confidence in future profits. The drop in expected future profit from new investment leads to a decrease in aggregate demand, which means that the aggregate demand curve shifts leftward from AD_0 to AD_1.

"You can best understand what happens next by imagining that the curve AD_0 can be peeled off the page so that it no longer exists. I mean, this is reasonable because, after all, the factors that created it no longer exist! Now before any adjustments take place, this leaves us with the curves SAS_0 and AD_1, and with the price level of 100. At this price level, there is a surplus of goods and services: SAS_0 shows that the quantity of real GDP supplied is equal to $12 trillion, but the AD_1 curve shows that the quantity of real GDP demanded is only $10 trillion. Firms find their inventories piling up. In this case, they cut prices to try to sell the output, and the price level falls. Once the price level reaches 95, there is no longer a surplus of output and firms stop cutting their prices. This, then,

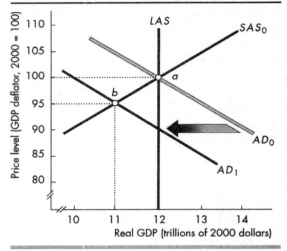

FIGURE **11.16**
You're the Teacher Question 1

is the new equilibrium, with a price level of 95 and a real GDP of $11 trillion.

"The key here is that the price level falls *because* the *AD* curve shifted. The fall in the price level did *not* shift the *AD* curve. In addition, the fall in the price level does not shift the *SAS* curve. If you want, you can think that we have moved along the SAS_0 curve from point *a* to point *b* (that is, from the old equilibrium point to the new equilibrium point), but the key thing is that the *SAS* curve has not shifted! After all, SAS_0 tells us that when the price level is 100, then $12 trillion of goods and services are supplied and when the price level is 95, then $11 trillion of goods and services are supplied. The slope of the *SAS* curve — and not a shift of the *SAS* curve — shows us that, when the price level falls, so, too, does the quantity of goods and services supplied."

2. "I'm really glad that you're starting to catch on because I like having a friend in class. Now that you understand what happens at the start, it won't be hard to see the rest of the story.

"You're right that what we called point *b* in Figure 11.16 can't be the end of the story. So far the only thing that has happened is that the price level has fallen and we've moved along SAS_0 to a lower level of real GDP. From the firms' standpoint, the prices of the things they sell have fallen, but their costs haven't changed. As a result, their profits are being squeezed. This is why they cut production. But, as they were cutting back on output, they were firing and laying off workers. Point *b* is a below full-employment equilibrium, with more unemployment than the natural rate. So workers start to accept lower wages and, in general, the prices of resources start to fall.

"Whenever we get to a below full-employment equilibrium, these sorts of adjustments occur. And as the prices of resources such as the money wage rate fall, firms find their profits starting to bounce back. As a result, they are willing to increase their supply of goods and services even if the price level doesn't change. For instance, even if the price level stays at 95, because their costs are falling, firms are willing to produce more than \$11 trillion of goods and services. To reflect this change, the *SAS* curve *shifts* rightward. As long as the money wage rate continues to fall, the *SAS* curve continues to shift rightward.

"Suppose that eventually the *SAS* curve has shifted from SAS_0 to SAS_1 in Figure 11.17. In this case, just like in Figure 11.16, where we pretended to erase the AD_0 curve once it was no longer relevant, in Figure 11.17 we can now pretend to erase the SAS_0 curve because the fall in the money wage rate makes SAS_1 the relevant curve. So Figure 11.17 shows us that the new equilibrium will occur at point *c*, where SAS_1 intersects AD_1. The price level is 90 and real GDP is \$12 trillion.

"The new level of real GDP is on the *LAS* curve; that is, the new equilibrium level of GDP is equal to potential real GDP. This situation is a full-employment equilibrium so unemployment is back at its natural rate, eliminating downward pressure on money wages. So money wages stop falling, which means that the *SAS* curve stops shifting rightward. As a result, point *c* is the new long-run equilibrium point. Compared to the initial point *a*, at point *c*, once all the adjustments are completed, we see that the price level is lower (90 versus 100), but that real GDP is the same (both are \$12 trillion)."

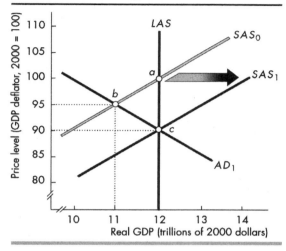

FIGURE **11.17**
You're the Teacher Question 2

Chapter Quiz

1. Which curve is vertical?
   a. The *AD* curve.
   b. The *SAS* curve.
   c. The *LAS* curve.
   d. None of the above.

2. The short-run aggregate supply curve shifts right-ward when
   a. the price level rises.
   b. the price level falls.
   c. the money wage rate rises.
   d. the level of potential GDP increases.

3. A change in the money wage rate
   a. shifts the *AD* curve.
   b. shifts the *SAS* curve.
   c. shifts the *LAS* curve.
   d. causes a movement along the *SAS* curve.

4. Short-run equilibrium is always at the point where the
   a *AD* curve crosses the *LAS* curve.
   b. *LAS* curve crosses the *SAS* curve.
   c. *AD* curve crosses the *SAS* curve.
   d. None of the above because the short-run equilib-rium point is always moving.

5. Aggregate demand increases when
   a. investment spending increases.
   b. government expenditure increases.
   c. net exports increase.
   d. All of the above increase aggregate demand.

6. Short-run aggregate supply increases. Hence the price level _____ and real GDP _____.
   a. rises; increases
   b. rises; decreases
   c. falls; increases
   d. falls; decreases

7. An inflationary gap occurs when
   a. GDP is below full-employment GDP.
   b. GDP equals full-employment GDP.
   c. GDP is above full-employment GDP.
   d. The *AD* curve shifts leftward.

8. Which of the following is <u>NOT</u> a reason why the aggregate demand curve slopes downward?
   a. Wealth effect.
   b. Intertemporal substitution effect.
   c. International substitution effect.
   d. Real wage effect.

9. In the short run, a temporary increase in oil prices _____ the price level and _____ real GDP.
   a. raises; increases
   b. raises; decreases
   c. lowers; increases
   d. lowers; decreases

10. Which of the following does <u>NOT</u> shift the aggre-gate demand curve?
    a. A decrease in the quantity of money.
    b. An increase in consumption expenditure.
    c. An increase in taxes.
    d. A rise in the price level.

The answers for this Chapter Quiz are on page 266

Chapter 12 EXPENDITURE MULTIPLIERS: THE KEYNESIAN MODEL*

■ Fixed Prices and Expenditure Plans

In the very short run, firms do not change their prices and they sell the amount that is demanded. As a result:

♦ The price level is fixed.

♦ GDP is determined by aggregate demand.

Aggregate planned expenditure is the sum of *planned* consumption expenditure, *planned* investment, *planned* government expenditure, and *planned* exports minus *planned* imports.

GDP and aggregate planned expenditures have a two-way link: An increase in real GDP increases aggregate planned expenditures, and an increase in aggregate expenditures increases real GDP.

Consumption expenditure, C, and saving, S, depend on disposable income (**disposable income**, YD, is income minus taxes plus transfer payments), the real interest rate, wealth, and expected future income.

The **consumption function** is the relationship between consumption expenditure and disposable income. Figure 12.1 illustrates a consumption function.

♦ The amount of consumption when disposable income is zero ($1 trillion in Figure 12.1) is called *autonomous consumption*. Consumption above this amount is called *induced consumption*.

♦ The **marginal propensity to consume** (*MPC*) is the fraction of a *change* in disposable income that is consumed, or $MPC = \dfrac{\Delta C}{\Delta YD}$ where Δ means "change in."

FIGURE 12.1
The Consumption Function

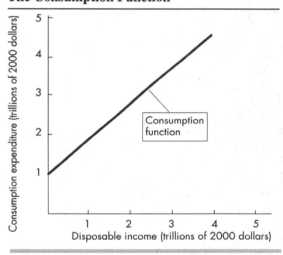

♦ The slope of the consumption function equals the *MPC*. The slope of the U.S. consumption function is about 0.9.

♦ Changes in the real interest rate, wealth, or expected future income shift the consumption function.

Consumption varies when real GDP changes because changes in real GDP change disposable income.

The **saving function** is the relationship between saving and disposable income. The **marginal propensity to save** (*MPS*) is the fraction of a change in disposable income that is saved, or $MPS = \dfrac{\Delta S}{\Delta YD}$.

The sum of the *MPC* plus *MPS* equals 1.

Domestic imports are determined in the short run mainly by U.S. GDP. The **marginal propensity to import** is the fraction of an increase in real GDP spent on imports.

■ Real GDP with a Fixed Price Level

FIGURE **12.2**

Aggregate Expenditure

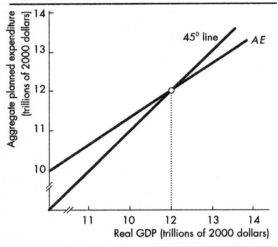

The aggregate expenditure schedule shows how aggregate planned expenditure depends on real GDP. The aggregate expenditure curve plots the aggregate expenditure schedule. Figure 12.2 illustrates an aggregate expenditure curve, $AE = C + I + G + NX$, where NX is exports minus imports.

♦ **Induced expenditure** is the sum of the components of aggregate expenditure,(consumption expenditure minus imports) that change with GDP.

♦ **Autonomous expenditure** is the sum of the components of aggregate expenditure that do not change when real GDP changes. In Figure 12.2 autonomous expenditure is $10 trillion.

Equilibrium expenditure is the level of aggregate expenditure that occurs when aggregate *planned* expenditure equals real GDP. In Figure 12.2 the equilibrium expenditure is the point at which the 45° line crosses the *AE* line, or $12 trillion.

♦ If real GDP exceeds equilibrium expenditure, unplanned inventories accumulate; if real GDP is less than equilibrium expenditure, inventories are drawn down in an unplanned manner.

■ The Multiplier

A change in autonomous expenditure creates an additional change in induced expenditure. The **multiplier** is the amount by which a change in autonomous expenditure is multiplied to determine the change in

equilibrium expenditure and real GDP. The multiplier is larger than 1.0 because a change in autonomous expenditure also changes induced expenditure.

♦ With no income taxes or imports, the multiplier equals $\frac{1}{(1-MPC)}$, or, equivalently, $\frac{1}{MPS}$.

♦ Income taxes and imports shrink the multiplier.

♦ Imports and income taxes reduce the slope of the *AE* curve. With them the multiplier equals
$$\frac{1}{(1 - \text{slope of the } AE \text{ curve})}.$$

♦ A business cycle expansion occurs when autonomous expenditure increases and the multiplier effect increases equilibrium expenditure; a business cycle recession occurs when autonomous expenditure decreases.

■ The Multiplier and the Price Level

The *aggregate expenditure curve* (*AE*) shows the relationship between aggregate planned expenditure and disposable income; the *aggregate demand curve* (*AD*) shows the relationship between the aggregate quantity of goods demanded and the price level. The *AD* curve is derived from the *AE* curve.

♦ An increase in the price level shifts the *AE* curve downward and equilibrium expenditure decreases.

FIGURE **12.3**

Increase in the Price Level and the *AE* Curve

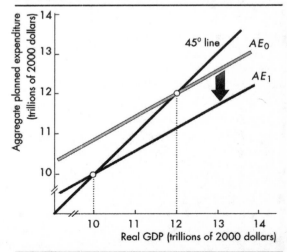

♦ Figure 12.3 illustrates this effect: When the price level rises from 130 to 170, the *AE* curve shifts from AE_0 to AE_1 and equilibrium expenditure decreases from \$12 to \$10 trillion.

♦ Figure 12.3 shows that, when the price level is 130, the aggregate quantity demanded is \$12 trillion and, when the price level is 170, the aggregate quantity demanded is \$10 trillion. These are two points on the AD curve in Figure 12.4.

FIGURE **12.4**
Increase in the Price Level and the AD Curve

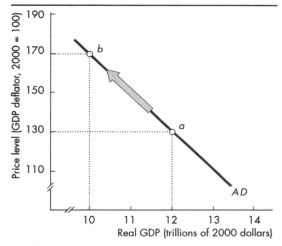

♦ An increase in the price level leads to a movement along the aggregate demand curve. Figure 12.4 shows how an increase in the price level from 130 to 170 lead to a movement along the AD curve from point *a* to point *b*. The AD curve does *not* shift in response to a change in the price level.

♦ The AD curve shifts when autonomous expenditure changes for any reason other than a change in the price level. For instance, a change in investment or government expenditure shifts the AD curve.

♦ The size of the shift in the AD curve equals the multiplier times the change in autonomous expenditure. Figure 12.5 shows this result, where the AD curve shifts rightward and the multiplied change in equilibrium expenditure is equal to the length of the double-headed arrow, \$2 trillion.

♦ The change in real GDP is less than the shift in the AD curve. In Figure 12.5 the shift in the AD curve is \$2 trillion. The increase in the price level reduces the increase in GDP; in the short run, real GDP in the figure increases by only \$1 trillion.

FIGURE **12.5**
Increase in Aggregate Demand

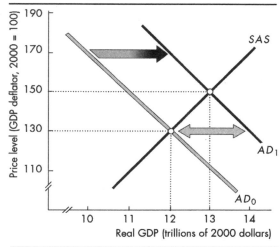

♦ In the long run, real GDP returns to potential real GDP and does not change as a result of a change in aggregate demand. In the long run, the multiplier is zero.

Helpful Hints

1. **AUTONOMOUS AND INDUCED EXPENDITURE :** Autonomous expenditure is independent of changes in real GDP, whereas induced expenditure varies as real GDP changes. In general, a change in autonomous expenditure creates a change in real GDP, which in turn creates a change in induced expenditure. The induced changes are at the heart of the multiplier effect.

2. **THE INTUITION OF THE MULTIPLIER :** The concept of the multiplier is very important. An initial increase in autonomous expenditure, such as invest-ment, increases real GDP directly, but that is not the end of the story. The initial increase in real GDP generates an increase in induced expenditure, which further increases real GDP and thus creates further increases in (induced) expenditure. Induced expenditure occurs because the increase in real GDP created by the increase in autonomous expenditure raises disposable income. For instance, an increase in investment purchases of computers raises the incomes of workers who are hired to manufacture the additional computers. Then, the

increase in disposable income increases these work-ers' (induced!) consumption expenditures.

3. **THE MULTIPLIER AND THE AGGREGATE SUPPLY CURVE :** The multiplier shows the change in equi-librium expenditure. So, if the multiplier is 5.0 and investment (a component of autonomous expendi-ture) increases by $10 billion, the equilibrium ex-penditure increases by $50 billion.

However, an increase in the equilibrium expendi-ture of $50 billion does not necessarily mean that equilibrium real GDP also increases by $50 billion. The change in equilibrium real GDP depends on the interaction of aggregate demand and aggregate supply. The $50 billion increase in equilibrium ex-penditure implies that the *AD* curve shifts right-ward by $50 billion, but this shift is one part of the picture. Depending on the aggregate supply curve, real GDP could increase by an amount close to $50 billion (if the *SAS* curve is relatively flat) or by an amount less than $50 billion (how much less de-pends on the steepness of the *SAS* curve).

Questions

■ True/False and Explain

Fixed Prices and Expenditure Plans

1. A change in disposable income shifts the consump-tion function.

2. The marginal propensity to consume equals con-sumption divided by disposable income.

3. The sum of the marginal propensity to consume and the marginal propensity to save equals 1.

Real GDP with a Fixed Price Level

4. When real GDP increases, induced expenditure increases along the *AE* curve.

5. Planned aggregate expenditure can be different than the actual aggregate expenditure.

6. Equilibrium expenditure occurs when aggregate planned expenditure equals real GDP.

7. When aggregate planned expenditure exceeds real GDP, inventories rise more than planned.

The Multiplier

8. An increase in autonomous expenditure leads to an induced increase in consumption expenditure.

9. With no taxes or imports, the multiplier equals
$$\frac{1}{(1 - MPS)}.$$

10. The larger the marginal propensity to consume, the smaller the multiplier.

11. If the slope of the *AE* curve is 0.8, the multiplier equals 5.0.

The Multiplier and the Price Level

12. An increase in investment shifts the *AE* curve up-ward and the *AD* curve rightward.

13. In the short run, an increase in investment expen-diture of $1 billion increases equilibrium GDP by more than $1 billion.

14. In the long run, an increase in investment expendi-ture of $1 billion increases equilibrium GDP by more than $1 billion.

■ Multiple Choice

Fixed Prices and Expenditure Plans

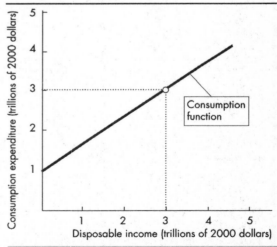

FIGURE **12.6**
Multiple Choice Question 1

1. What is the marginal propensity to consume, *MPC*, in Figure 12.6?
   a. 1.00.
   b. 0.90.
   c. 0.67.
   d. $3 trillion.

2. The fraction of a change in disposable income saved is called

a. the marginal propensity to consume.
b. the marginal propensity to save.
c. the marginal tax rate.
d. none of the above.

3. The *MPC* plus *MPS* equals

a. 1.
b. 0.
c. a number between 1 and 0.
d. a number not between 0 and 1.

4. Consumption expenditure increases when ___ increases.

a. the interest rate
b. the price level
c. real GDP
d. saving

5. Which of the following increases the amount a household saves?

a. A decrease in the household's current disposable income.
b. An increase in the household's expected future income.
c. An increase in the household's net taxes.
d. A decrease in the household's expected future income.

6. Which of the following shifts the consumption function downward?

a. An increase in current disposable income.
b. An increase in future expected income.
c. An increase in wealth.
d. A decrease in wealth.

7. An increase in expected future income ____ consumption expenditure and ____ saving.

a. increases; increases
b. increases; decreases
c. decreases; increases
d. decreases; decreases

Real GDP with a Fixed Price Level

8. The aggregate expenditure curve shows the relationship between aggregate planned expenditure and

a. government expenditure.
b. real GDP.
c. the interest rate.
d. the price level.

9. Autonomous expenditure is <u>NOT</u> influenced by

a. the interest rate.
b. taxes.
c. real GDP.
d. any variable.

10. If unplanned inventories rise, aggregate planned expenditure is

a. greater than real GDP and firms increase their output.
b. greater than real GDP and firms decrease their output.
c. less than real GDP and firms increase their output.
d. less than real GDP and firms decrease their output.

11. If aggregate planned expenditure exceeds real GDP, in the short run,

a. aggregate planned expenditure will increase.
b. real GDP will increase.
c. the price level will fall to restore equilibrium.
d. exports decrease to restore equilibrium.

The Multiplier

12. If investment increases by $200 and, in response, equilibrium expenditure increases by $800,

a. the multiplier is 0.25.
b. the multiplier is 4.0.
c. the slope of the *AE* curve is 0.25.
d. None of the above.

13. The multiplier equals

a. 1/(slope of *AE* curve).
b. $MPC/(1 - MPC)$.
c. $MPS/(MPC)$.
d. 1/(1 − slope of *AE* curve).

14. If the slope of the *AE* curve is 0.80, the multiplier equals
    a. 10.0.
    b. 5.0.
    c. 2.0.
    d. 0.5.

15. If the slope of the *AE* curve is 0.75 the multiplier equals
    a. 1.33.
    b. 1.50.
    c. 2.00.
    d. 4.00.

16. An increase in autonomous expenditure shifts the *AE* curve
    a. upward and leaves its slope unchanged.
    b. upward and makes it steeper.
    c. upward and makes it flatter.
    d. downward and makes it steeper.

17. An increase in income taxes ___ the magnitude of the multiplier.
    a. increase
    b. do not change
    c. decrease
    d. sometimes increase and sometimes decrease

18. A recession begins when
    a. the multiplier falls in value because the marginal propensity to consume has fallen in value.
    b. autonomous expenditure increases.
    c. autonomous expenditure decreases.
    d. the marginal propensity to consume rises in value, which boosts the magnitude of the multiplier.

The Multiplier and the Price Level

19. An increase in the price level shifts the *AE* curve ____ and ____ equilibrium expenditure.
    a. upward; increases
    b. upward; decreases
    c. downward; increases
    d. downward; decreases

20. A fall in the price level leads to
    a. a downward shift in the aggregate expenditure curve and a movement along the aggregate demand curve.
    b. an upward shift in the aggregate expenditure curve and a rightward shift in the aggregate demand curve.
    c. an upward shift in the aggregate expenditure curve and a movement along the aggregate demand curve.
    d. a movement along both the aggregate expenditure curve and the aggregate demand curve.

21. The multiplier is 2.0 and, owing to an increase in expected future profit, investment increases by $10 billion. The increase in investment and the multiplier result in the *AD* curve
    a. shifting rightward by exactly $20 billion.
    b. shifting rightward by more than $20 billion.
    c. shifting rightward by less than $20 billion.
    d. not shifting and the *SAS* curve shifting rightward by $20 billion.

22. The multiplier is 2.0 and, owing to an increase in expected future profit, firms increase their investment by $10 billion. As long as the *SAS* curve is not horizontal, in the short run, equilibrium real GDP will
    a. increase by $20 billion.
    b. increase by more than $20 billion.
    c. increase by less than $20 billion.
    d. be unaffected.

23. The multiplier is 2.0 and, owing to an increase in expected future profit, investment increases by $10 billion. If potential real GDP is unaffected, in the long run, equilibrium real GDP will
    a. increase by $20 billion.
    b. increase by more than $20 billion.
    c. increase by less than $20 billion.
    d. be unaffected.

24. Investment increases by $10 billion. In the short run, which of the following increases the effect of this change on equilibrium real GDP?
    a. A smaller value for the marginal propensity to consume.
    b. The presence of income taxes.
    c. A steeper short-run aggregate supply curve.
    d. A flatter short-run aggregate supply curve.

■ Short Answer Problems

1. Explain why the *MPC* plus the *MPS* sum to 1.
2. What is the difference between autonomous and induced expenditure?
3. Suppose that aggregate planned expenditure is greater than real GDP so that inventories are decreasing. If prices are sticky, explain the process by which equilibrium expenditure is achieved.

TABLE **12.1**

Aggregate Expenditure Components

Real GDP	Consumption expenditure	Investment	Government expenditure
0.5	0.2	0.3	0.2
1.0	0.6	0.3	0.2
1.5	1.0	0.3	0.2
2.0	1.4	0.3	0.2
2.5	1.8	0.3	0.2

4. Table 12.1 shows the components of aggregate expenditure in the nation of Woodstock. All quantities are in billions of 2000 dollars. Woodstock has no foreign trade and no taxes.

   a. Plot these components of aggregate expenditure in Figure 12.7. Label the lines.

TABLE **12.2**

Aggregate Expenditure

Real GDP (billions of 2000 dollars)	Aggregate expenditure (billions of 2000 dollars)
0.5	———
1.0	———
1.5	———
2.0	———
2.5	———

   b. Complete Table 12.2 to show aggregate expenditure in Woodstock.

   c. Use Table 12.2 and plot the aggregate expenditure line in Figure 12.7. Label it *AE*.

   d. Draw a 45° line in Figure 12.7. What is equilibrium expenditure in Woodstock?

   e. Use either Figure 12.7 or Table 12.1 to determine the equilibrium consumption expenditure, investment, and government purchases.

FIGURE **12.7**

Short Answer Problem 4

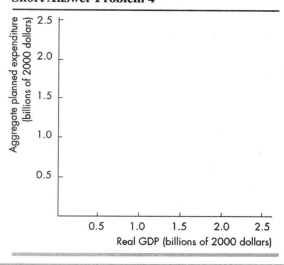

TABLE **12.3**

New Aggregate Expenditure Components

Real GDP	Consumption expenditure	Investment	Government expenditure
0.5	0.2	0.4	0.2
1.0	0.6	0.4	0.2
1.5	1.0	0.4	0.2
2.0	1.4	0.4	0.2
2.5	1.8	0.4	0.2

5. Continuing with the Woodstock nation, investment increases by $0.1 billion to $0.4 billion, as shown in Table 12.3.

   a. Taking into account the increase in investment, complete Table 12.4 to show aggregate expenditure in Woodstock.

TABLE **12.4**

New Aggregate Expenditure

Real GDP (billions of 2000 dollars)	Aggregate expenditure (billions of 2000 dollars)
0.5	———
1.0	———
1.5	———
2.0	———
2.5	———

b. What is the new equilibrium level of expenditure? What is the increase in equilibrium consumption expenditure? Equilibrium investment? Equilibrium government purchases?

c. Compared to problem 4, what is the increase in consumption expenditure? In investment? In government purchases?

d. What is Woodstock's multiplier? How does the fact that the multiplier exceeds 1.0 relate to your answers to part (c)?

6. Suppose there are no income taxes or imports. In this case, explain why the multiplier is larger if the marginal propensity to consume is larger.

TABLE **12.5**

The *MPC*, *MPS*, and Multiplier

MPC	MPS	Multiplier
0.9	____	____
0.8	____	____
0.7	____	____
0.6	____	____
0.5	____	____

7. a. Assuming there are no income taxes or imports, complete Table 12.5.

b. Based on Table 12.5, how does a decrease in the size of the *MPC* affect the multiplier?

8. The island nation of Wet has an aggregate expenditure curve with a slope of 0.75.

a. Investment increases by $20 billion. Before prices change, what is the change in equilibrium expenditure?

b. By how much and in what direction does the aggregate demand curve shift?

c. Suppose that instead of being 0.75, the slope of the *AE* curve is 0.90. With this higher slope, what is the change in equilibrium expenditure? The shift in the aggregate demand curve?

d. In the short run, prices rise. Without giving a precise numeric answer, what is the effect of the higher price level on the change in equilibrium

expenditure? The shift in the aggregate demand curve?

9. Briefly explain what the *AE* curve illustrates and how it is related to the *AD* curve.

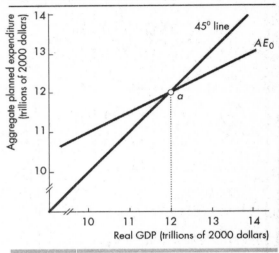

FIGURE **12.8**

Short Answer Problem 10 (a)

10. Figure 12.8 shows the aggregate expenditure curve when the price level is 110. When the price level rises to 120, the *AE* curve shifts vertically downward from AE_0 by $1 trillion. When the price level falls to 100, the *AE* curve shifts vertically upward from AE_0 by $1 trillion.

a. Draw two new *AE* curves in Figure 12.8 for the price levels of 100 and 120. What are the equilibrium levels of aggregate expenditure for these two price levels? Label as *b* the equilibrium point when the price level is 100 and as *c* the equilibrium when the price level is 120.

b. Use Figure 12.8 to obtain three points, *a*, *b*, and *c*, on the aggregate demand curve. Plot these three points in Figure 12.9 (on the next page). Assume that the aggregate demand curve is linear and draw the *AD* curve in Figure 12.9

FIGURE **12.9**

Short Answer Problem 10 (b)

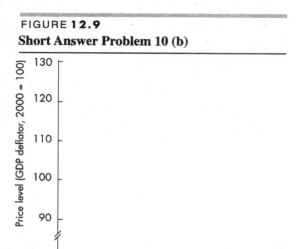

■ **You're the Teacher**

1. "I've got something of an idea about how the multiplier, *AD*, *SAS*, and *LAS* curves all fit together, but I know I'm still a little confused. Remember when I helped you in our other class? C'mon, don't you still owe me for that? Can you help me with this stuff?" Well, you actually might owe your friend some help. And, after all, your friend *is* asking you about a lot of material that is really important. So pay back your debt by explaining to your friend how these topics all fit together by using the example of an increase in investment. Explain how the shift in the *AD* curve is determined, what the short-run effects are on the price level and real GDP, and what the long-run effects are on the price level and real GDP.

Answers

■ True/False Answers

Fixed Prices and Expenditure Plans

1. **F** A change in disposable income creates a movement along the consumption function, not a shift in it.

2. **F** The marginal propensity to consume equals the *change* in consumption divided by the *change* in disposable income.

3. **T** Because $MPC + MPS = 1$, the formulas for the multiplier, $\dfrac{1}{(1 - MPC)}$ and $\dfrac{1}{MPS}$, are equivalent.

Real GDP with a Fixed Price Level

4. **T** The increase in GDP induces increases in aggregate expenditure. Indeed, that is why the AE curve has a positive slope.

5. **T** If the economy is not in equilibrium, actual aggregate expenditure is different from planned aggregate expenditure.

6. **T** The question gives the definition of equilibrium expenditure.

7. **F** When aggregate planned expenditure exceeds real GDP, inventories fall because more goods are being purchased than are being produced.

The Multiplier

8. **T** The question presents the essential reason why the multiplier is larger than 1 in value.

9. **F** With no taxes and imports, using the MPC, the multiplier is $\dfrac{1}{(1 - MPC)}$, while using the MPS, the multiplier is $\dfrac{1}{MPS}$.

10. **F** The larger the marginal propensity to consume, the larger is the change in consumption resulting from any change in disposable income, which causes the multiplier to be larger.

11. **T** When the slope of the AE curve is 0.8, the multiplier equals $1/(1 - 0.8)$, which is 5.0.

The Multiplier and the Price Level

12. **T** Any increase in autonomous expenditure *not* the result of a change in the price level shifts the AE curve upward and the AD curve rightward.

13. **T** An increase in investment creates a larger increase in GDP because of the multiplier.

14. **F** In the long run, the economy returns to potential GDP, so the long-run change in GDP is zero.

■ Multiple Choice Answers

Fixed Prices and Expenditure Plans

1. **c** The MPC is $(\Delta C)/(\Delta YD)$, which here is ($2 trillion)/($3 trillion) = 0.67.

2. **b** The question presents the definition of the marginal propensity to save.

3. **a** The fact that $MPC + MPS = 1.0$ means that knowing a value for one (say, the MPC) allows us to calculate the value of the other.

4. **c** An increase in real GDP induces increases in consumption expenditure.

5. **d** When people expect less income in the future than they did before, they respond by increasing their savings in order to (partially) make up for the newly recognized shortfall in future income.

6. **d** A decrease in wealth makes people poorer, so they decrease their consumption expenditure.

7. **b** As people perceive that their income will be higher in the future, they increase current spending and decrease current saving.

Real GDP with a Fixed Price Level

8. **b** The aggregate expenditure curve shows that, as real GDP increases, so does the quantity of planned expenditure.

9. **c** The definition of autonomous expenditure is expenditure that is not affected by changes in real GDP.

10. **d** If unplanned inventories rise, aggregate planned expenditure is less than production, that is, is less than GDP. In response to the unplanned rise in inventories, firms reduce their level of production and real GDP decreases.

11. **b** If aggregate planned expenditure exceeds real GDP (aggregate production), inventories decline. In response, to rebuild their inventories, firms increase their production and GDP increases.

The Multiplier

12. **b** The multiplier here is 4.0 because 4.0 is the amount by which the change in autonomous spending is multiplied to give the change in equilibrium expenditure.

13. **d** Answer (d) is the formula for the multiplier.

14. **b** The multiplier is $\dfrac{1}{(1 - \text{slope of } AE \text{ curve})}$, which means that the multiplier equals 5.0.

15. **d** Comparing the answer to this question with that for 14 shows that as the slope of the AE decreases in magnitude, so does the multiplier.

16. **a** An increase in autonomous expenditure shifts the AE curve upward; a decrease shifts it downward.

17. **c** Higher income taxes reduce the effect a change in real GDP has on disposable income and thereby reduce the magnitude of the induced change in consumption expenditure.

18. **c** When autonomous expenditure decreases, firms' inventories pile up, so firms decrease production and real GDP decreases.

The Multiplier and the Price Level

19. **d** An increase in the price level decreases consumption expenditure, thereby shifting the AE curve downward and hence decreasing the equilibrium level of expenditure.

20. **c** The change in the price level leads to a *shift* in the AE curve and a *movement along* the AD curve.

21. **a** The rightward shift in the AD curve equals the multiplied impact on equilibrium expenditure. In this case it is $(2.0) \times (\$10 \text{ billion}) = \$20$ billion, as illustrated in Figure 12.10 by the increase in the quantity of real GDP demanded from $50 billion to $70 billion.

22. **c** The AD curve shifts rightward by $20 billion but the SAS curve slopes upward. So in the short run, the increase in the equilibrium level of real GDP is less than $20 billion. Figure 12.10 illustrates this situation, where the $20 billion rightward shift in the AD curve creates only a $10 billion increase in equilibrium GDP.

23. **d** In the long run, real GDP returns to potential GDP without any long-run effect on real GDP. In Figure 12.10 in the long run real GDP returns to the potential GDP of $50 billion.

FIGURE 12.10
Multiple Choice Questions 21, 22, 23

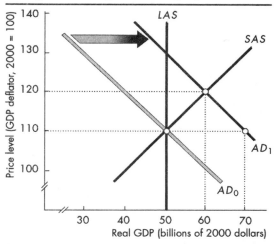

24. **d** The flatter the SAS curve, the less prices rise and the larger is the increase in equilibrium GDP and aggregate expenditure.

■ Answers to Short Answer Problems

1. Only two things can be done with a dollar change, say an increase, in disposable income: Spend it (all or part) or save it (all or part). The *MPC*, or marginal propensity to consume, indicates the fraction of the dollar change in disposable income that is spent on consumption, whereas the *MPS*, or marginal propensity to save, indicates the fraction of the dollar that is saved. Because consumption and saving are the only two uses to which the dollar can be put, the two fractions must sum to one.

2. Autonomous expenditure does not change when real GDP changes, whereas induced expenditure does change.

3. In the discussion of aggregate expenditure and equilibrium expenditure in this chapter, we assume that individual prices are fixed so that the price level is fixed. This "thought experiment" allows us to develop the economic model of the components of aggregate expenditure without worrying about the complication of price level changes. As a result, when we discuss how firms adjust to unwanted decreases in their inventories, we assume that firms respond by raising production, without prices changing. Hence when prices are fixed, equilibrium expenditure is attained by an increase in output.

FIGURE **12.11**

Short Answer Problem 4 (a) and (c)

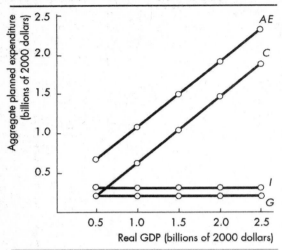

4. a. Figure 12.11 shows the consumption line, *C*, the investment line, *I*, and the government expenditure line, *G*.

TABLE **12.6**

Aggregate Expenditure

Real GDP (billions of 2000 dollars)	Aggregate expenditure (billions of 2000 dollars)
0.5	0.7
1.0	1.1
1.5	1.5
2.0	1.9
2.5	2.3

   b. Table 12.6 shows the schedule of aggregate expenditure. Aggregate expenditure equals the sum of consumption expenditure, investment, and government expenditure. When GDP is, say, $1.0 billion, aggregate expenditure equals $0.6 billion + $0.3 billion + $0.2 billion, or $1.1 billion.

   c. The aggregate expenditure curve, *AE*, is plotted in Figure 12.11. It is the vertical sum of the *C* + *I* + *G* curves in the figure.

FIGURE **12.12**

Short Answer Problem 4 (d)

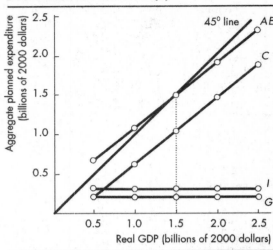

   d. Figure 12.12 shows the 45° line. The equilibrium level of expenditure equals $1.5 billion because the *AE* line crosses the 45° line at that point.

   e. In Figure 12.12 the dotted line indicating the equilibrium level of expenditure shows that the equilibrium level of consumption expenditure is $1.0 billion, the equilibrium level of investment is $0.3 billion, and the equilibrium level of government expenditure is $0.2 billion. Alternatively, in Table 12.1, the data in row 3, the row for which GDP is $1.5 billion, give the same answers for consumption expenditure, investment, and government expenditure.

TABLE **12.7**

New Aggregate Expenditure

Real GDP (billions of 2000 dollars)	Aggregate expenditure (billions of 2000 dollars)
0.5	0.8
1.0	1.2
1.5	1.6
2.0	2.0
2.5	2.4

5. a. Table 12.7 shows the new schedule of aggregate expenditure. These expenditures are obtained in the same way as those in Table 12.6 in problem 4: At each level of real GDP, add consumption

expenditure, investment, and government expenditure.

b. The new equilibrium expenditure is $2.0 billion because that level of aggregate expenditure equals real GDP. The equilibrium level of consumption is $1.4 billion; investment, $0.4 billion; and government expenditure, $0.2 billion.

c. Consumption expenditure increased by $0.4 billion, from $1.0 billion to $1.4 billion. Investment increased by $0.1 billion, from $0.3 billion to $0.4 billion. But government expenditure did not change.

d. The multiplier is 5.0: The $0.1 billion increase in investment created a $0.5 billion increase in aggregate expenditure. The $0.5 billion increase in aggregate expenditure can be divided into a $0.1 billion (autonomous) increase in investment and a $0.4 billion (induced) increase in consumption expenditure.

6. Any initial increase in autonomous expenditure generates a direct increase in equilibrium expenditure. The basic idea of the multiplier is that this initial increase in aggregate expenditure generates *further* increases in aggregate expenditure as increases in consumption expenditure are induced. In each round of the multiplier process, the increase in spending, and thus the further increase in aggregate expenditure, are determined by the marginal propensity to consume. Because a larger marginal propensity to consume means a larger increase in aggregate expenditure at each round, the total increase in equilibrium expenditure is greater. So, the multiplier is larger if the marginal propensity to consume is larger.

TABLE **12.8**

The *MPC*, *MPS*, and Multiplier

MPC	MPS	Multiplier
0.9	0.1	10.0
0.8	0.2	5.0
0.7	0.3	3.3
0.6	0.4	2.5
0.5	0.5	2.0

7. a. Table 12.8 completes Table 12.5. Because *MPC* + *MPS* = 1.0, *MPS* = 1.0 − *MPC*. For the first row, *MPS* = 1.0 − 0.9 = 0.1. The multipliers can be calculated using either of two equivalent formulas, multiplier $= \dfrac{1}{(1-MPC)} = \dfrac{1}{MPS}$.

b. As Table 12.8 shows, when the *MPC* falls in size, so too does the multiplier.

8. a. The multiplier formula $\dfrac{1}{(1-\text{slope of } AE \text{ curve})}$ shows that the multiplier in Wet is equal to $\dfrac{1}{(1-0.75)} = 4.0$. So the change in equilibrium expenditure is (4.0)($20 billion), or $80 billion.

b. The aggregate demand curve shifts by an amount equal to the change in equilibrium expenditure. Equilibrium expenditure increases by $80 billion, so the aggregate demand curve shifts rightward by $80 billion.

c. If the slope of the *AE* curve is 0.90, the multiplier is 10.0. Hence, in this case, equilibrium expenditure increases by (10.0)($20 billion) = $200 billion, and the aggregate demand curve shifts rightward by $200 billion.

d. When prices start to rise, the aggregate expenditure curve shifts downward. (The higher prices decrease consumption expenditure.) The downward shift in the aggregate expenditure curve reduces equilibrium expenditure. However, the aggregate demand curve does *not* shift. Instead, a movement occurs along the aggregate demand curve to a lower level of equilibrium real GDP.

9. The *AE* curve and the *AD* curve are quite different curves. The *AE* curve answers the question: For a given price level, how is equilibrium expenditure determined? When the price level rises, aggregate planned expenditure decreases so that the *AE* curve shifts downward and equilibrium expenditure decreases. Aggregate demand is different: It relates the quantity of real GDP demanded to differing values of the price level. In other words, the *AD* curve uses the results derived using the *AE* curve to show how equilibrium expenditure changes when the price level changes.

10. a. Figure 12.13 (on the next page) shows the aggregate expenditure curve for price levels of 100 (AE_1) and 120 (AE_2). The equilibrium points are *b* and *c*, and the equilibrium levels of expenditure are $14 trillion and $10 trillion, respectively.

FIGURE 12.13
The AE Curves

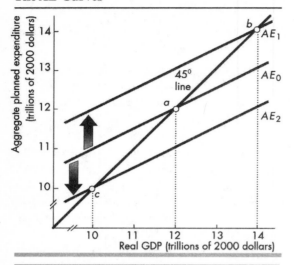

FIGURE 12.14
The AD Curve

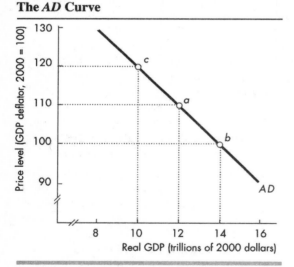

b. Figure 12.14 shows the three points on the *AD* curve. When the price level is 100, the aggregate quantity demanded is the equilibrium expenditure of $14 trillion (point *b*); when the price level is 110, the aggregate quantity demanded is the equilibrium expenditure of $12 trillion (point *a*); and when the price level is 120, the aggregate quantity demanded is $10 trillion (point *c*).

■ You're the Teacher

1. "Wow, you're asking about a lot of stuff. Are you sure that I owe you *that* much?

"Let's tackle your questions by thinking about the situation in which investment increases by $10 billion. Why did investment increase? I don't know; maybe because expectations of future profits increased; maybe because the interest rate dropped. Whatever the reason, though, it increased by $10 billion. Now, let's also say that the slope of the *AE* curve equals 0.67.

"The first thing we can do is to calculate the multiplier. We know that the multiplier equals

$$\frac{1}{(1 - \text{slope of } AE \text{ curve})},$$ so in this case we get

$$\frac{1}{(1 - 0.67)} = 3.0.$$ In other words, we know that the multiplier is 3.0 and that the $10 billion increase in investment leads to a (3.0)($10.0 billion) = $30.0 billion increase in equilibrium expenditure.

"Now I need to draw a figure; let's call it Figure 12.15. Check it out. Before investment increased, the economy was in equilibrium at point *a*. Here the initial aggregate demand curve, AD_0, crossed the short-run aggregate supply curve, SAS_0, and the long-run aggregate supply curve, *LAS*. The equilibrium price level was 110 and the level of real GDP was $60 billion.

FIGURE 12.15
Short-Run Increase in Aggregate Demand

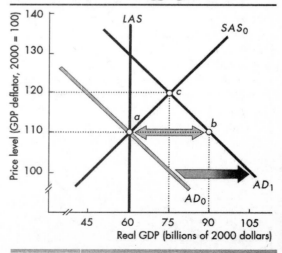

"Okay, now pay attention because here's where your questions start: The increase in investment shifts the *AD* curve rightward, and the size of the shift equals the change in equilibrium expenditure. In other words, the *AD* curve shifts rightward to AD_1, and the size of the shift equals $30 billion. The shift is the difference between point *b* and point *a* along the double headed arrow; this difference is $30 billion. So the *AD* curve shifts rightward by the multiplied impact on equilibrium expenditure.

"But a key point is that, in the short run, real GDP doesn't increase by all $30 billion. It would increase by the entire $30 billion only if prices did not change. But, in the short run, prices are going to start to change. And as they rise, people reduce their consumption expenditures, and the equilibrium amount of expenditure doesn't change by the entire $30 billion; it changes by something less. Figure 12.15 shows that the short-run equilibrium — where AD_1 crosses SAS_0— is at point *c*. And at point *c*, real GDP increases by (only) $15 billion, to $75 billion. Why don't we go to point *b*? Because, in the short run, the price level has increased, from 110 to 120.

"But, look, point *c* can't be the end of the story. At point *c*, the price level has increased, but money wages haven't changed. As more time passes, workers negotiate higher wages, which take into account the higher prices. And as money wage rates rise, the short-run aggregate supply curve shifts leftward.

"The final part of the story is illustrated in Figure 12.16. Here the *SAS* curve has shifted leftward and the new, long-run equilibrium point is *d*, where the *AD* curve crosses the *LAS* curve and the *SAS* curve, SAS_1. Thus at point *d*, we've returned to the long-run equilibrium because prices *and* money wages have both adjusted: Real GDP has returned to potential GDP ($60 billion) and the price level has increased to 130.

"I think Table 12.9 shows some results that can help you tie all these changes together. In it I've listed the four points shown in the figures I've drawn. Basically, we begin at point *a*. Then the increase in investment starts to move us to point *b*. If

prices are sticky long enough, the multiplier process will have time to complete itself and we'll get to point *b*. But in the short run, prices rise and so we move to point *c*, where prices but not money wages have changed. And then, from point *c*, money wages start to adjust and we eventually move from point *c* to point *d*, where both prices and money wages have risen. Point *d* is the final, long-run equilibrium.

"Look, your question required a really long answer, so how about you springing for the pizza the next time we buy some?"

FIGURE 12.16
Long-Run Increase in Aggregate Demand

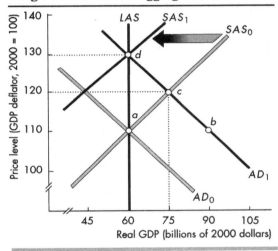

TABLE 12.9
Different Points

Point	Situation
a	Initial equilibrium
b	Price level constant, money wage constant
c	Price level increased, money wage constant
d	Price level increased, money wage increased

Chapter Quiz

1. Included in aggregate expenditure are
   a. consumption, saving, and government expenditure.
   b. consumption expenditure, investment, and government expenditure.
   c. investment, saving, and net exports.
   d. investment, government expenditure, and disposable income.

2. When the consumption function lies above the 45° line,
   a. saving is positive.
   b. saving is negative.
   c. consumption expenditure is negative.
   d. disposable income is negative.

3. Expenditure that depends on the level of income is
   a. actual expenditure.
   b. induced expenditure.
   c. autonomous expenditure.
   d. equilibrium expenditure.

4. If the MPS = 0.1 and there are no taxes and no imports, then the multiplier equals
   a. 10.0.
   b. 5.0.
   c. 1.0.
   d. None of the above.

5. If prices are fixed and the multiplier is 5, an increase in investment spending of $10 billion increases equilibrium expenditure by
   a. $50 billion.
   b. $10 billion.
   c. $5 billion.
   d. $2 billion.

6. If prices are fixed and the slope of the AE curve is 0.80, a $5 billion increase in investment increases equilibrium expenditure by
   a. $25 billion.
   b. $15 billion.
   c. $10 billion.
   d. None of the above.

7. A decrease in the price level
   a. shifts the AE curve upward.
   b. shifts the AE curve downward.
   c. does not shift the AE curve.
   d. perhaps shifts the AE curve depending on whether the MPC is greater than or less than the MPS.

8. An increase in investment spending shifts the AD curve _____ by a greater distance when the slope of the AE curve is _____.
   a. rightward; larger
   b. rightward; smaller
   c. leftward; larger
   d. leftward; smaller

9. In the long run, the multiplier
   a. is greater than 1.0 in value.
   b. equals 1.0 in value.
   c. is precisely twice the short-run multiplier.
   d. equals 0.

10. A change in _____ does not change autonomous expenditure.
    a. the price level.
    b. the interest rate.
    c. real GDP.
    d. any economic variable.

The answers for this Chapter Quiz are on page 266

Chapter 13 U.S. INFLATION, UNEMPLOYMENT, AND BUSINESS CYCLES *

Key Concepts

■ The Evolving U.S. Economy

Real GDP and the price level have changed dramatically over time in the U.S. economy. Both real GDP and the price level have grown over time.

♦ Sustained growth in real GDP results from growth in potential GDP, owing to increases in the labor force, capital stock, and advances in technology.

♦ Persistent inflation occurs when aggregate demand grows faster than long-run aggregate supply.

♦ Growth in real GDP is not steady but goes in cycles because aggregate demand and short-run aggregate supply do not increase at the same rate.

From 1960 to 1967, growth in real GDP was rapid and inflation was low. In the 1970s, inflation was generally high and growth in real GDP was slow. From 1983 to 1990, growth in real GDP was steady and inflation was moderate. After the 1991 recession, the economy expanded and inflation was low until the recession of 2001. Since then growth in real GDP was been somewhat slow and the inflation rate has remained moderate.

■ Inflation Cycles

An inflation that starts from an initial increase in aggregate demand is a **demand-pull inflation.**

♦ Figure 13.1 illustrates the start of a demand-pull inflation. The increase in aggregate demand raises the price level from 110 to 120.

♦ With no further increase in aggregate demand, eventually the money wage rate rises and short-run aggregate supply decreases. The price level rises to

FIGURE 13.1
Start of a Demand-Pull Inflation

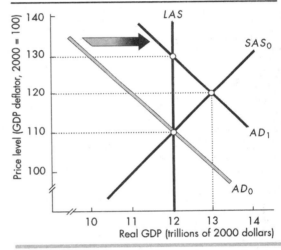

130 and then stops. This process is a one-time change in the price level.

♦ For the inflation to become established, the rightward shift in the AD curve needs to continue. Persistent Fed policy of increasing the quantity of money results in persistent rightward shifts in the AD curve. Monetary growth is necessary for a demand-pull inflation.

The United States experienced demand-pull inflation that started in the 1960s and lasted through the middle of the 1970s.

A **cost-push inflation** starts as the result of an increase in costs. Money wage rates and the cost of raw materials, such as oil, are the main sources of cost-push inflation.

♦ The cost hike decreases short-run aggregate supply, raising the price level and decreasing GDP. The combination of a rise in the price level and a decrease in real GDP is called **stagflation**.

♦ If nothing else changes, there is a one-time increase

in the price level. To create a persisting inflation, something else must change: The Fed must respond.

♦ If in response to the short-run decline in GDP, the Fed cuts the interest rate and increases the quantity of money, aggregate demand increases and the price level rises still higher.

♦ The rise in the price level created by the increase in aggregate demand invites another cost hike. If it occurs and aggregate demand increases again, a cost-push inflation is occurring.

The United States experienced cost-push inflation in the late 1970s when OPEC hiked the price of oil higher and the Fed initially responded with an expansionary monetary policy.

FIGURE 13.2
Expected Inflation

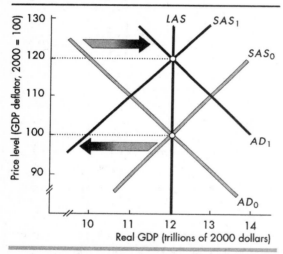

A **rational expectation** is a forecast based on all relevant information and it is the most accurate forecast possible. If people correctly expect an increase in aggregate demand, the money wage rate rises to reflect the higher price level. Figure 13.2 illustrates this case. The increase in aggregate demand to AD_1 is matched by a higher wage rate that decreases short-run aggregate supply to SAS_1. GDP remains equal to potential GDP and the expected inflation does not affect real GDP.

If aggregate demand increases more than people expect, unexpected inflation occurs and real GDP exceeds potential GDP. If aggregate demand increases less than expected, the decrease in short-run aggregate supply exceeds the increase in aggregate demand. As a result, real GDP is less than potential GDP.

■ Inflation and Unemployment: The Phillips Curve

A **Phillips curve** shows a relationship between the inflation rate and the unemployment rate. There is a short-run Phillips curve and a long-run Phillips curve.

The **short-run Phillips** curve shows the relationship between the inflation rate and the unemployment rate holding constant the expected inflation rate and natural unemployment rate. Moving along the short-run Phillips curve, the expected inflation rate and natural unemployment rate do not change.

FIGURE 13.3
Short-Run and Long-Run Phillips Curves

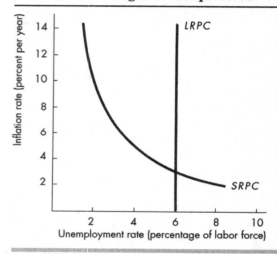

♦ Figure 13.3 shows a short-run Phillips curve, labeled *SRPC*. Along a short-run Phillips curve, higher inflation is associated with lower unemployment.

♦ The short-run Phillips curve is related to the short-run aggregate supply curve. A surprise increase in aggregate demand moves the economy upward along the *SAS* curve, leading to a higher price level — hence higher inflation — and an increase in real GDP — hence lower unemployment.

♦ A decrease in the expected inflation rate shifts the short-run Phillips curve downward by the amount of the decrease in expected inflation.

A **long-run Phillips curve** shows the relationship between the inflation rate and unemployment rate when the inflation rate equals the expected inflation rate.

♦ Figure 13.3 shows a long-run Phillips curve, labeled *LRPC*. It is vertical at the natural unemployment rate (6 percent in the figure).

♦ Both the short-run and long-run Phillips curves shift if the natural unemployment rate changes. For instance, if the natural unemployment rate increases by 1 percentage point, both the Phillips curves shift rightward by 1 percentage point.

In the United States, changes in the expected inflation rate and the natural unemployment rate have shifted the Phillips curves.

■ The Business Cycle

FIGURE **13.4**
Mainstream Business Cycle Theory

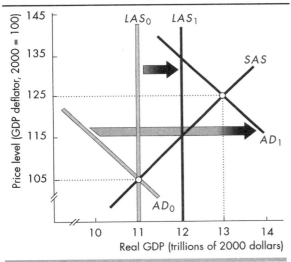

Mainstream business cycle theory concludes that the business cycle is the result of aggregate demand growth fluctuating around the steady growing potential GDP. Figure 13.4 illustrates the mainstream theory. (For simplicity, short-run aggregate supply remains constant.) Potential GDP has grown, so the long-run aggregate supply curve shifts from LAS_0 to LAS_1. Aggregate demand, however, has grown even more, from AD_0 to AD_1. As a result, the price level rises from 105 to 125 and real GDP increases from $11 billion to $13 billion. Real GDP is (temporarily) higher than potential GDP of $12 trillion. The economy is a strong expansion accompanied by higher than expected inflation.

The three mainstream business cycle theories differ in what they regard as the source of the fluctuations in aggregate demand and the role played by sticky money wages.

♦ The **Keynesian cycle theory** regards fluctuations in investment driven by fluctuations in business confidence as the main sources of fluctuations in aggregate demand. The money wage rate is sticky.

♦ The **monetarist cycle theory** sees fluctuations in consumption expenditure and investment driven by fluctuations in the growth rate of the quantity of money as the main sources of fluctuations in aggregate demand. The money wage rate is sticky.

♦ The **new classical cycle theory** says that the money wage rate and the position of the SAS curve are determined by a rational expectation of the price level, which is determined by the intersection of the AD curve and the LAS curve. Only unexpected fluctuations in aggregate demand bring fluctuations in real GDP.

♦ The **New Keynesian cycle theory** asserts that money wages are set at many past dates so the rational expectation of the price level at many past dates determines the SAS curve. Both currently expected and unexpected fluctuations aggregate demand bring fluctuations in real GDP.

The **real business cycle theory** (RBC theory) regards random fluctuations in productivity as the main source of economic fluctuations.

♦ The impulse in RBC theory is technological changes that affect the growth rate of productivity.

♦ The RBC mechanism is a change in productivity that affects investment demand and labor demand. During a recession, both decrease. The decrease in investment demand lowers the demand for loanable funds. As a result, the equilibrium quantity of loanable funds and investment decrease and the real interest rate falls. The fall in the real interest rate creates an *intertemporal substitution* effect that decreases the supply of labor. With both the demand and supply of labor decreasing, employment falls. The fall in employment and productivity decrease potential GDP so that the real GDP decreases and the economy is in a recession. Changes in the quantity of money have no effect on real GDP or employment.

Criticisms of the RBC theory are that:

♦ Money wages are sticky.

♦ The intertemporal substitution effect is too weak to account for large fluctuations in employment.

♦ Productivity shocks, as measured, are correlated with factors that change aggregate demand.

Defenses of the RBC theory are that:

♦ It explains both business cycles and economic growth.

♦ It is consistent with microeconomic data concerning labor supply, labor demand, and investment demand.

Helpful Hints

1. **LINKS BETWEEN AGGREGATE SUPPLY AND THE PHILLIPS CURVE :** The Phillips curve and the *AS/AD* model are closely linked. Consider an unexpected increase in aggregate demand. In the short run, a movement occurs along the *SAS* curve. The price level rises, and real GDP increases above potential GDP. The rise in the price level means that inflation occurs, and the increase in GDP means that the unemployment rate falls. Hence the unexpected increase in aggregate demand has resulted in a movement along the short-run Phillips curve, with higher inflation and unemployment falling to below its natural rate.

GDP, in the long run, cannot remain greater than potential GDP. Tight conditions in the labor market (and other resource markets) result in the money wage rate (and other resource prices) rising to reflect the higher price level. So, in the *AS/AD* model, the rise in the money wage rate shifts the *SAS* curve leftward. Real GDP returns to the vertical *LAS* curve and equals potential GDP.

In terms of the Phillips curve, the unemployment rate cannot remain below its natural rate. Therefore as inflation continues and people come to expect it, the higher inflation rates are built into money wages (and the prices of other resources). The short-run Phillips curve shifts upward as people revise the amount of inflation they expect. The unemployment rate returns to the vertical long-run Phillips curve and equals the natural rate.

There are strong links between the *AS/AD* model and the Phillips curve. In the short run, the increase in real GDP is associated with a drop in unemployment. In the long run, as real GDP returns to potential GDP in the *AS/AD* model, unemployment similarly returns to the natural rate in the Phillips curve model.

Questions

■ True/False and Explain

The Evolving U.S. Economy

1. Since 1960, there have been about as many years during which the price level rose as years during which the price level rose.

Inflation Cycles

2. Demand-pull inflation starts with an increase in aggregate demand.

3. An inflation that starts with an expansionary monetary policy is a cost-push inflation.

4. Cost-push inflation results in stagflation.

5. By itself, a one-time increase in the price of oil creates an ongoing inflation.

6. If an increase in aggregate demand is anticipated correctly, inflation will not occur.

Inflation and Unemployment: The Phillips Curve

7. The short-run Phillips curve shows that, if the inflation rate rises and the expected inflation rate does not change, the unemployment rate falls.

8. The long-run Phillips curve shows that higher inflation lowers unemployment.

9. An increase in the expected inflation rate shifts the short-run Phillips curve upward and the long-run Phillips curve rightward.

10. Changes in the natural unemployment rate shift both the short-run and the long-run Phillips curves.

11. Data for the United States show that the short-run Phillips curve has not shifted during the last three decades.

The Business Cycle

12. The mainstream business cycle theories assert that fluctuations in aggregate demand growth are the source of business cycles.

13. The factor driving the business cycle in the Keynesian theory of business cycles are changes in business confidence.

14. According to the new classical cycle theory, an expected decrease in aggregate demand leads to a recession.

15. The new Keynesian theory of the business cycle stresses intertemporal substitution.

16. According to the real business cycle theory, the source of a recession is a slowdown in the growth rate of the quantity of money.

■ Multiple Choice

The Evolving U.S. Economy

1. For the U.S. economy,
   a. business cycles are no longer a problem because the last complete business cycle occurred in the 1970s.
   b. since 1960, the highest growth rate of real GDP has been achieved after the end of the 2001 recession.
   c. both real GDP and the price level have risen since 1960.
   d. inflation peaked in the 1960s and has generally fallen since then.

Inflation Cycles

2. Demand-pull inflation occurs when
   a. aggregate demand increases persistently.
   b. aggregate supply and aggregate demand decrease persistently.
   c. the government increases its purchases.
   d. oil prices increase substantially.

3. In a demand-pull inflation, the *AD* curve shifts _____ and the *SAS* curve shifts _____.
   a. rightward; rightward
   b. rightward; leftward
   c. leftward; rightward
   d. leftward; leftward

4. Which of the following shifts the aggregate demand curve rightward year after year?
   a. A one-time tax cut.
   b. A one-time increase in government purchases of goods and services.
   c. Inflation.
   d. Growth in the quantity of money.

5. Cost-push inflation might start with
   a. a rise in money wage rates.
   b. an increase in government purchases.
   c. an increase in the quantity of money.
   d. a fall in the prices of raw materials.

6. A rise in the price level owing to an increase in the price of oil
   a. definitely triggers a cost-push inflation.
   b. definitely triggers a demand-pull inflation.
   c. might trigger a cost-push inflation.
   d. might trigger a demand-pull inflation.

7. Which of the following statements about a cost-push inflation is correct?
   a. Cost-push inflation starts when an increase in aggregate demand "pushes" costs higher.
   b. Cost-push inflation might start with a rise in the price of raw materials, but it requires increases in the quantity of money to persist.
   c. To persist, cost-push inflation needs a continual series of cost hikes with no change in aggregate demand.
   d. The United States has never experienced a cost-push inflation.

8. Once a cost-push inflation is underway, the *AD* curve shifts _____ and the *SAS* curve shifts _____.
   a. rightward; rightward
   b. rightward; leftward
   c. leftward; rightward
   d. leftward; leftward

9. A correctly expected increase in aggregate demand that causes a correctly expected increase in inflation leads to _____ in short-run aggregate supply and ___ in real GDP.
   a. an increase; an increase
   b. a decrease; an increase
   c. a decrease; no change
   d. a decrease; a decrease

10. If the aggregate demand curve shifts rightward less than expected,
    a. expectations could not be rational expectations.
    b. real GDP will be less than potential GDP.
    c. the real interest rate will be lower than expected.
    d. the real wage rate will be lower than expected.

Inflation and Unemployment: The Phillips Curve

11. The short-run Phillips curve shows the relationship between
    a. the price level and real GDP in the short run.
    b. the price level and unemployment in the short run.
    c. inflation and unemployment when expected inflation equals the actual inflation.
    d. inflation and unemployment when expected inflation does not change.

12. The long-run Phillips curve shows the relationship between
    a. the price level and real GDP in the long run.
    b. the price level and unemployment in the long run.
    c. inflation and unemployment when expected inflation equals the actual inflation.
    d. inflation and unemployment when expected inflation does not change.

Use Figure 13.5 for the next four questions.

FIGURE **13.5**
Multiple Choice Questions 13, 14, 15, 16

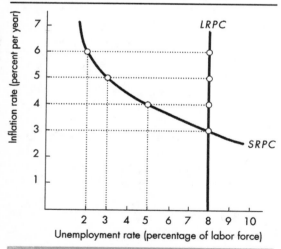

13. In the above figure, what is the natural unemployment rate?
    a. 2 percent.
    b. 3 percent.
    c. 5 percent.
    d. 8 percent.

14. Based on Figure 13.5, what is the expected inflation rate?
    a. 3 percent.
    b. 4 percent.
    c. 5 percent.
    d. 6 percent.

15. If people's expected inflation rate does not change, for an inflation rate of 5 percent, what is the short-run unemployment rate?
    a. 2 percent.
    b. 3 percent.
    c. 5 percent.
    d. 8 percent.

16. After people's expected inflation rate completely adjusts, for an inflation rate of 5 percent, what is the long-run unemployment rate?
    a. 2 percent.
    b. 3 percent.
    c. 5 percent.
    d. 8 percent.

17. A rise in the expected inflation rate leads to ____ in the long-run Phillips curve and ____ in the short-run Phillips curve.
    a. an upward shift; no shift
    b. a leftward shift; an upward shift
    c. no shift; no shift
    d. no shift; an upward shift

18. A rise in the natural unemployment rate leads to a ____ in the long-run Phillips curve and ____ in the short-run Phillips curve.
    a. rightward shift; no shift
    b. leftward shift; a rightward shift
    c. rightward shift; a rightward shift
    d. leftward shift; a leftward shift

The Business Cycle

19. The mainstream business cycle theories all assert that the main factor leading to business cycles is fluctuations in the growth of
    a. aggregate demand.
    b. short-run aggregate supply.
    c. long-run aggregate supply.
    d. expectations.

20. In the monetarist cycle theory, business cycles are the result of fluctuations in
    a. productivity.
    b. businesses' animal spirits.
    c. expectations
    d. the quantity of money

21. According to the new classical cycle theory and the new Keynesian cycle theory, if the Federal Reserve unexpectedly hikes the interest rate and so decreases the quantity of money during a recession,
    a. nothing will happen because the recession is already occurring.
    b. the recession will tend to deepen, as aggregate demand unexpectedly decreases.
    c. the recession will tend to end because aggregate supply unexpectedly increases.
    d. the recession will tend to end because aggregate demand unexpectedly increases.

22. Which of the following is the impulse in the real business cycle theory?
    a. An unexpected change in aggregate demand.
    b. A change by the Fed in the growth rate of the quantity of money.
    c. A change in expectations about future sales and profits.
    d. A change in the growth rate of productivity.

23. The intertemporal substitution effect refers to the idea that
    a. a higher real wage rate increases the quantity of labor supplied.
    b. a higher real wage rate decreases the quantity of labor supplied.
    c. a higher real interest rate increases the supply of labor.
    d. the demand for labor depends on the money wage rate, not the real wage rate although the supply of labor depends on the real wage rate.

24. According to the _____ theory of business cycles, a change in the monetary growth rate has no effect on real GDP.
    a. Keynesian
    b. monetarist
    c. new Keynesian
    d. real business cycle

◼ Short Answer Problems

1. People do not expect the price level to change when the Fed unexpectedly cuts the interest rate so that the quantity of money unexpectedly increases. What is the effect on the price level and real GDP? Be sure to tell what happens to the aggregate demand curve and short-run aggregate supply curve.

2. Explain how the events in problem 1 could lead to a demand-pull inflation spiral.

3. Explain the differences between the short-run Phillips curve and the long-run Phillips curve.

TABLE **13.1**

Phillips Curve

Inflation rate (percent per year)	Unemployment rate (percent of labor force)
3	7
4	6
5	5
6	4

FIGURE **13.6**

Phillips Curves

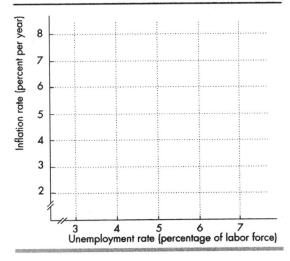

4. Table 13.1 shows the Phillips curve when the expected inflation rate is 4 percent. The natural unemployment rate is 6 percent, and the actual inflation rate is 4 percent.
   a. In Figure 13.6, draw the short-run Phillips curve (label it $SRPC_0$) and the long-run Phillips curve (label it $LRPC$).

b. Suppose that the inflation rate rises to 6 percent and, immediately after the increase, the expected inflation rate does not change. What is the unemployment rate?

5. Continuing with the situation in part (b) of problem 4, when the inflation rate rises to 6 percent, suppose that after a year the expected inflation rate rises to 5 percent.

   a. In Figure 13.6, draw the new short-run Phillips curve that results from the change in the expected inflation rate. Label this Phillips curve $SRPC_1$.

   b. If the inflation rate remains at 6 percent, after inflation expectations have increased to 5 percent, what is the unemployment rate?

6. Continuing with the situation in Problem 4, suppose that, two years after the inflation rate increased to 6 percent, expected inflation rises to 6 percent.

   a. In Figure 13.6, draw the new short-run Phillips curve that results from the change in the expected inflation rate to 6 percent. Label this Phillips curve $SRPC_2$.

   b. If the inflation rate remains at 6 percent, after the expected inflation rate has increased to 6 percent, what is the unemployment rate?

TABLE **13.2**

Theories and Fluctuation Sources

Theory	Source
Keynesian	
Monetarist	
New classical	
New Keynesian	
Real business cycle	

7. Complete Table 13.2 by listing the impulse that each theory stresses as the primary cause of economic fluctuations.

8. Suppose that aggregate demand increases so that the *AD* curve shifts rightward.

   a. According to the Keynesian cycle theory, what factor is the most likely cause of the increase in aggregate demand? What is the effect on real GDP and the price level?

   b. According to the monetarist cycle theory, what factor is the most likely cause of the increase in aggregate demand? What is the effect on real GDP and the price level?

   c. According to the new classical cycle theory, what is the effect on real GDP and employment if the increase in aggregate demand was expected? If the increase was unexpected?

   d. According to the new Keynesian cycle theory, what is the effect on real GDP and employment if the increase in aggregate demand was expected? If the increase was unexpected?

   e. According to the real business cycle theory, what is the effect on real GDP and employment of the increase in aggregate demand?

■ **You're the Teacher**

1. "Even before I read this chapter, I thought that business cycles were important. But one thing that I just can't understand is why economists can't figure out which theory of business cycles is correct. That's so important, I'd have thought they would know which theory is right! Are economists stupid or what?" Your friend has a rather jaundiced view of economists' intelligence. You would certainly like to set your friend straight about how bright economists are by explaining why the cause(s) of business cycles aren't totally known.

Answers

■ True/False Answers

The Evolving U.S. Economy

1. **F** During *each* year after 1960 the price level has risen so that the inflation rate has been positive.

Inflation Cycles

2. **T** With the initial increase in aggregate demand, the price level starts to rise.

3. **F** An increase in the monetary growth rate increases aggregate demand and results in demand-pull inflation.

4. **T** When the short-run aggregate supply decreases, stagflation occurs.

5. **F** Unless the Fed increases the quantity of money, a one-time increase in the price of oil creates a one-time increase in the price level.

6. **F** If the increase in aggregate demand is expected, real GDP does not change. The price level, however, rises so inflation occurs.

Inflation and Unemployment: The Phillips Curve

7. **T** Along the short-run Phillips curve, higher inflation rates lower the unemployment rate.

8. **F** The long-run Phillips curve is vertical, indicating that in the long run higher inflation does not lower unemployment.

9. **F** The increase in expected inflation shifts the short-run Phillips curve upward but does not shift the long-run Phillips curve.

10. **T** If the natural unemployment rate increases, *both* the short-run and long-run Phillips curves shift rightward; if the natural unemployment rate decreases, both curves shift leftward.

11. **F** Data show several shifts in the Phillips curve because of changes in the expected inflation rate and in the natural rate of unemployment.

The Business Cycle

12. **T** While they differ in their details, all the mainstream theories focus on fluctuations in aggregate demand growth as the factor that leads to business cycles.

13. **T** Because businesses' confidence about the future can change so rapidly, Keynes said that it was subject to "animal spirits."

14. **F** A decrease in aggregate demand leads to a recession only if it is unexpected.

15. **F** The real business cycle theory stresses intertemporal substitution.

16. **F** Monetarists assign importance to a slowdown in the growth rate of the quantity of money. Real business cycle economists assert that changes in the quantity of money do not create business cycle fluctuations.

■ Multiple Choice Answers

The Evolving U.S. Economy

1. **c** Real GDP has risen because the U.S. economy has experienced economic growth; the price level has risen because the U.S. economy also has experienced inflation.

Inflation Cycles

2. **a** Demand-pull inflation results when the demand for goods increases, thereby "pulling up" the price level.

3. **b** Aggregate demand increases, which raises the price level. Hence money wages rise and short-run aggregate supply decreases.

4. **d** Growth in the quantity of money means that the quantity of money in the economy continually increases, which persistently shifts the *AD* curve rightward.

5. **a** Cost-push inflation starts with a factor that decreases aggregate supply.

6. **c** The oil price increase might trigger a cost-push inflation if the Fed responds by cutting the interest rate and increasing the growth rate of the quantity of money.

7. **b** A rise in the price of a resource can kick off a cost-push inflation, but to persist the inflation must be ratified by persistent expansionary monetary policy.

8. **b** Once a cost-push inflation is underway, aggregate demand increases short-run aggregate supply decreases, which are the same changes that occur when a demand-pull inflation is underway.

9. **c** The higher inflation leads to higher money wages, which decrease short-run aggregate supply and results in no change in real GDP.

10. **b** If the *AD* curve shifts rightward less than expected, the price level is lower than expected, which means that real wages are higher than expected. Firms respond by cutting production so that real GDP is less than potential GDP.

Inflation and Unemployment: The Phillips Curve

11. **d** Answer (d) is the definition of the short-run Phillips curve.

12. **c** Answer (c) is the definition of the long-run Phillips curve. Comparing this question with question 11 shows the important role played by inflation expectations.

13. **d** The *LRPC* is vertical at the natural unemployment rate, 8 percent.

14. **a** The *SRPC* crosses the *LRPC* at the level of expected inflation.

15. **b** In the short run, the economy moves along its *SRPC* so that the increase in the inflation rate reduces the unemployment rate to 3 percent.

16. **d** In the long run, the economy returns to the *LRPC* and unemployment returns to its natural rate, or 8 percent here.

17. **d** The long-run Phillips curve shifts only when the natural unemployment rate changes; the short-run Phillips curve shifts when the natural unemployment rate changes *and* when the expected inflation rate changes.

18. **c** Both Phillips curves shift rightward by the amount of the increase in the natural unemployment rate.

The Business Cycle

19. **a** While the theories differ on the factor that cause the fluctuations in aggregate demand growth, the theories all agree that these fluctuations result in business cycles.

20. **b** Monetarists assert that the factor creating business cycles is changes in the growth rate of the quantity of money.

21. **b** According to these theories, unexpected decreases in aggregate demand decrease GDP.

22. **d** The real business cycle theory asserts that the impulse leading to business cycles is changes in the growth rate of productivity.

23. **c** Basically, the higher real interest rate boosts the return from savings, so, in order to earn more

and thus save more, people increase their supply of labor when the real interest rate rises.

24. **d** Real business cycle theory asserts that only real factors can affect real GDP.

■ Answers to Short Answer Problems

1. The cut in the interest rate and increase in the quantity of money shift the aggregate demand curve rightward. If the price level is not expected to change, the short-run aggregate supply curve remains unchanged. Then the increase in aggregate demand raises the price level and increases real GDP.

2. The higher price level leads to demands for higher money wages. Higher money wage rates push up the costs of production and shift the *SAS* curve leftward, leading to a further rise in the price level and a drop in real GDP. A demand-pull inflation spiral could result if the Federal Reserve again cuts the interest rate and increases the quantity of money. In this case, the *AD* curve continues to shift rightward, triggering leftward shifts in the *SAS* curve and leading to an ongoing inflation.

3. The short-run Phillips curve applies when the expected inflation rate is constant. Therefore the short-run Phillips curve slopes downward so that if the inflation rate rises (and hence real wages fall) unemployment falls.

The long-run Phillips curve applies when the expected inflation rate has fully adjusted to reflect changes in the actual inflation rate. In other words, along the long-run Phillips curve, the expected inflation rate equals the actual inflation rate. The long-run Phillips curve, therefore, is vertical at the natural unemployment rate. Along the long-run Phillips curve, a rise in the actual inflation rate is matched by an equivalent rise in the expected inflation rate (so that the real wage rate is constant) and thus the unemployment rate remains constant at the natural rate.

4. a. Figure 13.7 (on the next page) shows the short-run and long-run Phillips curves.

   b. If the inflation rate rises to 6 percent and the expected inflation rate remains at 4 percent, the economy moves along the Phillips curve $SRPC_0$ to point *a* and the unemployment rate falls to 4 percent.

FIGURE **13.7**
Phillips Curves

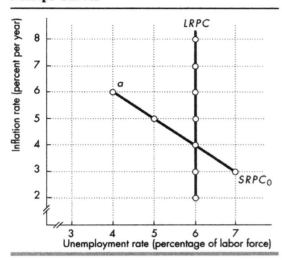

FIGURE **13.8**
Phillips Curves

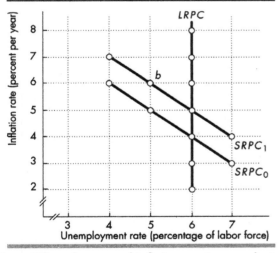

5. a. When the expected inflation rate increases by 1 percentage point, the *SRPC* shifts upward by 1 percentage point. In Figure 13.8 the short-run Phillips curve shifts from $SRPC_0$ to $SRPC_1$.

   b. When the expected inflation rate is 5 percent, the relevant Phillips curve is $SRPC_1$. So if the inflation rate is (still) 6 percent, the economy is at point *b* on $SRPC_1$, and the unemployment rate becomes 5 percent. When the inflation rate does not change, an increase in the expected inflation rate raises the unemployment rate.

FIGURE **13.9**
Phillips Curves

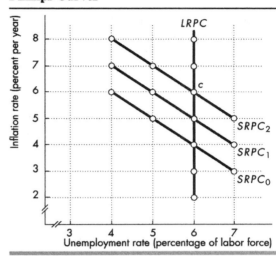

6. a. The new *SRPC* (when expected inflation is 6 percent) is in Figure 13.9 as $SRPC_2$.

   b. When the expected inflation rate rises to 6 percent, the unemployment rate is 6 percent. When the expected inflation rate is 6 percent, $SRPC_2$ is the relevant short-run Phillips curve. Hence when the inflation rate is 6 percent, the economy is at point *c* on $SRPC_2$. Alternatively, when the expected inflation rate is 6 percent *and* the actual inflation rate is 6 percent, the economy is on its long-run Phillips curve, *LRPC*, because the actual and expected inflation rates are equal. So the economy is at point *c* on *LRPC*.

TABLE **13.3**
Theories and Fluctuation Source

Theory	Source
Keynesian	Changes in business confidence
Monetarist	Changes in the monetary growth rate
New classical	Unexpected changes in aggregate demand
New Keynesian	Changes in aggregate demand that were unexpected when labor contracts were signed
Real business cycle	Changes in productivity growth

7. Table 13.3 shows the source that each theory

stresses as the primary cause of business cycle economic fluctuations.

8. a. In the Keynesian cycle theory, aggregate demand most likely increased because business confidence rose, thereby increasing investment. Real GDP increases and the price level rises.

   b. According to the monetarist cycle theory, the most likely cause of the increase in aggregate demand is an increase in the growth rate of the quantity of money. Real GDP increases and the price level rises.

   c. In the new classical cycle theory only unexpected changes in aggregate demand affect real GDP and employment. If people expect the change in aggregate demand, the money wage rate rises so that so that the short-run aggregate supply decreases. The price level rises but real GDP does not change. If the increase in aggregate demand was unexpected, then the money wage rate does not change. As a result, the short-run aggregate supply does not change. The price level rises and real GDP increases.

   d. According to the new Keynesian cycle theory, even though the increase in aggregate demand is expected, it becomes expected only *after* some wage contracts have been signed. The increase in aggregate demand money was unexpected when the contracts were signed. Hence the expected increase in aggregate demand still raises the price level and increases real GDP. If the increase in aggregate demand was unexpected, then the price level rises and real GDP increases.

   e. According to the real business cycle theory, the aggregate supply curve is the vertical long-run aggregate supply so that real GDP is equal to potential GDP. The increase in aggregate demand has no effect on the long-run aggregate supply, so real GDP does not change. The price level, however, rises.

■ You're the Teacher

1. "Look, economists really are smart. They're working on something that is *incredibly* complex. Let me give you an example: Economists would like to know how much a change in the quantity of money affects real GDP. Think of all the different possibilities. Man! Monetarists say that changes in the quantity of money can have large effects. New classical economists think that only unexpected changes can affect real GDP. And the real business cycle theory says that changes in the quantity of money have no effect. Just like you said, this range of answers sure covers all the bases!

"But, think about what we'd have to do to determine which answer is correct: Basically, we'd have to change the quantity of money and nothing else. That is, government expenditures couldn't change, the price of oil couldn't change, technology couldn't change — nothing could change. If any of these other things varied, real GDP might change because of that factor, not because of the change in the quantity of money. If we could conduct this type of 'controlled' experiment, we could figure out exactly how changes in the quantity of money affected real GDP. Do you think anyone will get to conduct this experiment? Of course not! So economists have to try to disentangle all the different things that affect real GDP and unemployment. All these things — taxes, government expenditures, technology, oil prices, interest rates — change every day, and each might have an impact on GDP. Isolating the effect of any one of them is nearly impossible.

"Economists do the best they can because they know the importance of figuring out which theory is right. And, you know, I think that working on this issue might actually be a real kick; I'm thinking about switching majors to economics! Becoming an economist can give me to chance to really help make a bunch of people's lives a lot better off. So, if I switch majors, you know that economists have to be really smart!"

Chapter Quiz

1. If this year's price level exceeds last year's price level,
   a. inflation occurred.
   b. inflation accelerated.
   c. deflation occurred.
   d. deflation accelerated.

2. A demand-pull inflation can be *started* by _____; a cost-push inflation can be *started* by _____.
   a. an increase in the price of oil; an increase in the price of oil
   b. a decrease in money wages; an increase in government expenditure
   c. an increase in the quantity of money; an increase in the price of oil
   d. an increase in the quantity of money; an increase in the quantity of money

3. To *continue*, a demand-pull inflation needs a continuing _____; to *continue*, a cost-push inflation needs a continuing_____.
   a. increase in the price of oil; increase in the price of oil
   b. decrease in money wage rates; decrease in money wage rates
   c. increase in the quantity of money; increase in the quantity of money
   d. increase in government expenditure; decrease in government expenditure

4. The relationship between unemployment and inflation is illustrated by
   a. the *AD* curve.
   b. the *LAS* curve.
   c. the *SAS* curve.
   d. the Phillips curves.

5. For a cost-push inflation to occur, higher oil prices must be accompanied by
   a. lower investment.
   b. higher tax rates.
   c. low government expenditure.
   d. higher growth in the quantity of money.

6. According to the mainstream business cycle theories, if the inflation rate turns out to be lower than expected real GDP
   a. decreases.
   b. does not change.
   c. increases.
   d. might change, but more information is needed about the direction the *AD* curve shifts.

7. In a demand-pull inflation, money wage rates rise because _____ in aggregate demand creates a labor _____.
   a. an increase; shortage
   b. an increase; surplus
   c. a decrease; shortage
   d. a decrease; surplus

8. The short-run Philips curve crosses the long-run Phillips curve at the
   a. natural interest rate.
   b. nominal interest rate.
   c. actual inflation rate.
   d. expected inflation rate.

9. What influence shifts *both* the short-run and long-run Phillips curve rightward?
   a. An increase in the expected inflation rate equal to the increase in the actual inflation.
   b. A decrease in the expected inflation rate equal to the decrease in the actual inflation rate.
   c. An increase in the natural unemployment rate.
   d. A decrease in the natural unemployment rate.

10. Only unexpected changes in aggregate demand lead to business cycle fluctuations according to the _____ theory.
    a. Keynesian business cycle
    b. monetarist business cycle
    c. new classical business cycle
    d. real business cycle

The answers for this Chapter Quiz are on page 266

5 THE ECONOMY IN THE SHORT RUN

Mid-Term Examination

■ **Chapter 11**

1. When real GDP exceeds potential GDP, then
   a. there is a recessionary gap.
   b. the economy is at its long-run equilibrium.
   c. there is an inflationary gap.
   d. the short-run aggregate supply curve has shifted rightward.

2. The long-run aggregate supply curve is
   a. vertical.
   b. positively sloped.
   c. negatively sloped.
   d. horizontal.

3. A decrease in government expenditure shifts
   a. the long-run, but not the short-run, aggregate supply curve leftward.
   b. the short-run, but not the long-run, aggregate supply curve leftward
   c. both the long-run and the short-run aggregate supply curves leftward.
   d. the aggregate demand curve leftward.

4. An increase in potential GDP
   a. shifts the *LAS* curve rightward and does not shift the *SAS* curve.
   b. shifts the *LAS,* the *SAS,* and the *AD* curves rightward.
   c. shifts the *AD* curve rightward.
   d. shifts the *LAS* and *SAS* curves rightward.

■ **Chapter 12**

5. On the 45° diagram, consumption expenditure is measured as
   a. a horizontal distance.
   b. a vertical distance.
   c. the area of a triangle.
   d. the area of a rectangle.

6. When the consumption function lies above the 45° line, households
   a. spend all of any increase in income on consumption.
   b. consume more than their disposable income.
   c. save some portion of their disposable income.
   d. save all of any increase in income.

7. Expenditure that depends on the level of income is
   a. spurious expenditure.
   b. equilibrium expenditure.
   c. induced expenditure.
   d. autonomous expenditure.

8. Suppose the slope of the *AE* curve is 0.90. Then a $100 billion increase in autonomous spending causes equilibrium expenditure to
   a. decrease by $100 billion.
   b. increase by $100 billion.
   c. increase by $900 billion.
   d. increase by $1,000 billion.

■ **Chapter 13**

9. A cost-push inflation is characterized by
   a. continuing increases in the quantity of money.
   b. continuing increases in real GDP.
   c. a one-time increase in government expenditure.
   d. All of the above are characteristics of cost-push inflation.

10. A demand-pull inflation requires persistent increases in
    a. tax rates.
    b. real wages.
    c. the quantity of money.
    d. government expenditure.

11. In the mainstream business cycle model, expansions are created by rightward shifts of the _____ curve that increase real GDP and _____ the price level.
    a. aggregate demand; lower
    b. aggregate demand; raise
    c. short-run aggregate supply; raise
    d. long-run aggregate supply; lower

12. The short-run Phillips curve _____; the long-run Phillips curve _____.
    a. slopes downward; slopes downward
    b. slopes upward; slopes upward
    c. is horizontal; is vertical
    d. slopes downward; is vertical

Answers

■ Mid-Term Exam Answers

1. c;   2. a;   3. d;   4. d;   5. b;   6. b;   7. c;   8. d;   9. a;   10. c;   11. b;   12. d.

Chapter 14 FISCAL POLICY*

Key Concepts

■ The Federal Budget

The **federal budget** is an annual statement of the government's expenditures and tax revenues. Using the federal budget to achieve macroeconomic objectives such as full employment, sustained economic growth, and price level stability is **fiscal policy**.

The President proposes a budget to Congress, Congress passes budget acts, and the President vetoes or signs the acts. The **Employment Act of 1946** commits the government to strive for full employment. The **Council of Economic Advisers** is a group of economists who monitor the economy and keep the President and the public informed about the current state of the economy and the best available forecasts of where it is heading.

♦ Tax revenues are received from four sources: personal income taxes, social security taxes, corporate income taxes, and indirect taxes. The largest source of revenue is the personal income tax.

♦ Outlays are classified as transfer payments, expenditures on goods and services, and interest payments on the debt. The largest expenditure item is transfer payments.

The government's budget balance equals tax revenues minus outlays.

♦ A **budget surplus** occurs if tax revenues exceed outlays; a **budget deficit** occurs if tax revenues are less than outlays; and a **balanced budget** occurs if tax revenues equal outlays.

♦ The U.S. government had a budget deficit from 1980 to 1997. Between 1998 to 2001 the government had a budget surplus but by 2002 the budget was back in deficit.

♦ **Government debt** is the total amount that the government has borrowed. As a percentage of GDP, the debt declined after World War II until 1974, increased until the mid 1990s, fell until 2002 and has risen since then.

♦ Most nations have government budget deficits.

■ The Supply Side: Employment and Potential GDP

The effects of fiscal policy on employment, potential GDP, and aggregate supply are called **supply-side effects**. The labor market determines the quantity of labor employed and the production function shows how much real GDP is produced by this amount of employment. When the labor market is in equilibrium, the amount of GDP produced is potential GDP.

An income tax decreases the supply of labor, which increases the before-tax wage rate and decreases the after-tax wage rate. The tax creates a **tax wedge** between the (higher) before-tax wage rate and the (lower) after-tax wage rate. Taxes on consumption expenditure also add to the overall tax wedge because they raise the prices of goods and services and so lower the real wage rate. The U.S. tax wedge is relatively small.

♦ An increase in the tax rate decreases the supply of labor, so it decreases equilibrium employment and potential GDP.

The **Laffer curve** is the relationship between the tax rate and the amount of tax collected. If tax rates are high enough, an increase in the tax rate decreases potential GDP by enough so that the total tax revenue collected decreases. In the United States, it is unlikely that the tax rate is this high, so in the United States an increase in the tax rate increases total tax revenue.

---

* This chapter is Chapter 30 in *Economics*.

■ The Supply Side: Investment, Saving, and Economic Growth

The earlier chapter on measuring GDP showed that investment is financed by saving, S, government saving, $T - G$, and foreign borrowing, $(M - X)$:

$$I = S + (T - G) + (M - X)$$

Private saving, PS, is $S + (M - X)$, so

$$I = PS + (T - G)$$

Saving is the sum of private saving plus government saving. A tax on interest income decreases private saving and thereby decreases the supply of loanable funds. The supply of loanable funds curve shifts leftward. The tax drives a wedge between the after-tax interest rate received by savers and the interest rate paid by borrowers. The tax decreases the equilibrium quantity of saving and investment. By decreasing investment, the tax lowers the economic growth rate.

Government saving, $T - G$, adds to private saving if the government has a budget surplus or subtracts from it if the government has a budget deficit. If the government budget deficit increases, the immediate effect decreases saving and shifts the supply of loanable funds curve leftward. The real interest rate rises and the equilibrium quantity of investment decreases.

♦ The tendency for a government budget deficit to decrease investment is called a **crowding-out effect**.

♦ The crowding-out effect can be offset by the **Ricardo-Barro equivalence** effect, which occurs when private saving changes to offset any change in government saving. The Ricardo-Barro effect says that a government budget deficit *decreases* government saving but means higher taxes in the future, so taxpayers *increase* their private saving in order to be able to pay the higher future taxes.

■ Generational Effects of Fiscal Policy

Generational accounting is an accounting system that measures the lifetime tax burden and benefits of each generation. To compare the value of taxes that will paid in the future and the benefits that will be received in the future, generational accounting uses **present values**, the amount of money that, if invested today, will grow to equal a given future amount when the interest it earns is taken into account.

Fiscal imbalance is the present value of the government's commitments to pay benefits minus the present value of its tax revenues. The U.S. government's fiscal imbalance was estimated as $45 trillion, a major part of which is from future Social Security payments.

Generational imbalance is the division of the fiscal imbalance between the current and future generations assuming that the current generation will enjoy the current levels of taxes and benefits. The current generation will pay 43 percent of the fiscal imbalance and future generations will pay 57 percent of the fiscal imbalance.

Foreign borrowing means that the United States owes an international debt. In June, 2006 the U.S. international debt is $5.2 trillion, with $2.2 trillion of the debt in the form of U.S. government securities.

■ Stabilizing the Business Cycle

Discretionary fiscal policy is a policy action initiated by an act of Congress; **automatic fiscal policy** is a change in fiscal policy caused by the state of the economy. Government fiscal policies can have multiplier effects:

♦ An increase in government expenditure increases aggregate demand. The **government expenditure multiplier** is the magnification effect of a change in government expenditure on aggregate demand.

♦ A decrease in taxes increases disposable income, which increases consumption expenditure and aggregate demand. The **autonomous tax multiplier** is the magnification effect of a change in autonomous taxes on aggregate demand. It is smaller in magnitude than the government expenditures multiplier.

♦ The **balanced budget multiplier** is the magnification effect on aggregate demand of a simultaneous change in government expenditure and taxes that leaves the budget balance unchanged. An increase in government expenditure increases aggregate demand by more than an equal-sized increase in taxes decreases aggregate demand, so on net aggregate demand increases and the balanced budget multiplier is positive.

Fiscal policy can be used to change real GDP so that it equals potential GDP. If real GDP is less than potential GDP, a recessionary gap exists and expansionary fiscal policy, such as an increase in government expenditure or a decrease in tax revenues, can be used. Expansionary policy shifts the AD curve rightward. The multiplier effect means that the aggregate demand curve shifts rightward by an amount that exceeds the initial

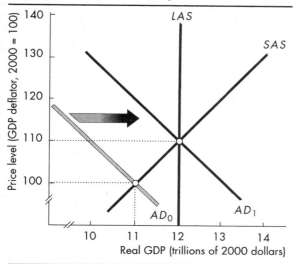

FIGURE 14.1
Expansionary Fiscal Policy

expansionary fiscal policy. Figure 14.1 shows how the fiscal policy eliminates a recessionary gap by increasing real GDP and raising the price level. The rightward shift of the aggregate demand curve is comprised of the initial increase in government expenditure or tax cut *plus* the multiplier effect.

If real GDP exceeds potential GDP, an inflationary gap exists and contractionary fiscal policy, such as a decrease in government expenditures or a tax hike, can be used. Contractionary policy shifts the *AD* curve leftward. The multiplier effect means that the aggregate demand curve shifts leftward by an amount that exceeds the initial contractionary fiscal policy. Real GDP decreases so that the inflationary gap is closed and the price level falls.

Lags limit the use of discretionary fiscal policy:

♦ The recognition lag, which is the time that it takes time to determine which fiscal policy actions are needed.

♦ The law-making time lag, which is the time that it takes Congress time to pass a fiscal policy change.

♦ The impact lag, which is the time it takes from passing a fiscal policy change to when the effects on real GDP are felt.

Automatic fiscal policy occurs because some tax receipts and expenditures change whenever real GDP changes. **Automatic stabilizers** are mechanisms that help stabilize GDP and operate without the need for explicit action.

Induced taxes are taxes that change when GDP changes. **Needs-tested spending** is spending that allows qualified people and businesses to receive benefits. Needs-tested spending changes when GDP changes.

Both induced taxes and needs-tested spending decrease the magnitude of the multiplier effects. The smaller the multipliers, the more moderate are expansions and recessions.

Induced taxes and needs-tested spending mean that the amount of the budget deficit changes with the business cycle. The deficit increases during a recession as induced taxes fall and needs tested spending increases.

The **structural surplus or deficit** is the budget balance that would occur if the economy were at full employment and real GDP equaled potential GDP. The **cyclical deficit or surplus** is the actual deficit or surplus minus the structural deficit or surplus. This latter part of the deficit is the result of the business cycle.

HELPFUL HINTS

1. **MULTIPLIERS :** The expenditure multiplier was discussed two chapters ago. This chapter continues the discussion by introducing additional multipliers, such as the government expenditure multiplier and autonomous tax multiplier. *All* multipliers exist for the same reason: An initial autonomous change that affects people's disposable income leads them to change their consumption expenditure. In turn, the consumption changes affect other people's income, which creates yet more induced changes in consumption expenditure. So, for *all* multipliers, aggregate demand changes because of the initial autonomous change and because of the further induced changes in consumption expenditure.

Questions

■ True/False and Explain

The Federal Budget

1. The Council of Economic Advisers proposes the federal government's budget to Congress.

2. If tax revenues exceeds government outlays, the government has a budget deficit.

3. The federal government has run small budget surpluses for most of the last two decades.

4. Most nations have a government budget deficit.

The Supply Side: Employment and Potential GDP

5. Increasing the income tax rate decreases potential GDP.

6. The tax wedge in the United States is larger than the tax wedge in the United Kingdom and in France.

7. Increasing the tax rate always increases tax revenue

The Supply Side: Investment, Saving, and Economic Growth

8. Investment can be financed only through private saving.

9. Increasing the tax rate on interest income decreases saving but increases equilibrium investment.

10. An increase in the government deficit can crowd out private investment.

Generational Effects of Fiscal Policy

11. Generational accounting measures a generation's lifetime tax burden and government benefits.

12. It is predicted that the current generation will pay about 75 percent of the current fiscal imbalance.

Stabilizing the Business Cycle

13. The autonomous tax multiplier shows that a tax cut decreases aggregate demand.

14. If GDP is less than potential GDP, a tax cut or an increase in government expenditures can return GDP to potential GDP.

15. One factor hindering the use of fiscal policy is the law-making time lag.

16. Induced taxes are an example of an automatic stabilizer.

17. Over a business cycle, the structural deficit rises and falls.

■ Multiple Choice

The Federal Budget

1. In the United States today, which of the following is the largest source of revenue for the federal government?
   a. Corporate income tax
   b. Personal income tax
   c. Indirect tax
   d. Government deficit

2. What is the largest component of federal government outlays?
   a. Transfer payments
   b. Expenditures on goods and services
   c. International purchases
   d. Interest on the debt

3. Suppose that the federal government's outlays in a year are $2.5 trillion, and that its tax revenues for the year are $2.3 trillion. The government is running a budget
   a. surplus of $2.3 trillion.
   b. surplus of $0.2 trillion.
   c. deficit of $0.2 trillion.
   d. deficit of $2.5 trillion.

4. Which of the following is largest?
   a. Federal government outlays.
   b. Federal government tax revenues.
   c. The budget deficit.
   d. Total government debt.

5. Currently the United States has a budget _____ and Japan has a budget _____.
   a. surplus; surplus
   b. surplus; deficit
   c. deficit; surplus
   d. deficit; deficit

The Supply Side: Employment and Potential GDP

6. An increase in the income tax rate
   a. increases potential GDP.
   b. can eliminate the income tax wedge.
   c. increases the demand for labor.
   d. decreases the supply of labor.

7. The tax wedge measures the gap between
   a. potential GDP and real GDP.
   b. before-tax and after-tax wage rates.
   c. the demand for labor and the supply of labor.
   d. government spending and tax revenues.

8. Most economists believe that in the United States an increase in the tax rate
   a. increases total tax revenue.
   b. does not change total tax revenue.
   c. decreases total tax revenue.
   d. probably changes total tax revenue but the direction of the change is ambiguous.

The Supply Side: Investment, Saving, and Economic Growth

9. If consumption expenditure is $7 trillion, saving by households is $1 trillion, the government surplus is $1 trillion, and net exports is −$2 trillion, what is investment?
   a. $7 trillion
   b. $4 trillion
   c. $3 trillion
   d. $2 trillion

10. An increase in the tax on interest income _____ the supply of saving and _____ the equilibrium amount of investment.
    a. increases; increases
    b. increases; decreases
    c. decreases; increases
    d. decreases; decreases

11. An increase in _____ can crowd out investment.
    a. the government budget deficit
    b. the government budget surplus
    c. the strength of the Ricardo-Barro effect
    d. private saving supply

Generational Effects of Fiscal Policy

12. Generational accounting shows that the present value of the government's commitments to pay benefits are _____ the present value of its taxes.
    a. greater than
    b. equal to
    c. less than
    d. not comparable to

13. It is estimated that the current generation will pay _____ percent of the fiscal imbalance and future generations will pay _____ percent.
    a. 89; 11
    b. 50; 50
    c. 43; 57
    d. 18; 82

Stabilizing the Business Cycle

14. A hike in income taxes is an example of
    a. discretionary fiscal policy.
    b. automatic fiscal policy.
    c. expansionary fiscal policy.
    d. a multiplier in action.

15. If government expenditure is increased by $200 billion and simultaneously taxes increase by $200 billion, then
    a. potential GDP increases.
    b. aggregate demand does not change.
    c. aggregate demand increases.
    d. aggregate demand decreases.

16. If the economy has a recessionary gap, in order to restore full employment an appropriate fiscal policy is
    a. a tax hike.
    b. a cut in government expenditures.
    c. an increase in government expenditures.
    d. a decrease in the autonomous tax multiplier.

17. Once the multiplier effect is taken into account, which of the following policies decreases aggregate demand the most?
    a. A $10 billion increase in government expenditures.
    b. A $10 billion decrease in government expenditures.
    c. A $10 billion tax increase.
    d. A $10 billion decrease in government expenditures combined with a $10 billion tax decrease.

18. How do induced taxes, such as the income tax, affect the size of the multiplier effects?
    a. Induced taxes increase the size of the multiplier.
    b. Induced taxes have no effect on the size of the multiplier.
    c. Induced taxes reduce the size of the multiplier.
    d. The answer depends on the presence or absence of needs-tested spending in the economy in addition to induced taxes.

19. Which of the following happens automatically if the economy goes into a recession?

  a. Government expenditures on goods and services increase.
  b. Income taxes rise.
  c. A budget surplus falls.
  d. Needs-tested spending falls.

20. If the federal government's budget is in deficit even when the economy is at full employment, the deficit is said to be

  a. persisting.
  b. non-cyclical.
  c. discretionary.
  d. structural.

■ Short Answer Problems

1. How has the U.S. budget surplus and deficit changed over the past two decades?

2. As a percentage of GDP, how has the federal government debt changed since 1940?

3. Explain the effect on potential GDP of an increase in taxes on labor income.

4. What is the tax wedge?

5. Figure 14.2 shows the market for loanable funds. The government's budget is balanced.

  a. Show the effect of a $400 billion government budget deficit if there is no Ricardo-Barro effect. How much investment is crowded out by the deficit?

  b. How does the Ricardo-Barro effect change the results of a budget deficit?

6. Igor has been elected to lead Transylvania. Igor's first action is to hire a crack team of economists and to ask them what fiscal policy he should propose.

  a. If Transylvania has an inflationary gap, what fiscal policies should Igor's economists propose?

  b. If Transylvania has a recessionary gap, what fiscal policies should Igor's economists propose?

  c. Because the legislature decides to meet only at night, it takes a year to get a fiscal policy in place in Transylvania. Suppose that Igor's economists predict that next year, without any government policy, Transylvania will have a recessionary gap. The government passes a fiscal policy that is designed to correct a recessionary

FIGURE 14.2
Short Answer Problem 5

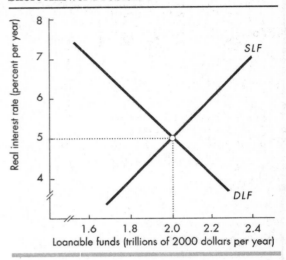

gap. However, the prediction is incorrect and without any government policy Transylvania actually would have had a full employment equilibrium. What happens when the fiscal policy, based on the incorrect prediction, takes effect?

  d. As Igor is sent packing back to his night job, explain to him what other factors might have hindered the success of his fiscal policy.

FIGURE 14.3
Short Answer Problem 7

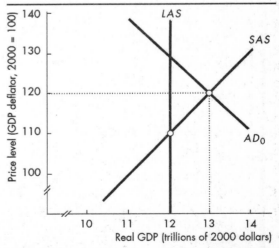

7. In Figure 14.3, show the effect of an increase in taxes that restores the economy to potential GDP. Assume there is no effect on potential GDP itself from the change in taxes.

8. What is the difference between a cyclical budget deficit and a structural budget deficit?

■ You're the Teacher

1. "These multipliers are kind of cool, and I've studied them until I really understand them. But there's just one point that still puzzles me: How come the government can't use its fiscal policy to eliminate fluctuations in GDP brought by changes in investment? I'd think that this policy would be a good one for the government to follow!" Your friend has certainly hit on a good point; now what's a good answer?

Answers

■ True/False Answers

The Federal Budget

1. **F** The President proposes the budget to Congress. The Council of Economic Advisers helps the President by monitoring the economy and offering policy proposals.

2. **F** A budget deficit occurs when tax revenues fall short of government outlays.

3. **F** Since 1980, the federal government ran a budget surplus only between 1998 and 2001.

4. **T** Most nations have government budget deficits.

The Supply Side: Employment and Potential GDP

5. **T** Increasing the income tax rate decreases the amount of full employment, which decreases potential GDP.

6. **F** The income tax wedge in the United States is smaller than that in the United Kingdom and much smaller than that in France.

7. **F** The Laffer curve shows that if the tax rate is high enough, increasing it decreases tax revenue.

The Supply Side: Investment, Saving, and Economic Growth

8. **F** Government saving also can finance investment.

9. **F** Increasing the tax rate on interest income decreases saving, which increases the equilibrium real interest rate and decreases equilibrium investment.

10. **T** The increase in the government deficit decreases the total supply of loanable funds, which raises the equilibrium real interest rate and decreases equilibrium investment.

Generational Effects of Fiscal Policy

11. **T** The question gives the definition of generational accounting.

12. **F** It is predicted that the current generation will pay about 43 percent of the fiscal imbalance.

Stabilizing the Business Cycle

13. **F** A tax cut increases aggregate demand and the autonomous tax multiplier shows that the increase in aggregate demand exceeds the initial cut in taxes.

14. **T** A tax cut or an increase in government expenditures increases aggregate demand and thereby increases real GDP.

15. **T** The law-making time lag reflects the fact that it usually takes Congress a long time to change taxes or government purchases.

16. **T** Another automatic stabilizer is needs-tested spending.

17. **F** The structural deficit shows what the deficit would be if real GDP equaled potential GDP.

■ Multiple Choice Answers

The Federal Budget

1. **b** Personal income taxes are the largest source of revenue, followed by social security taxes.

2. **a** Transfer payments are by far the largest component of federal government outlays.

3. **c** The government's deficit equals its outlays, $2.5 trillion, minus its taxes, $2.3 trillion.

4. **d** The total government debt is near $7 trillion, which dwarfs federal government outlays (approximately $2.9 trillion), tax revenues (about $2.5 trillion), and the current deficit (about $400 billion).

5. **d** Although both Japan and the United States have government budget deficits, as a fraction of GDP the Japanese deficit is much larger than the U.S. deficit.

The Supply Side: Employment and Potential GDP

6. **d** Because the tax hike decreases the supply of labor, equilibrium employment decreases and so does potential GDP.

7. **b** An income tax lowers the after-tax wage rate so that it is less than the before tax-wage rate.

8. **a** Though it is possible for the tax rate to be so high that an increase in it lowers tax revenue, most economists think that in the United States the tax rate is not that high.

The Supply Side: Investment, Saving, and Economic Growth

9. **b** Investment equals the sum of private saving, $1 trillion, plus government saving, $1 trillion, plus foreign borrowing, which is the negative of net exports, $2 trillion.

10. **d** The tax on interest income lowers the return from saving, so it decreases the supply of saving and thereby decreases the equilibrium quantity of investment.

11. **a** A government deficit decreases the supply of loanable funds, and so raises the real interest rate and decreases the equilibrium quantity of investment.

Generational Effects of Fiscal Policy

12. **a** Currently generational accounting estimates that the present value of the government's commitments to pay benefits exceeds the present value of its taxes by about $45 trillion.

13. **c** It is estimated that the current generation will pay 43 percent of the fiscal imbalance, leaving more than half to be paid by future generations.

Stabilizing the Business Cycle

14. **a** Because the tax increase does not occur automatically, it is a discretionary fiscal policy.

15. **c** The balanced budget multiplier shows that an increase in government purchased balanced by an identical increase in tax revenue increases aggregate demand.

16. **c** A recessionary gap needs an expansionary policy to offset it, so an increase in government expenditures is the correct policy.

17. **b** Both the decrease in government expenditures and the increase in taxes decrease aggregate demand, but the government expenditures multiplier is larger than the autonomous tax multiplier, so the decrease in government expenditures has a larger effect on aggregate demand.

18. **c** Induced taxes reduce the change in disposable income that results from a change in GDP. So induced taxes decrease the amount of induced consumption that results from a change in GDP and thereby reduce the size of the multipliers.

19. **c** During a recession, tax revenues fall and transfer expenditures rise, thereby decreasing a budget surplus.

20. **d** A structural deficit is a deficit that exists even when the economy is producing at full employment.

■ Answers to Short Answer Problems

1. For most of the past two decades, the United States has had a government budget deficit. The deficit was particularly large during the middle of the 1980s. It began to shrink toward the end of the late 1980s, but rose once again in the early 1990s. Then in the middle of the 1990s to 1996 the deficit was reduced until 1998 when there was a budget surplus. The surplus lasted until 2001, after which a deficit remerged.

2. As a fraction of GDP, the government debt rose from 1940 through 1946 to its highest point ever. Then from 1946 to the beginning of the 1980s, the government debt fell as a fraction of GDP. From 1980 until the middle of the 1990s, the fraction rose. It then fell after the middle of the 1990s until 2001 when it has started to rise once again.

3. An increase in taxes on labor income decreases potential GDP. An increase in these taxes decreases the supply of labor. As a result, the full-employment equilibrium quantity of labor decreases, which decreases potential GDP.

4. The tax wedge is the difference between the before-tax wage rate and the after-tax wage rate. A tax on labor income increases the before-tax wage rate but decreases the after-tax wage rate, thereby creating the tax wedge. In addition, taxes on consumption expenditure also increase the tax wedge because these taxes raise the prices of goods and services and thereby further decrease the after-tax real wage.

5. a. Figure 14.4 (on the next page) shows the effect of the $400 billion government deficit. The government deficit decreases saving by $400 billion and so shifts the supply of loanable funds curve leftward by $400 billion. As the figure shows, the equilibrium real interest rate rises from 5 percent to 6 percent and the equilibrium quantity decreases from $2.0 trillion to $1.8 trillion. So the $400 billion deficit crowds out (decreases) $200 billion of investment.

FIGURE **14.4**
Short Answer Problem 5

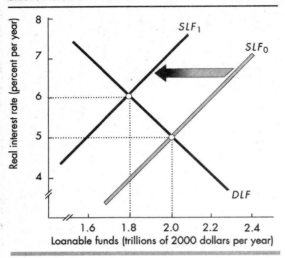

Loanable funds (trillions of 2000 dollars per year)

b. The Ricardo-Barro effect says that people change their saving to offset the effect of a government deficit. In the extreme, people increase their saving by the full amount of the deficit, in which case the supply of loanable funds curve does not shift so that investment and the real interest rate do not change. In a less extreme case, the saving increase offsets only some of the deficit, so the supply of loanable funds curve still shifts leftward, but by a smaller amount. As a result, the real interest rises less and investment decreases less that they would in the absence of the Ricardo-Barro effect.

6. a. In an inflationary gap, real GDP exceeds potential GDP, so contractionary policies are appropriate. Igor's economists should suggest a decrease in government expenditures or an increase in taxes.

b. In a recessionary gap, real GDP is less than potential GDP, so expansionary policies are appropriate. Igor's economists should suggest an increase in government expenditures or a decrease in taxes.

c. Because Igor's economists predict the presence of a recessionary gap, the policies they suggest are expansionary policies: An increase in government expenditures and/or a tax cut. Both policies increase aggregate demand. But Transylvania is already at full employment when these policies take effect, so the increase in aggregate

demand pushes Transylvania into an equilibrium with an inflationary gap. Real GDP exceeds potential GDP and the price level rises.

d. Igor lost his job because of the difficulty of economic forecasting combined with the law-making lag. Other lags that hamper fiscal policy are the recognition lag, which is the time it takes to figure out that fiscal policy actions are needed, and the impact lag, which is the time between when a fiscal policy change is passed and when its effects on real GDP are felt. All these lags make fiscal policy difficult.

FIGURE **14.5**
Short Answer Problem 7

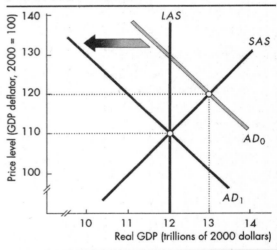

Real GDP (trillions of 2000 dollars)

7. Figure 14.5 shows the effect of an increase in taxes. The increase in taxes decreases aggregate demand so that the aggregate demand curve shifts from AD_0 to AD_1. The price level falls from 120 to 110 and real GDP decreases so that it becomes equal to potential GDP, $12 trillion.

8. A budget deficit can be divided into a cyclical budget deficit and a structural budget deficit. The structural deficit is the deficit that would exist if the economy were at potential GDP. The cyclical deficit is the deficit that results because the economy is not a full employment. Basically the cyclical deficit is the result of the business cycle.

■ You're the Teacher

1. "Yeah, I think the multipliers are cool, too. I didn't have the foggiest idea about them until we started studying them in class.

   "But look, let's talk about your question. I think the main deal here is that it's hard for the government to respond in a timely and appropriate fashion. One problem is the time required for the government to enact fiscal policy changes. As the text points out, the federal budget is proposed by the President early in the year and the final spending bills are signed by the President late in the year. It's got to take time to change the federal budget. I bet that one reason for the delay is the complexity of the budget and the budgeting process. Another reason is politics. You know how *we* disagree about who to vote for! Well, the political parties might agree that, say, tax cuts are needed, but disagree on precisely which taxes should be cut and by how much.

   "Also, it can't be real easy to know what is the correct policy to pursue. Some observers might think that we are headed for a recession, and others believe that a strong expansion will occur over the next year or so. And who knows what potential GDP really is? I mean, it's a great concept for us to learn because it helps us get a lot of ideas straight, but in the real world it's got to be hard to know what potential GDP equals. So again I can see political parties squabbling — one thinking that we are below potential GDP and need expansionary policies to lower unemployment and the other thinking we are above potential GDP and need contractionary policies to limit inflation.

   "So, I guess there are probably some reasons why the government doesn't use its fiscal policy to eliminate business cycles even though it would be great if the government could do so."

Chapter Quiz

1. A balanced budget occurs when the government's
   a. outlays exceeds its tax revenues.
   b. outlays equal its tax revenues.
   c. outlays are less than its tax revenues.
   d. total debt equals zero.

2. As a fraction of GDP, the public debt
   a. has risen each year for the past 50 years.
   b. has fallen each year for the past 50 years.
   c. both rose and fell after 1974 and today is higher than it was in 1974.
   d. generally rose until about 1974 and today is lower than it was in 1974.

3. Which of the following is a problem with using fiscal policy to stabilize the economy?
   a. Implementing fiscal policy might be slow.
   b. Congress can act too quickly and so the policy might be inappropriate.
   c. Government expenditures have only an indirect effect on aggregate demand.
   d. The Fed must determine whether the policy is correct.

4. An increase in government expenditures shifts the
   a. *LAS* curve rightward.
   b. *SAS* curve leftward.
   c. *AD* curve rightward.
   d. *AD* curve leftward.

5. If taxes on labor income are cut, then
   a. the *AD* curve shifts leftward.
   b. the tax wedge shrinks in size.
   c. potential GDP decreases.
   d. employment decreases because people no longer need to work as long to pay their taxes.

6. The presence of income taxes _____ the magnitude of the government expenditure multiplier and _____ the magnitude of the autonomous tax multiplier.
   a. increases; increases
   b. increases; does not change
   c. decreases; does not change
   d. decreases; decreases

7. Income taxes and transfer payments
   a. act like economic shock absorbers and stabilize fluctuations in income.
   b. prevent the economy from moving toward equilibrium.
   c. increase the impact of changes in investment and net exports.
   d. increase the economy's growth rate.

8. If the government increases its expenditure by $10 billion and increases its taxes by $10 billion, the *AD* curve
   a. shifts rightward.
   b. does not shift.
   c. shifts leftward.
   d. might shift depending on whether the tax hike increases or decreases aggregate demand.

9. By definition, a discretionary fiscal policy
   a. requires action by the Congress.
   b. is triggered by the state of the economy.
   c. must involve changes in government purchases.
   d. must involve changes in taxes.

10. If a tax cut has large effects on the supply of capital and labor, then it
    a. definitely increases potential GDP.
    b. definitely does not change potential GDP.
    c. definitely decreases potential GDP.
    d. might change potential GDP, but the direction of the change is uncertain.

The answers for this Chapter Quiz are on page 266

15 MONETARY POLICY*

■ Monetary Policy Objectives and Framework

♦ The goals of monetary policy are to achieve "maximum employment, stable prices, and moderate long-term interest rates." Price stability is the key for achieving these goals. Price stability creates low inflation, which leads to low nominal interest rates and real GDP close to potential GDP.

♦ The means of monetary policy to attain its goals is by keeping the growth rate of the quantity of money in line with the growth rate of potential GDP.

To determine if the goal of stable prices is being achieved, the Fed uses the **core inflation rate**, the inflation rate calculated using the *core CPI*, which removes food and fuel prices from the CPI. The core inflation rate is more stable than the CPI inflation rate. A core inflation rate of between 1 and 2 percent a year is generally assumed to be equivalent to price stability.

To determine if the goal of maximum employment is being achieved, the Fed looks at a large number of indicators but the key is the output gap, the percentage deviation of real GDP from potential GDP. The Fed tries to minimize the output gap.

♦ The **Federal Open Market Committee** (FOMC) is the Fed's main policy-making group. The FOMC meets 8 times a year and the Fed releases the minutes of each meeting 3 weeks after the meeting.

■ The Conduct of Monetary Policy

A **policy instrument** is a variable the Fed can target with precision using its policy tools. The Fed could target either the quantity of money, the exchange rate, or the short-term interest rate. Only one of these variable can be targeted at a time. The Fed chooses to target a short-term interest rate, the **federal funds rate** which is the interest rate on overnight loans of reserves that banks make to each other. By targeting this interest rate, the Fed will change it in line with the Fed's policy. When the Fed changes the federal funds rate, it generally does so by a quarter of a percentage point.

For its monetary policy, the Fed can use an instrument rule or a targeting rule:

♦ An **instrument rule** is a decision rule for monetary policy that sets the policy instrument at a level that is based on the current state of the economy. The Taylor rule is an instrument rule. The **Taylor rule** states that the federal funds rate should be set according to the inflation rate and the output gap according to the formula

$$FFR = 2 + INF + 5(INF - 2) + 0.5GAP$$

where *FFR* is the federal funds rate, *INF* is the inflation rate, and *GAP* is the output gap, all measured in percentages.

♦ A **targeting rule** is a decision rule for monetary policy that sets the policy instrument at a level that makes the forecast of the ultimate policy goal equal to its target. For instance, the Fed could set the federal funds at the level which makes the expected inflation rate equal to its target level.

The Fed uses *open market operations*, the purchase or sale of government securities by the Fed, to achieve its target.

♦ When the Fed buys government securities, banks' reserves increase. When the Fed sells government securities, banks' reserves decrease.

---

* This chapter is Chapter 31 in *Economics*.

The federal fund rate is determined by the equilibrium in the market for banks' reserves. The Federal Reserve can hit its federal funds interest rate target by using its open market operations to change the quantity of reserves in the market. If the Fed wants to lower the federal funds rate, it increases the quantity of reserves by buying government securities; if the Fed wants to raise the federal funds rate, it decreases the quantity of reserves by selling government securities.

■ Monetary Policy Transmission

The Fed's actions ripple through the economy. A lower federal funds rate:

♦ Lowers other short-term interest rates.

♦ Decreases the *U.S. interest rate differential* (the U.S. interest rate relative to the interest rates in other countries) and thereby lowers the exchange rate, which then increases net exports and aggregate demand.

♦ Increases the quantity of money and increases bank loans. The increase in bank loans increases the supply of loanable funds and (temporarily) lowers the long-term real interest rate.

♦ Increases investment and consumption expenditure, which both increase aggregate demand. A multiplier process follows, which further increases aggregate demand.

♦ Increases aggregate demand, as illustrated in Figure 15.1, so that real GDP growth and the inflation rate increase.

Real GDP growth and the inflation rate both slow when the Fed raises the interest rate.

If real GDP is less than potential GDP there is a recessionary gap. In this case, the Fed lowers the federal funds rate in order to increase aggregate demand and thereby increase real GDP and employment. If real GDP exceeds potential GDP, there is an inflationary gap. In this case the Fed raises the federal funds rate to decrease aggregate demand and thereby lower the price level and avoid inflation.

The actual links between the Fed's policy and changes in real GDP are loose and have lags. The changes in the federal funds rate must work though many sectors to change the real long-term interest rate and that change depends on how inflation expectations change. While these changes are working out, still other factors might change, making monetary policy difficult.

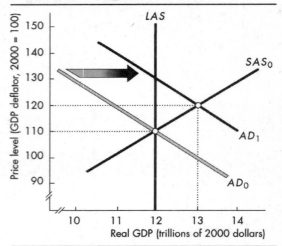

FIGURE 15.1
Effect of Lowering the Federal Funds Rate

■ Alternative Monetary Policy Strategies

The Fed's monetary policy strategy is to target the federal funds interest rate. There are four alternatives the Fed could use but has rejected:

♦ Monetary Base Instrument Rule — The Fed could set a target level for the monetary base. The **McCallum Rule** makes the growth rate of the monetary base respond to the long-term average growth rate of real GDP and medium term changes in the velocity of circulation of the monetary base. The Fed believes that the demand for money is too unstable to use this rule.

♦ Money Targeting Rule — The Fed could target the quantity of money, perhaps using Milton Friedman's **k-percent rule** which makes the quantity of money grow at *k* percent a year, where *k* equals the growth rate of potential GDP. The Fed believes that the demand for money (and the velocity of circulation) are too unstable to use this strategy.

♦ Exchange Rate Targeting Rule — The Fed could target the exchange rate. A fixed exchange gives the Fed no control over the U.S. inflation rate. A crawling peg exchange rate requires that the Fed be able to distinguish when the **real exchange rate**, the relative price of U.S. produced goods to foreign produced goods, changes, which is difficult.

♦ Inflation rate targeting — The Fed could use **inflation rate targeting**, in which the Fed would make a public commitment to meet an explicit in-flation target and then explain how its policy ac-tions will achieve that target. Other central banks use inflation rate targeting. The advantage of this policy is that it makes the goals of monetary policy explicit and makes accountability easy. The Fed believes that its implicit targeting has done at least as well as an explicit inflation rate targeting rule.

Helpful Hints

1. **ROLE OF THE LOANABLE FUNDS MARKET :** The loanable funds market plays a key role in transmit-ting monetary policy from the initial change in the federal funds rate to the ultimate change in real GDP and the price level. One point to keep in mind about this transmission mechanism and the loanable funds market is the point that banks' loans are a supply of loanable funds. When the Fed changes the federal rate using an open market op-eration, the Fed changes banks' reserves, which then changes the quantity of loans they can make. So if the Fed buys government securities, it is sell-ing reserves to banks, which will lead the banks to increase their loans and, as a result, increase the supply of loanable funds.

It also is important to keep in mind that the effect on the interest rate in the loanable funds market is a short-run effect. In the short run, the real interest rate adjusts so that the loanable funds market is in equilibrium. For instance, if the Fed lowers the fed-eral funds rate, the (real) supply of loanable funds increases and, in the short run, the real interest rate falls. However in the long run it is the price level that adjusts so that the loanable funds market is in equilibrium. So in the long run, the real interest will return to its initial value and the price level will rise, thereby reducing the real supply of loanable funds back to its initial amount.

Questions

■ True/False and Explain

Monetary Policy Objective and Framework

1. The Fed's key goal is achieving price level stability.

2. The core inflation rate is the inflation rate of fuel and food prices.

3. The Federal Reserve never reveals its monetary policy.

The Conduct of Monetary Policy

4. The Fed has chosen to use the monetary base as its policy instrument.

5. The Taylor rule specifies that the federal funds rate should depend on the inflation rate and output gap.

6. When the Federal Reserve buys government securi-ties, banks' reserves increase.

7. When the Federal Reserve buys government securi-ties, it shifts banks' demand curve for reserves rightward.

Monetary Policy Transmission

8. Higher interest rates affect consumption expendi-ture, investment, and net exports.

9. By controlling the federal funds rate, the Fed has tight control over the long-term real interest rate.

10. A decrease in the federal funds rate increases aggre-gate demand.

11. To fight inflation, the Fed will raise the federal funds rate.

12. If the Fed changes its monetary policy, the imme-diate effect is to change short-run aggregate supply and shift the *SAS* curve.

13. One factor that makes it difficult to conduct mone-tary policy is the time lags in the monetary policy transmission process.

Alternative Monetary Policy Strategies

14. It is technically impossible for the Federal Reserve to monetary base instrument rule.

15. A *k*-percent rule means that the Federal Reserve should select some value, "*k*," for the inflation rate and then target the inflation rate.

16. If the Fed used an exchange rate targeting rule of fixing the exchange rate, then it would be unable to control the U.S. inflation rate.

17. Monetary policy must focus on actual variables, such as inflation or unemployment, and cannot be concerned with people's inflation expectations.

■ Multiple Choice

Monetary Policy Objective and Framework

1. Which of the following is <u>NOT</u> one of the Fed's monetary policy goals?
   a. Conducting open market operations.
   b. Promoting maximum employment.
   c. Insuring price stability.
   d. Keeping long-term interest rates moderate.

2. The core inflation rate
   a. is almost always lower than the actual CPI inflation rate.
   b. is almost always higher than the actual CPI inflation rate.
   c. fluctuates less than the actual CPI inflation rate.
   d. cannot be compared to the actual CPI inflation rate.

The Conduct of Monetary Policy

3. Which of the following is <u>NOT</u> one of the Fed's potential policy instruments?
   a. The federal funds rate.
   b. The quantity of the monetary base.
   c. The exchange rate.
   d. The inflation rate.

4. For its policy instrument(s), the Fed chooses to use
   a. only the quantity of the monetary base.
   b. the quantity of the monetary base and the federal funds rate.
   c. only the federal funds rate
   d. the federal funds rate and the exchange rate

5. If the Fed expects that setting the federal funds rate at 4 percent will allow it to achieve its ultimate policy goal of the inflation rate equaling 1 percent, then the Fed is using
   a. a targeting rule.
   b. an instrument rule.
   c. a variation of the Taylor rule.
   d. a policy target instrument.

6. An open market sale of government securities by the Fed _____ banks reserves and _____ the federal funds rate.
   a. increases; raises
   b. increases; lowers
   c. decreases; raises
   d. decreases; lowers

7. When the federal funds interest rate is 6 percent, the quantity of reserves demanded is $100 billion. If the quantity of reserves is actually $110 billion, then the
   a. demand for reserves increases and the demand for reserves curve shifts rightward.
   b. demand for reserves decreases and the demand for reserves curve shifts leftward.
   c. federal funds rate rises.
   d. federal funds rate falls.

Monetary Policy Transmission

8. If the Fed raises the federal funds
   a. investment and consumption expenditure decrease.
   b. the price of the dollar rises on the foreign exchange market and so net exports decrease.
   c. a multiplier process that affects aggregate demand occurs.
   d. All of the above answers are correct.

9. If the Fed lowers the federal funds
   a. the long-term real interest rate rises.
   b. aggregate demand decreases.
   c. the exchange rate falls.
   d. the quantity of money decreases.

10. If the Fed raises the federal funds rate, the quantity of money _____ and the supply of loanable funds _____.
    a. increases; increases
    b. increases; decreases
    c. decreases; increases
    d. decreases; decreases

11. In order to combat inflation, the Fed will _____ the federal funds rate and as a result, the quantity of loans _____.
    a. lower; decreases
    b. lower; increases
    c. raise; decreases
    d. raise; increases

12. To eliminate an inflationary gap, the Fed will _____ the federal funds rate and, as a result, aggregate demand _____.
    a. raise; increases
    b. raise; decreases
    c. lower; increases
    d. lower; decreases

13. The Fed's actions to fight a recession shift the
    a. aggregate demand curve rightward.
    b. aggregate demand curve leftward.
    c. long-run aggregate supply curve rightward.
    d. long-run aggregate supply curve leftward.

14. A fall in the federal funds rate shifts the
    a. *AD* curve rightward.
    b. *SAS* curve rightward.
    c. *LAS* curve rightward.
    d. *AD* curve leftward.

15. If the Fed lowers the federal funds rate, it _____ the price level and _____ real GDP.
    a. raises; increases
    b. raises; does not change
    c. raises; decreases
    d. does not change; increases

Alternative Monetary Policy Strategies

16. The McCallum rule is an example of
    a. a monetary base instrument rule.
    b. a money targeting rule.
    c. an exchange rate targeting rule.
    d. an inflation targeting rule.

17. A primary reason the Fed does not use a *k*-percent rule targeting money growth is because the Fed believes that
    a. such a rule would give it no control over the U.S. inflation rate.
    b. such a rule would make inflation expectations unmanageable.
    c. the demand for money has large and unpredictable shifts.
    d. real GDP would no longer respond to changes in the federal funds rate.

18. If the Fed adopted inflation rate targeting, it would make an explicit commitment to achieving an inflation target. In addition, the Fed also would intervene in the foreign exchange market to fix the U.S. exchange rate.
    a. Both sentences are true.
    b. Only the first sentence is true.
    c. Only the second sentence is true.
    d. Both sentences are false.

■ Short Answer Problems

FIGURE **15.2**
Short Answer Problem 1

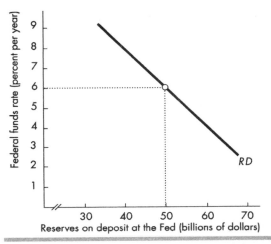

1. The quantity of reserves is $50 billion and the market for reserves is in equilibrium, as illustrated in Figure 15.2.
    a. What is the equilibrium federal funds rate?
    b. If the Fed wants to lower the federal funds rate to 4 percent, what must it do? Draw this change in Figure 15.2.

FIGURE **15.3**
Short Answer Problem 2

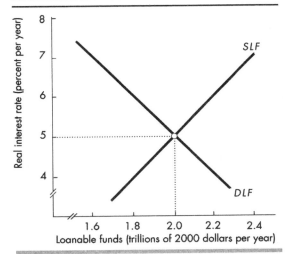

2. In Figure 15.3, show the effect raising the federal funds rate has in the market for loanable funds. Why is there this effect?

3. Explain how the Fed lowers the federal funds rate. Then explain how lowering the federal funds rate affects the quantity of money and the supply of loanable funds.

4. Explain how lowering the federal funds rate affects the U.S. exchange rate.

5. Explain how lowering the federal funds rate affects consumption and investment.

FIGURE **15.4**

Short Answer Problem 6

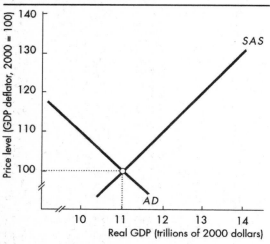

6. In Figure 15.4 show how a decrease in the federal funds rate affects the price level and real GDP.

7. Igor has been put charge of the Fed. Igor likes this job because it involves using his brain rather than collecting them. Igor thinks that the inflation rate is too high. If Igor convinces the rest of the members of the FOMC that his concern is correct, what policy action the Fed will take and how does this action affect the economy?

8. Why can't the Fed precisely guide the U.S. economy and avoid both recessions and inflations?

■ **You're the Teacher**

1. Your friend is talking: "I know that the Fed tries to keep prices stable, long-term interest rates at a reasonable level, and employment close to full employment. But the book says that all three of these goals can be achieved if the Fed concentrates on price stability. How in the world can this be?" This question is both interesting and important. Answer it for your friend so that your friend can see its importance.

Answers

■ True/False Answers

Monetary Policy Objective and Framework

1. **T** If the Fed meets its goal of price stability, then its goals of maximum employment and moderate long-term interest rates are easier to achieve.
2. **F** The core inflation is calculated using the core CPI which *omits* fuel and food prices.
3. **F** The minutes of each FOMC meeting are made public three weeks after the meeting.

The Conduct of Monetary Policy

4. **F** The Fed has chosen to use the federal funds rate as its policy instrument.
5. **T** The Taylor rule an instrument rule that tells to what the Fed should set the federal funds rate.
6. **T** When the Fed buys government securities, the Fed pays for these purchases by increasing banks' reserves.
7. **F** The Fed's purchase of government securities increases the quantity of reserves but does not shift the demand curve for reserves.

Monetary Policy Transmission

8. **T** Higher interest rates ripple through the economy, affecting many sectors.
9. **F** The Fed has no direct control over the crucial long-term real interest rate.
10. **T** Changing aggregate demand is part of the ripple effect of monetary policy.
11. **T** By raising the federal funds rate, aggregate demand decreases which lowers the price level.
12. **F** The short-run aggregate supply does not immediately change.
13. **T** The time lags mean that determining the proper policy is difficult because the policy must be what *will* be needed in the future rather than what *is* needed in the present..

Alternative Monetary Policy Strategies

14. **F** The Fed could, if it so desired, use a monetary base instrument rule.
15. **F** The *k*-percent rule is that the Fed should set the growth rate of the quantity of money equal to *k* percent where *k* percent equals the growth rate of potential GDP.

16. **T** The inability to control the U.S. inflation rate is why the Fed does not use a fixed exchange targeting rule.
17. **F** People's inflation expectations are a crucial component of monetary policy.

■ Multiple Choice Answers

Monetary Policy Objective and Framework

1. **a** Conducting open market operations is how the Fed operates to meet its monetary policy goals.
2. **c** The core inflation rate removes the influence of changes in the prices of food and fuels. Because these prices are quite variable, the core inflation rate fluctuates less than the actual CPI inflation rate.

The Conduct of Monetary Policy

3. **d** The inflation rate is one of the Fed's goals, not one of its instruments.
4. **c** The Fed *could* use either the federal funds rate, the quantity of money, or the exchange rate as its policy instrument. The Fed chooses the use the federal funds rate.
5. **a** The Fed is setting its policy instrument, the federal funds rate, at the level that makes the forecast of its policy goal, the inflation rate, equal to the Fed's target for this goal.
6. **c** The open market sale decreases banks' reserves, which raises the federal funds rate.
7. **d** There is a surplus of reserves so the federal funds rate will fall until it reaches its new equilibrium.

Monetary Policy Transmission

8. **d** Each of the answers describes one of the ripples from the Fed's policy.
9. **c** By lowering the federal fund rate, in the foreign exchange market the demand for U.S. dollars decreases so the exchange rate falls.
10. **d** To raise the federal funds rate the Fed sells U.S. government securities, which decreases banks' reserves, thereby decreasing their loans and the quantity of money.
11. **c** By raising the federal funds rate and decreasing the quantity of loans, the Fed decreases aggregate demand.
12. **d** An inflationary gap means that real GDP exceeds potential GDP, so by raising the federal

funds rate the Fed decreases aggregate demand and real GDP.

13. **a** By shifting the aggregate demand curve rightward, the Fed increases real GDP, thereby offsetting the recession.

14. **a** A fall in the federal funds rate increases aggregate demand, thereby shifting the *AD* curve rightward.

15. **a** The *AD* curve shifts rightward so in the economy moves along its upward sloping *SAS* curve to a higher price level and increased real GDP.

Alternative Monetary Policy Strategies

16. **a** The McCallum rule would determine how the monetary base grows.

17. **c** If the demand for money shifts unpredictably, then the effect on the economy of changes in the quantity of money becomes unpredictable.

18. **b** The first sentence accurately describes part of an inflation rate targeting rule. The second sentence, however, describes one of the alternative exchange rate targeting rules.

■ Answers to Short Answer Problems

FIGURE **15.5**
Short Answer Problem 1

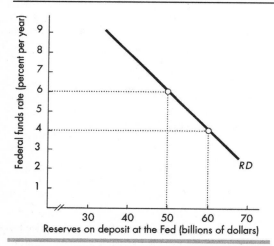

1. a. The equilibrium federal funds rate is 6 percent because that is the rate which sets the quantity of reserves demanded equal to the quantity supplied.

   b. To change the federal funds rate to 4 percent, the Fed must increase the quantity of reserves to $60 billion, as illustrated in Figure 15.5.

FIGURE **15.6**
Short Answer Problem 2

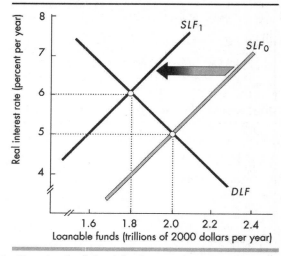

2. To raise the federal funds rate, the Fed will sell government securities to banks, thereby decreasing banks' reserves. When banks' reserves decrease, banks cut back on their loans, which decreases the supply of loanable funds. Figure 15.6 shows the effect in the loanable funds market. The supply curve of loanable funds shifts leftward, from SLF_0 to SLF_1 and the real interest rate rises, in the figure from 5 percent per year to 6 percent per year.

3. In order to lower the federal funds rate, the Fed conducts open market operations in which it buys U.S. government securities. When the Fed buys government securities, it pays for these purchases by increasing banks' reserves. Banks then have excess reserves, which they loan. As a result, the quantity of money increases and the supply of loanable funds also increases.

4. Lowering the federal funds rate lowers the U.S. exchange rate. With the lower U.S. interest rates, the U.S. interest rate differential falls. As a result, foreign savers demand fewer U.S. dollars because they will buy fewer U.S. assets. And U.S. savers supply more dollars in order to buy foreign exchange to use to purchase foreign assets. The decrease in demand for U.S. dollars coupled with the increase in the supply of U.S. dollars lowers the U.S. exchange rate.

5. Lowering the federal funds rate increases consumption expenditure and investment. To lower the federal funds rate, the Fed conducts open market operations and buys U.S. government securities.

When the Fed buys government securities, it pays for these purchases by increasing banks' reserves. Banks then have excess reserves, which they loan so the supply of loanable funds increases. The increase in the supply of loanable funds lowers the real interest rate. The fall in the real interest then increases consumption expenditure and investment.

FIGURE 15.7
Short Answer Problem 6

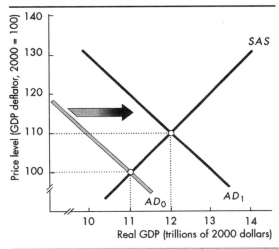

6. If the Fed cuts the federal funds rate, the quantity of money and loans increases. The supply of loanable funds increases so that the long-term real interest rate falls. As a result, consumption expenditure, investment, and net exports all increase, thereby increasing aggregate demand. The increase in aggregate demand means the aggregate demand curve shifts rightward, from AD_0 to AD_1 in Figure 15.7. The price level rises, in the figure from 100 to 110, and real GDP increases, in the figure from \$11 trillion to \$12 trillion.

7. Because he thinks the inflation rate is too high, Igor wants to decrease aggregate demand in order to lower the price level and thereby slow the inflation rate. The proper policy for Igor to propose is for the Fed to raise the federal funds rate. To raise the federal funds rate the Fed sells government securities to banks, thereby decreasing banks' reserves. When banks' reserves decrease, banks cut back on their loans, which decreases the supply of loanable funds and raises the long-term real interest rate. In turn, the higher real interest rate decreases consumption expenditure and investment. The U.S. exchange

rate rises, which decreases net exports. As a result of the decrease in consumption expenditure, investment, and net exports, aggregate demand decreases, thereby lowering the price level and slowing the inflation rate. (The decrease in aggregate demand also decreases real GDP.)

8. The Fed faces two related issues that make it impossible for the Fed to guide the economy so as to constantly avoid both recession and inflation. First, the links in the chain that connect monetary policy actions, that is, changes in the federal funds rate, with the ultimate change in real GDP and the price level are loose and indirect. In particular, the Fed's change in the federal funds rate must first change banks' loans, which then must impact the loanable funds market to change the real interest rate. Then the change in the real interest rate must change investment, consumption, and/or net exports in order to affect aggregate demand. Finally the change in aggregate demand changes the price level and real GDP. If *any* of these links breaks, the policy has no effect. The second issue the Fed faces is that the time it takes for all the adjustments to work out can be long and can be variable. As a result, when the impact is finally felt on real GDP and the price level, the economic environment might have changed. The change in the environment means that the policy might be counterproductive, that is, the policy might reinforces recessionary or inflationary forces that have arisen since the policy was undertaken.

■ You're the Teacher

1. "This is a great question. Here is a great answer! First off, in the short run these goals *can* conflict with each other and price stability is not the perfect answer. For instance, if there is a recessionary gap, we know that the Fed can lower the federal funds rate with the result that real GDP increases and the price level rises. In this case, the Fed has boosted employment but at the cost of raising the price level and so increasing the inflation rate. What the book says, however, is that in the *long run* achieving price stability helps the Fed reach its other goals so that in the long run these goals do not conflict. I think seeing how price stability gives moderate long-term interest rates is pretty quick. After all, the nominal interest rate equals the real interest rate plus the expected inflation rate. In the long run, the Fed can't

affect the real interest rate—remember that 'classical dichotomy' from some chapters ago that you asked me about? And now if prices are stable, then the expected inflation rate will be low, maybe even zero. So the nominal interest rate will surely be almost as low as possible if prices are stable. Now, what about achieving maximum employment? Well, the deal is that we get maximum employment when people make the best decisions about working and firms make the best decisions about hiring. These deci-

sions are easier to make if prices are stable because then people and firms don't have to try to figure out how inflation will affect them in the future. If prices are stable, we get maximum employment. So, at least in the long run, it all boils down to price stability in order to keep inflation and inflation expectations as low as possible."

Chapter Quiz

1. If the Fed is trying to fight a recession, it will
   a. lower the inflation rate.
   b. lower the federal funds rate.
   c. raise the U.S. exchange rate.
   d. decrease the quantity of money.

2. When the Fed raises the federal funds rate,
   a. aggregate demand decreases.
   b. the long-term real interest rate falls.
   c. the quantity of loans increases.
   d. net exports increase.

3. The Taylor rule says that the
   a. Fed should allow the quantity of money to grow at a constant rate.
   b. Fed should target the exchange rate by setting a crawling peg.
   c. federal funds rate should depend on the inflation rate and the output gap.
   d. exchange rate should be kept fixed in order for the Fed to have the maximum influence on the federal funds rate.

4. The Fed's actions to fight a recessionary gap shift the
   a. aggregate demand curve rightward.
   b. aggregate demand curve leftward.
   c. long-run aggregate supply curve rightward.
   d. long-run aggregate supply curve leftward.

5. If banks' reserves increase, the
   a. demand for loanable funds increases.
   b. demand for loanable funds decreases.
   c. supply of loanable funds increases.
   d. supply of loanable funds decreases.

6. If the Fed purchases U.S. government securities, the federal funds rate _____ and the quantity of banks' loans _____.
   a. rises; increases
   b. rises; decreases
   c. falls; increases
   d. falls; decreases

7. Which of the following is an objective of monetary policy?
   a. to conduct open market operations
   b. to choose the proper policy instrument
   c. to promote stable prices
   d. to insure equilibrium in the market for reserves

8. The k-percent rule is an example of
   a. a monetary base instrument rule.
   b. a money target rule.
   c. an exchange rate targeting rule.
   d. an inflation rate targeting rule.

9. If the Fed hikes the federal funds rate, then the quantity of money _____.
   a. increases
   b. does not change.
   c. decreases
   d. probably changes, but without more information it is not possible to determine if it increases, decreases, or does not change

10. If the Fed raises the federal funds rate, the growth rate of real GDP _____ and the inflation rate _____.
    a. speeds up; rises
    b. speeds up; falls
    c. slows down; rises
    d. slows down; falls

The answers for this Chapter Quiz are on page 266

Part Review 6 MACROECONOMIC POLICY

Mid-Term Examination

■ **Chapter 14**

1. If federal government outlays exceed tax revenues,
   a. there is a government budget surplus.
   b. there is a government budget deficit.
   c. the federal government debt must be decreasing.
   d. the premise of the question is incorrect because by law federal government outlays must equal tax revenues.

2. A tax on labor income ____ employment and ____ potential GDP.
   a. increases; increases
   b. increases; decreases
   c. decreases; increases
   d. decreases; decreases

3. The government expenditure multiplier is the magnification effect of a change in government expenditure of goods and services on
   a. potential GDP.
   b. short-run aggregate supply.
   c. aggregate demand.
   d. all of the above.

4. An example of a contractionary fiscal policy is
   a. a tax hike.
   b. an increase in government expenditures on goods and services.
   c. an increase in the budget deficit.
   d. an increase in needs-tested spending.

■ **Chapter 15**

5. An increase in the federal funds rate
   a. increases aggregate demand.
   b. raises the price level.
   c. decreases the supply of loanable funds.
   d. increases investment.

6. If the Fed wants to fight inflation, the Fed will
    a. raise the federal funds rate.
    b. lower the federal funds rate.
    c. increase investment.
    d. decrease the government budget deficit.

7. If the Fed buys government securities in the open market, the federal funds
   rate _____ and the supply of loanable funds _____.
    a. rises; increases
    b. rises; decreases
    c. falls; increases
    d. falls; decreases

8. The core inflation rate
    a. is more volatile than the total inflation rate.
    b. is the inflation rate the Federal Reserve uses to help it determine whether
       price stability is being achieved.
    c. equals the total inflation rate minus the inflation from housing and medical
       care.
    d. is the only factor the Federal Reserve uses when determining its monetary
       policy.

Answers

■ Mid-Term Exam Answers

1. b;   2. d;   3. c;   4. d;   5. c;   6. a;   7. c;   8. b.

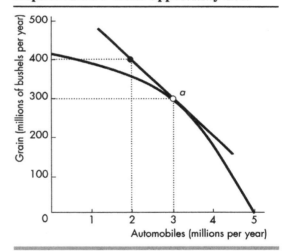

FIGURE **16.1**

Slope of the *PPF* is the Opportunity Cost

Chapter 16 TRADING WITH THE WORLD*

Key Concepts

■ Patterns and Trends in International Trade

The goods and services we buy from producers in other nations are our **imports**; the goods and services we sell to people in other nations are our **exports**. Most U.S. exports and imports are manufactured goods. Trade in goods accounts for most of U.S. international trade; trade in services (travel and transportation) accounts for the rest.

Trade has accounted for an increasingly large fraction of total output in the United States. **Net exports** is the value of exports minus the value of imports. In 2006, the value of U.S. imports exceeded that of U.S. exports.

■ The Gains from International Trade

Comparative advantage is the factor that drives international trade. Countries can produce anywhere on their production possibility frontier (*PPF*) curve. Figure 16.1 shows a *PPF* for a nation producing at point *a*.

♦ The *PPF's* slope is (Δbushels of grain)/(Δcars), with Δ meaning "change in." The slope, which is 100 bushels of grain per automobile, equals the opportunity cost of one more automobile at point *a*.

♦ A country has a **comparative advantage** in the production of a good if the country can produce it at a lower opportunity cost than any other country.

A country can gain by buying the goods from other nations that the nations produce at the lowest opportu-

nity cost and selling the goods it produces at the lowest opportunity cost to the other countries.

♦ A nation gains from trade by specializing in production of goods for which it has a comparative advantage and trading for other goods.

♦ With international trade, a nation receives a higher relative price for the goods it exports and pays a lower relative price for the goods it imports. The **terms of trade** is the quantity of exports that a nation must pay for its imports.

♦ International trade allows all nations to consume *outside* their *PPFs*. The added consumption is the gains from trade.

---

*This is Chapter 32 in *Economics*.

Some trade involves similar goods. There are two reasons for trade in similar goods:

♦ Diversified tastes — people demand many similar but slightly different products.

♦ Economies of scale — average total cost declines with output.

A nation can specialize in the production of one of the similar goods and capture economies of scale by trading the good throughout the world.

■ International Trade Restrictions

Governments restrict trade to protect domestic industries. The main methods used to restrict trade are:

♦ **Tariffs** — a tax imposed by the importing country when an imported good crosses its boundary.

♦ **Nontariff barrier** — any action other than a tariff that restricts international trade.

Today, U.S. tariffs are low compared to their historical levels. The **General Agreement on Tariffs and Trade** (GATT) is an international agreement designed to reduce tariffs. The **World Trade Organization**, to which the United States belongs, requires that nations more closely obey GATT rules. The **North American Free Trade Agreement** (NAFTA) is a 1994 agreement between the U.S., Canada, and Mexico that will remove most tariffs between these nations over a 15-year period.

Figure 16.2 illustrates the effects of a tariff.

♦ A tariff decreases the supply of the imported good. The new supply curve with the tariff lies above the old supply curve by the amount of the tariff (the length of the arrow).

♦ The price rises from P_0 to P_1 and the quantity decreases from Q_0 to Q_1. The government gains revenue as indicated in the figure. The tariff reduces the gains from trade and creates inefficiency.

♦ By decreasing imports to the domestic economy, foreigners can buy less from the domestic economy. The drop in the value of domestic exports equals the drop in the value of domestic imports.

Quotas and voluntary export restraints are nontariff barriers.

♦ **Quota** — a quantitative restriction on the maximum amount of a good that can be imported.

♦ **Voluntary export restraint** — an agreement between governments in which the exporting nation agrees to limit the volume of its exports. A VER is like a quota allocated to each exporter.

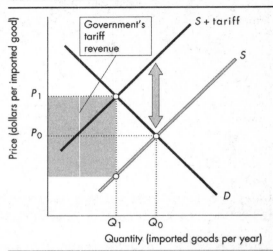

FIGURE 16.2
The Effect of a Tariff

Similar to tariffs, nontariff barriers raise the prices of imported goods and decrease the quantities imported. Unlike a tariff, the government gets no revenue from a nontariff barrier; the revenue from the higher price goes to importers in the case of quotas and to foreign exporters in the case of voluntary export restraints.

■ The Case Against Protection

Arguments in favor of protection are flawed. The arguments and their errors are:

♦ *National security* — the nation should protect industries that are necessary for its defense.
Error: Virtually every industry may be considered "vital" for defense; direct subsidies to targeted industries are more efficient than protection from international competition.

♦ **Infant-industry argument** — the nation should protect a young industry that will reap learning-by-doing gains in productivity and eventually be able to compete successfully in the world market.
Error: If the learning-by-doing benefits accrue only to the firms in the industry, this argument fails because these firms can finance their own start-ups; direct subsidies are more efficient.

♦ **Dumping** — the nation should protect an industry from foreign competitors who sell goods below cost.
Error: Determining when a firm sells below cost is very difficult; only global natural monopolies are able to sustain a monopoly; if the firm is a natural

monopoly, regulation is the more efficient way to restrain it.

- *Protection saves jobs* — imports cost U.S. jobs.
  Error: Free trade costs jobs in importing industries, but it creates them in exporting industries; tariffs that protect jobs in import-competing industries do so at an exceedingly high cost.

- *Cheap foreign labor* — tariffs are necessary to compete with cheap foreign labor.
  Error: U.S. labor is more productive than cheap foreign labor; U.S. firms can compete successfully in industries in which they have a comparative advantage because of their productivity relative to other nations.

- *Brings diversity and stability* — nations specialized in the production of one good might be subject to economic fluctuations.
  Error: The United States is not specialized; nations that are specialized can gain by such specialization and then diversify by investing abroad.

- *Lax environmental standards* — protection is needed to compete against nations with weak environmental standards.
  Error: Not all poor nations have weak standards; poor nations' concerns about the environment will increase when they grow richer through trade; currently poor nations might have a comparative advantage in pollution-intensive goods.

- *National culture* — protection is necessary to protect the nation's national culture.
  Error: Those clamoring for protection are simply "rent-seekers" involved in the country's national media outlets; many "American" producers of media are from other nations.

- *Rich nations exploit developing countries* — protection prevents developed nations from forcing people in poor nations to work for slave wages.
  Error: By allowing poor nations to trade with rich ones, wages in poor nations rise because of the increased demand for labor.

■ Why Is International Trade Restricted?

- The government collects revenue from tariffs. This revenue source is important in developing nations.

- Some people are harmed by international trade and so they lobby politicians to limit free trade.

Helpful Hints

1. **DOES PROTECTION SAVE JOBS ?** This argument is popular but incorrect. Imposing a tariff on imports costs jobs in export industries. We lose jobs because foreigners, unable to sell as much to us, are thus unable to buy as much from us. Hence our export industries shrink, or fail to grow as much as otherwise.

   Moreover, saving the jobs in the import-competing industry comes at a very high cost. For example, protection in the textile industry annually costs American residents $221,000 per job; in the automobile industry, $105,000 per job; in dairy products, $220,000 per job; and in steel, $750,000 per job. These costs greatly exceed the wages in these jobs. Just as it would be foolish to spend $221,000 to obtain $45,000, so, too, is it foolish for the nation to protect jobs when the cost of the protection exceeds the wages paid for the jobs!

2. **WHY DOES PROTECTION PERSIST ?** Gains from free trade can be considerable, so why do countries impose trade restrictions? The key is that, although free trade creates overall benefits to the economy as a whole, there are both winners and losers. The winners gain more in total than the losers lose, but the latter tend to be concentrated in a few industries. In other words, the gains from free trade are spread amongst many people — so the gain per person is small — while the costs are concentrated amongst only a few people— so the costs per person are large.

   Because of this concentration, free trade is resisted. Even though trade restrictions benefit only a small minority while the overwhelming majority are harmed, implementation of trade barriers is not surprising. The cost of a particular trade restriction to each of the majority individually is quite small, but the benefit to each of the few individually large. So the minority has a strong incentive to have a restriction imposed, whereas the majority has little incentive to expend time and energy in resisting a trade barrier. The net result is that governments frequently wind up restricting free trade, even though the restrictions cost their nations more than they benefit it.

Questions

■ True/False and Explain

Patterns and Trends In International Trade

1. Nations can trade goods but not services.

2. The United States is a large importer and exporter of manufactured goods.

3. In 2006, the value of American imports exceeded the value of American exports.

The Gains from International Trade

4. Each nation's opportunity cost of producing any good or service is the same.

5. A nation has a comparative advantage in a good if it can produce the good at a lower opportunity cost than other nations.

6. Trade allows a nation to consume a combination of goods and services that lie beyond its *PPF*.

7. Only the nation exporting a good gains from trade.

8. Nations do not trade similar goods.

9. Firms can capture economies of scale with international trade.

International Trade Restrictions

10. Tariffs in the United States are at an all-time high.

11. Economists generally agree that high tariffs improve a nation's standard of living.

12. When governments impose tariffs, they increase their consumers' welfare.

13. A quota and a voluntary export restraint on an imported good both raise its price.

The Case Against Protection

14. The only argument for protection without any error is the infant-industry argument.

15. U.S. workers can compete with lower paid foreign workers in industries in which the U.S. has a comparative advantage.

16. International trade lowers wages in poor nations.

Why Is International Trade Restricted?

17. Free international trade benefits some citizens and harms others.

■ Multiple Choice Questions

Patterns and Trends In International Trade

1. Which of the following is a U.S. service export?
   a. A U.S. citizen buys dinner while traveling in Switzerland.
   b. A Canadian buys a cap while in Canada.
   c. A Swiss citizen buys a computer made in the United States.
   d. A Mexican citizen spends the night in a motel while visiting the United States.

2. In 2006
   a. trade in services accounted for about 50 percent of total U.S. exports.
   b. agricultural products accounted for over 50 percent of total U.S. exports.
   c. the U.S. government rejected the NAFTA treaty.
   d. U.S. imports were greater in value than U.S. exports.

The Gains from International Trade

3. Musicland and Videoland produce two goods, CDs and DVDs. Musicland has a comparative advantage in the production of CDs if in Musicland
   a. fewer DVDs must be given up to produce 1 CD than in Videoland.
   b. less labor is required to produce 1 CD than in Videoland.
   c. less capital is required to produce 1 CD than in Videoland.
   d. less labor and capital are required to produce 1 CD than in Videoland.

4. International trade allows a nation to
   a. produce and consume at a point beyond its *PPF*.
   b. produce at a point beyond its *PPF* but not consume at a point beyond its *PPF*.
   c. consume at a point beyond its *PPF* but not produce at a point beyond its *PPF*.
   d. neither produce nor consume at a point beyond its *PPF*.

5. The maximum gains from trade occur when
   a. there is no international trade.
   b. each nation produces according to its comparative advantage and trades with other nations.
   c. each nation uses tariffs rather than quotas.
   d. each nation uses quotas rather than tariffs.

Figures 16.3 and 16.4 show production in two nations, Solaris and Chaff. Production is taking place at point *a* in Solaris and at point *b* in Chaff. Use these figures for the next four questions.

FIGURE **16.3**
Production in Solaris

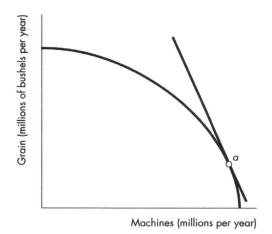

FIGURE **16.4**
Production in Chaff

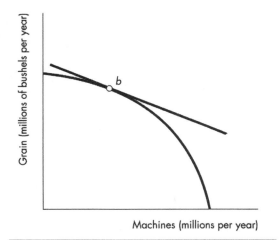

6. The slope of the *PPF* at point *a* in Solaris is 200 bushels of grain per machine; the slope of the *PPF* at point *b* in Chaff is 15 bushels of grain per machine. Without trade between the nations, what is the opportunity cost of a machine in Solaris?
   a. The cost is 200 bushels of grain.
   b. The cost is $1/200$ bushels of grain.
   c. The cost is 15 bushels of grain.
   d. The cost is $1/15$ bushel of grain.

7. Without trade between the nations, what is the opportunity cost of a machine in Chaff?
   a. The cost is 200 bushels of grain.
   b. The cost is $1/200$ bushels of grain.
   c. The cost is 15 bushels of grain.
   d. The cost is $1/15$ bushel of grain.

8. Solaris has a comparative advantage in _____, and Chaff has a comparative advantage in _____.
   a. machines; grain
   b. grain; machines
   c. machines and grain; neither good
   d. neither good; machines and grain.

9. Once Solaris and Chaff begin to trade, Solaris exports _____ to Chaff and Chaff exports _____ to Solaris.
   a. machines; grain
   b. grain; machines
   c. machines and grain; neither good
   d. neither good; machines and grain

10. International trade based on comparative advantage can allow each country to consume
    a. more of the goods it exports, but always less of the goods it imports.
    b. more of the goods it imports, but always less of the goods it exports.
    c. more of the goods it exports and imports.
    d. less of the goods it exports and imports.

11. The combination of diversified tastes and economies of scale can account for
    a. a nation importing and exporting similar products.
    b. why tariffs create inefficiency.
    c. specialization according to comparative advantage.
    d. the result that free trade allows nations to consume at points beyond their *PPF* even though they cannot produce at points beyond their *PPF*.

International Trade Restrictions

12. A tariff is
    a. a government imposed limit on the amount of a good that can be exported from a nation.
    b. a government imposed barrier that sets a fixed limit on the amount of a good that can be imported into a nation.
    c. a tax on a good imported into a nation.
    d. an agreement between governments to limit exports from a nation.

13. Who benefits from a tariff on a good?
    a. Domestic consumers of the good
    b. Domestic producers of the good
    c. Foreign governments
    d. Foreign producers of the good

14. Suppose that the United States imports only textiles from Mexico and exports only computers to Mexico. If the United States imposes a tariff on Mexican textiles, the U.S. textile industry _____ and the U.S. computer industry _____.
    a. expands; expands
    b. expands; does not change
    c. expands; contracts
    d. contracts; expands

15. When does the government gain the most revenue?
    a. When it imposes a tariff.
    b. When it imposes a quota.
    c. When it negotiates a voluntary export restraint.
    d. The amount of revenue it gains is the same with a tariff and a voluntary export restraint.

The Case Against Protection

16. The (false) idea that an industry should be protected because of learning-by-doing until it is large enough to compete successfully in world markets is the _____ argument for protection.
    a. absolute advantage
    b. infant industry
    c. dumping
    d. diversity

17. Selling a product in a foreign nation at a price less than its cost of production is called
    a. infant industry exploitation.
    b. absolute advantage.
    c. dumping.
    d. net exporting.

18. When a rich nation buys a product made in a poor nation, in the poor nation the demand for labor _____ and the wage rate _____.
    a. increases; rises
    b. increases; falls
    c. decreases; rises
    d. decreases; falls

19. Which of the following is a valid reason for protecting an industry?
    a. The industry is unable to compete with low-wage foreign competitors.
    b. The industry is necessary to diversify the nation's production.
    c. Protection keeps richer nations from exploiting the workers of poorer countries.
    d. None of the above reasons is a valid reason for protection.

Why Is International Trade Restricted?

20. Which of the following statements about the gains from international trade is correct?
    a. Everyone gains from international trade.
    b. Some people gain from international trade and some lose, though overall the gains exceed the losses.
    c. Some people gain and some people lose from international trade; overall the losses exceed the gains.
    d. Everyone loses from international trade.

Short Answer Problems

FIGURE 16.5
Short Answer Problem 1

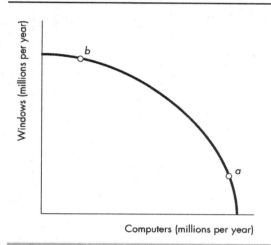

1. Two nations, Disc and Chip, have the same *PPF*. Both nations produce only two goods, windows and computers. Figure 16.5 shows their current production points: Disc at point *a* and Chip at point *b*.
   a. In which nation is the opportunity cost of a window lowest? In which is the opportunity cost of a computer lowest? Explain how you arrived at your answer.
   b. Which nation has a comparative advantage in producing windows? In producing computers? Why?
   c. If Disc and Chip trade, which nation would export windows? Which would export computers? Why?

2. A nation produces only wheat and computer chips. It has a comparative advantage in chips. Draw a production possibility frontier and use it to show how the nation specializes and the gains from trade.

3. How does a tariff on an imported good affect the domestic price of the good? The quantity of the good imported? The quantity of the good produced domestically?

4. How does a quota on an imported good affect the domestic price of the good, the quantity imported, and the quantity produced domestically?

5. How does a tariff on imports affect the exports of the country?

TABLE 16.1
Market for Watches in Norolex

Price (dollars per watch)	Quantity demanded (millions of watches)	Quantity supplied (millions of watches)
$20	65	15
25	60	20
30	55	25
35	50	30
40	45	35
45	40	40
50	35	45

6. Table 16.1 gives the domestic supply and demand schedules for watches for the nation of Norolex.
   a. Draw the supply and demand schedules in Figure 16.6.
   b. What is the equilibrium price?
   c. How many watches are produced in Norolex? How many are purchased by consumers in Norolex?

FIGURE 16.6
Short Answer Problems 6 and 7

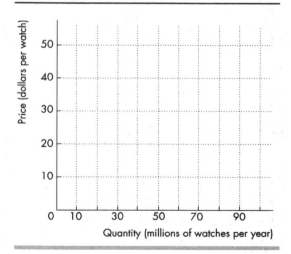

TABLE 16.2
Supply Schedule of Watches with Trade

Price (dollars per watch)	Quantity supplied in Norolex (millions of watches)	Quantity supplied by Switch (millions of watches)	Total quantity supplied (millions of watches)
$20	15	20	___
25	20	25	___
30	25	30	___
35	30	35	___
40	35	40	___
45	40	45	___
50	45	50	___

7. Norolex now trades with another nation, Switch. Switch exports watches to Norolex. Switch's export supply schedule is in Table 16.2 along with Norolex's domestic supply schedule.

   a. Complete Table 16.2 by determining the total supply schedule of watches.

   b. Graph the total supply schedule in Figure 16.6, which already contains the domestic supply and demand schedules you graphed from the previous question.

   c. What is the new equilibrium price of a watch?

   d. How many watches are produced in Norolex? How many are purchased by consumers in Norolex? How many are imported?

8. The watch industry in Norolex is unhappy with the situation after trade with Switch has occurred. The watch industry lobbies the government to impose a $15 per watch tariff on imports from Switch.

   a. Complete Table 16.3, which shows how the tariff affects imports from Switch.

   b. Using your answers from Table 16.3, complete Table 16.4, which shows the new total supply schedule after the tariff has been imposed.

   c. After the tariff is imposed, what is the equilibrium price of a watch in Norolex?

   d. How many watches are produced in Norolex? How many watches are purchased by consumers in Norolex? How many watches are imported?

   e. Relative to the situation in problem 6, explain who has gained from the tariff and who has lost. Explain why the gainers have gained and the losers have lost.

TABLE 16.3
Short Answer Problem 8 (a)

Price (dollars per watch)	Pre-tariff quantity supplied by Switch (millions of watches)	Post-tariff quantity supplied by Switch (millions of watches)
$20	20	5
25	25	10
30	30	15
35	35	___
40	40	___
45	45	___
50	50	___

TABLE 16.4
Short Answer Problem 8 (b)

Price (dollars per watch)	Quantity supplied in Norolex (millions of watches)	Quantity supplied by Switch (millions of watches)	Total quantity supplied (millions of watches)
$20	15	5	___
25	20	10	___
30	25	15	___
35	30	___	___
40	35	___	___
45	40	___	___
50	45	___	___

■ You're the Teacher

1. "I understand the stuff about comparative advantage. But I can't see how the United States can compete with nations like Mexico, where the wages are so low. We have to protect our high wages by keeping Mexican products out of our markets." Your friend thinks he understands comparative advantage, but he does not. Help him understand comparative advantage. Explain how American firms can compete with Mexican companies.

2. After you explain the error in question 1, your friend makes another mistake: "OK, now I see how U.S. firms can compete. But, still, international trade can't be good. After all, if this trade helps Mexico, we must lose. So I still think that international trade should be banned." Explain to your friend how international trade benefits both America and Mexico.

Answers

■ True/False Answers

Patterns and Trends In International Trade

1. **F** Services, such as travel abroad, transportation, and insurance, can be traded internationally.

2. **T** The majority of U.S. imports and U.S. exports are manufactured goods.

3. **T** In 2006, as throughout the 1980s and 1990s, the value of U.S. imports exceeded the value of U.S. exports.

The Gains from International Trade

4. **F** Because nations have different opportunity costs, international trade can raise the welfare of *each* nation.

5. **T** The question presents the definition of comparative advantage.

6. **T** The nation gains from trade because it can consume a combination of goods and services that lie beyond its *PPF*.

7. **F** All nations engaged in international trade gain from the trade.

8. **F** Diversity of tastes and economies of scale account for the considerable international trade that takes place in similar goods.

9. **T** Long production runs, which create economies of scale, can be sold internationally.

International Trade Restrictions

10. **F** Tariffs in the United States are near an all-time low.

11. **F** Economists agree that tariffs reduce a nation's standard of living.

12. **F** By raising the price of imported goods, tariffs harm consumers.

13. **T** Tariffs, quotas, and voluntary export restraints all limit the quantity of imports and thus all raise the price of imports.

The Case Against Protection

14. **F** All arguments for protection are flawed.

15. **T** In industries with a comparative advantage, higher productivity more than offsets higher wages, so American firms can successfully compete.

16. **F** International trade *raises* wages in poor nations.

Why Is International Trade Restricted?

17. **T** Free trade benefits consumers and workers (and firms) in exporting industries. It harms workers (and firms) in import-competing industries.

■ Multiple Choice Answers

Patterns and Trends In International Trade

1. **d** The Mexican resident has purchased a service, lodging, from an American firm.

2. **d** The value of U.S. imports exceeded the value of U.S. exports in 2006 and in most recent years.

The Gains from International Trade

3. **a** The opportunity cost of a good is the number of other goods that must be foregone to increase production of the good.

4. **c** With or without international trade, producing at points beyond the *PPF* is impossible, but international trade allows consumption to occur at points beyond the *PPF*.

5. **b** Free trade with production taking place according to comparative advantage creates the maximum gains from trade.

6. **a** The opportunity cost equals the slope of the *PPF* because the slope is the opportunity cost, in terms of grain, of producing 1 more machine.

7. **c** For the reason outlined in the answer to question 6, the opportunity cost of a machine in Chaff is 15 bushels of grain.

8. **b** The opportunity cost of grain is less in Solaris, and the opportunity cost of a machine is less in Chaff.

9. **b** Each nation exports the good in which it has a comparative advantage.

10. **c** By specializing in the products with a comparative advantage and trading with other nations, the nation can consume more of both the goods it imports and the goods it exports.

11. **a** By specializing in the production of one good that is similar to another and then exporting the good, a firm can capture economies of scale and satisfy people's desires for its particular variation of the good.

International Trade Restrictions

12. **c** Answer (c) is the definition of a tariff.

13. **b** Domestic producers gain because the price of the product rises.

14. **c** The textile industry gains from the tariff, and the computer industry loses.

15. **a** Unlike tariffs, the government gets no revenue from quotas and voluntary export restraints.

The Case Against Protection

16. **b** The description in the problem is the definition of the infant industry argument for protection.

17. **c** Although often alleged, dumping is difficult to prove because it is difficult to determine whether a firm is selling below its cost.

18. **a** By increasing the demand for the goods produced in the poor nation, the demand for labor increases, thereby raising the wage rate in that nation.

19. **d** All of the reasons offered for protection are faulty.

Why Is International Trade Restricted?

20. **b** Because the overall gains exceed the overall loses, in principle the losers from international trade can be compensated so that, on balance, everyone gains from the trade.

■ Answers to Short Answer Problems

1. a. The opportunity cost of a window is lowest in Disc. The opportunity cost of a computer is lowest in Chip.

   Figure 16.7 demonstrates these result. The opportunity cost of a computer equals the magnitude of the slope of the line tangent to the *PPF*. In Figure 16.7, the magnitude of the slope of the line tangent at point *b* is less than the magnitude of the line tangent at point *a*. Hence the opportunity cost of a computer is less at point *b*, which is where Chip produces. The opportunity cost of a window equals the inverse of the slopes of these lines, so the opportunity cost of a window is less at point *a*, which is Disc's production point.

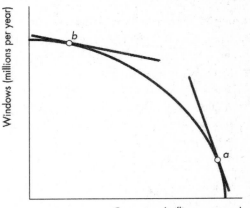

FIGURE **16.7**
Short Answer Problem 1

Windows (millions per year)

Computers (millions per year)

   b. Disc has a comparative advantage in producing windows because its opportunity cost of producing a window is less than Chip's opportunity cost. Similarly, Chip has a comparative advantage in producing computers.

   c. Disc would export windows and Chip would export computers because these are the goods for which each nation has a comparative advantage. Alternatively, windows are relatively cheaper in Disc, so Disc will export Windows. Computers are relatively less expensive in Chip, so Chip will export computers.

2. Figure 16.8 (on the next page) shows the situation in the nation. In the figure, before trade the nation initially produces and consumes *W* bushels of wheat and *C* chips. Without trade, the amount of wheat consumed equals the amount produced and the number of chips consumed equals the number produced. Once the nation trades, it changes its production of wheat and chips. With trade, the nation increases its production of computer chips and decreases its production of wheat. This change is illustrated in Figure 16.8, where the nation produces C_p chips and W_p bushels of wheat. However, the nation does not consume these amounts of chips and wheat. Instead, it exports chips and imports wheat

FIGURE 16.8
Short Answer Problem 2

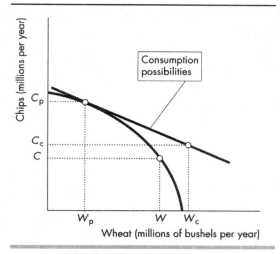

so that it consumes (along its consumption possibilities line) C_c computer chips and W_c bushels of wheat. Note that the nation consumes fewer chips than it produces and more wheat than it grows.

The gains from trade are illustrated in Figure 16.8 because with trade the nation consumes more chips *and* more wheat than it consumed without trade. (Compare the initial consumption bundle of C chips and W bushels of wheat to the post-trade bundle of C_c chips and W_c bushels of wheat.) International trade has allowed this nation to increase its consumption of *all* goods, which makes its inhabitants better off.

3. A tariff on an imported good raises its price to domestic consumers because the foreign export supply decreases. As the domestic price of the good climbs, the quantity of the good demanded decreases, so the quantity imported decreases. The rise in the domestic price leads to an increase in the quantity of the good produced domestically.

4. The effect of a quota on the domestic price of the good, the quantity imported, and the quantity of the good produced domestically are exactly the same as the effects of a tariff discussed in the answer to short answer problem 3. The difference is that with a tariff the rise in the domestic price occurs because foreigners decrease their supply of the good at all prices (that is, the foreign supply curve with the tariff lies above the initial supply curve without the

tariff). A quota, however, forces the export supply curve to become vertical at the quota amount.

5. When a country imposes a tariff on its imports, the volume of its imports shrink, and the volume of its exports to other countries shrinks by the same amount. A tariff limits the amount of goods that other nations can sell to the first country and also lowers the price the other nations receive for their products. So when a nation limits its imports, foreign nations cannot afford to buy as many exports from the first country, so the tariff decreases the nation's exports.

FIGURE 16.9
Short Answer Problem 6

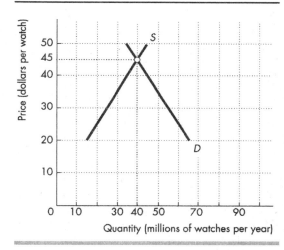

6. a. Figure 16.9 shows the demand and supply schedules.

   b. Either from Figure 16.9 or from the demand and supply schedules, the equilibrium price with no international trade is $45 because at this price the quantity demanded equals the quantity supplied.

   c. With no trade, forty million watches per year are produced domestically, and so 40 million watches per year are purchased by consumers in Norolex.

7. a. Table 16.5 (on the next page) shows the total supply schedule. At any price, the total quantity supplied in Norolex equals the sum of the quantity produced in Norolex plus the quantity supplied by Switch.

TABLE **16.5**

Short Answer Problem 7 (a)

Price (dollars per watch)	Quantity supplied in Norolex (millions of watches)	Quantity supplied by Switch (millions of watches)	Total quantity supplied (millions of watches)
$20	15	20	<u>35</u>
25	20	25	<u>45</u>
30	25	30	<u>55</u>
35	30	35	<u>65</u>
40	35	40	<u>75</u>
45	40	45	<u>85</u>
50	45	50	<u>95</u>

FIGURE **16.10**

Short Answer Problem 7

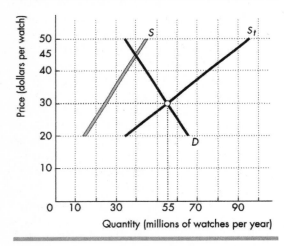

TABLE **16.6**

Short Answer Problem 8 (a)

Price (dollars per watch)	Pre-tariff quantity supplied by Switch (millions of watches)	Post-tariff quantity supplied by Switch (millions of watches)
$20	20	5
25	25	10
30	30	15
35	35	<u>20</u>
40	40	<u>25</u>
45	45	<u>30</u>
50	50	<u>35</u>

TABLE **16.7**

Short Answer Problem 8 (b)

Price (dollars per watch)	Quantity supplied in Norolex (millions of watches)	Quantity supplied by Switch (millions of watches)	Total quantity supplied (millions of watches)
$20	15	5	<u>20</u>
25	20	10	<u>30</u>
30	25	15	<u>40</u>
35	30	<u>20</u>	<u>50</u>
40	35	<u>25</u>	<u>60</u>
45	40	<u>30</u>	<u>70</u>
50	45	<u>35</u>	<u>80</u>

b. Figure 16.10 shows the total supply curve, S_t, the initial supply curve, and the demand curve.

c. The new equilibrium price of a watch is $30.

d. At the equilibrium price of $30, consumers in Norolex buy 55 million watches per year. At this price, watch firms in Norolex produce 25 million watches. The difference between the total quantity of watches purchased and the total quantity produced, 30 million watches per year, is imported from Switch.

8. a. Table 16.6 shows how the tariff affects the supply schedule of imports from Switch. A $15 per watch tariff lowers the receipts of the firms in Switch by $15 per watch. Hence when the price,

including the tariff, is $35 a watch, the watch companies receive only $20 per watch. As the initial supply schedule shows, when the Switch watch companies receive $20 per watch, they supply 20 million watches. The remainder of the supply schedule is calculated similarly.

b. The new total supply schedule equals the sum of the Norolex supply schedule plus the new, post-tariff Switch supply schedule. Table 16.7 shows the new total supply schedule.

c. The equilibrium price of a watch is $35.

d. At the price of $35, consumers buy 50 million watches per year. Firms in Norolex produce 30 million watches per year. Imports from Switch are 20 million watches per year.

e. The watch firms and their workers in Norolex have gained. With the tariff, they produce more watches and receive a higher price. The Norolex government also has gained because it obtains revenue from the tariff, $300 million. (The tariff revenue equals the tariff, $15 per watch, multiplied by the number of watches imported, 20 million.) Consumers in Norolex and the Switch watch manufacturing firms and their workers have lost. Consumers have lost because they must pay a higher price for a watch ($35 with the tariff compared to $30 without the tariff) and so respond by purchasing fewer watches. Switch firms and workers have lost because the lower price they receive for a watch leads them to produce fewer watches for export (20 million with the tariff versus 30 million without).

■ You're the Teacher

1. "Look, you don't have the main idea here. Let's use some numbers because they should help you catch on. Suppose that American wages are 10 times higher than Mexican wages. Now, it's also a fact that American workers are more productive than Mexican workers. Let's take two industries. In the first, call it industry A, suppose that American workers are 2 times as productive as Mexican ones; in the second, say, industry B, American workers are 20 times as productive. In industry A, American firms won't be able to compete with Mexican firms. Sure, our workers are twice as productive, but they are paid ten times as much. Therefore American firms will lose out in this industry. But in industry B, American companies firms will drive Mexican ones out of business. Even though our workers are paid 10 times as much as Mexican workers are paid, they produce 20 times as much as Mexican workers produce. So the per unit cost of the good is less in the United States, so American firms are going to be able to compete and compete successfully.

"The United States won't be able to compete successfully with Mexico in producing every type of good or service but the reason is that the United States does not (and cannot) have a comparative advantage in all goods and services even though it might well have an absolute advantage. But in the industry with the comparative advantage — industry B in my example — the United States is going to be able to compete and to win the competition."

2. "Well, I'm glad you're catching onto some of the ideas of this chapter, but you're missing another key point. The chapter explains how trade allows all nation to consume more goods and services than it can produce. Remember the diagrams showing how a nation can consume more of everything if it trades? Obviously, this fact has to make nations engaged in international trade better off.

"But there's also another a way to tackle this point. I read somewhere that 'trade is not a zero-sum game.' Here's what that means: If you and I voluntarily agree to a trade, like I'll trade my economics notes for your chemistry notes, the trade has to make us both better off. After all, if the trade didn't make me better off, I wouldn't agree to it and if it didn't make you better off, you wouldn't agree to it. This type of trade will enable both of us to raise our grades: me in chemistry and you in economics.

"Well, it's the same idea with trading between nations. Suppose that we import a VCR from Mexico and the Mexicans use the money we sent them to buy 50 bushels of wheat from Kansas. Essentially, we've traded the 50 bushels of wheat for the VCR. If this trade didn't make us better off, we wouldn't do it. So, too, for the Mexicans involved: If they didn't want the wheat more than the VCR, they won't agree to the transaction. And, as the chapter explained, if we specialize in wheat and Mexico in VCRs, we both will be able to consume more wheat and more VCRs than if we produced VCRs and wheat and Mexico produced VCRs and wheat.

"Or think about this more generally. For two potential trading partners to be willing to trade, they must have different comparative advantages, that is, different opportunity costs. Then they will trade and *both* parties will gain. If the countries do not trade, each faces and must pay its own opportunity costs. The price at which trade takes place will be somewhere between the opportunity costs of the two nations. With trade, the country with the lower opportunity cost of the good in question gains because it receives a price above its opportunity cost. Similarly, the country with the higher opportunity cost gains because it pays a price below its opportunity cost.

"You know, I think this is really cool. What it shows is that just as trade between us makes both of us better off, trade between nations makes both nations better off."

Chapter Quiz

1. It is ____ to import a service and it is ____ to export a service.

   a. possible; possible
   b. possible; not possible
   c. not possible; possible
   d. not possible; not possible

2. The U.S. balance of trade is the value of ____ and has been ____ in recent years.

   a. imports minus the value of exports; positive
   b. exports minus the value of imports; positive
   c. imports minus the value of exports; negative
   d. exports minus the value of imports; negative

3. A *PPF* has corn on the vertical axis and computers on the horizontal axis. The opportunity cost of an additional computer is the magnitude of the

   a. slope of a ray from the origin to the *PPF*.
   b. inverse of the slope of a ray from the origin to the *PPF*.
   c. slope of the *PPF*.
   d. inverse of the slope of the *PPF*.

4. Between two nations, to determine whether a nation has a comparative advantage in a product, it is necessary to compare the

   a. total amount produced in each nation.
   b. opportunity costs in the nations.
   c. total demand for the products in each nation.
   d. None of the above.

5. If a nation does *not* trade with the rest of the world, its consumption possibility frontier

   a. is identical to its *PPF*.
   b. lies outside its *PPF*.
   c. lies inside its *PPF*.
   d. has no particular relationship to its *PPF*.

6. The direct effect of a tariff is to restrict ____ and benefit ____.

   a. exports; producers
   b. exports; consumers
   c. imports; producers
   d. imports; consumers

7. The United States today imposes an average tariff of approximately

   a. 4 percent on imports.
   b. 4 percent on exports.
   c. 40 percent on imports.
   d. 40 percent on exports.

8. When a quota is imposed, the difference between the domestic price and the world price is collected by

   a. the domestic government.
   b. the foreign government.
   c. domestic consumers.
   d. domestic importers of the good.

9. It is possible for expensive U.S. labor to compete successfully against less expensive foreign labor because U.S. labor

   a. pays taxes in the United States.
   b. can travel abroad to produce the goods in other nations.
   c. frequently belongs to powerful labor unions that protect their interest.
   d. is more productive.

10. If a poor nation exports a good to a rich nation, in the poor nation wages in the export sector ____ and employment ____.

   a. rise; increases
   b. rise; decreases
   c. fall; decreases
   d. fall; increases

The answers for this Chapter Quiz are on page 266

■ **Chapter 16**

1. If the United States has an excess of exports over imports, the United States has
   a. a negative net exports balance that is financed by U.S. lending to foreigners.
   b. a negative net exports balance that is financed by U.S. borrowing from foreigners.
   c. a positive net exports balance that is financed by U.S. lending to foreigners.
   d. a positive net exports balance that is financed by U.S. borrowing from foreigners.

2. If an efficient country trades with the rest of the world, it produces at a point that lies
   a. inside its production possibilities frontier.
   b. on its production possibilities frontier.
   c. outside its production possibilities frontier.
   d. either inside or outside its production possibilities frontier.

3. When the full effects are considered, a reduction in tariffs would
   a. decrease imports and increase exports.
   b. increase imports and decrease exports.
   c. increase imports and exports.
   d. decrease imports and exports.

4. Which of the following earns revenue for the domestic government?
   a. Tariffs.
   b. Quotas.
   c. Voluntary export restraints.
   d. Subsidies.

Answers

■ Mid-Term Exam Answers

1. c;   2. b;   3. c;   4. a.

Final Exams

Exam 1

1. Of the following, which would *not* be included in GDP?
   a. Your purchase of a haircut.
   b. Your purchase of a used textbook for this course.
   c. Your investment of $100 in a savings account at your bank.
   d. Neither b nor c would be included in GDP.

2. Which points in a production possibilities frontier are both attainable and inefficient?
   a. Points beyond the frontier.
   b. Points on the frontier.
   c. Points within the frontier.
   d. Both points on and within the frontier.

3. Suppose a heat wave in the South causes millions of chickens to commit suicide. Keeping in mind that only live chickens can be sold to be processed into food, as a result of the heat the equilibrium price of a chicken dinner ____ and the equilibrium quantity ____.
   a. rises; increases
   b. probably changes, but in an ambiguous direction; decreases
   c. rises; probably changes, but in an ambiguous direction
   d. rises; decreases

4. If the government's budget deficit increases and there is no Ricardo-Barro effect, then the
   a. supply of loanable funds decreases.
   b. supply of loanable funds increases.
   c. demand for loanable funds decreases.
   d. demand for loanable funds increases.

5. According to the quantity theory, changes in the growth rate of the quantity of money lead to changes in the inflation rate. Using the new classical cycle theory, if the public expects aggregate demand to increase, then the increase in aggregate demand has no effect on the unemployment rate.
   a. Both sentences are true.
   b. The first sentence is true; the second sentence is false.
   c. The first sentence is false; the second sentence is true.
   d. Both sentences are false.

6. If the inflation rate is 10 percent and the real interest rate is 3 percent, the nominal interest rate is approximately
   a. 30 percent
   b. 7 percent
   c. 13 percent
   d. 3.3 percent

7. The stage of the business cycle during which output is falling is
   a. the recession.
   b. the expansion.
   c. the peak.
   d. the trough.

8. The supply curve for pizza does <u>NOT</u> shift if there is a change in the
   a. number of sellers of pizza.
   b. technology used to produce pizza.
   c. price of pizza.
   d. price of resources (such as cheese) used to produce pizza.

9. If the government's tax revenues are $1,050 billion and its total outlays are $1,000 billion, the government has a
    a. deficit of $50 billion
    b. surplus of $50 billion
    c. deficit of $900 billion
    d. surplus of $950 billion

10. An assumption of the neoclassical growth theory is that
    a. in the long run, people earn only a subsistence real wage rate.
    b. all technological advances are the result of people's deliberate actions.
    c. the economy-wide return to capital diminishes as more capital is accumulated.
    d. knowledge is not subject to diminishing returns.

11. Fiscal policy includes a change in
    a. the quantity of money.
    b. the price level.
    c. the unemployment rate.
    d. tax rates.

12. Suppose the slope of the *AE* curve is 0.9. If investment decreases by $20 billion, then the *AD* curve
    a. shifts rightward by $200 billion.
    b. shifts leftward by $200 billion.
    c. shifts rightward by $20 billion.
    d. shifts leftward by $20 billion.

13. As we move along a production possibilities frontier producing more and more of a good, the opportunity cost of producing extra units of this good _____.
    a. falls
    b. does not change
    c. rises
    d. may rise, fall, or not change

14. GDP equals
    a. aggregate expenditure.
    b. aggregate income.
    c. the value of the aggregate production in a country during a given time period.
    d. all of the above

For the next two questions, suppose the government increased its expenditures on goods, that is, *G* increases. In the short run, the economy moves along the short-run *AS* curve; in the long-run it moves along the long-run *AS* curve.

15. In the short run, the price level ____ and real GDP ____.
    a. rises; increases
    b. rises; does not change
    c. does not change; increases
    d. rises; decreases

16. In the long run, the price level ____ and real GDP ____.
    a. rises; increases
    b. rises; does not change
    c. does not change; increases
    d. rises; decreases

17. The federal funds rate is the interest rate that
    a. the Federal Reserve charges banks for loans from the Federal Reserve.
    b. banks charge the Federal Reserve for loans from the banks.
    c. banks charge each other for the loan of reserves.
    d. None of the above.

18. An increase in unemployment compensation payments means that the opportunity cost to unemployed workers from searching for jobs decreases. When the cost of searching for jobs decreases, unemployed workers will be more likely to accept job offers.
    a. Both sentences are true.
    b. The first sentence is true; the second sentence is false.
    c. The first sentence is false; the second sentence is true.
    d. Both sentences are false.

19. What type of unemployment would include a high school graduate who has just entered the labor force and is looking for a job?
    a. frictional
    b. structural
    c. cyclical
    d. excessive

20. Output is at its highest point at _____ and this is followed by _____.
    a. the recession; the trough.
    b. an expansion; a recession
    c. the peak; a recession.
    d. the peak; an expansion.

21. The most *common* way the Fed has of increasing the quantity of money is by
    a. raising the required reserve ratio.
    b. lowering the required reserve ratio.
    c. buying a government security.
    d. selling a government security.

22. According to the _____ theory of business cycles, a change in the growth rate of the quantity of money has no effect on real GDP.
    a. Keynesian cycle theory
    b. monetarist cycle theory
    c. new Keynesian cycle theory
    d. real business cycle

23. Which of the following is included in the investment component of GDP?
    a. Microsoft's purchase of stock in IBM.
    b. GE's investment of $100,000 in a savings account at its bank.
    c. Ford Motor's purchase of a factory previously owned by GM.
    d. Leonardo's Pizza's (a local pizza restaurant) purchase of a new pizza oven.

24. The exchange rate changes from 100 yen per dollar to 130 yen per dollar. The yen has _____ against the dollar and the dollar has _____ against the yen.
    a. depreciated; appreciated
    b. depreciated; depreciated;
    c. appreciated; appreciated
    d. appreciated; depreciated

25. Which theory is characterized by the conclusion that people receive only a subsistence wage rate?
    a. The classical theory of growth.
    b. The Monetarist theory of business cycles.
    c. The Keynesian theory of business cycles.
    d. The neoclassical theory of growth.

26. A lot of trade between nations involves trading similar goods (that is, the U.S. both imports and exports automobiles to Japan). Which of the following is *not* a reason for trade in similar goods?
    a. Diversified tastes.
    b. Absolute advantage.
    c. Economies of scale.
    d. None of the above because they are all reasons why nations trade similar goods..

27. A decrease in the expected future exchange rate shifts the demand curve for U.S. dollars _____ and the supply curve of U.S. dollars _____.
    a. rightward; rightward
    b. rightward; leftward
    c. leftward; rightward
    d. leftward; leftward

28. When the Federal Reserve buys a government security, banks' reserves will _____.
    a. increase
    b. not change
    c. decrease
    d. possibly change, depending on whether the Fed purchased the security from a bank or from another seller

29. Suppose that the growth rate of velocity is 1 percent, the growth rate of the quantity of money is 7 percent, and the growth rate of real GDP is 3 percent. Then the inflation rate is
    a. 8 percent.
    b. 6 percent.
    c. 5 percent.
    d. While the inflation rate can be calculated using the numbers given, none of the answers given above are correct.

30. The price of cheese used to produce pizza rises. As a result of the increase in cost, the equilibrium relative price of a pizza _____ and the equilibrium quantity produced _____.
    a. rises; increases
    b. rises; decreases
    c. falls; increases
    d. falls; decreases

Exam 2

1. If the government cuts taxes on labor income, potential GDP _____ and the *LAS* curve shifts _____.
   a. increases; rightward
   b. increases; leftward
   c. decreases; rightward
   d. decreases; leftward

2. The situation of the price level rising and GDP falling — stagflation — could be the result of the
   a. *AD* curve shifting leftward.
   b. *AD* curve shifting rightward.
   c. *SAS* curve shifting leftward.
   d. *SAS* curve shifting rightward.

3. Which of the following *shifts* the *SAS* curve leftward?
   a. an increase in the price level
   b. a decrease in the price level
   c. an increase in money wages
   d. a decrease in money wages

4. An unexpected increase in the inflation rate _____
   the unemployment rate and an expected increase in
   the inflation rate _____ the unemployment rate.
   a. raises; raises
   b. raises; does not change
   c. lowers; does not change
   d. lowers; lowers

5. In the short-run, when the Fed lowers the federal
   funds rate, the price level _____ and real GDP
   _____.
   a. rises; increases
   b. rises; decreases
   c. falls; increases
   d. falls; decreases

6. Neoclassical growth theory
   a. asserts that in the long run people are paid a sub-
      sistence wage
   b. concludes that growth rates of different nations
      must differ.
   c. predicts that economic growth will be perpetual.
   d. assumes technological progress is the result of
      chance.

7. Open-market operations are the purchase or sale of
   government securities by commercial banks.
   a. True
   b. False

8. An increase in consumers' income shifts the _____
   curve for normal goods _____.
   a. demand; leftward
   b. demand; rightward
   c. supply; leftward
   d. supply; rightward

9. Suppose that people decide eating pizza is stylish
   and simultaneously a new pizza oven is invented that
   lowers the cost of producing a pizza. The relative
   price of a pizza _____ and the quantity _____.
   a. rises; increases
   b. falls; increases
   c. probably changes, but in an ambiguous direc-
      tion; increases
   d. rises; probably changes, but in an ambiguous
      direction

10. Which of the following factors does **NOT** *shift* the
    AD curve?
    a. a change in government expenditures
    b. a change in the quantity of money
    c. a change in taxes
    d. a change in the price level

11. The most expansionary fiscal policy of the following
    is the one that
    a. lowers government expenditure and lowers taxes.
    b. raises government expenditure and lowers taxes.
    c. raises government expenditure and raises taxes
       even more.
    d. raises taxes.

12. An increase in households' saving increases the
    _____ and _____ the real interest rate.
    a. supply of loanable funds; raises
    b. supply of loanable funds; lowers
    c. demand for loanable funds; raises
    d. demand for loanable funds; lowers

13. When would the U.S. exchange rate rise the most?
    a. When the supply of and demand for U.S. dollars increase.
    b. When the supply of U.S. dollars increases and the demand for them decreases.
    c. When the supply of U.S. dollars decreases and the demand for them increases.
    d. When the supply of and demand for U.S. dollars decrease.

14. What type of unemployment includes an individual who is unemployed because of a general downturn in economic activity?
    a. Frictional unemployment
    b. Structural unemployment
    c. Cyclical unemployment
    d. Trough unemployment.

15. Along the path of the business cycle, real GDP rises during _____, then reaches _____, and then _____.
    a. a recession; a peak; an expansion
    b. an expansion; a peak; a recession
    c. a trough; an expansion; a peak
    d. a recession; a trough; an expansion

16. Which of the following is the factor that leads to business cycles in the Keynesian cycle theory?
    a. An unexpected change in aggregate demand.
    b. A change by the Fed in the growth rate of the quantity of money.
    c. A change in business confidence about future sales and profits.
    d. An unexpected change in the growth rate of productivity.

17. Which growth theory concludes that in the long run people are be paid a subsistence wage rate?
    a. The classical growth theory
    b. The neoclassical growth theory
    c. The new growth theory
    d. The Keynesian cycle theory

18. Which theory concludes that economic growth can continue indefinitely?
    a. The classical growth theory.
    b. The Keynesian cycle theory.
    c. The new growth theory.
    d. The neoclassical growth theory.

19. The government sector deficit is $75 billion and the private sector deficit is $25 billion. Hence net exports equals
    a. −$100 billion.
    b. −$75 billion
    c. −$50 billion.
    d. −$25 billion.

FIGURE 1

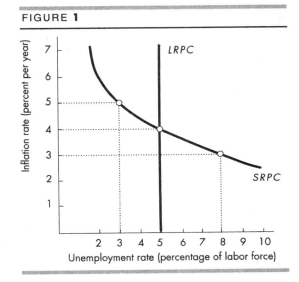

20. In the figure, the expected inflation rate is
    a. 5 percent.
    b. 4 percent.
    c. 3 percent.
    d. None of the above

21. In the figure, the natural unemployment rate is
    a. 3 percent.
    b. 5 percent.
    c. 8 percent.
    d. None of the above.

22. An increase in the productivity that increases the demand for labor _____ potential GDP and shifts the *LAS* curve _____.
    a. decreases; rightward
    b. decreases; leftward
    c. increases; rightward
    d. increases; leftward

23. Along which curve does the price level change but not the money wage rate?
    a. The *AD* curve.
    b. The *SAS* curve.
    c. The *LAS* curve.
    d. None of the above.

24. If the slope of the *AE* curve equals 0.9, what does the expenditure multiplier equal?
    a. 10.0.
    b. 9.0.
    c. −10.0.
    d. −9.0.

25. If the price index last year is 200 and next year is 220, the inflation rate between the years is
    a. 220 percent
    b. 200 percent
    c. 20 percent
    d. 10 percent

26. If the Fed lowers the federal funds rate, the quantity of loans _____ and the quantity of money _____.
    a. increases; increases
    b. increases; decreases
    c. decreases; increases
    d. decreases; decreases

27. A nation's investment must be financed by
    a. national saving only.
    b. the government's budget deficit.
    c. borrowing from the rest of the world only.
    d. national saving plus borrowing from the rest of the world.

28. Suppose that capital per hour of labor increases by 21 percent while real GDP per hour of labor increases by 12 percent. The change in technology increased real GDP per hour of labor by _____.
    a. 21 percent
    b. 17 percent
    c. 12 percent
    d. 5 percent

29. The maximum gains from international trade occur when
    a. there is no such trade.
    b. each nation produces according to its comparative advantage and trades with other nations.
    c. each nation uses tariffs rather than quotas to restrict trade.
    d. each nation uses quotas rather than tariffs to restrict trade.

30. In the United States, over the last two decades, the demand for labor has
    a. increased more than the supply of labor has increased.
    b. increased less than the supply of labor increased.
    c. increased while the supply of labor has decreased.
    d. decreased while the supply of labor has increased by more.

Answers

■ Final Exam 1 Answers

1. d; 2. c; 3. d; 4. a; 5. a; 6. c; 7. a; 8. c; 9. b; 10. c;
11. d; 12. b; 13. c; 14. d; 15. a; 16. b; 17. c; 18. b; 19. a; 20. c;
21. c; 22. d; 23. d; 24. a; 25. a; 26. b; 27. c; 28. a; 29. c; 30. b.

■ Final Exam 2 Answers

1. a; 2. c; 3. c; 4. c; 5. a; 6. d; 7. b; 8. b; 9. c; 10. d;
11. b; 12. b; 13. c; 14. c; 15. b; 16. c; 17. a; 18. c; 19. a; 20. b;
21. b; 22. c; 23. b; 24. a; 25. d; 26. a; 27. d; 28. d; 29. b; 30. a.

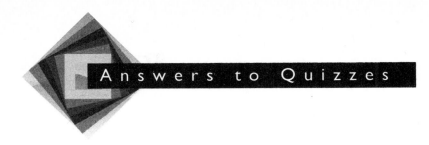

Answers

■ Chapter 1
1. c;   2. c;   3. c;   4. a;   5. d;   6. a;   7. c;   8. c;   9. d;   10. d.

■ Appendix
1. c;   2. c;   3. a;   4. c;   5. c;   6. c;   7. c;   8. d;   9. b;   10. b.

■ Chapter 2
1. b;   2. d;   3. b;   4. d;   5. a;   6. a;   7. d;   8. b;   9. c;   10. d.

■ Chapter 3
1. d;   2. d;   3. b;   4. b;   5. c;   6. b;   7. c;   8. a;   9. b;   10. b.

■ Chapter 4
1. a;   2. a;   3. a;   4. b;   5. b;   6. c;   7. c;   8. c;   9. c;   10. d.

■ Chapter 5
1. b;   2. c;   3. a;   4. a;   5. c;   6. d;   7. b;   8. d;   9. d;   10. c.

■ Chapter 6
1. d;   2. a;   3. c;   4. a;   5. b;   6. c;   7. a;   8. c;   9. b;   10. d.

■ Chapter 7
1. c;   2. d;   3. a;   4. d;   5. a;   6. a;   7. c;   8. c;   9. d;   10. c.

■ Chapter 8
1. d;   2. d;   3. d;   4. d;   5. c;   6. c;   7. c;   8. b;   9. c;   10. b.

■ Chapter 9
1. a;   2. b;   3. d;   4. a;   5. a;   6. a;   7. d;   8. c;   9. b;   10. c.

■ Chapter 10
1. c;   2. b;   3. c;   4. b;   5. b;   6. a;   7. a;   8. b;   9. a;   10. c.

■ Chapter 11
1. c;   2. d;   3. b;   4. c;   5. d;   6. c;   7. c;   8. d;   9. b;   10. d.

■ Chapter 12
1. b;   2. b;   3. b;   4. a;   5. a;   6. a;   7. a;   8. a;   9. d;   10. c.

■ Chapter 13
1. a;   2. c;   3. c;   4. d;   5. d;   6. a;   7. a;   8. d;   9. c;   10. c.

■ Chapter 14
1. b;   2. c;   3. b;   4. c;   5. b;   6. d;   7. a;   8. a;   9. a;   10. a.

■ Chapter 15
1. b;   2. a;   3. c;   4. a;   5. c;   6. c;   7. c;   8. b;   9. c;   10. d.

■ Chapter 16
1. a;   2. d;   3. c;   4. b;   5. a;   6. c;   7. a;   8. d;   9. d;   10. a.

Conclusion SHOULD YOU MAJOR IN ECONOMICS?*

Should You Take More Economic Courses?

Now that you have learned about supply and demand, employment and unemployment, government policies, the Fed, and good old Igor (at least in the Study Guide you learned about Igor!), it is time to look to the future.

♦ Should studying economics be part of your future?

♦ Should you take more classes or maybe even major in economics?

♦ What about graduate school in economics?

Economists generally assume that people make rational choices to maximize their own well-being. There is no reason to drop this assumption now. The purpose of this chapter is to help you make that rational maximizing choice by providing low-cost information. Let us assess the benefits and see whether they outweigh the costs of studying economics.

Benefits from Studying Economics

■ Knowledge, Enlightenment, and Liberation

As John Maynard Keynes, a famous British economist, said, "The ideas of economists ... both when they are right and when they are wrong, are more powerful than is commonly understood. Indeed the world is ruled by little else. Practical men, who believe themselves to be quite exempt from any intellectual influences, are usually the slaves of some defunct economist." Studying economics is a liberating and enlightening experience.

---

* This section was written by Robert Whaples of Wake Forest University and updated by Mark Rush.

It's better to bring your ideas out in the open, to confront and understand them, rather than to leave them buried.

■ Knowledge, Understanding, and Satisfaction

Many of the most important problems in the world are economic. Studying economics gives you a practical set of tools to understand and solve them. Every day, on television and in the newspapers, we hear and read about big issues such as economic growth, inflation, unemployment, international trade relations, the latest moves by the Fed, the most recent tax or spending bill, the environment, and the future of Social Security. Your introduction to economics shows that learning economics will let you watch the news or pick up a newspaper and better understand these issues. As an added bonus, economics helps you understand smaller, more immediate concerns, such as: How much Spam should I buy? Is skipping class today a good idea? Should I put my retirement funds in government bonds or in the stock market? After all, as the famous author George Bernard Shaw put it, "Economy is the art of making the most of life." Mick Jagger, the lead singer of the "Rolling Stones" and who dropped out of the London School of Economics, complains that he "can't get no satisfaction." Maybe he should have studied more economics? The economic way of thinking will help you maximize your satisfaction.

■ Career Opportunities

All careers are not equal. While the wages in many occupations have not risen much lately, the wages of "symbolic analysts" who "solve, identify, and broker problems by manipulating symbols" are soaring.[1] These people "simplify reality into abstract images that can be rearranged, juggled, experimented with, communicated to other specialists, and then, eventually, transformed back into reality." Their wages have been rising as the globalization of the economy increases the demand for their insights and as technological developments (especially computers) have enhanced their productivity. Economists are the quintessential symbolic analysts as we manipulate ideas about abstractions such as supply and demand, cost and benefits, and equilibrium.

You can think of your training in economics as an exercise regimen, a workout for your brain. You will use many of the concepts you will learn in introductory economics during your career, but it is the practice in abstract thinking that will really pay off.

In fact, most economics majors do not go on to become economists. They enter fields that use their analytical abilities, including business, management, insurance, finance, real estate, marketing, law, education, policy analysis, consulting, government, planning, and even medicine, journalism, and the arts. A recent survey of 100 former economics majors at my university included all of these careers. If you want to verify that economics majors graduate to successful and rewarding careers, just ask your professors or watch what happens to economics majors from your school as they graduate.

Census statistics show that across the nation, economics majors earn more than most other majors. Table 1, from a 1998 study by the U.S. Bureau of Labor Statistics, shows that in 1993 (the most recent data available) middle-aged men with bachelor's degrees in economics earned more than those with all but a handful of other undergraduate degrees. Among women, economics was the *highest* earning major. (see Table 1)

That's the long-run picture. The short-run view looks much the same. In 2003 the average annual starting salary of economics and finance majors was $40,084. While this is lower than the salaries for those with degrees in computer science, engineering, and some other sciences, it is a couple of thousand dollars higher than salaries for those with degrees in business administration. Moreover, the entry-level salary of economics majors beats the entry-level salary of social science and humanities majors by a wide margin, as Table 2 shows. These numbers are updated annually, so feel free to look up the latest statistics. (In addition, the employment rate of economics majors is higher than that of many other majors, such as those in the humanities and other social sciences.)

The widening earnings gap between economics and similar majors helps explain why enrollments in economics are climbing. Since 1996 the number of

TABLE 1

**Median Earnings by College Major
Women and Men, Age 35-44 (1993)**

	Women	Men
Accounting	$39,843	$49,502
Agriculture	28,752	36,758
Biological/Life Sciences	34,245	41,179
Business (except accounting)	34,638	44,867
Chemistry	37,501	44,994
Computer and information services	43,757	50,510
Economics	**49,175**	**49,378**
Education	27,988	34,470
Engineering	49,072	53,287
English language and literature	30,296	38,297
Health/medical technologies	35,526	36,269
History	30,553	38,095
Liberal arts/general studies	32,073	39,625
Pharmacy	48,428	50,480
Psychology	32,301	40,718
Sociology	29,532	37,250

Source: Daniel Hacker, "Earnings of College Graduates: Women Compared with Men," *Monthly Labor Review*, March 1998.
http://stats.bls.gov/opub/mlr/1998/03/art5full.pdf
Note: Figures are for those with a bachelor's degree.

TABLE 2

**Average Annual Starting Salary Offers
by College Major, 2003**

Chemical Engineering	$51,853
Computer Science	47,419
Economics/Finance	**40,084**
Business	37,122
Marketing	34,628
History	32,108
English	30,157
Criminal Justice	29,234
Psychology	27,454

Source: National Association of Colleges and Employers, jobweb.
http://www.jobweb.com/SalaryInfo/03summerss.htm

economics degrees awarded in the United States has jumped about 14 percent, with similar trends in Canada and Australia.[2]

Even if you aren't planning on getting a job right out of college, economics can be a valuable major. Economics degrees are looked upon very favorably by MBA programs and law schools. Over one-third of economics graduates enter professional programs within two years of their undergraduate degree, divided equally between business and law. In fact, an analysis of Law School Admission Test (LSAT) scores from the 1990s showed that among the fourteen college majors with more than 2,000 students taking the exam, economics majors did the *best*. The average score of 155.3 topped second-place history (154.0), as well as English (153.7), Psychology (151.9), Political Science (151.6), Communications (150.7), Sociology (149.3), and Business Administration (148.6).[3]

A *Wall Street Journal* article announced that "Economics, Once a Perplexing Subject, Is Enjoying a Bull Run at Universities." Economics is not a vocational training program, preparing you for a single line of work. Instead, the career benefits of an economics major are so great because economics teaches you to *think* and thinking is what's ultimately rewarded in our dynamic economy.

The Costs of Studying Economics

Because the "direct" costs of studying economics (tuition, books, supplies) aren't generally any higher or lower than the direct costs of other courses, indirect costs will be the most important of the costs to studying economics.

■ Forgone Knowledge

If you study economics, you can't study something else. This forgone knowledge could be very valuable.

■ Disutility

If you dislike studying economics because you find it boring, tedious, or unenlightening in comparison to other subjects, then the opportunity cost is even higher because your overall level of satisfaction falls. (I know that this is rare, but it does occasionally happen).

■ Time and Energy

Economics is a fairly demanding major. Although economics courses do not generally take as much time as courses in English and history (in which you have to read a lot of long books) or anatomy and physiology (in which you have to spend hours in the lab and hours memorizing things), they do take a decent amount of time. In addition, some people find the material "tougher" than most subjects because memorizing is not the key. In economics (like physics), analyzing and solving are the keys. The rigor of the major is an obstacle for many.

■ Grades

As Table 3 shows, grades in introductory economics courses are usually a notch lower than grades in some other majors, including other social sciences and the humanities.[4] On the other hand, grades in economics are generally higher than grades in the sciences and math. Grades in introductory economics courses are generally a hair lower than grades in introductory courses to other majors, including other social sciences and the humanities.

TABLE 3

Average Grades and Grade Distribution by College Major

Department	Mean Grade	% Above B+	% Below B−
Music	3.16	44	21
English	3.12	27	12
Psychology	3.02	28	23
Philosophy	2.99	29	21
Art	2.95	29	24
Political science	2.95	24	23
Economics	2.81	20	31
Chemistry	2.66	17	44
Math	2.53	22	46

Caveat Emptor (Buyer Beware): Interpreting Your Grades Is Not Straight Forward

High grades provide direct satisfaction to most students, but they also act as a signal about the student's ability to learn the subject material. Unfortunately, because the grade distribution is not uniform across departments, you might be confused and misled by your grades. You might think that you are exceptionally good at a subject because of a high grade, when in fact nearly everyone gets a high grade in that subject. The important point here is that you should be informed about your own school's grade distribution. Just because you got a B in economics and an A in history does not necessarily mean that your comparative advantage is in learning history rather than economics. Everyone — or virtually everyone — might receive an A in history. Earning a B or a C in economics could mean that it is the best major for you because high grades are much harder to earn in economics. It is fun to have a high GPA in college, but maximizing GPA should not be your goal. Maximizing your overall well-being is probably your goal, and this might be obtained by trading off a tenth or so of your GPA for a more rewarding major — perhaps economics.

In assessing the tradeoffs, you'll notice that mean departmental grades are higher where average earnings are lower. Employers know which departments grade harder. A recent article on grade patterns concluded that "those students who attend college primarily as a route to a better paying job should understand that 'easy' courses may be no bargain in the long run." [5]

Potential Side Effects from Studying Economics

Studying economics has some potential side effects. I'm not sure whether they are costs or benefits and will let you decide.

■ Changing Ideas about What Is Fair

A recently completed study compared students at the beginning and end of the semester in an introductory economics course.[6] It found that by the end of the semester, significantly more of the students thought that the functioning of the market is "fair." This was especially true for female students. The results were consistent across a range of professors who fell across the ideological spectrum.

For example, the proportion of students who regarded it as unfair to increase the price of flowers on a holiday fell almost in half. The proportion that favored government control over flower prices, rather than market determination, fell by over 60 percent. The study ar-

gues that these responses do not reflect changes in deep values, but instead represent the discovery of previous inconsistencies and their modification in the light of new information learned during the semester.

■ Changing Behavior

Many people believe that the study of economics changes students' values and behavior. Some observers think that it changes them for the worse. Others disagree. In particular, it is argued that economics students become more self-interested and less likely to cooperate, perhaps because they spend so much time studying economic models, which often assume that people are self-interested. For example, one study reports experimental evidence that economics students are more likely than nonmajors to behave self-interestedly in prisoners' dilemma games and ultimatum bargaining games.[7]

This need not mean that studying economics will change you, however. Another study compares beginning freshmen and senior economics students and concludes that economics students "are already different when they begin their study of economics."[8] In other words, students signing up for economics courses are already different; studying economics doesn't change them. However, there are reasons to question both of these conclusions, because it is not clear whether these laboratory experiments using economic games reflect reality. One experiment asked students whether they would return money that had been lost. It found that economics students were more likely than others to say that they would keep the cash.

However, what people say and what they do are sometimes at odds. In a follow-up experiment, this theory was tested by dropping stamped, addressed envelopes containing $10 in cash in different campus classrooms. To return the cash, the students had only to seal the envelopes and mail them. The results were that 56 percent of the envelopes dropped in economics classes were returned, while only 31 percent of the envelopes dropped in history, psychology and business classes were sent in.[9] Perhaps economics students are less selfish than others!

Obviously, no firm conclusions have been reached about whether or how studying economics changes students' behavior.

Costs versus Benefits

Suppose that you've weighed the costs and benefits of studying economics and you've decided that the benefits are greater than or equal to the costs. Obviously, then, you should continue to take economics courses. If you can't decide whether the benefits outweigh the costs, then you should probably collect more information — especially if it is good but inexpensive. In either case, read the rest of this section.

The Economics Major

The study of economics is like a tree. The introductory microeconomics and macroeconomics courses you begin with are the tree's roots. Most colleges and universities require that you master this material before you go on to any other courses. The way of thinking, the language, and the tools that you acquire in the introductory course are usually reinforced in intermediate microeconomics and macroeconomics courses before they are applied in more specialized courses that you take. The intermediate courses are the tree's trunk. Among the specialized courses that make up the branches of economics are econometrics (statistical economics), financial economics, labor economics, resource economics, international trade, industrial organization, public finance, public choice, economic history, the history of economic thought, mathematical economics, current economic issues, and urban economics. The branches of the tree vary from department to department, but these are common. It will pay to check your college bulletin and discuss these courses with professors and other students.

Graduate School in Economics

■ Preparing for Graduate School in Economics

You can prepare for graduate school in economics by taking several math classes. This would probably include at least two years of calculus plus a couple of courses in probability and statistics and linear/matrix algebra. Ask your advisor about the particular courses to take at your college. In addition, the mathematical economics and econometrics courses in the economics department are essential. (*Helpful hint*: Even if you aren't going to graduate school, these mathematical courses can be valuable to you, just as more economics courses can be valuable for nonmajors.)

If your school offers graduate level economics courses, you might want to sit in on a few to get accustomed to the flavor of graduate school.

Most graduate programs require strong grades in economics, a good score on the Graduate Record Examination (GRE), and solid letters of recommendation. It is a good idea to get to know a few professors very well and to go above and beyond what is expected so that they can write glowing letters about you.

■ Financing Graduate School

Unlike some other graduate and professional degree programs, you probably won't need to pile up a massive amount of debt while pursuing a Ph.D. in economics. Most Ph.D. programs hire their economics graduate students as teaching or research assistants. Teaching assistants begin by grading papers and running review sessions and can advance to teaching classes on their own. Research assistants generally do data collection, statistical work, and library research for professors and often jointly write papers with them. Most assistantships will pay for tuition and provide you with enough money to live on.

■ Where Should You Apply?

The best graduate school for you depends on a lot of things, especially your ability level, geographical location, areas of research interests, and, of course, financing. You should talk with your professors about ability level and areas of research. In addition, there are informative articles that give overall departmental rankings and rankings by subfield. See especially Richard Dusansky and Clayton J. Vernon, "Rankings of U.S. Economics Departments," *Journal of Economic Perspectives*, Vol. 12, no. 1, Winter 1998, pp. 157-170, Jerry G. Thursby, "What Do We Say about Ourselves and What Does It Mean? Yet Another Look at Economics Department Research," *Journal of Economic Literature*, Vol. 38, no. 2, June 2000, pp. 383-404, and John Tschirhart, "Ranking Economics Departments in Areas of Expertise," *Journal of Economic Education*, Vol. 20, no. 2, Spring 1989, pp. 199-222. There will probably be more up-to-date rankings by the time you apply. Ask a professor or reference librarian to help you track them down. For smaller specialties (e.g., economic history, urban economics) it is especially important to get up-to-date information on any particular program.

■ What You Will Do in Graduate School

Most graduate programs in economics begin with a year of theory courses in macroeconomics and micro-economics. After a year you will probably take a series of tests to show that you have mastered this core theory. If you pass these tests, in the second and third year of courses you will take more specialized subjects and perhaps take lengthy examinations in a couple of sub-fields. After this you will be required to write a dissertation —original research that will contribute new knowledge to one of the fields of economics. These stages are intertwined with work as a teaching and/or research assistant, and the dissertation stage can be quite drawn out. In the social sciences the median time that it takes for a student to complete the Ph.D. degree is about 7.5 years.[10] Be aware that a high percentage (roughly 50 percent) of students do not complete their doctoral degree.

■ What Is Graduate School Like?

Graduate school in economics comes as a surprise to many students. The material and approach are distinctly different from what you will learn as an undergraduate. The textbooks and journal articles you will read in graduate school are often very theoretical and abstract. A good source of information is sitting in on courses or reading the reflections of recent students. See especially *The Making of an Economist* by Arjo Klamer and David Colander (Boulder, Colo.: Westview Press, 1990).

The Committee on Graduate Education in Economics (COGEE) undertook an important review of graduate education in economics and reported its findings in the September 1991 issue of the *Journal of Economic Literature*. COGEE asked faculty members, graduate students, and recent Ph.D.s to rank the most important skills needed to be successful in the study of graduate economics. At the top of the list were analytical skills and mathematics, followed by critical judgment, the ability to apply theory, and computational skills. At the bottom of the list were creativity and the ability to communicate. If you are interested in economic issues but do not have the characteristics required by graduate economics departments, consider other economics-related fields, such as graduate school in public policy. Many economics majors go to business schools to obtain an MBA and are often better prepared than students who have undergraduate degrees in business.

Economics Reading

If decide to make studying economics part of your future, or if you're hungry for more economics, you should immediately begin reading the economic news and books by economists. Life is short. Why waste it watching TV?

The easiest way to get your daily recommended dose of economics is to keep up with current economic events. Here are a few sources to pick up at the newsstand, bookstore, or library over your summer or winter break.

■ The *Wall Street Journal*

Many undergraduates subscribe to the *Wall Street Journal* (WSJ) at low student rates. Join them! Your professor will probably have student subscription forms. Not only is the WSJ a well-written business newspaper, but it also has articles on domestic and international news, politics, the arts, travel, and sports, as well as a lively editorial page. Reading the WSJ is one of the best ways to tie the economics you are studying to the real world and to prepare for your career.

■ Magazines and Journals

The Economist, a weekly magazine published in England, is available at a student discount rate. Pick up a copy at your school library and you will be hooked by its informative, sharp writing. *Business Week* is also well worth the read.

Also recommended are *The American Enterprise, The Cato Journal, Challenge,* and *The Public Interest*, four quarterlies that discuss economic policy. Finally, there is the *Journal of Economics Perspectives*, which is published by the American Economic Association and written to be accessible to undergraduate economics students.

■ Books by Economists

I recently asked a group of economics professors from across the country the following question: "A bright, enthusiastic student who has just completed introductory economics comes up to you, the professor, and asks you to recommend an economics book for reading over the summer. What do you suggest?"

Here is what they suggested that you, the bright, enthusiastic student, should read:

■ Top Choices

Milton Friedman, *Capitalism and Freedom*.
Steven Levitt and Stephen Dubner, *Freakonomics*.
Steve Landsburg, *The Armchair Economist: Economics and Everyday Life*.

■ Other Good Choices

Alan Blinder, *Hard Heads, Soft Hearts: Tough-Minded Economics for a Just Society*.
Hernando de Soto, *The Mystery of Capital: Why Capitalism Triumphed in the West and Failed Everywhere Else*.
Robert Frank, *Luxury Fever: Why Money Fails to Satisfy in an Era of Excess*.
David Friedman, *Hidden Order: The Economics of Everyday Life*.
Susan Lee, *Hands Off: Why the Government Is a Menace to Economic Health*.

In addition, Adam Smith's *The Wealth of Nations* is a must read for every student of economics. Written in 1776, it is the most influential work of economics ever. Its insights are still valuable today.

■ Economic Fiction

For those with a taste for fiction, choices include:
Marshall Jevons, *Murder at the Margin*, *The Fatal Equilibrium*, and *A Deadly Indifference*. A trio of economics-based murder mysteries. Use your economic theory to solve the crime.

Russell Roberts, *The Invisible Heart*. An economics-based romance novel! "Can Laura love a man with an Adam Smith poster on his wall?"
Russell Roberts, *The Choice: A Parable of Free Trade and Protectionism*.
Jonathan Wight, *Saving Adam Smith: A Tale of Wealth, Transformation, and Virtue*.

Endnotes

1. This term is used by Robert Reich in *The Work of Nations*. The quote is from p. 178.
2. John J. Siegfried and David K. Round, "International Trends in Economics Degrees during the 1990s," *Journal of Economic Education*, Vol. 32, no. 3, Summer 2001, pp. 203-18.
3. Michael Nieswiadomy, "LSAT Scores of Economics Majors," *Journal of Economic Education*, Vol. 29, no. 4, Fall 1998, pp. 377-79.
4. Richard Sabot and John Wakeman-Linn, "Grade Inflation and Course Choice," *Journal of Economic Perspectives*, Vol. 5, no. 1, Winter 1991, pp. 159–170.
5. Donald G. Freeman, "Grade Divergence as a Market Outcome," *Journal of Economic Education*, Vol. 30, no. 4, Fall 1999, pp. 344-51.
6. Robert Whaples, "Changes in Attitudes about the Fairness of Free Markets among College Economics Students," *Journal of Economic Education*, Vol. 26, no. 4, Fall 1995.
7. Robert H. Frank, Thomas Gilovich, and Dennis T. Regan, "Does Studying Economics Inhibit Cooperation?" *Journal of Economic Perspectives*, Vol. 7, no. 2, Spring 1993, pp. 159–171.
8. John R. Carter and Michael D. Irons, "Are Economists Different, and If So, Why?" *Journal of Economic Perspectives*, Vol. 5, no. 2, Spring 1991, pp. 171–177.
9. "Economics Students Aren't Selfish, They're Just Not Entirely Honest," *Wall Street Journal*, January 18, 1995, B1.
10. See Ronald Ehrenberg, "The Flow of New Doctorates," *Journal of Economic Literature*, Vol. 30, June 1992, pp. 830–875. If breaks in school attendance are included, this climbs to 10.5 years. Of course, some students attend only part time, and most have some kind of employment while completing their degrees.